Paving Paradise

THE FLORIDA HISTORY AND CULTURE SERIES

UNIVERSITY PRESS OF FLORIDA

Florida A&M University, Tallahassee
Florida Atlantic University, Boca Raton
Florida Gulf Coast University, Ft. Myers
Florida International University, Miami
Florida State University, Tallahassee
New College of Florida, Sarasota
University of Central Florida, Orlando
University of Florida, Gainesville
University of North Florida, Jacksonville
University of South Florida, Tampa
University of West Florida, Pensacola

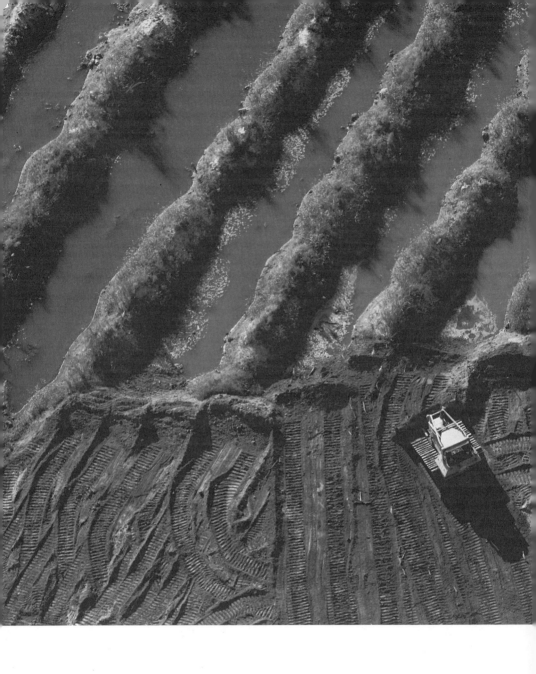

University Press of Florida

Gainesville Tallahassee Tampa Boca Raton Pensacola Orlando Miami Jacksonville Ft. Myers Sarasota

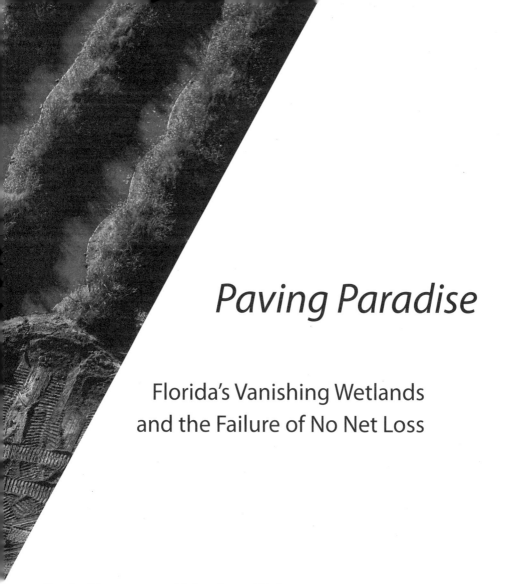

Paving Paradise

Florida's Vanishing Wetlands
and the Failure of No Net Loss

Craig Pittman and Matthew Waite

Foreword by Raymond Arsenault and Gary R. Mormino, Series Editors

For Sherry, Sean, and Cameron—CP

For Nancy, Paige, and Brady—MW

Copyright 2009 by Craig Pittman and Matthew Waite
Printed in the United States of America. This book is printed on Glatfelter
Natures Book, a paper certified under the standards of the Forestry
Stewardship Council (FSC). It is a recycled stock that contains 30 percent
post-consumer waste and is acid-free.

13 12 11 10 09 08   6 5 4 3 2 1

Library of Congress Cataloging-in-Publication Data
Pittman, Craig.
Paving Paradise : Florida's vanishing wetlands and the failure of no net loss /
Craig Pittman and Matthew Waite ; foreword by Raymond Arsenault and Gary
R. Mormino.
p. cm. — (The Florida history and culture series)
Includes bibliographical references.
ISBN 978-0-8130-3286-3 (alk. paper)
1. Wetlands—Florida. 2. Wetland conservation—Government policy—
Florida. I. Waite, Matthew, 1975- II. Title.
QH105.F6P58 2008
333.91'81309759—dc22   2008018548

The University Press of Florida is the scholarly publishing agency for the State
University System of Florida, comprising Florida A&M University, Florida
Atlantic University, Florida Gulf Coast University, Florida International
University, Florida State University, New College of Florida, University of
Central Florida, University of Florida, University of North Florida, University
of South Florida, and University of West Florida.

University Press of Florida
15 Northwest 15th Street
Gainesville, FL 32611-2079
www.upf.com

Contents

Foreword   vii
Acknowledgments   ix
Abbreviations   xiii

Prologue: The Numbers Game   1
 1. "The National Emblem of Florida"   7
 2. A Reasonable Curb   18
 3. "Let Us Try"   31
 4. Marco Island & Bonita Springs   46
 5. Six Percent Saviors   61
 6. "The Joy of Life"   78
 7. The Promise, Plus   90
 8. Images of Loss   101
 9. The Myth of Mitigation   108
10. Turning a Minus into a Plus   128
11. "A Mine Is a Terrible Thing to Waste"   142
12. Let Sleeping Watchdogs Lie   166
13. The Cussing Congressman   191
14. Loopholes and Sinkholes   217
15. Dirty Water   237
16. Banking on Phony Numbers   251
17. Toward a More Honest System   275

Appendix A. Satellite Imagery Methodology   285
Appendix B. Accuracy Assessment Tables   291
Notes   293
Selected Bibliography   339
Selected Sources on Remote Sensing   345
Index   347
Series List   353

Foreword

Paving Paradise: Florida's Vanishing Wetlands and the Failure of No Net Loss is the latest volume in a series devoted to the study of Florida history and culture. During the past half-century, the burgeoning population and increased national and international visibility of Florida have sparked a great deal of popular interest in the state's past, present, and future. As a favorite destination of countless tourists and as the new home for millions of retirees and transplants, modern Florida has become a demographic, political, and cultural bellwether. Florida has also emerged as a popular subject and setting for scholars and writers. From avenging hurricanes to disputed elections, from tales of the Everglades to profiles of Sunbelt cities, Florida has become irresistible.

The Florida History and Culture Series provides an attractive and accessible format for Florida-related books. As co-editors of the series, we are committed to the creation of an eclectic but carefully crafted set of books that provides the field of Florida studies with a new focus. It is our hope that this focus will encourage Florida writers to consider the broader implications and context of their work. The series includes standard academic monographs, as well as works of synthesis, memoirs, and anthologies. Books dealing with Florida history predominate, but we encourage authors researching Florida's environment, politics, literature, and popular or material culture to submit their manuscripts as well. Each book offers a distinct personality and voice, but the ultimate goal of the series is to foster a broad sense of community and collaboration among Florida scholars.

In recent years, readers of the *St. Petersburg Times* have become familiar with the probing environmental journalism of Craig Pittman and Matthew Waite. Combining careful research, solid writing, and investigative flair, they have addressed the challenges and dilemmas of environmental policy in the Sunshine State. Now, with the publication of *Paving Paradise*, a major element of their important work will reach a broader audience of scholars, policy makers, and concerned citizens.

The subject at hand is the state's vanishing wetlands—and the policy of "no net loss" that was established in 1989 to resolve the wetlands crisis. That policy, the authors maintain, has been a dismal failure, despite seventeen years of broad popular support and political hype. "The result," they conclude, "is a taxpayer-funded program that creates the illusion of environmental protection while doing little to stem the destruction of precious natural resources." Year after year, the wetlands slip away, yet few politicians or bureaucrats have been willing to acknowledge this troubling reality. Many readers will find *Paving Paradise* a profoundly disturbing book. But, like several environmental books previously published in the Florida History and Culture Series—*The Everglades: An Environmental History* (1999) by David McCally, *The Mosquito Wars: A History of Mosquito Control in Florida* (2004), by Gordon Patterson, *Paradise Lost? The Environmental History of Florida* (2005), edited by Jack E. Davis and Raymond Arsenault, and *Losing It All to Sprawl: How Progress Ate My Cracker Landscape* (2006), by Bill Belleville—Pittman and Waite's timely study offers information and insights that no civic-minded Floridian can afford to ignore.

Gary Mormino and Raymond Arsenault
University of South Florida, St. Petersburg
Series Editors

Acknowledgments

Although our two names are listed as authors of this book, behind us stands an army of people whose support made this book possible.

Craig wants to thank his wife Sherry, who has put up with his muddy boots, late hours, and constant yammering about mitigation. He contends that her continuing love for him, in spite of all this, is so miraculous as to prove the existence of God. He also wants to thank his father, a surveyor who taught him from an early age how government really works, and his mother, who taught him to appreciate nature, especially the particularly wacky human kind often found in Florida.

Matt wants to thank his wife Nancy, who has been a wonderful mother to two beautiful children, even when the kitchen table was covered in remote sensing textbooks and academic papers. She has lovingly feigned interest in particle physics when her husband excitedly explained it. The whole reason he wanted to write this book was so he could take the first copy and hand it to his parents. It is a small step toward repaying them for reading to their sons every night, giving the gift of a lifelong love of the written word.

Some of the others who made our "Vanishing Wetlands" series in the *St. Petersburg Times*, and thus this book, a reality include:

- Tom Scherberger, the editor who saw the possibilities in a rough idea, gave us a green light when other editors had been doubtful and then shepherded our reporting for nearly two years until our initial stories finally made it into the paper. Other editors who worked on our follow-up stories (and vastly improved them) were Richard Bockman and Marilyn Garateix.
- Neil Brown, the *Times'* executive editor, whose unshakable faith in the value of this story led to an unprecedented commitment of time, money, and resources. Neil took such a personal interest in our work that he not only helped edit the stories, he even wrote many of the headlines.

- Ace researcher Caryn Baird, who tracked down court records, academic studies, home phone numbers, government reports—in short, she found us everything but D. B. Cooper's briefcase. We would be remiss if we did not mention the other researchers who pitched in as well: Angie Drobnic Holan, Cathy Wos, and Carolyn Edds. A special shout-out goes to former *Times* reporter Julie Hauserman, who unearthed some crucial information from the state archives.
- Photographer Lara Cerri, whose dedication to capturing just the right image sometimes required staking out wetlands well before dawn (and before we would ever dream of waking up).
- Graphic artists Dana Oppenheim and Jeff Goertzen who displayed an unending professionalism when a couple of yahoos handed them years of reporting and asked for clear and sophisticated graphics and illustrations in weeks, sometimes days. They delivered every time, and we thank them.
- Web designer Lee Glynn, who has taken a truly massive amount of material and turned it into one of the most stunning Web presentations we have ever seen, often on short notice, and page designers Amy Hollifield and Paul Alexander, who performed similar feats of magic with the printed product.
- University of South Florida professor Barnali Dixon, who patiently explained concepts not covered in your standard liberal arts education—sometimes repeatedly—and provided invaluable guidance from the project's very beginnings and Florida State University professor J. B. Ruhl, who generously shared his data on mitigation banking and the projects that were buying bank credits.
- All the dedicated state and federal employees who talked to us, on the record, to explain how the system had gone wrong.
- The cadre of lawyers and wetland experts who advised us, reminisced for us, and sometimes loaned us books, particularly David White, Jan Goldman-Carter, Julie Sibbing, Robin Lewis, John Thomas, Tom Reese, Jeff Ruch, and Royal Gardner. Roy made the most valuable contribution of them all: He called Craig in 2001 to recommend reading a new report the National Research Council had just produced on wetlands losses in America. That call led to everything that followed, including this book. We are also grateful to Steve Davies, editor and publisher of the *Endangered Species & Wetlands Report*, and to the Environmental Law Institute's *National Wetlands Newsletter* for providing us access to their archives.

- *Times* corporate attorney Alison Steele, who helped soothe our first-time-author jitters and aided us with a host of potentially troublesome details.

And last but most certainly not least, we thank University of South Florida professor Gary Mormino, a fan of our series, who urged the University Press of Florida to turn it into a book and introduced us to its terrific editor-in-chief, John Byram.

Craig Pittman and Matthew Waite

Abbreviations

CEQ	Council on Environmental Quality
DEP	Department of Environmental Protection
DER	Department of Environmental Regulation
DOT	Department of Transportation
EIS	Environmental Impact Statement
EPA	Environmental Protection Agency
FAA	Federal Aviation Administration
FEMA	Federal Emergency Management Agency
FHBA	Florida Home Builders Association
FOIA	Freedom of Information Act
GAO	Government Accountability Office
GIS	Global Information Systems
NAACP	National Association for the Advancement of Colored People
NEPA	National Enviromental Policy Act
NRC	National Research Council
NRDC	Natural Resources Defense Council
NMFS	National Marine Fisheries Service
NWI	National Wetlands Inventory
OPPAGA	Office of Program Policy Analysis and Government Accountability
PHEM	Panther Habitat Evaluation Model
ROD	Record of Decision
SJRWMD	St. Johns River Water Management District
UMAM	Uniform Mitigation Assessment Method
USACE	Unites States Army Corps of Engineers
USGS	United States Geological Survey
WERC	Water Enhancement and Restoration Coalition
WRAP	Wetlands Rapid Assessment Protocol

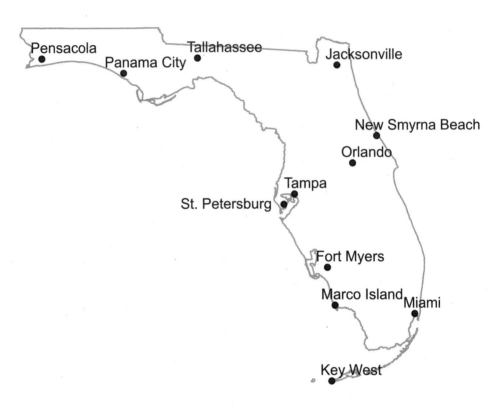

Map 1. Florida, pinpointing key areas discussed in the text.

Prologue

The Numbers Game

There is a strong interest in keeping the number high and none in keeping it correct. . . . These numbers are generated by the demand that the government appear to know a great deal more than it actually does.

—Peter Reuter, "The (Continued) Vitality of Mythical Numbers," *Public Interest*, Spring 1984

∾

Gale Norton needed some good news.

For five tumultuous years, the silver-haired Norton had served as secretary of the U.S. Department of the Interior. From the day in 2001 that President George W. Bush appointed her to oversee the nation's parks, wildlife, Indian tribes, and public lands, she had been embroiled in controversy. Environmentalists condemned her for trying to open up Arctic wilderness to oil drilling. Federal judges cited her twice for contempt of court. Her department became mired in a nasty scandal involving a Washington lobbyist named Jack Abramoff that would eventually lead to her second-in-command pleading guilty to lying to Congress. Her inspector general was conducting an investigation of the agency's top management that would soon produce still more unflattering headlines. When Norton announced her resignation in 2006, the president of the environmental group Defenders of Wildlife put out a press release containing just two words: "Good riddance."

Yet Norton was determined to leave office on a positive note. On March 30, 2006, her next-to-last day on the job, she called a press conference to announce a truly impressive accomplishment: the achievement of something called "no net loss."

Ever since the Clean Water Act became law in 1972, America's wetlands were supposed to be protected from destruction. Yet somehow America kept on destroying its swamps, bogs, and marshes. So in 1989, then president George H. W. Bush vowed to turn the tide. He promised that from then on, there would be "no net loss" of wetlands. The promise of no net loss was so politically popular that the presidents who followed, Democrat and Republican, also made it their policy.

For 17 years, politicians had been promising to reverse the loss of the nation's dwindling wetlands. No net loss was an easy promise to make, but it was difficult to carry out. Wetlands kept getting in everyone's way. Every year thousands of acres of swamps were still being converted into new suburbs, golf courses, highways, mines, farms, big-box stores.

But now, at last, Norton was ready to announce that the elusive goal of no net loss had been reached. In fact, a new report from her department said that between 1998 and 2004—during the largest real estate boom in American history—the lower 48 states had actually gained wetlands. The report found an estimated 191,750 acres of new wetlands nationwide.

At her press conference, a smiling Norton called this "good news not only for biologists but for all of us. We all depend on wetlands as the nurseries of life."

But then the reporters—who before the press conference had been briefed by clearly annoyed activists from the National Wildlife Federation—began questioning Norton's numbers. Weren't most of those wetland "gains" not really wetlands? Weren't they actually artificial ponds? Ornamental fountains? Golf course water hazards, even? Wasn't it true that, without all those artificial ponds, the numbers in the report said just the opposite of what Norton had just announced—namely, that the nation was still losing tens of thousands of acres of natural, life-sustaining wetlands?

Norton's smile faded.

"Ponds," she snapped, "are getting a bad rap."

Sure, there was an increase in the number of man-made ponds, she said, but "people like having ponds as an amenity. Ponds are being more widely used for stormwater runoff or for other reasons, and that is beneficial. That is something that adds wetlands. Again, they may not be the highest-value wetlands, but the fact that people value wetlands and they take private actions to add wetlands is something we view as positive."

Norton's elastic definition of wetlands prompted some waggish news coverage. The *New York Times* ran a story headlined, "Fewer Marshes + More Man-Made Ponds = Increased Wetlands." *Field & Stream* magazine snorted, "You Call This a Wetland?" Florida's largest daily newspaper, the *St. Petersburg*

Times, ran side-by-side pictures of a stormwater retention pond and a cypress swamp under a headline that asked, "Are These Both Wetlands?" Someone posted the story on the snarky "Fark.com" Web site with the tag "Asinine," where it drew more than 160 comments about whether Norton knew the difference between a swamp and a hole in the ground.

On the satirical Comedy Central cable show *The Colbert Report*, host Stephen Colbert contended that the Bush Administration should be praised for taking such a bold stand. "They're simply nurturing the word 'wetlands' to give it the freedom it needs to mean what they need it to," Colbert explained with a straight face. "This way, wetlands may not be growing, but the 'idea' of wetlands is . . . by counting any form of moist dirt." To underline his point, the screen next to him flashed a picture of a Chia Head sprouting greenery labeled "Wetland."

But it wasn't just the definition of wetland that was being stretched to the breaking point. The numbers used for the report's conclusion were being stretched, too.

One of the reporters who covered Norton's press conference was a sharp-eyed newsletter publisher named Steve Davies who produces a monthly publication called the *Endangered Species & Wetlands Report*. Davies tracked down the report's author, a biologist named Thomas Dahl, and quizzed him about one odd line he had noticed in a footnote on page 46: "The coefficient of variation expressed as a percentage is 89.1 percent for the net gain estimate."

Davies asked the author what that meant in English. Dahl, a widely respected scientist who works for the U.S. Fish and Wildlife Service's National Wetlands Inventory, told Davies that the note meant that the acres of wetlands counted for the report could be 89 percent higher . . . or 89 percent lower than the stated figure.

"That's a fairly large standard error," Dahl told Davies.

Given the political pressure to come up with a particular answer in the report, Davies later joked, another term for that is "a bald-faced lie."

It is also sadly typical of the way government officials have treated the protection of wetlands over the past 30 years: as a numbers game, a way to keep everyone distracted by happy promises of a green future while allowing the continued destruction of the nation's swamps, marshes, and bogs.

The result is a taxpayer-funded program that creates the illusion of environmental protection while doing little to stem the destruction of precious natural resources.

☙

As reporters for the *St. Petersburg Times*, we wrote about Norton's press conference as part of a continuing series of stories on Florida's wetlands. Our series originated in 2003 with a decision to test whether no net loss was really working in Florida. It seemed like the ideal test case.

Florida's wetlands lack the appeal of Florida's beaches. The chamber of commerce isn't running ads featuring sunsets over the salt marshes. The legislature hasn't created a special license plate to raise money for buying up cypress domes. Nevertheless, Florida's wetlands are a wonder to behold. Florida has 10.5 million acres of them, more than any state other than Alaska. A larger percentage of Florida's land surface is occupied by wetlands than any other state. And it possesses a greater diversity of wetland types than the other 49 states, ranging from the tupelo swamps of the Panhandle to the tidal flats of the Keys.

Such a wide array can be overwhelming, even for scientists. For instance, most of the 1990 reference book *Ecosystems of Florida* is dry and clinical, but the chapter titled "Swamps" begins by giddily rattling off a list of wetland types that sounds like a demented jump-rope rhyme: "Heads, galls, domes, bogs, sogs, bays, strands and hammocks . . ." Then, sobering up a bit, the author notes that because of a lack of research "most of Florida's swamps are as much a mystery now as they were when first described."

The state has so many wetlands that are scattered so widely, developers say they can't possibly avoid them.

"You can't do anything in Florida and not impact under an acre," Chandler Morse of the National Home Builders Association told us.

In fact, the flawed report Norton was touting singled out the Sunshine State as having a special problem with its wetlands being wiped out: "Development conflicts with wetlands in rapidly growing areas of Florida were particularly evident. In some instances, these developments were also responsible for the creation of residential lakes and ponds used for water retention and aesthetics."

In other words, the report said Florida was rapidly swapping its swamps for stormwater ponds.

Selling Florida swampland to unsuspecting buyers dates back at least to the 1920s, but it's still going on. Often developers will excavate a wetland to create their stormwater retention pond or golf course water hazard, then use the dirt from the excavation to fill in the wetlands where the houses and golf course will be built. Sometimes they have to get even more creative with their use of fill.

In parts of fast-growing Pasco County on the state's west coast, new houses sit atop mounds of fill that can be four or five feet high. Each yard contains a second, smaller grass-covered knoll of fill. Under it is the septic tank. When the weather is dry, the contour of the yard looks like a mowing challenge, but that's all.

After hurricane season arrives June 1, though, rain often pours down in proportions that even Noah might regard as excessive. The yards fill with water, and the houses and septic tanks perch above the surface like small islands, to the surprise and dismay of new homeowners suddenly trapped by the rising flood.

Now the two mounds of fill make more sense, especially the smaller one. An inundated septic tank doesn't work.

"You buy a $500,000 house, you want to use the septic tank," explained Pasco resident Jennifer Seney, whose front yard is usually wet enough to sprout cypress trees.

Wet or dry, every inch of Florida's landscape is under tremendous development pressure. In 2004, Florida issued building permits for more new housing than any other state. Local governments approved a total of 250,000 new houses, condos, and apartments—nearly 50,000 more than California, a state that has twice the population and nearly three times the land area.

Put another way, Florida permitted one out of every seven new housing units in the United States in 2004, with a total estimated value of $36 billion. Most of that development is not taking place in the cities but in suburban and rural areas. By 2010, experts predict, more than one million acres of Florida's remaining farmland will be converted to urban uses.

So we wondered: facing such an intense drive to develop every piece of available land and the legal requirement to protect so many acres of swamps and marshes, how could federal officials ensure that Florida was not seeing a net loss wetlands?

We spent three years chasing the answer to that question—nagging federal and state officials, quizzing congressmen and state legislators, e-mailing biologists, rooting through untold boxes of government records, and slogging through marshes and swamps slated for extinction. We also pored over satellite imagery, built spreadsheets, and dug through law books, Federal Register notices, and academic studies.

We discovered a topsy-turvy world where a minus can equal a plus, dry land masquerades as wet, and supposedly scientific test results don't count if they yield an undesirable answer.

We found politicians from both parties who pay lip service to protecting the environment but really only care how quickly their contributors can get permits.

And we found regulators whose work costs the taxpayers millions of dollars, yet they say their only power is to delay wetland destruction, not deny it.

"It's a huge scam," one of them told us.

In short, what we found was not what the authors of the Clean Water Act had in mind 30 years ago.

It's more like what George Washington would have wanted.

1

"The National Emblem of Florida"

Back before he was the Father of His Country, George Washington was just another small businessman scuffling for work, a surveyor measuring and mapping the Virginia Colony. At one point, he surveyed the perimeter of the 2,000-square-mile Great Dismal Swamp and declared it "a glorious paradise" full of fish and game.

Then he joined a consortium in 1764 whose business plan called for using slaves to drain that "glorious paradise" and convert it to farms.

Back then, the vast expanse of land that would someday become the 50 United States contained an abundance of swamps, bogs, and marshes—nearly 392 million acres of muck and mud and mire. There were 221 million acres of wetlands alone in what would become the lower 48 states.

Not until halfway through the 20th century did anyone begin to grasp how important they were. No one knew back in Washington's day that one acre of wetland can hold up to 1.5 million gallons of floodwaters. Wipe out a wetland and we lose that storage capacity, so that when flooding hits it causes expensive damage to homes, stores, and offices.

No one knew until recently that for every 2.7 miles of wetland that a hurricane crosses, its storm surge is reduced by a foot. Nor did anyone know the valuable role wetlands play in recharging the supply of drinking water in the underground aquifer. By one estimate, a 500,000-acre swamp provides $25 million worth of aquifer recharge and flood storage—for free.

No one knew back then the role wetlands play in filtering out pollution flowing through them, removing up to 90 percent of some of the most common pollutants. And no one appreciated then how they provide a haven for fish and wildlife, some of it commercially valuable. Nowadays more than 70 percent of America's $111 billion annual fishing industry is based on wetland-dependent species.

And of course no one knew of the role wetlands play in absorbing carbon, storing as much as 40 percent of the earth's carbon output, thus combating the rise of global warming.

Instead, throughout most of U.S. history, "wetlands" were synonymous with "wasteland." Every swamp and bog was considered a noxious obstacle to settlement and transportation, a home to vermin and disease, a refuge for fearsome marauders—in short, a place to be avoided or, if possible, wiped out. Even the air of the swamps was supposed to be sickening, spawning a miasma of malaria and other diseases.

Because wetlands often existed near the mouths of rivers or on the edges of lakes, they got in the way of settling this new country. New York, Boston, and New Orleans were founded atop filled wetlands, as was the nation's new capital, named for its first drainer-in-chief.

Back then the common terms for draining or filling in wetlands were "reclamation" and "internal improvement," suggesting that what was going on was for the good of the populace. Florida's early settlers believed they needed a lot of reclamation. Across Florida's 35 million acres of land were some 21 million acres of wetlands, meaning almost three-fourths of the state was inundated at least part of the year.

That was a tad too damp for even John James Audubon. When the pioneer naturalist visited Florida in 1832, he was dumbstruck by its enormous flocks of colorful flamingos and roseate spoonbills, but complained that the places where they lived were just too mucky for a man to bear.

"The general wildness, the eternal labyrinth of waters and marshes, interlocked and apparently never ending, the whole surrounded by interminable swamps—all these things had a tendency to depress my spirits, notwithstanding some beautiful flowers, rich looking fruits, a pure sky and ample sheets of water at my feet," he wrote to his editor. Ever since childhood, he wrote, he had pictured Florida in his mind as "the garden of the United States," but now realized it was "a garden where all that is not mud, mud, mud is sand, sand, sand . . ."

Because so much of Florida's interior seemed so forbidding, when Florida became a state in 1845 its population of 65,500 was clumped in crude settlements here and there along the coast in places like St. Augustine, Tampa, and Pensacola. Overland travel usually required struggling through the blank places on the map. It was easier to take a boat around the coast, but no faster.

Small wonder, then, that Florida's political leaders viewed its enormous quantity of swampland—classified at the time as federal property—as a serious impediment to their plans for the state's future growth and, of course, their own future success.

Florida became a state in part because of a real estate deal. To interest territories in joining the Union, Congress offered to hand over control of 500,000 acres of federal land on the spot. Florida's most prominent politician of the time, David Levy Yulee, pushed hard for statehood so Florida could take charge of so much land. After he became one of Florida's first two U.S. senators, Yulee pushed the federal government to hand over even more land. He contended that if Florida could get the federal government to deliver all that swamp, the state could sell it to developers who would reclaim it and resell it to settlers. Then the state could use the money from selling its swampland to finance a railroad to transport people and goods across the state from the Atlantic Ocean to the Gulf of Mexico. One reason Yulee found this plan so appealing is because he expected to go into the railroad business.

So in 1850, in an effort spearheaded by Senator Yulee, Florida joined with a dozen other soggy states in persuading Congress to pass the Swamp and Overflowed Lands Act, which handed over every inch of federal wetlands to those states for "reclamation." By 1854, Congress had awarded nearly 65 million acres of swamps to 15 states with an eye toward draining them as fast as they could. Eventually, Florida was awarded a total of 20 million acres of land classified as "wet and unfit for cultivation."

Shortly thereafter the Florida legislature passed a law that handed over more than 3,000 acres of land and up to $10,000 in bonds for every mile of track that a railroad laid. By then Yulee, the true force behind passage of the new law, had founded a new railroad line to take advantage of it. Yulee's railroad made a profit its first year in business—thanks to a contract for carrying the mail, awarded by a committee that Yulee just happened to serve on.

Giving away millions of acres of wetlands to the states, which then handed them over to private individuals with few strings attached, was an ill-considered move for which the nation continues to pay a price.

"Of approximately 65 million acres of wetlands given to the states, nearly all are now in private ownership," government biologists Samuel Shaw and C. Gordon Fredine wrote in the groundbreaking 1956 circular that first suggested using the term "wetlands" for swamps and bogs and marshes. "The landowners can do with them as they wish. It is unfortunate that water-conservation and waterfowl-protection areas were not selected and set aside for public benefit at numerous locations before the lands were transferred from federal ownership.

If this had been the case, the government would not now be in the position of buying these 'wastelands' at high prices."

Florida's government did its best to give away every acre of its swamps. In fact it did too good a job. In a move that was to become a hallmark of Florida real estate practices, state officials by 1883 had handed out deeds to 17.5 million acres—even though at that point the state held title to only 14.7 million acres.

Still, it took a long time for "reclamation" to make much of a dent in Florida's extensive wetlands. Thirty years after the Swamp and Overflowed Lands Act, a visitor from out of state grumbled that "from what I have observed, I should think Florida was nine-tenths water, and the other tenth a swamp."

As late as the 1940s, Florida's landscape remained so inhospitable that it was the least populated state in the South. Air conditioning was a rarity. Theme parks were unheard of. Mosquitoes swarmed everywhere, held in check by little but the slap of a hand.

The folks who did the most to wipe out Florida's swamps were farmers. They dammed creeks and streams and dug ditches to drain the wetlands, creating pastures and fields for growing row crops. Loggers could be almost as destructive, clear-cutting entire cypress forests and floating the logs downriver to busy sawmills.

As the state grew, road building crews took a toll on the wetlands too. They would scoop out the muck on one or both sides of a route to build up the road bed, creating a highway bordered by a canal for flood control. If—as happened with the construction of the Tamiami Trail across the Everglades—the road happened to dam the natural flow of a swamp, so much the better.

When in the early 20th century scientists discovered that the source of malaria was not some floating miasma in the air of the swamps but rather the mosquitoes that swarmed there, government crews did their best to get rid of any standing water where the mosquitoes bred. They dug ditches that drained the swamps and even squirted oil on the surface of any remaining water to kill the larvae and everything else.

Meanwhile, real estate entrepreneurs came up with a way to create something out of what seemed like a whole lot of nothing. They sent big dredging machines rumbling up to a stretch of marshland or even open water to scoop out the stuff from the bottom, pile it up, and spread it out to fill any low-lying areas, then go back for more. Through the miracle of dredge-and-fill, wetlands became dry land.

The king of dredge-and-fill development in Florida was Carl Fisher, a half-blind daredevil from the Midwest who built the Indianapolis Speedway, planned the first transcontinental highway, and made a fortune selling gas-powered car headlights that occasionally blew up his factories.

When he brought his young bride, Jane, to tour some land he'd bought in Florida in 1912, all she saw were bug-infested mangrove swamps.

"I refused to find any charm in this deserted strip of ugly land rimmed with a sandy beach," Jane later wrote. "But Carl was like a man seeing visions."

What he saw was a way to make his mile-long "strip of ugly land" into a development paradise. Fisher spent up to $50,000 a day—nearly a million in today's figures—dredging up the bottom of Biscayne Bay, piling it up to build what became Miami Beach. He dispatched black laborers to chop down the mangroves. Then he filled in the swamps and, atop the fill, built houses, hotels, golf courses, even polo fields, all just in time for the 1920s real estate boom.

Humorist Will Rogers labeled Fisher's dredges "all-day suckers" and joked that "Carl rowed the customers out in the ocean and let them pick out some nice smooth water where they would like to build, and then he would replace the water with an island, and today the dredge is the national emblem of Florida."

Charles Green Rodes refined Fisher's technique into an art form. Along the New River in Fort Lauderdale, Rodes dredged a series of canals at right angles to the river, then used the fill to create a series of small peninsulas that reached into the water like grasping fingers. Each little peninsula became a cul-de-sac. Each lot along the street backed up to a newly dug canal so it could be sold as waterfront property. Their backyard docks provided homeowners with access not only to the New River but to the whole East Coast.

Rodes' finger-island idea proved so profitable it was copied throughout the state, most notably in Cape Coral, near Fort Myers, where dredge-and-fill work that wiped out 18,000 acres of wetlands in the 1960s created some 400 miles of finger canals along the Caloosahatchee River—and so many backyard docks for boats that now zoom along the river that Lee County frequently leads the state in boat-related manatee deaths.

Developers had a strong incentive to create more land in the 1920s as Florida real estate prices climbed to breathtaking heights. Thousands of would-be wheeler-dealers flocked to South Florida to cash in, buying options on lots that existed only on a blueprint, expecting to resell them at a huge markup before making any actual payments. The hyperbole employed to sell lots reached breathtaking heights too—a ditch to drain Coral Gables became "40 miles of inland waterway," while the lots along the stagnant canal became "waterfront" estates.

So many land speculators flooded Miami that "city fathers had been forced to pass an ordinance forbidding the sale of property in the street, or even the showing of a map, to prevent inordinate traffic congestion," Frederick Lewis Allen later wrote. "Motor-busses roared down Flagler Street, carrying 'prospects' on free trips to watch dredges and steam-shovels converting the outlying mangrove swamps and the sandbars of the Bay of Biscayne into gorgeous Venetian cities for the American homemakers and pleasure-seekers of the future. . . . The whole strip of coast line from Palm Beach southward was being developed into an American Riviera; for sixty-odd miles it was being rapidly staked out into fifty-foot lots. The fever had spread to Tampa, Sarasota, St. Petersburg, and other cities and towns on the West Coast. "

This is when the state's reputation for shady real estate deals involving swampland earned its spot in the American museum of stereotypes. In the movie *The Cocoanuts*—released in 1929, after the Florida real estate bubble burst and a pair of hurricanes dealt a near-fatal blow to whatever market was left—Groucho Marx tries to pass off a swamp as a subdivision, telling a potential customer, "You can have any kind of a home you want. You can even get stucco. Oh, how you can get stucco."

Still, over the following decades millions of people poured into Florida because Fisher and his successors found a way to make the place look like something it wasn't, a fantasyland of easy living and balmy breezes for $10 down and $10 a month.

The Florida fantasy reached its apotheosis in the mid-1960s when entertainment mogul Walt Disney sent representatives to secretly buy up 27,000 swampy acres in Orange and Osceola counties—a land mass twice the size of Manhattan that was 75 percent under water during the summer (which is why Disney acquired it for just $5 million).

When Walt himself surveyed the cypress trees and dark water, though, he announced, "No no, this won't do." The water had to be blue, he said, to match the color in his imagination. With enough money, his consultants assured him, it could be whatever he wanted.

To make it happen, Disney persuaded the Florida legislature to create a local government, the Reedy Creek Improvement District, which had the power to issue tax-free bonds, yet was answerable only to its largest landowner.

Turning all those wetlands into Walt Disney World required the Reedy Creek district to build 40 miles of drainage canals, 18 miles of levees, and 13 water-control structures—although the canals were artfully disguised as meandering streams. Excavating the 200-acre, 10-foot-deep Seven Seas Lagoon that now greets visitors to the Magic Kingdom yielded enough fill dirt to raise the theme park 12 feet above the surrounding countryside.

All this dredge-and-fill development began to take its toll, though.

In St. Petersburg, for instance, dredge-and-fill converted so much of Boca Ciega Bay to dry land that in 1957 Governor LeRoy Collins quipped that "pretty soon we are going to have to drill to find water here."

By 1964, developers creating new waterfront had converted more than 12 percent of Boca Ciega Bay's 20,000 acres into filled land. They did it by digging up the bottom from another 5,000 acres. Although the bay had once been one of the state's most productive fisheries, by 1966 biologists testified that the fish population had been so damaged by pollution and loss of habitat that the local fishing industry was now losing $1.4 million a year.

It wasn't just private developers who got rid of the swamps. Floridians got the federal government's help in altering the landscape. For instance, cattlemen wanted government help in changing the Kissimmee River, which once meandered 103 miles within a one- to two-mile-wide floodplain that was about 56 miles long. Amid the oxbows were some 35,000 acres of wetlands.

"The river and floodplain were not discreet and independent ecosystems, and the ebb and flow of their life was closely interrelated," a government report noted years later. "In November, ducks and probers, such as snipe and ibis, fed in the sloughs, potholes and wet prairies in upland areas near the tree line. Many of the same populations used the potholes, oxbows, backwaters of the floodplain in February, and the river and the deepest marshes and cypress swamps near the river in May."

Then along came the U.S. Army Corps of Engineers, which in the name of controlling floods to aid the ranchers straightened out the river's bends, forcing the water to shoot straight south into Lake Okeechobee. They eliminated 20,000 of the 35,000 acres of floodplain wetlands, and the only objection came from wildlife experts who bemoaned the loss of duck habitat.

The result, Corps officials conceded in 1991, was bad not just for ducks but for everyone. They noted their work had caused "diminished floodplain diversity, reduction in waterfowl and wading bird usage of the floodplain, and loss of habitat for forage, as well as larger riverine fish species. . . . Lack of flow associated with a meandering river system has degraded water quality, led to excessive sedimentation of river substrates, diminished habitat quality and diversity, and [led to] degradation of river biological communities."

In other words, without the oxbows and wetlands, the river was turned into a polluted ditch—in the name of progress.

Somehow the forces of progress and civilization always hung a bull's-eye on Florida's swamps. When the Dade County Port Authority was looking for a good location for a new airport that would be bigger than the four largest airports in America combined, it chose a spot in the Big Cypress Swamp, in the western headwaters of the Everglades. This was not an unusual move in the postwar era. Airports in Washington, New York, Philadelphia, Seattle, Salt Lake City, and Los Angeles are all built on what used to be wetlands, because the swamps generally offered wide-open spaces and no neighbors to complain about the noisy jets.

In 1968, the port authority bought a 39-square-mile site just north of Everglades National Park and quickly built a training runway, laying down the first of what were supposed to be many big, long slabs of asphalt. The "Everglades jetport," as the port authority called it, would have runways six miles long, with jets taking off every minute. Then, for easy access to the site from both coasts, the authority wanted a 1,000-foot-wide transportation corridor built from coast to coast. The corridor would include a new interstate highway, a high-speed mass transit system, even a "recreational waterway" for airboats and waterfoils.

From this very large seed of publicly funded construction, supporters expected to see a lush growth of highly profitable private real estate development—commercial properties to serve the jetport and residential properties for the employees and executives.

"By the year 2000, if one were to take the authority seriously, the site would have been ready to assume its manifest destiny as a spaceport for commercial rocket launching and recoveries, a sort of Cape Kennedy-by-the-Cypress," reported American Heritage magazine.

Port authority officials, still thinking about wetlands in terms of "reclamation" and "internal improvement," saw nothing wrong with their plans.

"Big Cypress Swamp is just typical South Florida real estate," said the authority's assistant director. "It's private property; eventually it's going to be put to human use."

But then a curious thing happened: people stood up for a swamp.

The chairman of the Flood Control District, which oversaw the pumps and levees and canals that handled the flow of water through South Florida, became alarmed that the proposed highway through the jetport site would block the flow of the River of Grass into Everglades National Park. He wrote letters sounding a warning to more than 100 influential people, stirring up the first protests against the project.

Then the president of the National Parks and Conservation Association published an article in his organization's magazine, trumpeting the dangers the park now faced from the jetport. That prompted 21 hunting, outdoor, and conservation groups and two unions to organize a consortium called the Everglades Coalition to battle the project. They got the attention of President Nixon's interior secretary as well as Congress, which held hearings.

Working behind the scenes to organize the battle against the jetport was a tall, lanky aide to Republican Governor Claude Kirk named Nathaniel Reed. Reed was the son of a New York theater producer whose family developed Jupiter Island, the winter playground of rich families. Reed grew up fishing in Hobe Sound and fell in love with Florida's natural bounty. Standing six foot five with a patrician nose and piercing blue eyes, in repose he looked like a fragile wading bird. But when defending the environment, he could roar like an angry bear.

Reed's most crucial ally in stopping the jetport was a tenacious former television reporter named Joe Browder. The ex-journalist knew how to work the publicity machine. He persuaded reporters from *Life, Look, Time,* and NBC's *Today* show to come down to Florida and cover the controversy, ensuring the jetport issue would get national attention. A Sierra Club official wrote later that the Big Cypress battle had "generated more notoriety, more conservationist ire, and more concern about environmental values than any single public works project conceived in this nation, anywhere, at any time."

In rounding up allies, Browder even approached a famous Miami author for help. But Marjory Stoneman Douglas, whose 1947 bestseller *Everglades: River of Grass* had first brought the state's most famous marsh to a national audience, demurred. Nobody would listen to some half-blind old lady, the 78-year-old writer said. People only pay attention to organizations.

"Well," Browder retorted, "why don't you start an organization?"

So she did, founding Friends of the Everglades with dues of $1 a year so anyone could join. Douglas not only denounced the jetport, she transformed herself into Florida's environmental conscience. She spent the next 30 years—until her death at 108—fearlessly confronting local, state, and federal officials, wagging her finger at them like Jiminy Cricket in a floppy garden-club hat.

Before long the jetport fight turned nasty. All the complaints about the environmental damage that would result just made the project's advocates dig in their heels.

"Alligators make nice shoes and pocketbooks," growled Florida's transportation secretary. "I'm not really concerned about the alligators. And I don't miss seeing the dinosaur either."

The director of the port authority jeered that to keep the conservationists happy, he would build them an astrodome for butterfly chasing. He boasted that "a new city is going to rise up in the middle of Florida. You're going to have one whether you like it or not."

Browder, with the help of a pioneering scientist named Art Marshall, compiled a list of 119 questions about the project's potential environmental impact, including fuel spills, air pollution, and future development. When Dade County officials held a meeting to answer the questions, though, the replies were repeatedly evasive: "The answer to that question is under study."

Finally an angry Reed leaped to his feet and berated the mayor for wasting their time. The mayor responded by branding Reed and Browder "white militants."

What killed the jetport at last was a combination of science and politics. The science came from the nation's first-ever environmental impact statement, supervised by a U.S. Geological Survey senior scientist named Luna Leopold, son of *Sand County Almanac* author Aldo Leopold. Leopold, working with Marshall, produced a study that concluded that the jetport would produce 4 million gallons of sewage and 1.5 million gallons of industrial waste a day, as well as scatter 10,000 tons of air pollutants across the Big Cypress-Everglades watershed.

Add to that the projected residential and commercial community of 150,000 people expected to sprout around the jetport, the report noted, and the end result seemed obvious: "Development of the proposed jetport and its attendant facilities will lead to land drainage and development for agriculture, industry, housing, transportation and services in the Big Cypress Swamp which will inexorably destroy the South Florida ecosystem and thus Everglades National Park."

Subsequent scientific studies reached similar conclusions. As a result, Reed convinced Governor Kirk to declare that the jetport belonged somewhere else.

Meanwhile then president Richard Nixon, whose administration was helping to pay for the jetport, decided to halt construction. Nixon didn't do it out of any heartfelt environmental concern but to bolster his bid for reelection by stealing the thunder from a potential opponent who had latched onto the jetport issue. Then, to make sure the killed-off jetport plan stayed dead, the federal government bought a big chunk of Big Cypress and turned it into a wilderness preserve.

The salvation of Big Cypress Swamp marked one of the first major triumphs of America's budding environmental movement, a movement that would soon lead to a new law to protect all of its swamps and marshes and bogs—and a compromise that would ultimately undermine those good intentions.

2

A Reasonable Curb

In the 200 years it took to transform 13 disorganized colonies into the most powerful country in the world, Florida lost nearly half its swamps, bogs, and marshes. Other states ditched and drained and filled a greater percentage of their wetlands: California, for instance, eliminated 90 percent. But acre for acre, Floridians wiped out more of their wetlands than any other state—roughly nine million acres.

However, as the battle over the Everglades jetport showed, the tide was about to turn. By the end of the 1960s, water pollution problems were becoming unavoidably obvious. Two-thirds of the country's lakes, rivers, and coastal waters had been declared unsafe for fishing or swimming. Lake Erie was biologically dead. The Detroit River contained six times the recommended healthy limit for mercury.

To make the danger as plain (and smelly) as possible, the nation's waterways were plagued by a record number of fish kills. The largest one ever documented left 26 million dead fish littering the surface of Florida's Lake Thonotosassa, killed by the waste spewing from four food-processing plants.

Then, to provide a vivid symbol of how foul America's water had become, Ohio's heavily polluted Cuyahoga River caught fire. It wasn't the first time it had happened, but this time the news caught the public's attention, even inspiring a bitterly satirical song by Randy Newman.

With the dawning of the first Earth Day in 1970, the nation clamored for the government to do something to clean up the air and water. A host of new laws ensued, including the Clean Air Act. But coming up with a law to halt water pollution took a little longer.

Congress had tried before to do something about water pollution. It passed a law back in 1948 called the Federal Water Pollution Control Act, offering loans to help pay for new sewage plants. But it left the job of stopping pollution to the states, and so everyone continued dumping waste into the nearest river.

Another law that Congress passed back at the turn of the century could have been used to stop polluters. But the government never really enforced it.

In 1899 a senator from Maine named William P. Frye sponsored a bill to clear up navigational problems in the nation's waterways. Cities and businesses would routinely dump garbage, sewage, even animal carcasses into rivers and lakes, obstructing boats trying to get by. To halt the practice, the federal agency in charge of maintaining the nation's waterways, the U.S. Army Corps of Engineers, drafted the Rivers and Harbors Act for Frye, and he convinced his colleagues to pass it. Two sections of the act, Section 10 and Section 13, became important precursors for future laws on water pollution.

The act's Section 13, sometimes known as the Refuse Act, forbade dumping "any refuse matter of any kind or description" in a navigable waterway without government permission. Customs officials and Corps personnel had the power to arrest violators, who could be charged with a misdemeanor. The penalty: fines of up to $2,500 per violation and even jail time. And as an incentive for whistleblowers, Frye's law said any citizen who reported a violation could collect up to half of the fine as a reward.

"No modern environmental law matched Section 13's resolute Victorian clarity," one modern historian has observed.

But for decades Section 13 was enforced only intermittently. It was viewed by federal officials as a minor component of the Rivers and Harbors Act. Meanwhile Section 10 got all the attention.

Section 10 said that anyone who wanted to put something in a waterway that might obstruct navigation must first get permission from the Corps. Administering Section 10 spurred the Corps to set up a national permitting program, the first one in the country's history. Rarely did the Corps turn anyone down, however.

Six decades after Frye's law passed, government officials suddenly discovered what Section 13, the Refuse Act, could do. In a 1960 case, the U.S. Supreme Court held that an Illinois steel mill had violated the Refuse Act by illegally filling up the Calumet River with its waste. The court ruled the government could use the act to force a polluter to halt its discharges.

Then, in 1966, the high court broadened the act's reach even further with a case out of Florida. Standard Oil Company had spilled airplane fuel into the St. Johns River. Federal prosecutors charged the company with violating the Refuse Act. A district judge tossed out the charges, finding that commercially valuable fuel did not meet the definition of "refuse." But on appeal, the U.S. Supreme Court ruled that the law covered "all foreign substances and pollutants."

"This case comes to us at a time in the nation's history when there is greater concern than ever over pollution—one of the main threats to our free-flowing rivers and to our lakes as well," Supreme Court Justice William O. Douglas wrote in the 6 to 3 majority opinion.

Armed with the two Supreme Court opinions, federal officials could attack any water pollution problem in America using the Refuse Act. In one nationally publicized case, Interior Secretary Walter Hickel even used the act in 1970 to sue Florida Power and Light for allowing a power plant to discharge large amounts of superheated water into Biscayne Bay, causing thermal pollution.

While the Corps was slow to employ the Refuse Act, Section 10 did give it another surprisingly powerful weapon it could employ in the war on pollution—and in March 1967, Army Col. Robert P. Tabb lit its fuse. The subsequent explosion continues to reverberate four decades later.

Back then, Florida was still selling off pieces of submerged land to Carl Fisher wannabes. In the 1950s a pair of well- connected Florida developers named Alfred Zabel and David Russell bought 11.5 acres of submerged land in Boca Ciega Bay. They planned to dredge up the bottom and dump the fill into the water to create a kidney-shaped chunk of dry land that would stretch about 1,200 feet into the bay. They could then use the new land to expand Zabel's Causeway Mobile Home Park.

Far larger dredge-and-fill projects had been approved for Boca Ciega Bay in the past. Dredge-and-fill projects were so numerous by 1957 that a *St. Petersburg Times* editorial noted that an up-to-date map showed "an incredible profusion of black slivers thrust lengthwise into the water, so numerous in places that the bay appeared to have been segmented by a series of dams."

Zabel was a town councilman in a St. Petersburg suburb called South Pasadena, while Russell was a socially prominent restaurateur, motel owner, and cofounder of an exclusive private school named Admiral Farragut Academy. He sometimes referred to himself as "Captain." The pair expected smooth sailing for their project.

But by the time Zabel and Russell came along, the damage that such developments caused had become quite evident. Many local residents opposed their proposal. The opponents showed up at a 1958 Pinellas County Commission meeting ready to combat the project armed with the latest technology: color slides showing how previous dredging projects had turned the bay muddy and foul, producing a stench at low tide.

The developers' reaction could be summed up as, "Too bad."

"A lot of people don't like what my clients proposed to do," Zabel and Russell's attorney told county commissioners, "but it is their property, and they have a right to develop it as long as no adverse material effects result."

Pinellas County commissioners could see the "adverse material effects" in the slides, though. They voted unanimously to turn down the dredge-and-fill permit, but the developers sued. The Florida Supreme Court overruled the county's decision 4 to 3.

Now, with their local permit in hand, the developers figured they would have no trouble getting their Section 10 permit from the Corps. Filling in their little piece of the bay would have no effect on navigation, and the Corps had not seen any problem with all those other, larger bay dredging projects.

But the Corps and the U.S. Fish and Wildlife Service had recently signed a formal agreement that the Corps would consult with the agency any time a dredge-and-fill project might affect wildlife. Mindful of Pinellas County's rather loud misgivings about the Zabel-Russell project's impact on the rest of the bay, the Corps sought the wildlife agency's opinion.

That's how the permit application landed on the desk of a young Interior Department lawyer named Tom Jorling. Known for being both intelligent and intense, Jorling was not just a lawyer. A former science teacher, Jorling also held a degree in the fledgling field of ecology. When Jorling read through the application, he didn't like what he saw, and he convinced his bosses to put up a fight.

"We got my superiors to agree that they should turn it into a significant case and make the case that the Corps should turn down the permit," Jorling recalled.

Now both the Interior Department and St. Petersburg residents were voicing objections to the permit. Col. Tabb, a West Point grad who had seen action at Omaha Beach during World War II, waded straight into the controversy by convening a public hearing at St. Petersburg's Bayfront Center. About 100 people showed up, most of them opposed to the project and to what it would do to what one called the "poor little ol' beat up bay."

To the developers' surprise, on March 14, 1967, Col. Tabb denied the permit. Not only was the denial unusual, so was the reason. While the dredge-and-fill would do nothing to upset navigation, Tabb wrote, he turned the permit down because of "the feeling of the Department of the Army that issuance of the permit would result in a distinctly harmful effect on the fish and wildlife resources of Boca Ciega Bay." Jorling's argument had convinced the colonel.

Naturally, the developers sued. The Corps was represented by the U.S. Justice Department, which based its legal brief on Jorling's work.

Figure 1. In 1967 Col. Robert Tabb denied businessmen Alfred Zabel and David Russell a dredge and fill permit for environmental reasons, establishing the importance of favoring the public interest over a developer's profit. (Photograph courtesy of *St. Petersburg Times*.)

The case was heard by U.S. District Judge Isaac Benjamin "Ben" Krentzman Jr., a stocky, gray-haired man who had grown up in the Florida Panhandle town of Milton, the son of a Jewish store owner and a Methodist mother. Now an elder in the Presbyterian Church, the judge—an Army lieutenant colonel during World War II—was known for his autocratic courtroom manner and his expertise in admiralty law. Krentzman ruled against the Corps, finding that Section 10 permits should only be concerned with hazards to navigation, not environmental degradation. Perhaps people interested in conservation would disagree, wrote the judge—who happened to be an avid fisherman himself—but if so, they should go change the law.

When the Justice Department appealed Krentzman's ruling, a three-judge panel from the New Orleans–based Fifth Circuit Court of Appeals convened at the old post office in Jacksonville to hear the arguments. Somehow a discussion of the importance of preserving Boca Ciega's seagrass beds as fish nurseries turned into a debate over whether the government was penalizing private property owners just so fish could have sex.

"The federal government is trying to come in and say I must let grass grow on my land so as not to interfere with the love life of little fishes," the developers' attorney told the appellate judges.

The judges were not swayed by the aquatic sex-life argument. In July 1970, the Fifth Circuit Court of Appeals ruled that Tabb was right to deny the permit. The government had a responsibility to examine any factor that might affect interstate commerce, the court noted, and then pointed out: "Dredge and fill projects are activities which may tend to destroy the ecological balance and thereby affect commerce substantially."

When the ruling was announced, "many in the Corps were just as surprised as the developer," a top Corps attorney later wrote.

By the time the appeals court had issued its ruling, Captain Russell was dead of a heart attack, but ex-councilman Zabel persisted. He tried to get the U.S. Supreme Court to hear the case. In February 1971, the high court declined to take the appeal, allowing the Fifth Circuit's ruling to stand. Zabel did not live to see his final defeat. Like Russell, he died from a heart attack before the Supreme Court decision.

The case of *Zabel v. Tabb* set an important precedent: the federal government could deny a dredge-and-fill permit based on environmental grounds, putting the public interest ahead of private profit—a revolutionary concept in environmental regulation.

The notion that the federal government had had the power all along to stop water pollution using a law passed in 1899 outraged many in the growing environmental movement. Pete Seeger even wrote a song criticizing the Corps for failing to stop pollution, although "The Eighteen Ninety-Nine" didn't catch on quite as strongly as "If I Had a Hammer."

With the public demanding the government do something to clean up its waterways, President Nixon tried to score political points by creating the Refuse Act Permit Program in 1970. The program set up a two-tiered permit process. Nixon gave the Corps the job of granting permits for the discharge or deposit of anything that went into a stream or water body. But Nixon's newly created Environmental Protection Agency, not the Corps, would determine whether the discharge would affect water quality.

Potential polluters were told they had just six months to get a permit. So by December 1971, nearly 20,000 Refuse Act permit applications had poured into the Corps. It quickly processed 11,000 and shipped them over to the fledgling EPA for water quality determinations. That's where the whole process bogged down.

The EPA had approved just 21 of them before a Sierra Club member, upset that one of the 21 was a permit to pollute his favorite canoeing river, filed suit. U.S. District Judge Aubrey Robinson issued a ruling halting the whole program, and it never got started again.

By then, though, another senator from Maine was leading the charge for a far stronger water pollution law.

At six foot four, with his wavy hair and stiff manner, Edmund Muskie looked more like a prosperous mortician than an ambitious politician. The son of Polish immigrants, Muskie grew up in a mill town where the local factory routinely dumped its waste in the river. He learned early on that there's a connection between the environment and the economy. As governor of Maine, Muskie tried to lure a manufacturer to the town of Bedford on the Saco River, only to lose out to another state because, the company said, the Saco was already too polluted.

By 1971, Muskie was widely considered the frontrunner for the Democratic presidential nomination. In September, *Time* magazine put him on the cover with a headline declaring he had the nomination all locked up. Although *Time* didn't mention it, Muskie's greatest strength was his ability to round up bipartisan support for groundbreaking environmental legislation like the Clean Air Act. He became known as the Senate's "Mr. Clean."

About a month after that particular *Time* magazine hit the newsstands, Muskie's Public Works Committee produced a bill that dealt with water pollution. In November 1971, the bill—then known simply as the amendments to the 1948 Federal Water Pollution Control Act—passed the Senate with no dissent. The House passed a less stringent version. All through the summer of 1972 a conference committee worked to hammer out a compromise, meeting nearly 40 times, usually starting early in the morning and going late into the night. It broke only for the two parties' political conventions.

Despite some backstage maneuvering by the Nixon Administration to kill the bill, on October 4, 1972, Muskie unveiled the final result. He noted that in 13 years in the Senate "I have never before participated in a conference which has consumed so many hours, been so arduous in its deliberations, or demanded so much attention to detail from the members."

By then Muskie's presidential campaign had come unraveled after a disastrous finish in the Florida primary in February 1972. He was victimized by

Nixon's "plumbers" and their dirty tricks, blew his cool in the face of attacks on his wife by a New Hampshire newspaper, and repeatedly fumbled his attempts to connect with young voters opposed to the Vietnam War. As gonzo journalist Hunter S. Thompson wrote in *Rolling Stone*, Muskie campaigned "like a farmer with terminal cancer trying to borrow money on next year's crop." Another candidate, George McGovern, won the Democratic nomination (and the right to be crushed by the Nixon reelection juggernaut).

Now, only a month before the presidential election, Muskie was no longer distracted by his own campaign and could concentrate on his water pollution bill. He called for final passage, casting the issue in the direst of terms: "Man, no less than the peregrine falcon and the mountain lion, is an endangered species."

As usual, Muskie had lined up bipartisan support for his bill, in this case led by Howard Baker, the folksy Republican senator from Tennessee, who called the bill "far and away the most significant and promising piece of environmental legislation ever enacted by the Congress." It sailed through the Senate on a unanimous vote and drew only 10 "nays" in the House.

Nixon's own EPA secretary was pushing for him to sign it, but he vetoed the bill anyway. Nixon said he didn't object to cleaning up pollution, but rather to the cost—an estimated $24 billion to help cities and counties across the nation stop dumping raw sewage into rivers, bays, and streams. That was $18 billion more than he wanted to spend.

The bill's sponsors, determined to override the veto, contrasted Nixon's concern for mere dollars with their own concern for the human cost of coping with a polluted world.

"Can we afford clean water?" Muskie asked his colleagues. "Can we afford rivers and lakes and streams and oceans which continue to make life possible on this planet? Can we afford life itself?"

And Baker asked, "If we cannot swim in our lakes and rivers, if we cannot breathe the air God has given us, what other comforts can life offer us?"

Hours after Nixon's veto, just before Congress was set to adjourn, both houses of Congress again took up the water pollution bill. For the first time since Nixon had taken office, and only three weeks before he won reelection by an overwhelming margin, Congress overrode a presidential veto. The votes were not even close—52 to 12 in the Senate and 247 to 23 in the House.

The new law—later to be known simply as the Clean Water Act—said no one could discharge pollution into the nation's waterways without getting federal permission. The goal was to reduce pollution to "restore and maintain the chemical, physical, and biological integrity of our nation's waters." The law optimistically called for a "zero discharge of pollutants" into the nation's rivers and streams by 1985.

It wasn't just the law's aim that was broad. It also marked an attempt to extend further than ever before the federal government's reach into regulating interstate commerce, to cover every conceivable source of water pollution.

In the past, federal laws related to the nation's waterways such as the Rivers and Harbors Act confined themselves solely to places where boats could float. In the 19th century that was the primary method of carrying freight long distances, so a river's navigability matched up well with the government's power to regulate interstate commerce under the U.S. Constitution.

While the 20th century brought new forms of commerce, the old navigability standard still applied—until Congress passed this new law in 1972. The law mentioned "navigable waters," but it also included a new phrase, "waters of the United States."

That second phrase was intended to cover pretty much everything that's wet, because water pollution could come from just about anywhere.

As Representative John Dingell, R-Michigan, explained in presenting the conference committee report on the bill: "Thus, this new definition clearly encompasses all water bodies, including main streams and their tributaries, for water quality purposes. No longer are the old, narrow definitions of navigability . . . going to govern matters covered by this bill."

The authors of the new law were particularly concerned about halting the loss of wetlands to dredging and filling, said Leon Billings, who as Muskie's chief aide was one of the new law's primary architects. The other architect was Tom Jorling, now working for Senator Baker as minority counsel on the Senate committee writing the bill. Because of his past work on the *Zabel v. Tabb* case, Jorling was well aware of the shortcomings of the Rivers and Harbors Act. So was Billings, who was frustrated with the Corps' reluctance to block more dredge-and-fill projects the way Col. Tabb did.

Billings and Jorling inserted language in the act's Section 404 that equated the dumping of fill dirt into a swamp with pumping toxic chemicals into a river: it was prohibited unless the developer first obtained government permission.

"It was an effort to give much more explicit statutory authority over dredge and fill," Jorling recalled 30 years later.

But it wasn't all that explicit, really—for one thing, Section 404 didn't actually use the word "wetlands." After all, as the recent fight over the Everglades jetport had shown, not everyone valued swamps. Instead, all the new law said was that the government could "issue permits . . . for the discharge of dredged or fill material into the navigable waters at specified disposal sites."

And then there was that part about "waters of the United States"—what did that really mean? Did it extend beyond coastal mangroves all the way inland to the freshwater swamps?

The ambiguity meant that regulators had to feel their way at first, said Vance Hughes, one of the first attorneys hired by the EPA to enforce environmental laws. The first big test case involved yet another dredge-and-fill project in St. Petersburg, this time a new subdivision called Harbor Isles proposed by a rakish and combative developer named Robert Wray and his partner, lawyer W. Langston Holland.

Wray, the son of a former city attorney, grew up along the shores of Tampa Bay, wading barefoot through the clear water to look for clams. He still enjoyed fishing and scuba diving, but that didn't stop him from planning a $45-million dredge-and-fill development covering about 281 acres of a section of the bay called Papys Bayou.

When more than 500 people signed a petition opposing his plans to excavate 1.3 million cubic yards of spoil from the bay for his subdivision, Wray said he didn't want to hurt the environment either.

"There's nobody around here who loves nature any more than I do," Wray told a reporter. "I still challenge anyone to show me a better project. This is going to be the best project in St. Petersburg."

State biologists reported that Wray and Holland had "chosen to develop in a rich estuarine area whose very nature precludes tolerance of human disturbance." But the developers got their permits—one from the county, one from the state, and a Section 10 permit from the Corps—and set to work dredging the bay bottom and dumping spoil in the mangroves.

That's when popular opposition to using submerged land for private profit led to a new legal fight, using the newly passed law.

"I got a call from the U.S. attorney in Tampa: There was a development beginning in the mangroves in Papys Bayou, and the locals were incensed by the drag lines dredging up all this dirt and putting it into the mangroves," recalled Hughes, who was based in the EPA's Atlanta office. "So I went down there and filed for a temporary restraining order" under Section 404 of the new water pollution law.

This was a risky move, since no one was sure whether Section 404 really protected swamps and marshes that lay inland. But Hughes believed Dingell's comments and other indications from the congressional record showed that this was what the new law was intended to cover.

"The developer showed up with three prominent lawyers," Hughes said. "They were caught off-guard by the argument we put together. We had some good expert witnesses who explained what the effects were."

The experts who talked about the dire effects of dredge and fill were a big hit with the presiding judge: the autocratic Krentzman, again—the same judge who had ruled against the environment in *Zabel v. Tabb*. Hughes said Krentzman quickly grasped Hughes' line of reasoning and saw what the destruction of the mangroves would mean to all the wildlife that depended on them. Hughes figured it was because of the judge's interest in fishing, but Krentzman's prior experience with *Zabel v. Tabb* probably didn't hurt.

At the December 1973 hearing, Krentzman ruled for the EPA's request for a temporary restraining order to stop Holland and Wray from any further unpermitted dredge-and-fill work above the mean high water line, and he upheld the EPA position in subsequent proceedings.

"Congress and the courts have become aware of the lethal effect pollution has on all organisms," Judge Krentzman wrote in an opinion that cited the Fifth Circuit's *Zabel v. Tabb* decision. "Weakening any of the life support systems bodes disaster for the rest of the interrelated life forms. To recognize this and yet hold that pollution does not affect interstate commerce unless committed in navigable waters below the mean high water line would be contrary to reason."

Krentzman's decision in *U.S. v. Holland* "gave us, early on, a foundation to regulate polluters on a very broad plain," Hughes said.

With Krentzman's ruling in hand, Hughes then teamed up with Jim Range, a young clerk in the Miami U.S. Attorney's Office, to go after similar dredge-and-fill operations in the Florida Keys, too. Hughes compared the strategy to the one employed by the Allies in beating Germany during World War II: "It was sort of an Eastern Front and a Western Front."

Along with his law degree, Range also had a master's degree in aquatic biology that made him eager to enlist in Hughes' war on dredge-and-fill development.

"I was quite interested in the fact that they were ripping the devil out of the Keys," said Range, a native of Tennessee. "Then Vance shows up and says, 'We need to do something about what's happening in Monroe County.'"

During the first hearing on their first case together, Range said he was extremely nervous, a feeling that turned to fear when the judge invited him and the developer's attorney back to his chambers. He thought perhaps the judge was angry with him.

"Well, I walk in," Range said, "and over his head's a great big bonefish, mounted, and I said to myself, 'Everything's going to be all right.'"

Sure enough, another angling judge had understood the environmental damage being wrought by the developers and ruled for the EPA.

Range figures he and Hughes took on six or seven more dredge-and-fill cases throughout 1974, hitting a home run every time they came to bat.

Their legal crusade against Florida dredge-and-fill developers did more than just protect the environment and establish the extent of the new law's power. It laid the groundwork for the 1977 revision of the Clean Water Act. The man in charge of handling the rewrite of Section 404 was Range, now chief aide to Senator Baker.

At the time, "404 was clearly on the chopping block," said Hughes, who by then had become an assistant EPA administrator in Washington. A series of controversial decisions involving wetlands protection had stirred up political opposition to Section 404's broad reach. The House had tried to scale back the law to cover only navigable waterways, and the Senate came within one vote— Senator Baker's, as it turned out—of eliminating Section 404 entirely.

Just five years after passing the original version, the idea of providing government protection for wetlands was still not an easy sell among some members of Congress, but Range and Baker were determined to give it a try.

"I remember being called into the cloakroom for a bipartisan meeting of senators," Range said. "I walked in and somebody said 'OK, this is the one.' And [Texas senator] John Tower said, 'OK, Jim, what is a wetland and why in the hell should I care? Is that all that mud down in South Texas that they been trying to get rid of since I was a boy?'"

Range said he started explaining to the diminutive Texas senator why wetlands were important, "and I could tell from the look on his face that he was somewhat incredulous." Finally, he said, Muskie or Baker grabbed his shoulder and told him that was enough. Somehow they got the new version through Congress with a revised, but still alive, Section 404, and President Jimmy Carter signed it, proclaiming, "The nation's wetlands will continue to be protected."

Given what he had seen happening in the Keys, Range said he knew Section 404 was one law that had to stay on the books when the revised Clean Water Act was passed.

"The bottom line was to try to stem what the scientific evidence of the day showed was a problem: a dramatic reduction in wetlands habitat around the nation," Range said. "What we wanted to do was show it was an environmentally sensitive activity and put some kind of reasonable curb on it."

Section 404 of the Clean Water Act marked a turning point in the way America dealt with environmental issues. Perhaps more importantly, it marked a change in how the government dealt with private property rights because, thanks to the Swamp and Overflowed Lands Act, most wetlands were not publicly owned.

"Federal regulation of wetlands was the first major step toward broad protection of landscape features," a National Academy of Sciences panel reported 20 years later. "Whereas regulation of air and water applies primarily to public or corporate entities, regulation of wetlands extends to individual property owners."

That, of course, is also where Section 404—or rather, the way it's carried out—has stumbled. Although wetlands that are left in their natural state provide broad benefits for the whole community, they are usually considered a drag on their owner's pocketbook. The conflict between what will benefit the general public and what will profit the individual property owner has frequently been settled by favoring the desires of the property owner.

The main trouble with the Clean Water Act, say critics, is that Congress handed the job of protecting the nation's wetlands to the least likely agency to act as a friend of the environment. It was the same agency that had at first refused to carry out the Refuse Act: the Corps of Engineers.

3

"Let Us Try"

Since its inception two centuries ago, the Corps of Engineers has built its reputation on manipulating nature to do man's bidding. The Corps has built dams, canals, and levees to alter the natural flow of waterways ranging from the Mississippi River to the Everglades. Its motto is "Essayons"—that's French for "Let us try," as opposed to "Wait, what's going to happen if we do that?"

Even though it has left a big mark on much of the American landscape, for the most part the taxpayers have no idea how this gargantuan federal agency is spending billions of dollars of their money.

"The Corps is in a strange position," said Chuck Hummer, longtime head of the Corps' national dredging program. "Most of the public doesn't recognize what it does and couldn't care less."

Originally formed by George Washington to fortify his positions during the Revolutionary War, the Corps early on controlled the fledgling military academy at West Point. As a result, it offered a growing nation a cadre of college-trained engineers able to turn the dreams of westward expansion into a buildable reality.

In 1824, Congress put the Corps in charge of surveying roads and canals needed for commerce as well as military purposes and authorized it to alter the course of the Mississippi and Ohio rivers to improve navigation. After getting that first green light, the Corps has never looked back. What was born as a military unit became in effect a public works bureaucracy, responsible for overseeing all kinds of nonmilitary missions—damming the Columbia River, building roads through Yellowstone National Park, finishing the Washington Monument.

Carl Fisher would have made a good Corps commander. According to an official Army history, in the 1880s the Corps "transformed the unsightly Potomac Flats" that lay just south of the Mall in Washington, D.C., by "dredging the river channel, dumping the spoil on the Flats, thus creating new land. . . . In

1897, Congress dedicated some 600 acres of reclaimed land, henceforth called West Potomac Park and East Potomac Park." Then the Corps planted the city's first cherry trees.

To boost its budget and influence, the Corps over the decades took on more and more construction work that had little to do with the Army's needs and more to do with accommodating politically powerful agricultural and development interests. From the 1930s to the 1960s it played a crucial role in remodeling Florida, drying out wetlands in the name of flood control so the land could be exploited. The Corps not only straightened the Kissimmee. It built a giant berm around Lake Okeechobee that starves the Everglades of its traditional source of water. And it created a maze of pumps and levees and canals through South Florida that still flushes an estimated one billion gallons of water a day out to sea at a time when Miami-Dade County's sprawl is starving for new water supplies.

True to its motto, the Corps was ready to try anything. At one point the Corps even proposed a complex scheme called the Four Rivers Project which called for converting four of Central Florida's major rivers—the Withlacoochee, the Hillsborough, the Ocklawaha, and the Peace—into straight-as-a-ruler canals just like the Kissimmee. (Fortunately for Central Florida's environment and drinking water supply, the plan never got enough traction to be carried out.)

That such a first-class destroyer of the natural landscape would be put in charge of protecting the nation's wetlands is just one more oddity of the Corps. As *Washington Post* reporter Michael Grunwald wrote in an award-winning investigative series in 2000, the Corps is the strangest agency in the federal government:

> It is an executive branch bureaucracy that takes marching orders from Congress, a military-run organization with an overwhelmingly civilian work force, an environmental regulator despised by environmentalists. The Corps has $62 billion worth of civil works projects underway—three times the federal spending on cancer research over the last decade.

As Grunwald noted, even its command structure is unusual. "The Corps of Engineers has this funny culture," said retired Col. Terry Rice, who spent more than 20 years in the Corps and ended his career in Florida. "There are 35,000 people in the Corps, 500 of them in the military—and they have all the leadership."

The Corps is commanded by a three-star general, called the chief of engineers. Below him are generals who oversee various regions. And below them are the colonels, like Rice, known as district engineers, who oversee each of the Corps' districts.

Each district engineer serves just three years before moving on, while the civilian workers may remain in their jobs for decades. As a result, the 38 districts all have their own culture, and they function somewhat independently of each other.

Rice said one of his predecessors in Jacksonville warned him about that, telling him: "What you have to understand is, you have incredible power to shape things. But your people don't want you to know that until it's time for you to leave." The staff knows the colonel will be gone shortly, so "their whole attitude is they want the district engineer to do as little as possible. They want the district engineer to be a figurehead. A new one comes in, they give him things to do" to keep him out of their hair, the retired colonel explained.

The Corps' military leadership answers to civilian officials at the Pentagon, and thus to the president. But its staff in each district is more concerned with what that area's congressman wants, because that's where the agency's funding comes from. Usually what Congress cares about is pork-barrel projects that boost politicians' reputations or their contributors' bank accounts.

"Most projects are initiated through the political process at the local level, and then sent through the review process," to see if they make economic sense, Chuck Hummer said. "Often it reflects political considerations over economic ones."

A good example of how the Corps could put its thumb on the scale to achieve a politically desired result was the Cross-Florida Barge Canal. The idea of digging a canal across the state was first conceived back in the early 1800s, when ships were major freight carriers around Florida and captains fretted about navigating through the treacherous passes of the Keys. A canal would give them the perfect short-cut through the Florida peninsula, a triumph of geometry over geography. But the alignment of money and political will to get the canal built didn't occur until the can-do, ask-not 1960s.

When the Corps did its study on the economic benefits of the canal project, the agency's leaders discovered that it no longer made economic sense to build a canal. Barges had long ago been replaced by trains and trucks as a way to move goods. But to keep the politicians happy, the Corps found a way to justify building it anyway. They invented a bogus benefit called "land enhancement" that made the numbers work, at least on paper. What "land enhancement" meant was that gouging a big hole in the land was supposed to make it more valuable.

Before a federal judge stopped the project in 1971, the Corps had flattened thousands of cypress trees and built a dam that backed up the Ocklawaha River for 16 miles, drowning a vast stretch of the Ocala National Forest—all based on that bogus benefits study. The damage has never been repaired.

By the late 1960s, people were beginning to notice the consequences of "Essayons." In a 1969 *Playboy* article, Supreme Court Justice William O. Douglas branded the Corps "Public Enemy No. 1." Former Interior secretary Stewart Udall wrote that the Corps was "rigidly trapped" by its own past: "Resembling brachiosaurus, a giant waterloving dinosaur with less brains per pound of flesh than any other vertebrate, the Corps has survived from the Jurassic Age of Engineering when dams, locks and dredged-out channels were deemed man's finest gifts to nature." And the fishing magazine *Field & Stream* denounced the Corps as "a greedy and overbearing cabal of compulsive dammers."

Even other federal agencies complained about its cavalier attitude toward nature. Bill Lake, a young attorney who worked for the Nixon White House's Council on Environmental Quality, told us that "one of the constant frustrations we had with the Corps of Engineers was that it was always engaged in environmentally destructive activities, but they didn't seem to have the same degree of interest when it came to the environmental part of their duties."

By 1971 Nat Reed, the former Florida gubernatorial aide who had battled the Everglades jetport, had moved up to a federal post as assistant secretary of the Department of the Interior. Reed testified before a congressional committee that he had recently stumbled across a Corps report that revealed "only one major stream in Delaware has not been channelized at least in part . . . and the Corps has authorization to work on that."

That led him to check on the Southern states, he told the congressmen. Reed said he was dismayed to discover the Corps had plans to alter 25,000 miles of stream channels there, too.

"A conservative estimate of the wooded wildlife habitat damaged or destroyed by these alterations," Reed warned the committee, "would be about 120,000 acres and could exceed 300,000 acres."

In 1974, a wealthy Belgian retiree from Stuart, Florida, named Martin Heuvelmans published what may be the most scathing denunciation of the Corps ever put between hard covers. Outraged by what the Corps had done to Lake Okeechobee, Heuvelmans wrote a book called *The River Killers* that blamed the Corps for everything but the Lindbergh kidnapping.

"The Corps is everywhere," he seethed. "The roar of its monstrous machines echoes throughout valley after valley, from the Atlantic to the Pacific. Where it can find a ripple on the water, the Corps is ready to 'improve' the situation with a dam or canal at the slightest political motivation. Its damn-dam foolishness . . . has reached virtually every major waterway in the United States."

His last chapter was titled simply, "Abolish the Corps."

The Corps leaders' reaction to the public's newfound passion for saving the environment ranged from bewilderment to hostility. In 1970, when Nixon signed the National Environmental Policy Act requiring all federal agencies to consider the environmental consequences of their actions, some of the Corps' leaders argued that the environmental movement was just a fad. They suggested finding a way to subvert or resist NEPA until the green fever passed.

This, then, was the agency to which Congress entrusted the protection of the nation's wetlands in 1972. Putting the Corps in charge of issuing wetlands permits was a necessary political compromise, Leon Billings told us. Without it, there may not have been a Clean Water Act.

"The Senate was inclined to give the permitting power to the EPA," Muskie's former aide explained, "but the House Committee on Public Works was strongly protective of the Corps. They wanted the Corps to have the power."

On paper, at least, this move made sense. The EPA was a brand new agency, created by Nixon just two years before. The Corps, on the other hand, already had a bureaucracy in place that was familiar with processing permits under the Rivers and Harbors Act.

Thus the Corps had seven decades of permitting experience that no other federal agency, especially the EPA, could claim Tom Jorling pointed out.

"At the time it was represented as the best managed agency in the federal government," Jorling told us. "The attitude then was: What they just need is a new direction."

The House members' less obvious motive, of course, was control. When a congressman said jump, the Corps asked only, "How high?" The EPA, on the other hand, was an unknown quantity, and answerable only to the president.

Still, the first time someone proposed putting the Corps instead of the EPA in charge of issuing dredge-and-fill permits, Muskie reacted angrily. "Mission-oriented agencies whose mission is something other than concern for the environment simply do not adequately protect environmental values," he snapped. "That is not their mission. They would do a disservice to their mission if they would try to act as environmental protectors. The mission of the Corps of Engineers is to protect navigation. Its mission is not to protect the environment."

But the long summer of conference committee meetings wore him down. In presenting the committee report to the full Senate on October 4, 1972, Muskie explained that the committee members "were uniquely aware of the process by which the dredge and fill permits are presently handled and did not wish to create a burdensome bureaucracy in light of the fact that a system to issue permits already existed."

So the act's Section 404 gave wetlands permitting power to the Corps—but there was a catch. As Muskie explained it, the committee had "agreed that the administrator of the Environmental Protection Agency should have the veto over the selection of the site for dredged spoil disposal and over any specific spoil to be disposed of in any selected site."

In other words, Congress expected the EPA to serve as a watchdog on the Corps' pro-business dinosaurs and make sure they did their job protecting the environment. Other agencies might recommend the Corps deny a Section 404 permit, but the EPA held the power to make the Corps stop in its tracks.

Unlike their reaction to NEPA, the Corps' leaders didn't shy away from taking on the job of protecting wetlands—but not because they cared all that much about saving them, Billings said.

"The Corps is very responsive to business and politicians and so forth who are interested in development," he explained. "Clearly they wanted to retain permitting power."

Still, at first the Corps hesitated to exercise that power to the full extent Congress had envisioned. As with NEPA, the Corps wasn't interested in carrying its "let us try" motto too far in helping the environment.

When Congress passes a new law, the agencies in charge of carrying it out must write a set of regulations spelling out how it will work. The first set of regulations the Corps wrote for Section 404 limited its jurisdiction to the same areas already covered by the Rivers and Harbors Act, which wasn't much. They wanted to deal only with wetlands that were "subject to the ebb and flow of the tide, and/or are presently, or have been in the past, or may be in the future susceptible for use for purposes of interstate or foreign commerce." To the Corps, Section 404 stopped at the mean high water line.

That meant an estimated 60 million acres of marsh, bog, and swamp—all freshwater wetlands—would remain unprotected by the 404 program.

But the case that Vance Hughes of the EPA had just prosecuted in Tampa federal court, *U.S. v. Holland,* said the Corps was wrong about what Section 404 covered. At Hughes' urging, Judge Krentzman read the legislative history of the new water pollution law and determined that it covered more than just navigable waterways. It covered "the waters of the United States," in the broad-

Figure 2. U.S. District Judge Ben Krentzman's March 1974 decision in *U.S. v. Holland* stated that the new water pollution law covered "the waters of the United States" in the broadest possible interpretation of that phrase, a ruling the EPA's top official called a "milestone." (Photograph courtesy of *St. Petersburg Times*.)

est possible interpretation of that phrase, just as Representative Dingell said it would. To limit the law's jurisdiction to the area below the mean high water line would thwart its aim, the judge wrote in his decision.

"Pollutants have been introduced into the waters of the United States without a permit and the mean high water mark cannot be used to create a barrier behind which such activities can be excused," Krentzman wrote. "The environment cannot afford such safety zones."

Krentzman's ruling in March 1974 set the stage for an assault on the Corps' overly cautious definition of its duties. In June, EPA administrator Russell Train fired off a letter to the chief of engineers, Lt. Gen. William Gribble, reminding him of the Holland case's "jurisdictional milestone" and calling Krentzman's ruling "a necessary step for the preservation of our limited wetland resources."

In August a top Justice Department official chimed in, urging the Corps to go along with the EPA's reading of the law. And the House Government Operations Committee weighed in too, urging the Corps to rewrite its regulations on jurisdiction to match "the congressional mandate that this term be given the broadest possible constitutional interpretation."

The Corps' response: Sure, we could protect all those wetlands, like the law says. But what if that infringes on people's property rights? Wouldn't this amount to "back-door land-use planning"? There were limits to "Let us try," and the Corps' leaders had no interest in becoming a bunch of zoning cops.

But the Corps' resistance to following the new law had stirred up environmental groups, including the Natural Resources Defense Council and the National Wildlife Federation. They heard about Krentzman's ruling and wanted to know more.

The NRDC's lawyers "got wind of what we did and sent a team down to Atlanta to talk to me about how we did it," Vance Hughes said. So the EPA lawyer shared everything he knew with the NRDC, essentially giving them the blueprints for pulling down the wall of faulty regulations that the Corps had built.

On August 16, 1974, the NRDC and the National Wildlife Federation filed suit against Secretary of the Army Howard "Bo" Callaway. The environmental groups made the same legal argument that Hughes had made: Section 404 applied to all the waters of the United States, not just the navigable ones.

Intervening on behalf of the plaintiff groups suing the Corps was an unusual ally: the state of Florida.

The motion filed in the case by the Florida Pollution Control Board and Florida Attorney General Robert Shevin accused the Corps of allowing developers to destroy "ecosystems of unique and major importance to the nation." The Florida motion cited Krentzman's ruling in *U.S. v. Holland* as one example of the Corps' failure to do its job.

Governor Reubin Askew and the Florida Cabinet even sent a resolution to Washington supporting the broadest constitutional interpretation of the Corps' regulatory power under Section 404 "in order to afford proper protection to Florida's vital wetlands."

Florida's enthusiastic participation in the lawsuit resulted from some savvy maneuvering by the NRDC representatives. Before filing their suit, they contacted a young attorney named David Gluckman, who in the past had represented environmental groups but now worked for the state Pollution Control Board. The NRDC's attorneys asked Gluckman "if I could get the state to help out, reasoning that this would be more impressive to the courts than just a 'do-gooder-wild-eyed-enviro' organization," Gluckman told us. He said Hughes offered some off-the-record, behind-the-scenes support from the EPA, which helped sealed the deal.

When Gluckman and other aides talked to Askew about the NRDC case, they found the straight-arrow governor from Pensacola was also receptive to jumping into the federal fray. Although Askew and the leaders of the state legislature were all members of the Democratic Party, he and the legislature didn't see eye to eye on some issues, and wetlands protection was one of them.

At the time Askew was elected in 1970, South Florida was in the grip of a historic drought. Alarmed, he convened a Governor's Conference on Water Management in South Florida at the Doral Hotel on Miami Beach. The 150-member panel, which included Marjory Stoneman Douglas and a young state senator named Bob Graham, produced a report that bluntly recommended, "There should be no further draining of wetlands for any purpose. . . . Wetlands are the most biologically productive of all lands."

So in 1973, Askew called for "protection by law of our wetland areas, both coastal and inland." But the legislature, which still viewed swamps as obstacles to progress, bottled the bill up in committee, and the dredges kept on working.

Now here was the Corps of Engineers, which could be using a new federal law to protect Florida's wetlands, and instead it was refusing to help—much to Askew's consternation.

"I was concerned about the lack of willingness on the part of the Corps to accept what they should be doing under their proper jurisdiction," Askew told us.

Besides, a lawsuit that gave a federal agency more power over wetlands might shake up those pro-development politicians and make a state wetlands law more palatable, Gluckman said.

Askew and the cabinet had some practical reasons for jumping into the case, too: the disagreement between the EPA and the Corps was hurting business. Developers like Robert Wray were building in freshwater swamps where the Corps said they needed no permit, and then Hughes and the EPA were slapping them with cease-and-desist orders, an Askew aide explained. As a result, "more and more confusion is growing in this area as to what is the jurisdiction," the aide told Askew and the cabinet. The only way to resolve the disagreement between the two agencies would be with a judge's ruling.

In court, Corps attorneys argued that expanding its regulatory program to cover freshwater wetlands would cost the taxpayers too much money. The agency would have to hire 1,750 new employees and boost its budget by $53 million a year, they contended. The Corps was significantly alone at the defense table, though. As the *Washington Post* noted at the time, both the EPA and the Justice Department said the Corps was off base.

The case went to U.S. District Judge Aubrey Robinson—the same judge who had halted the Refuse Act permitting program. After reviewing the legislative history just as Krentzman did, Judge Robinson came to the same conclusion Krentzman had. He found that Congress "asserted federal jurisdiction over the nation's waters to the maximum extent permissible under the Commerce Clause of the Constitution." The judge ordered the Corps to publish new regulations "clearly recognizing the full regulatory mandate of the Water Act."

NRDC general counsel Gus Speth later called it "the easiest lawsuit I've ever won. The Corps didn't have a prayer of sustaining their position. . . . It was a slam dunk."

The Corps did not appeal—but it didn't do exactly what the judge ordered, either.

Instead, disgruntled Corps leaders decided to scare America into revoking the 404 program. A general ordered up a press release designed to make the wetland permitting program sound like a bunch of jackbooted thugs were ready to clamp down on private property rights at the first sign of damp soil. The goal, according to a former Corps attorney, was to "provoke public interest in what the Corps perceived as a massive federal land-use control grab."

The press release, picked up by the wire services and carried in newspapers nationwide, incited an enormous backlash against not just wetlands protection but also against the Corps itself. Suddenly the press release didn't look like such a smart idea after all.

"It created a firestorm that, in a way, this issue has never recovered from," Speth said.

Gen. Gribble, the chief of engineers, fired off a letter to Governor Askew, warning about the ruling's "impact on you and the people of your state." Askew, a teetotalling Presbyterian elder, often displayed a limited tolerance for political manipulation. His scorching response blasted the Corps for putting out a press release that "has obfuscated the real importance and significance of your new responsibilities. These responsibilities relate, I believe, to the protection of our nation's irreplaceable natural wetlands so important to water quality and quantity, wildlife, fisheries and outdoor recreation."

The NRDC and other environmental groups mounted an opposition campaign that had the Corps' officials backpedaling. Train at the EPA and some members of Congress condemned the Corps for manufacturing a controversy instead of doing its job. The poor press officer who had written the release under a general's orders had to make a public apology. But no one was fired or disciplined.

Chastened at last, the Corps put out new regulations with a considerably broader definition of what it would regulate. Soon the Corps' wetland permitting business was booming. By the 1980s the Corps was handling more than

11,000 permits a year nationwide—and despite its past reluctance, the Corps now tried to do its job the way Congress had envisioned.

In the late 1970s, Florida developers who sought 404 permits were allowed to destroy a mere 14 percent of the wetland acreage they requested, according to a study by the National Marine Fisheries Service. The study found that the Corps was blocking 86 percent of the proposed wetlands destruction projects in Florida—exactly what the authors of Section 404 had hoped would happen, not to mention Governor Askew and the Florida Cabinet.

The Jacksonville office "had more denials than any other district in the country," recalled former Corps permit reviewer Haynes Johnson. If another federal agency, such as the EPA or the U.S. Fish and Wildlife Service, objected to a wetlands permit, "the Corps would tell the developer to work it out with the agencies and come back to us," Johnson recalled. "The project would get put on hold. That irritated some people."

Then came the Reagan Revolution.

Onetime California governor Ronald Reagan was elected president in 1980 as an enemy of Big Government and a friend of Big Business. Saving the environment took a back seat to boosting the nation's floundering economy. The people he initially picked to run the environmental agencies reflected his priorities.

Reagan's first selection to head the EPA, Anne Gorsuch Burford, once boasted that she reduced the book of clean water regulations from six inches thick to a mere half-inch. But after 22 months in office she resigned amid accusations she had manipulated the agency's Superfund to favor politically connected polluters. The EPA's assistant administrator resigned amid charges he kowtowed to the chemical industry. And the head of the hazardous waste section, who had complained in a memo about a colleague who was "systematically alienating the business community," went to jail for lying to Congress.

Reagan put the Interior Department under James Watt, who tried to turn public park land over to private developers and, when this plan met with opposition, compared his suffering to that of the Jews who were gassed at Auschwitz. When environmental groups objected to his plan to authorize the sale of coal from federal lands in five Western states, he said no one could criticize his decision because his coal advisory panel included "a black . . . a woman, two Jews, and a cripple."

Reagan wanted government to get off business' back. "Deregulation" became the buzzword—and wetlands protection became a primary target. The Corps' regulatory program "had become needlessly burdened by red tape that caused excessive delays in the processing of individual permit applications," according to an official Army history of the time. "Consequently, the program was designated for review by the Task Force on Regulatory Relief, chaired by Vice President George Bush."

The Reaganites would have loved to get rid of Section 404 entirely, said Jim Range. But Range's boss, Senate Majority Leader Baker, made it clear that he wouldn't stand for that.

"They knew that nothing on wetlands was going to move through the U.S. Senate," Range said. "I delivered that message to the White House."

Still, the 404 program could be hamstrung, and the civilian Reagan tapped to take charge of the Corps was eager to help tie it up. Reagan selected as the new assistant secretary of the Army for civil works a veteran dam-builder named William R. Gianelli. He had a degree in engineering and a Purple Heart from World War II—he had been shot while helping to build an airfield on Saipan. When Reagan was governor of California, Gianelli served as the head of the state Water Resources Department. But for nearly nine years since then, he had worked as a freelance consultant on water issues, making him less than sympathetic toward regulations that might hamper business.

Gianelli later said that his top priority when he took over the Corps was launching "a major reform of Section 404" because, he said, it was "simply not working." Not only were permits taking far too long to process, Gianelli said, but he also worried that applicants were not getting what he called "a fair shake." He was convinced the Corps was paying too much attention to environmental impacts. As a result "the applicants were being required to do much more than could be reasonably expected in order to get a project underway," he said.

Gianelli, a take-charge manager little burdened by self-doubt, agreed to lead the Bush committee's study of the 404 program. The goal was clear. "We were given certain mandates, among which was to modify the administrative processes so that the decisions could be reached in 60 days," he said.

His solution? Stop worrying so much about the environment.

The problem, as he saw it, was that when the EPA, National Marine Fisheries Service, and the Fish and Wildlife Service were concerned about the wetlands impact of a project, they could appeal a permit decision through a number of steps, culminating in an appeal to the secretary of the Army. Although the appeals might fail, the process itself took so long that developers often agreed to make changes that the agencies wanted, just to avoid a lengthy and expensive construction delay.

To Gianelli, that was tantamount to blackmail, and certainly not something that aided the economy. He also did not like it that sometimes the agencies would appeal the Corps' permit decisions based on things that had nothing to do with their own environmental mission. For instance, they might criticize a project's economic rationale, such as noting that there were already plenty of golf course subdivisions in an area, so there was no need for a new one that would wipe out crucial wetlands.

Gianelli and his deputy (and eventual replacement) Robert Dawson decided to limit the appeal process. Working with Burford, Watt, and other Reagan appointees, they cut a deal that said the only appeal of a permit would be straight to Gianelli himself, and the agencies could only appeal based on their own areas of expertise. The upshot was to give the Corps far more power to say yes to a permit and make it stick. It also undercut the clout that the other agencies had used to block permits that were bad for the environment.

Dawson, in testifying at a 1982 Senate committee hearing, said the changes he and Gianelli were making marked "a good first step in making the Corps' regulatory program more responsive to the public."

When Dawson started explaining to the senators about how 404 permits were taking way too long to process, Senator John Chafee, R-Rhode Island, interrupted him. "The objective of the program is not to get permits out quickly but to keep the nation's waters clean," barked Chafee, who had helped Muskie and Baker get the Clean Water Act passed. But Chafee's complaints failed to deter Gianelli and Dawson from pushing the changes through.

In fact, Gianelli made a personal visit to the Corps' Florida headquarters to tell them to get out their rubber stamps. The days of leading the nation in denials were officially over.

"He sat us down in Jacksonville and told us in no uncertain terms that he wanted us to process permits as quickly as possible, and he wasn't talking about denials," recalled Haynes Johnson, who was reviewing permits in that office.

To critics who complained that the "reforms" he advocated hampered wetlands protection under Section 404, Gianelli offered a simple, if bizarre, response: Section 404 wasn't supposed to protect wetlands, so gutting it wasn't an attack on wetlands protection.

"I believe the primary problem we have had on our regulatory reform is the perception that 404 is a wetlands protection measure, and it is no such thing," he said. Instead, he said "404 related to water quality . . . and was not a wetland protection measure, except in those cases where it could be demonstrated that destroying of the wetland does have some effect on water quality."

The Corps, like good soldiers, heard the orders from Gianelli and Dawson loud and clear. By 1984, the Marine Fisheries study found, the Corps was giving a green light to 64 percent of the requested wetlands destruction in Florida, an increase of 50 percent in just three years.

"It is our opinion that the Jacksonville district is decreasing the amount of time by decreasing the environmental review," said Ed Keppner, head of the NMFS regional office in St. Petersburg (and himself a former Corps employee).

"They definitely are on a bent to issue permits, and you can feel it," agreed Joe Carroll, Florida supervisor for the U.S. Fish and Wildlife Service.

Among the projects highlighted by the NMFS report was the Corps' approval of a 404 permit for filling in 4.2 acres of wetlands at MacDill Air Force Base in Tampa to create the air base's second golf course. Both the EPA and the fisheries agency contended that building a golf course—especially a second one—was not a good reason for destroying wetlands, and the course could be built elsewhere. What the Corps hadn't told the two federal agencies is that the Air Force had already done the work illegally and the Corps was issuing an after-the-fact permit saying it was all right.

A big part of the problem, the NMFS reported, was that Corps officials had come to regard permit applicants in Florida as their clients and wetland permits as products to be pushed along on a factory line as quickly as possible.

"The Army's regulatory program is so flawed it is no longer a usable tool to adequately protect wetlands," Assistant Secretary of the Interior G. Ray Arnett complained in a 1984 letter to Dawson.

Justice Department lawyers explained the end result of Gianelli and Dawson's reforms quite nicely in a 1984 legal brief: "Due to the magnitude of the program and its decentralized administration, effective implementation of Section 404 is highly dependent on voluntary compliance by landowners."

In other words, don't count on the Corps to act as the wetlands police. Anyone who's obeying the law is doing so of his or her own accord.

Section 404, designed to save wetlands, became instead a most permissive permitting program. In internal memos from the mid-1980s, Corps officials state flatly that their policy is "when in doubt, err in favor of the applicant not the environment."

Things went downhill quickly in Florida, where wetlands were constantly getting in the way of developers' plans. In a 1988 memo sent out to Corps employees in Florida, the Army's top civilian regulator in the state, John Adams, wrote that "it is Corps policy: 'When in doubt, do not regulate.' Therefore, do not create more work if you can avoid it."

That mindset has not changed. Even today, along with every 404 permit, the Corps' Jacksonville office sends out a "customer satisfaction survey" to the people who are destroying swamps and marshes.

Current and former Corps employees told us their agency has failed to do its job of saving wetlands.

"We're not protecting the environment," Vic Anderson, a Florida native and a 30-year veteran of the Corps' regulatory division, told us. "It's a make-believe program."

It wasn't always like this. There was a time when a courageous colonel took a stand for Florida's wetlands—and paid a big price for it.

4

Marco Island & Bonita Springs

In the early 1960s, Marco Island was a quiet slice of old Florida. Thick scrub and gumbo-limbo trees covered most of the island, the largest of the Ten Thousand Islands chain that stretches from Fort Myers down to the Keys. On three sides of the island, a wide fringe of tangled mangroves lined the shore. The fourth side offered a four-mile-long beach where sparkling white dunes rose up like mountains of sugar.

Only a narrow wooden bridge built in the 1930s connected the island to the mainland. Reaching the nearest town, Naples, required a 45-minute drive.

On the island, the closest thing to civilization was a pair of tiny fishing villages, Marco and Goodland, one of them with a rustic lodge for visiting anglers eager to test their luck with the tarpon, snook, and redfish that thrived just off the coast. But then Hurricane Donna hit in 1960, damaging the villages and covering parts of the island with 12 feet of water.

You couldn't be soft and live on Marco back then. As one history of the island explained, the remoteness of it "seemed to attract—to say it nicely— the pioneer . . . those with a few cards missing from their decks—union 'bad boys'—and individuals who could not fit in to more civilized surroundings."

There had once been a clamming factory, but then the clam beds were stripped bare one too many times and they didn't recover. A railroad once ran to the island, but after the clamming died off the rail line was abandoned. Except for a U.S. Air Force missile tracking station, nothing new had been built there for years.

Then along came the Mackle brothers. Elliott, Robert, and Frank Mackle Jr. had already made a mint off developing South Florida. The sons of a construction magnate, they had turned sleepy Key Biscayne into a resort for the rich, then created new communities in Deland, Daytona Beach, rural Hernando County, and Charlotte County. They counted among their friends President Nixon, financier Bebe Rebozo, and Florida senator George Smathers.

The Mackles spent $7 million to buy up most of Marco Island, and in 1964 they set in motion one of the most ambitious development plans in the state's history. Over the next 15 years, the Mackles planned to build 10,000 homes on 6,700 acres. They envisioned Marco as the crown jewel of their developments, with 8,000 waterfront lots and 90 miles of canals.

They knew they faced a challenge unlike anything they had taken on before. Soil borings found that the squishy muck went down 40 feet. The island had no central water or sewer, so most of the fresh water was trucked in. The first time company president Frank Mackle Jr. visited the beach, he was greeted by swarms of mosquitoes so bloodthirsty that he had to sprint back to his car to avoid being eaten alive.

Figure 3. The Mackle brothers—(left to right) Elliott, Robert, and Frank Jr.—worked together to turn the wilderness of Marco Island into a glittering resort that attracted politicians, celebrities, and sports stars. (Photograph courtesy of Deltona Corporation.)

To make their vision a reality, the Mackles would use two time-tested development methods: dredge-and-fill plus presold lots. By dredging and filling the wetlands, they could create dry land wherever they needed it. By selling the lots before anything was actually built, they could finance the construction. Developers had been doing both for decades, but never on the scale the Mackles had in mind.

They got their permits from the state and the Corps for the first phase, dubbed "Marco River," in 1964. The Corps took just nine days to approve the Section 10 permits for the dredging. The Mackles converted the old missile tracking station into their development headquarters and set to work.

Thanks to an extensive national advertising campaign, the grand opening in 1965 attracted some 25,000 people who wanted to see what all the hoopla was about. By opening day, the Mackles' work crews had already built a wellfield on the mainland, run a water line to the island, and constructed a sewer plant. They had also built 10 model homes that ranged in price from $19,800 to more than $40,000. Still, the Mackles promised to keep the island's essential character intact.

"Marco Island is the last large undeveloped tract of waterfront land in South Florida, and its rolling topography and tropical foliage give it a character unmatched in this part of the world," Frank Mackle Jr. told reporters on the eve of the grand opening. "We are determined that the community we build there will be fully in keeping with the island's natural beauty and ideal location."

Then the crews started building seawalls, chopping down the mangroves, and filling in the swamps. They were well on their way to turning Marco Island into a thriving retirement and recreation mecca, complete with golf courses, a shopping center, a yacht club, a ritzy hotel, and even their own air service to spray for mosquitoes.

But then the law changed, and a new sheriff arrived to enforce it.

ॐ

In 1975, a 44-year-old Army veteran named Col. Don Wisdom took charge of the Corps of Engineers office in Jacksonville. In his official dress-uniform portrait, Wisdom is flashing an aw-shucks grin like a Little Leaguer who just drove in the winning run.

But Wisdom was no kid. He had served two tours of duty in Vietnam with the elite Army Rangers. One contemporary writer described him as having "an air of crisp toughness about him," and noted that he "has been known to describe himself as 'a badass.'"

At the time, Wisdom was a unique figure in the Corps because he was more than an engineer. He had a master's degree from Pennsylvania State University in environmental studies. His previous posting was in Washington as the Corps' assistant director for military construction for environmental planning.

Before he headed south, Wisdom met with a Florida native knowledgeable on environmental issues, Interior Undersecretary Nat Reed—the same Nat Reed who had battled the Everglades jetport and criticized the Corps for straightening so many rivers. Reed briefed him on what to expect at his new post.

Wisdom's toughest challenge was bringing the new 404 wetlands permitting program to the place that needed it the most. His goal, he told us, was "to save the lifeblood of Florida, the wetlands."

The new colonel discovered that the Jacksonville staff was less interested in saving wetlands than they were in getting along with their regular customers. A subordinate later told Army historians he frequently had to step in between Wisdom and civilian employees who had been there before him and would remain long after he had moved on. Wisdom left "a lot of bruised feelings," his successor told us.

Wisdom says he spent a lot of time pushing his staff to give closer scrutiny to dredge-and-fill permits that until then had been approved with little fuss. Among the permit applications that they were already working on when Wisdom took charge were the final ones needed by the Mackles to complete their vision for Marco Island.

The Mackles' development company, Deltona Corp., was proposing three new developments on Marco Island, calling them Collier Bay, Big Key, and Barfield Bay. Collier Bay had already been partially constructed before the Corps caught Deltona doing dredge-and-fill without any 404 permits.

Big Key and Barfield Bay were planned for areas almost completely covered in mangroves and open water. Only 20 acres of Big Key was considered upland, and 91 acres of Barfield Bay wasn't already wet. To turn all the swamps and bay bottom into dry, buildable land, Deltona's plans called for digging 67 miles of canals through the mangroves and dredging 18.2 million cubic yards of fill, destroying more than 2,000 acres of wetlands and wiping out 54 linear miles of mangroves.

However, Deltona assured the Corps that this would in fact be good for the environment.

A consultant the company hired said that dead-end canals would produce more phytoplankton for fish food than all the mangroves that Deltona wanted to cut down. In fact, skeptical biologists with the National Marine Fisheries Service discovered that Deltona's consultant was claiming the new canals would produce twice as much phytoplankton as had ever been recorded before anywhere in Florida. The fisheries experts didn't buy it.

Still, Deltona had a reputation at the time for being more concerned about the environment than other Florida developers. The Mackles had persuaded the Corps to approve a Section 10 permit for one of its earlier phases over the objections of the Fish and Wildlife Service. The Corps said yes because the Mackles agreed to all sorts of conditions on the permit, "from building experimental mangrove islands to establishing a marine ecology lab to building ocean reefs to on and on," recalled Bernie Goode, then the civilian head of the regulatory office of the Corps in Jacksonville.

But the Corps included a warning in that 1969 permit: Don't count on getting any more of these. Look at what happened to Zabel and Russell up in Pinellas County.

"We had sent the signals that the next ones to come might not be so easy to come to a favorable conclusion," Goode said.

Undeterred, the Mackles kept on selling lots that didn't exist yet at Barfield Bay, Big Key, and Collier Bay. By 1970, they had sold 95 percent of all the lots in their master plan.

A year later, when the Mackles opened their 400-room hotel, the ceremonies featured Governor Askew, comedian Jaye P. Morgan, and the Goodyear blimp. The place had begun attracting sports celebrities—Gene Sarazen, Ara Parseghian, Joe Garagiola, and Bob Griese all bought property there. Some became part of the advertising campaign.

"Come to Marco Island—Florida's Primitive Paradise!" Garagiola told his broadcast audience.

"It's the Shangri-La of America," one resident told a national magazine.

To complete Shangri-La's development plan, the Mackles needed to build these last three subdivisions. The first hurdle was getting their permits from a state government headed up by a governor who called mangroves "the wonderlands of life." But Askew considered Frank Mackle a friend, so they talked about what kind of deal they could cut.

The governor, despite his pro-mangrove leanings, was convinced that the state had a moral obligation to allow Deltona to proceed with its development. After all, the state had not used its authority over interstate land sales to stop Deltona from selling so many lots that didn't exist yet. But Askew was determined to drive a hard bargain with Mackle, so he demanded the company turn over to the state thousands of acres of prime beach property, guaranteeing they would never be developed.

"Frank looked at me and he almost had tears in his eyes, and he said, 'If we do this, it's going to bankrupt us,'" Askew told us. "And I said, 'I hope not, but that's the price.'" The Mackles agreed to the swap, state permits in exchange for preserved beachfront, and that took care of the state's permission.

The Mackles figured that with their state permits in hand, getting through the Corps permit process would be a snap. To make sure everything went smoothly with the Ford Administration, they hired the former chairman of the Republican National Committee to represent their interests in Washington.

But their timing was atrocious. The Corps had just gone through the firestorm of the *NRDC v. Callaway* case over how to implement the new water pollution law. Now the permitting decision was in the hands of a colonel in Jacksonville who understood the environmental consequences of dredge-and-fill development and the requirements of Section 404. And every other federal agency was encouraging him to exercise his authority to stop the Mackles.

When Wisdom met with representatives of the EPA, Fish and Wildlife Service, and National Marine Fisheries Service, they urged him to deny all three permits because of the effect that so much wetland destruction would have on the environment throughout the Ten Thousand Islands.

Every big environmental group in the country, including the ones that had sued the Corps in 1975, lined up against Deltona too. The Audubon Society's busiest activist, Charles Lee, repeatedly visited the Corps office to lobby Wisdom and his staff to deny the permits. Lee called the Mackles' proposed development "one of the largest single acts of destruction ever to befall Florida's natural coastline." Frank Mackle Jr. dismissed such talk as "ecological nonsense."

Wisdom flew down to Naples to take an aerial tour of the site with the Mackles. From the plane, he could see what Marco Island looked like. He could see what would be lost if he said yes and what would be saved if he said no.

Still, Wisdom was torn. "I had pined over this, especially knowing the Mackles," he told us. He realized they weren't the evil, greedy despoilers that some environmental activists made them out to be. "They were only doing what they thought was right from a development standpoint," he said. "You couldn't fault those guys for that."

If Wisdom said yes, then the Mackles were headed for big profits. If Wisdom said no, they faced financial ruin. They had presold 4,000 home sites that could not be built. If no homes were built, they would have to return tens of millions of dollars to the would-be buyers.

Wisdom convened a two-day public hearing at Lely High School in Fort Myers. He and Goode sat on the stage in the high school auditorium for hours and listened to everyone who wanted to talk. Deltona bused in union workers—many toting signs that said "Unshackle Mackle!"—and they packed the room, arguing that denying the permits would cost them their jobs. Some of the buses also carried retirees who seemed befuddled about why they were there.

Meanwhile hundreds more, including members of the Audubon Society and the Environmental Defense Fund, showed up to oppose the permits. In all, some 1,300 people packed the September 1975 hearing to tell Wisdom what to do. The antagonism between the sides grew volatile, with Deltona's proponents blasting the environmental activists as nothing but a bunch of Communist-oriented birdwatchers who didn't own any property on Marco Island and thus should have no say in what happened there.

Thousands of people wrote to the Corps office in Jacksonville, making arguments for and against the project. Some letters were spurred by a letter-writing campaign mounted by environmental groups. Others were generated by a group of Belgians who had retired to Deltona's first Marco development and formed their own corporation to lobby for more amenities for their community—amenities that depended on the new projects being built.

Although the decision wasn't supposed to be a popularity contest, the flood of letters had an impact on Goode.

"I'd take them home and I would read them at night," Goode said. "I would share them with my wife. I would pray over this thing. I just kept moving back and forth, from one side of this fence to the other."

Some of the people who wrote and called the Corps were frustrated with the government's reluctance to say yes to Deltona's continued development of the island. One woman called Goode from Minnesota to say "that her husband has got arthritis so bad that if they don't get down there before next winter, she doesn't think he'll last, and why in the world can't you all give them those permits so they can build their lots down there," Goode recalled.

Then there was the young mother who showed up at Goode's desk one day carrying a nine-month-old baby. "She was terribly nervous," Goode said. "She had just driven from Fort Myers all the way to Jacksonville—I would guess about 10 hours, and with this little baby. And she said she just didn't know what else to do. She had to come talk to . . . somebody in the Corps of Engineers to please, for the sake of her son and her grandchildren, that there would be something left of Florida's coastal marshes, and she says, 'I'm not a member of the Audubon Society. I'm just a mother and I just have to talk to somebody and beg that something be done to stop this.'"

One group of observers watched the Corps' decision-making process with particular interest: developers who had 89 separate permit applications for similar projects up and down the Florida coast, which if approved would wipe out another 14,000 acres of wetlands. "We couldn't stand up against them if we didn't stand up against Deltona," Goode recalled. "It had to happen at Marco Island if we were going to stop this encroachment of housing into the coastal areas."

Despite the letters, despite the calls, despite the politics and the impact on other developers and his own sympathy for the Mackles, to Wisdom what carried the day was what he saw as his duty under the law.

"There was no choice," he said.

The regulations for carrying out the new pollution law said that a Section 404 permit should be denied if a project's purpose was not "water-dependent." In other words, if it didn't need to be located on a swamp, it should be built somewhere else. To Wisdom, the purpose of Deltona's project was

Figure 4. Jacksonville District Engineer Don Wisdom was hailed as a hero for the precedent-setting Marco Island decision, but he paid a price. (Photograph courtesy of U.S. Army Corps of Engineers.)

housing, and housing did not need to be built on top of a swamp to fulfill its purpose.

During his aerial tour of the island, Wisdom took notes but didn't let on to the Mackles what he was thinking. When he got back to Jacksonville, he huddled with Goode and the rest of his staff and crafted what he would say.

On October 16, 1975, Wisdom recommended approving a 404 permit for Collier Bay, but only Collier Bay. That one was already started, and so he figured the Mackles ought to be allowed to finish it. But he recommended the Corps deny the permits for Barfield Bay and Big Key because he had concluded the Mackles could build elsewhere and avoid destroying wetlands.

Because of the project's importance, Wisdom's report went straight to his superior officer, Maj. Gen. Carroll Letellier, in the Atlanta regional office of the Corps. Letellier was a builder first and foremost, having recently returned stateside from overseeing an engineering command in Europe working on $400 million in construction projects. His sympathies clearly lay with the Mackles.

Letellier said Wisdom was wrong and recommended approving all three permits. The purpose of the project was "waterfront development," Letellier wrote, so of course it had to be built on the water. The Mackles had already completed most of their Marco Island master plan, so they deserved the right to finish it all, he contended. Besides, turning them down might "constitute a substantial taking of property rights," he wrote.

The final decision rested with the chief engineer, Lt. Gen. Gribble, still smarting over the public relations debacle that his staff created after the Callaway ruling. With his wavy gray hair and dimpled chin, the 58-year-old Gribble looked like a Hollywood casting director's idea of a general, but his resume was genuinely impressive. He had graduated from West Point in 1941 and served in World War II under Gen. Douglas MacArthur during the hopscotch campaign to retake the Pacific islands from the Japanese. Since then, Gribble had overseen the construction of nuclear reactors and highways in Alaska, and he had run the Corps' engineering school.

Because of his background, Gribble thought of the Corps as a force for building and development, period. He admitted to subordinates that he was uncomfortable playing the role of a regulator telling landowners they could not build whatever they wanted. As for Marco Island—well, his own secretary had bought a lot there.

On March 17, 1976, Gribble invited both Wisdom and Letellier to Washington to make their arguments in person. Goode was there too, as were other generals and Corps lawyers.

Wisdom talked about what the law and the regulations required. Then Letellier played a trump card: a letter from Governor Askew asking the Corps to approve all three Deltona permits so the Mackles would donate all that pristine beach to the state. Letellier contended the Corps had to respect Askew's wishes and approve the permits because the governor spoke for the whole state.

Gribble turned to Wisdom and asked if that was true. No, Wisdom replied. Unlike other states, he pointed out, Florida did not invest all executive power in its governor. Instead the state was run by an elected cabinet, and the governor was merely one of its seven members.

At that point, Wisdom recalled, Letellier "sort of sank down in his chair." Further undercutting Letellier's position was the fact that—as Goode reminded Gribble in a memo—Governor Askew had supported the other side in *NRDC v. Callaway*. The staff found documents where Askew "went on and on about the national importance of protecting Florida's remaining wetlands," Goode said.

On top of all that, the head of the EPA, Russell Train, was now publicly threatening to use Section 404's veto power for the first time if the Corps approved Deltona's permits. If that happened, it was sure to revive all the previous year's controversy about the Corps' environmental insensitivity.

Still, Gribble told his staff that he was leaning toward Letellier's position. He believed that the federal government should overturn a state's decision only if state officials seemed to be acting irresponsibly. But he agreed with Wisdom that the issue boiled down to just one question: what was the Corps' duty under the law?

He ordered Corps attorney Bill Hedeman to work with the rest of the staff to outline a case for each of three options: approving all three permits; denying them all; or following Wisdom's recommendation to deny two and approve one. Then Gribble spent the next month digging through all the reports and comments on the project.

When the general was ready, his staff decided he would announce his decision on the Friday before Easter. The Corps notified the White House that the decision was forthcoming and also gave a heads-up to other federal agencies, including—as Deltona was a publicly traded company—the Securities and Exchange Commission.

"They must have overreacted because they suspended trading on Deltona that day and of course that sent vibes throughout the nation on tickertapes and was picked up rather quickly," Goode said.

Frank Mackle III was traveling on Deltona's corporate plane when the pilot told him about the SEC suspension. The Mackles were so certain the Corps would say yes that "bottles were opened and toasts were made," he recalled.

The next morning, April 15, 1976, the Corps held press conferences in Jacksonville and Washington to announce Gribble's decision. He had decided to uphold Wisdom's recommendation. Gribble denied the two permits to fill in the pristine mangrove swamps and approved only the third one to complete the already begun Collier Bay development.

Gribble told subordinates that it was the toughest decision he ever had to make. He didn't like the outcome, he said, but he did what the new law required. He favored environmental protection for the public over the desire of a developer to make a profit.

Gribble's six-page decision states flatly that "a housing/recreational development of the type envisioned . . . which will result in almost total destruction of these wetland areas is an unnecessary destruction of this wetland resource. . . . It is my opinion that the applicant has also failed to demonstrate that there are no other sites or construction alternatives to accomplish this housing development that involve less than the total destruction of the wetlands resources."

Sure, the state was in favor of it, Gribble wrote, but the other federal agencies were opposed, "and it is also our responsibility to rely on the views of those federal agencies which have the responsibility for assessing the impact of the proposed work on the values intended to be protected."

Besides, Gribble added, the Mackles should have known better than to try to get a project like this approved after what happened in *Zabel v. Tabb*: "Developers and lot purchasers were put on notice at that time that policies and decisions were changing and that the issuance of permits thereafter was not as predictable as it was when the first Marco River permit was issued for this development in 1964."

Deltona president Frank Mackle Jr. was flabbergasted. He had had no idea the Corps would turn his project down. "I am shocked and outraged," he announced in a formal press release. Months later he was still reeling, telling a magazine reporter: "It was absolutely astounding, the biggest miscarriage of justice in my lifetime. I still can't get over it. The Corps—they've been like us. They're engineers, our kind of people."

The phones at Deltona's headquarters began ringing off the hook as thousands of people who had bought lots that didn't exist now demanded their money back. Some threatened to sue. Meanwhile the banks that had loaned Deltona millions of dollars for building the hotel and other amenities were also demanding payment. The company teetered on the verge of bankruptcy. The Mackles tried to satisfy everyone as best they could, offering home sites in other parts of the state, or a note guaranteeing a refund in five years, even swapping company assets outright.

"We traded one guy for a bulldozer," Frank Mackle III said.

Askew, although he liked Col. Wisdom, felt disappointed and even somewhat betrayed by the Corps action. "I felt the denial was a repudiation of an agreement that everybody was supposed to be a part of," he said.

Deltona went to court to overturn the decision, arguing not only that the denial was wrong but that it had effectively taken away their property rights. They won at the trial court level, but on appeal the Fifth Circuit, as in *Zabel v. Tabb*, sided with the Corps. In 1982 the U.S. Supreme Court declined to hear the Deltona case. The Mackles had lost, and Gribble's decision stood because "Deltona could not show that the benefits of its proposed project outweighed the damage to the wetland resource," Army historians later wrote.

The Corps permit denial "ripped at the company and ripped at the family too," Frank Mackle III said. By then the oldest Mackle brother, Elliott, had retired, and the middle brother, Robert, was ready to shut down Deltona and join him. But the youngest brother, Frank Jr., was determined to keep the company afloat somehow. So the two remaining Mackles went their separate ways and never again did business together.

In public, Frank Mackle Jr. claimed the permit denial was little more than a small bump in the road to ultimate success for their Marco Island development.

"I don't want to seem like a Pollyanna and I don't want to minimize this thing, but I think it's a manageable problem," he told the *Miami Herald*.

In truth, though, he only barely staved off ruin. To pay back all the lot buyers and bankers, Frank Mackle Jr. sold his beloved hotel to the Marriott Corp. and dumped a lot of other properties as well. He completed the development of Collier Bay, and that was that for Marco Island. The rest of the land, where the 404 permits had been denied, he deeded over to the public in exchange for some property in Miami that he could develop. The mangrove swamps once targeted for destruction are now part of the Rookery Bay National Estuarine Research Reserve.

Col. Wisdom was acclaimed by Florida's environmentalists for standing up to the politically powerful Mackles. The Audubon Society gave him an award. The head of the Florida Wildlife Federation told a national magazine that, compared to other state and federal regulators, Wisdom was "like a nun in a cathouse." There was even talk of running him for governor.

But Wisdom did not emerge unscathed from the battle of Marco Island.

In his 26 years in the Corps, just like clockwork, Wisdom's name always showed up on the promotions list when it was his time to move up in rank. But in 1978, when he was due to be promoted to general, he was passed over. He blames retaliation by Letellier over the Marco Island permit decision.

"Of course," Wisdom said. "He got kicked in the crotch." Another general asked Wisdom to stay on for another three years, in hopes he would get another shot at his star, but Wisdom said no thanks. He retired as a colonel.

Now running a small environmental consulting firm on Florida's east coast, Wisdom says he has no regrets for taking a stand. "I had been taught you've got to go by your own thoughts and not just obey what you're told," he said.

The Marco Island decision shocked Corps leaders who took a dim view of the environmental movement. It hit them "like a ton of bricks," Corps attorney Bill Hedeman said. It showed them that the 404 program was really intended to protect wetlands—although some Corps officials were still not keen on the idea.

"Feelings around here are split," John Adams, Goode's replacement as the civilian boss of regulatory in Jacksonville, told a magazine reporter afterward. "Personally, I'm a little concerned that the federal government may be going too far."

Despite Adams' misgivings, the Marco Island decision—and the subsequent court rulings upholding it—became a precedent that was supposed to guide all future Corps decisions. Every permit application was supposed to meet the same test that Col. Wisdom used: Was the project something that had to be built in wetlands? Was it water dependent? If not, then there was a legal presumption that it ought to be built somewhere else, somewhere dry.

To get a permit from the Corps to build in a wetland, a developer would have to somehow overcome that presumption and prove that the project could not be built anywhere else. The Corps would have to analyze every project to see if there were alternative sites or configurations that would be less damaging to the environment.

But Wisdom's lost promotion marked a precedent as well.

"Don't you think that didn't send a message to the district engineers that followed him?" retired Corps dredging expert Chuck Hummer pointed out.

Fast-forward 20 years. In the 1990s the population of Southwest Florida boomed, and as a result the pace of wetlands destruction picked up speed too. The Corps issued permits to erase nearly 4,000 acres of wetlands in the western Everglades, even as its leaders talked of restoring the eastern side of the River of Grass.

The town of Bonita Springs led the state in new arrivals with household incomes of $150,000 and above. The newcomers were wealthy entrepreneurs and high-powered executives from major companies such as General Electric and Kodak, all ready to plunk down big bucks for a sumptuous McMansion next to the fairway. The economic incentive to wipe out Collier County's cypress swamps was a strong one.

"Wetlands get dried up with money," observed Danny Curran, a grizzled and talkative shrimper who grew up in Bonita Springs.

Upscale subdivisions—several of them built by a developer who later pleaded no contest to bribing Collier County commissioners—helped to choke off the natural sloughs that flowed into the nearby Imperial River. Once upon a time the wetlands flowing to the Imperial River protected that part of Bonita Springs from flooding, but now they were gone.

When torrential rains hit Collier County in the fall of 1995, the water tried to flow down to the river through its old sloughs, but it was blocked by the new subdivisions. The stormwater spilled out into areas that used to stay dry, causing widespread flooding that forced the evacuation of more than 1,000 people.

"Once it's full, it's gotta go somewhere," said Curran, who remembers driving to town with water rolling over the hood of his truck.

The Corps and the South Florida Water Management District—the same agencies that approved all the development in the wetlands—came up with a solution. They decided to spend $30 million of the taxpayers' money buying up homes and moving residents out of the area. Then the houses could be torn down and the land converted back to swamps.

Among the houses bought by the government was Curran's, even though that one did not flood (it was on stilts). Among those allowed to stay: houses in the subdivision built by the bribe-paying developer. In fact, the government offered to move Curran and his wife into one of that subdivision's new homes.

Given the Marco Island precedent, how could the Corps sign off on all the 404 permits that doomed Bonita Springs to flooding? Simple. The Corps showed developers how to get around its own rules.

When a project is not wetland dependent, as required by the Marco Island decision, then the Corps is supposed to consider alternative sites—places where the project could be built without harming wetlands. But if the project's purpose is drawn as narrowly as possible, then the number of alternative sites tends to shrink dramatically.

From 1990 to 2005, the top civilian in charge of the Corps' regulatory division in Florida was John Hall, a crusty paraplegic with a dry sense of humor and a doctorate in biology. He told us that the way to get around the Marco Island precedent is easy. It's all in the way you phrase the application. And, Hall said, Corps officials are happy to help developers with the phrasing.

Say you want to build a golf-course community on wetlands in the Jacksonville area, said Hall.

"Most people would say a residential golf community doesn't have to be located in wetlands," Hall explained. "So we work with the applicant on the purpose: 'A middle-income residential development built around a . . . 9-hole or 18-hole championship golf course.' Also they're targeting it for a particular demographic, right? I want to define the project purpose (to include that) and say 'in the greater metropolitan Jacksonville area.'"

That language serves to limit the search for alternative sites to pretty much the site the applicant wanted all along, Hall said. And if by chance a less damaging alternative still turns up, the Corps lets the applicant make the decision to reject it. That way, the Corps appears to comply with the letter of the law, while still allowing wetlands to be wiped out.

If the Corps really applied the Marco Island rule in Florida, longtime Corps biologist Vic Anderson told us, "probably 60 percent of these permits could be denied because they're not water dependent."

Instead, he said, "lot by lot we're allowing the piecemeal filling of Florida."

5

Six Percent Saviors

The busiest Corps of Engineers permitting operation in the world is headquartered in a Jacksonville office building rising 21 stories from the south bank of the St. Johns River.

The regulatory division of the Corps occupies the third floor of Two Prudential Plaza, sitting above other floors that since 2002 have also been leased by the taxpayers for use by the Corps. Those other floors are devoted to more traditional Corps duties—dredging shipping channels, operating the locks on canals, and managing the multi-billion-dollar project to restore the Everglades. All told, the Corps occupies 167,000 square feet of prime riverfront space in downtown Jacksonville.

Seventy people work for the regulatory division in Jacksonville. Their 700 or so colleagues on the other floors regard them as "kind of a bastard stepchild of the district," retired Col. Terry Rice, who served as the district engineer in the mid-1990s, told us. "They're kind of in opposition to everything that the other branches do. They don't fit."

From the gleaming windows of the Corps' regulatory office, there's a nice panorama across the St. Johns, with all the traffic rushing to and fro across the nearby Fuller Warren Bridge. Looking out provides a far more interesting view than looking in. A bird perched on the third-floor ledge would see a seemingly unending warren of cubicles where the carpet, chairs, and computers all come in shades of gray.

The first time we visited this bland palace in 2004, we noticed a big whiteboard amid the cubicles. Near the top of the board someone had written, "I'm so happy I can:," and then below that, other employees had contributed a series of bitterly sarcastic entries to complete the sentence. The top entry on the list: "Reload."

As we were escorted down a hallway, a heavyset, gray-haired man with sharp blue eyes and a neat mustache rolled his wheelchair to a halt in front us, blocking our way. Our guide introduced us to John Hall, who glared up at us for a second in silence.

Then he asked if we planned to produce a story called "The River Killers," outlining how corrupt Corps officials were getting rich off kickbacks from developers. We joked that that would explain their incredibly plush offices with the gold-plated doorknobs. He laughed, but not very hard.

"It takes an incredible amount of dedication to do what we do and put up with the crap we put up with every day," Hall said with a trembling voice. Then he rolled away.

When a new colonel arrives in Jacksonville, he may have only the dimmest understanding of how the regulatory side works. For 15 years, the man who taught them how to do their job was Hall.

"The first person to come talk to me when I got in was John Hall," recalled Rice, a 26-year veteran Corps officer who took charge of the Jacksonville office in 1994. "And my first reaction was: You mean the Corps does this? I had no earthly idea."

Rice said that during his three-year stint running the Jacksonville office, permitting issues took up most of his time and energy. Rice made a lot of controversial decisions, but he said, "I don't think I ever went against John."

From 1990 until his retirement in 2005, Hall commanded not only the staff

Figure 5. For 15 years, John Hall ran the largest regulatory division of the Corps. (Photograph courtesy of U.S. Army Corps of Engineers.)

in Jacksonville but another gaggle of employees scattered throughout the state in branch offices in places like Pensacola, Palatka, and Palm Beach, plus one in Puerto Rico. During the time Hall ran the largest regulatory office in the Corps, he frequently traveled the country to teach other Corps districts how to do their jobs. He has probably been the most influential national figure in the Corps' regulatory division.

"I'm a GS-15, the highest nonpolitical level you can reach," Hall boasted in one of a series of interviews he granted us after that first frosty encounter. The only other GS-15 in the Corps, he said, was the guy who headed up the Corps' regulatory division nationwide—a position that Hall himself held briefly in the late 1980s.

Hall grew up in Alexandria, Virginia, where his grandfather once lived in a house at the foot of the 333-foot Masonic tower honoring the first president. He graduated from the local high school and then earned a degree from George Washington University. With a doctorate in biology, he did some wetlands research at the University of Georgia but then decided academia didn't suit him. Instead, he went into government work, first for the National Oceanic and Atmospheric Administration, then for the Corps.

When we met him, polio had robbed him of the use of his legs, and divorce had left him living alone in a 940-square-foot condo, carefully chosen so that all the services he might need were within three blocks. His condo overlooked the St. Johns, so close to the river's edge that he joked he could fish from the balcony. He was also close enough to notice that, with every rainfall, a storm sewer gushed unfiltered pollution straight into the river.

Hall's hobby was sailing, but his work with the Corps occupied most of his waking hours. His private e-mail address showed his commitment: it began with "drwetlands." His consuming passion for his work could lead to bitter frustration when he ran up against what he perceived as bureaucratic foot-dragging by other government agencies.

"I've seen John just bawl in these meetings—just lose it," Rice said. "He can't understand why people can't do their jobs. He takes it personally."

His passion could also boil over into anger. Anyone who crossed him would feel the heat. In 2001 an EPA employee named Bruce Boler began repeatedly objecting to 404 permits in Lee and Collier counties, citing concerns about increased water pollution. Hall blew a gasket. The way Hall saw it, water quality was supposed to be the state's concern, not the EPA's. Hall believed Boler—who was highly critical of the Corps' permitting practices—was just trying to halt or delay new permits with frivolous objections.

"That really made me mad," Hall said. "I hate dealing with stupid people."

So Hall sent Boler's boss at the EPA an e-mail labeling him "a loose cannon." Then, at a meeting with Boler and other federal agency officials, Hall employed a visual aid to make the same point.

"Just as a sort of a joke, because I like nautical things, I own seven small saluting cannons," Hall recalled. "I brought one in—it had a barrel about eight inches long—I brought it in and dropped it on the floor and said, 'That's a loose cannon.'"

(Boler, who transferred to a less controversial job with the National Park Service in 2003, was no fan of Hall or the Corps, either: "The only thing they want to do is enable development.")

But Hall could also be refreshingly frank about the shortcomings of the permitting program. At a May 2004 public meeting in Fort Myers, Hall said he had spent 20 years trying to get his agency to do a better job of assessing the cumulative impact of wiping out 10 acres of wetlands here and 20 more over there—and the Corps still couldn't do it.

"I don't think anybody should trust the Corps of Engineers to know when you've gone so far that you shouldn't go any further," Hall said.

When an environmental activist commented that some of the things Hall was saying were disturbing, Hall replied, "I'm a disturbing guy."

In the late 1990s a sharp-tongued Lee County civic activist named Ann Hauck befriended Hall, exchanging letters and e-mails with him, even inviting him to dinner with her and her husband when he was visiting the area. Hauck, a redhead from Wisconsin who resembles a late-stage Katherine Hepburn, repeatedly warned Hall that the Corps was repeating the mistakes in the western Everglades that the Corps was supposed to be fixing in the eastern Everglades.

Sometimes they argued, to the point where Hall would stop responding to her e-mails for a while. But more often the crusty bureaucrat and the persistent rabble-rouser found some common ground in their distaste for pro-development local, state, and federal officials.

"Oh, I share your concerns about the urbanization of Florida," he told her in one 2004 e-mail. "And the 404 program can be a powerful tool to mold that urbanization, but NOT block it. Big money and big influence will always carry the day in American politics. It always has and always will."

With reporters, Hall tended to be more circumspect, although he could still be quite candid about the shortcomings of the permitting system. For instance, when we asked him about why the Corps charges only $100 for a 404 permit, regardless of whether it's a 20-acre housing development or a 50,000-acre mining project, he chuckled and said, "My suspicion is that it costs as much to process the checks as they bring in."

He offered us a straightforward analysis of what was wrong with Florida. All the Corps' woes, he said, stem from the fact that most of Florida's 67 counties "are striving really hard to improve their economic bases." For 20 years Florida law has required cities and counties to draw up comprehensive land-use plans for dealing with growth. But city and county officials have routinely granted variances that gave developers whatever they wanted, he said.

As a result, he said, one county official told him that his government's land-use plan was really whatever the Corps would permit. "They don't have any plan at all!" Hall grumbled. "They're depending on a regulatory agency to do their planning for them? Bullshit!"

All too often, he said local and state officials in Florida approve projects they know to be bad for the environment and then look to the Corps to stop it.

"Nobody has the guts to draw the line," he said.

In the past the Corps would take a stand regardless of state approval—on Boca Ciega Bay, on Marco Island. But these days a project that has already won approval from local and state officials is virtually certain to get a yes from the Corps, too, Hall explained. The way he described the process it sounded almost like a factory line: applications go in one end, then they're processed and come out the other end stamped approved.

"The Corps regulatory program is a command and control program, and it does what any command and control program tends to do," Hall said. "We get the application, we review it against the requirements that are set, and if it meets the requirements and satisfies the criteria, then the permit is issued."

∾

Despite the name of the agency, nearly all of the Corps of Engineers employees reviewing 404 permits are biologists. They're not engineers or architects trained in how developments should be designed. They're not experts in hydrology trained to spot how a development might cut off the flow of water. They're not accountants who could easily calculate the cost of building somewhere besides wetlands. But those are all jobs they have to do.

"We're not ideally equipped for this," Hall admitted. As a result, the Corps' regulators usually just trust the developers and their consultants to analyze if there are alternatives to building in wetlands to see if they meet the Marco Island test.

"It basically comes down to almost a gut feeling," Hall said. "Do you think you're really being told the truth here? And do you think their arguments are reasonable? . . . Eventually it comes down to some level of best professional judgment."

The exception to the all-biologist staff is a perpetually overworked man named Bob Barron. He's the only employee of the Jacksonville regulatory office with an engineering degree. When regulators need a study done involving lots of numbers and mapping, the job is invariably handed to Barron.

The first time we encountered Barron was at an environmental law conference held in a Tampa hotel ballroom in March 2004. A slim, animated man with close-cropped graying hair, Barron wore a dark suit, a red tie that was just a tad too short, and a goofy grin. He stood in front of a room full of environmental consultants and local government officials and talked for 30 minutes about wetland regulations.

At one point Barron mentioned the legal presumption that projects that don't need to be built in or near the water can be built somewhere other than wetlands—the basis, though Barron didn't mention it, for the Marco Island decision.

"That presumption doesn't really work well in Florida," Barron said.

∾

The first biologist the Corps hired in Florida to review permits was a firefighter's son named Vic Anderson, who then spent 30 years working for an agency he grew to despise. The Corps' wetland protection efforts are "pretty close to a complete failure," he told us.

A native of St. Petersburg, Anderson earned a degree in marine biology and worked for the National Marine Fisheries Service prior to joining the Corps in 1974. The day after he retired in 2004 to a dirt-road home in rural Polk County, the gray-bearded Anderson told us story after story about how he butted heads with Hall and other Corps higher-ups when he tried to follow the law rather than kowtow to permit applicants.

For instance, there was the time when the corporate giant W. R. Grace & Company applied for a permit to mine for phosphate in a large sawgrass marsh near Tampa known as Hooker's Prairie. Phosphate mining, which produces a key component of fertilizer, is a politically powerful industry in Florida. In reviewing the W. R. Grace permit, Anderson said, he very strictly applied the "alternatives" test that had killed Deltona's Marco Island project.

"There's no constraint on looking at practicable alternatives, especially if it's not a water-dependent activity," recalled Anderson. "So I suggested, 'stick to uplands, or mine for phosphate elsewhere—such as Morocco.' I said, 'We ought to deny this permit.'"

He was overruled.

"It's been my experience with the Corps of Engineers that it does not feel it represents the general public or the resources it's been given the duty to protect," Anderson said. "The attention is more on erring in the interest of the applicant."

But according to Hall, that's the way it's supposed to work. By bending over backward to help developers, miners, and other applicants to get their permits, the reviewers are simply complying with a longstanding Corps rule: every project seeking a permit is presumed to be in the public interest, unless the Corps can somehow prove otherwise.

"I think this is based on a fundamental precept of the American legal system: innocent unless proven guilty," Hall wrote us in an e-mail.

He said he has been including that presumption in every briefing he has given to the new colonels who have taken charge of the Jacksonville district for the past 15 years. It's even in the training manual given to new permit reviewers.

"A permit will be granted unless the [colonel] determines that it would be contrary to the public interest," the training manual says. "Thus to deny a permit . . . the burden of proof is on the Corps to show a proposal is contrary to the public interest."

Experts on wetlands law say both Hall and the manual have it backwards. We talked to three of them: Royal Gardner, who from 1989 to 1993 served as the Corps' top lawyer on wetlands issues and now is vice dean of the Stetson University School of Law in Gulfport, near St. Petersburg, as well as vice chair of the American Bar Association's Committee on Water Quality and Wetlands; Margaret "Peggy" Strand, former head of the U.S. Justice Department's environmental law section and editor of *The Wetlands Deskbook*, a widely used compendium of information about the 404 program; and Kim Diana Connolly, a professor who directs the environmental law clinic at the University of South Carolina and coeditor of the American Bar Association book *Wetlands Law and Policy: Understanding Section 404*.

They all pointed out that the Corps' own regulations say that "most wetlands constitute a productive and valuable public resource, the unnecessary alteration or destruction of which should be discouraged as contrary to the public interest."

"The general legal standard is that a permit applicant must prove that his project is in the public interest," Strand told us.

But when we told Hall what the legal experts said, he scoffed: "OK, that's their interpretation." He said he had been present when the regulations were written, so he knew what the authors' intent was—and it was for the Corps to side with the applicants.

"If it's a flawed reading of the regulations," Hall said stubbornly, "it is a nationwide flaw."

Still, before approving a permit, Corps biologists are supposed to run through a checklist known as the "public interest test," balancing such factors as preserving wetlands with the profits of the property owner. The roots of the public interest test go back to Col. Tabb's decision to reject Zabel and Russell's dredge-and-fill permit because the public interest was better served by protecting the environment.

But Vic Anderson said he and other Corps employees joked that it should be called a "special interest review," because somehow the answer always turned out to be saying yes to filling and killing the wetland.

The grind of churning out permit after permit to obliterate the wetlands they're supposed to save can take a toll on Corps biologists. One of them, Dale Beter of the Panama City office, pleaded with Bay County Commissioners via a personal email—mistakenly leaving his Corps of Engineers office information at the bottom of his signature—that their continual push for more condos was going to "ring the death knell for those who may want to see the water and remember the days when the resources seemed to never end."

Even Hall had to learn to go with the flow instead of battling the tidal wave of permits.

"In regulatory, I learned a lesson long ago," he wrote in an internal e-mail to one of his colonels. "Courage is to move forward with the best you can put together in a real time mode of operation. My skills are honed to the move ahead approach, simply doing the best you can. It has taken me a LONG time to realize and accept that."

❧

In contrast to Col. Wisdom's personal survey of Marco Island, these days Corps employees rarely leave the office to look at the wetlands they're allowing developers to wipe out. The 100 regulatory employees scattered around Florida are overwhelmed. Some juggle more than 200 permits at one time and cover a dozen or more counties, making site visits impossible.

"We rely on verbal descriptions, aerials, and photographs," said Charles "Chuck" Schnepel, who like Anderson was hired by the Corps in Florida 30 years ago. "We don't have time to go out and do three-hour inspections." Of course that means, once again, trusting applicants to tell them the truth.

The Corps not only issues more 404 permits in Florida than in any other state, it also issues permits for greater wetland losses than anywhere else.

When Corps officials from Florida talk to their colleagues in other states "everybody just can't believe the difference in each state," said Schnepel, who has a sarcastic drawl and a fondness for Hawaiian shirts. "The acreage of impacts that causes them to sit up and take notice is small compared to us."

Once, when Schnepel was at a conference outside Florida, he mentioned to a colleague from up north that he was reviewing a proposal to wipe out 2,200 acres of wetlands. The colleague was stunned at the scale of environmental damage, Schnepel told us.

How, he asked, could the Corps issue a permit so large? The answer, Schnepel replied, is simple: the permit application was filled out properly.

"The regulatory program doesn't say we're out here to deny permits," explained Schnepel, who runs the Corps' Tampa office. "It says we're out here to process them."

Really, he explained, the Corps' only power is to delay a permit's approval in the hopes of convincing a developer to modify his plans to lessen the environmental impact. But ultimately, if the developer persists, the answer will wind up being yes.

There are lots of tricks the Corps can employ in getting to yes. A common one involves cutting up a big project into small pieces which require more than one permit. The Corps will say that each segment has "independent utility," meaning there's no need to look at the total impact of the project because each segment can be built independently from the rest. Of course, once half of a project has been built, the rest has enough momentum going that approval becomes a foregone conclusion.

A prime example is the Scripps Research Institute. In 2003 Governor Jeb Bush announced that secret negotiations with the institute of La Jolla, California, had resulted in Scripps officials agreeing to build a new biotech campus in Palm Beach County in exchange for $300 million in state incentives. Bush trumpeted Scripps' decision as a way to stimulate new development in Palm Beach, predicting it would spark a 21st-century version of the California gold rush. County officials anticipated the Scripps facility would become the centerpiece of a massive laboratory-office-residential complex covering thousands of acres.

Scripps officials toured the county looking for a site, led by the head of Palm Beach County's Business Development Board, Greg Fagan. The site they selected was an orange grove called Mecca Farms, next door to the Loxahatchee National Wildlife Refuge. Fagan assured them there would be fewer problems with environmental permitting at that site than at any of the others they examined. Fagan did not mention he was part owner of a piece of land across the street and thus stood to profit from Scripps' selection of that site. Fagan's partners included the former head of the county's planning and zoning department.

Environmental groups were highly critical of the site, pointing out that it would put a sprawling development the size of downtown West Palm Beach in a previously undeveloped rural area that was miles from the roads, sewer lines, and other infrastructure that would be needed.

Among the most vocal critics: Nat Reed, now retired from government service and leading an antisprawl group called 1,000 Friends of Florida. Putting Scripps in such a remote spot "will torpedo both Palm Beach County's comprehensive plan and the state's comprehensive planning process," Reed warned.

But state and county officials demanded fast approval of the permits for the 1,919-acre Mecca Farms site. The Corps agreed to put the 404 permit on a fast track.

How to speed up such a large permit review? Split it up.

The county applied for a 404 permit for just the 535-acre Scripps Research Park, which would destroy 21 acres of ditches that had been built by the grove owner to drain the wetlands on the site. The permits for the rest of the project, including roads and other development that would have major wetland impacts, would come later. Although the EPA and other agencies objected, the Corps approved the permit for the 535 acres in just eight months, and the county broke ground to start construction.

The Florida Wildlife Federation and the Sierra Club sued, arguing that chopping Scripps into segments violated the Clean Water Act and other federal regulations. A few days after the groundbreaking, U.S. District Judge Donald Middlebrooks agreed.

"The inescapable conclusion from this record is that the Research Park Project was conceptualized as an integrated whole, progressing in phases, and that the 535-acre project was never intended to stand alone—not that is until time came to apply for a . . . permit," Judge Middlebrooks wrote.

Suddenly faced with a long construction delay, Scripps abandoned the Mecca Farms site and instead switched over to a spot on the Jupiter campus of Florida Atlantic University. That was the site Reed and the environmental groups had been pushing all along.

∾

When environmental groups sought a public hearing on the controversial Scripps permit, the Corps said no. The Corps does its work largely outside public view. It conducts no public debate and requires no vote in an open meeting. The public hearings that were a hallmark of the Zabel-Russell and Deltona permit denials are a thing of the past.

Because they're kept in the dark, most of Florida's 18 million residents have no idea of the influence the Corps has on their lives and futures. They don't know it's allowing vital swamps and marshes to be converted to convenience stores and office parks and apartments, and that they're likely to pick up the tab for the subsequent flooding and other problems. They have no idea how important it is to their future whether a bird colonel in Jacksonville says yes or no.

"There's no job out there besides commanding soldiers in combat where you can have a larger impact on people's quality of life," said Col. Robert Carpenter, a ruddy-faced Stanford grad who was in charge of the Jacksonville office of the Corps from 2003 to 2006.

The Corps does not completely ignore the public. It does mail notices about some permits to adjoining property owners, though they seldom realize what's at stake and take the time to respond.

"Every time you fill in one of these wetlands, that water's got to go somewhere," Vic Anderson said. Sometimes after the project wipes out the wetlands, he said, then the calls start pouring in—"Hey, my neighbor filled two wetlands and now my yard's flooded." By then, he said, it's too late.

The other way to find out what the Corps is doing is to look up the information on the Corps' Web site, where it lists public notices for projects that are under consideration. On July 1, 2004, for instance, the Web site offered 56 notices about permit applications on projects from all around the state. Many were for an acre or less, but when we added them all together they totaled more than 800 acres of wetlands. Nearly a year later, more than half had been approved and the rest were headed that way.

The applicants listed on this particular day ranged from big development companies to lowly mom-and-pop builders. One application was from the mighty St. Joe Company, Florida's biggest landowner and developer, seeking a permit for its new 499-home SummerCamp development in the Panhandle.

Another was from a Jacksonville homeowner who wanted to put about two feet of fill in slightly more than one-tenth of an acre of wetlands on the St. Johns so he could extend his backyard—and halt the flow of water from his neighbor's yard.

Many of the public notices revealed plans to turn a swamp into a subdivision. In Fort Myers, U.S. Homes wanted a permit to destroy 41 acres of wetlands in the Estero Bay watershed for a new 240-home development. A Flagler Beach developer sought an OK to destroy nearly 50 acres of the Black Branch Swamp to build a road and an industrial park in Bunnell. A Naples developer asked for a permit to destroy 46 acres of wetlands to create a subdivision called, of course, Cypress Landings.

Some were aimed at improving facilities as a way to create more business. The Collier County Airport Authority was asking for a permit to build a new runway at the Marco Island Executive Airport, which would require filling in 21 acres of mangrove wetlands. And an Ormond Beach church sought permission to dump fill in 13 acres of wetlands along the Tomoka River to expand its parking lot.

Some were for more basic work. The Seminole Tribe of Indians, for instance, wanted a permit to destroy about 100 acres of wetlands with a limestone mine to provide construction material for their Broward County reservation.

Several were for after-the-fact permits, the kind a developer applies for after being caught destroying wetlands without first getting a permit. There were no consequences to being caught—no fines, no criminal prosecution, nothing.

That's not unusual. In 2003 the family that owns the Winn-Dixie supermarket chain applied for a permit to wipe out 500 acres of wetlands along the Tomoka River to build a new city called Nocatee. The project generated a lot of controversy. Environmental groups filed a legal challenge to the state permit, but lost. Only a 404 permit from the Corps stood in the way of starting construction.

Because of the size of both the project and the controversy, a Corps permit reviewer named Mark Evans drove out from Jacksonville to the proposed new town to take a first-hand look at what would be destroyed. Evans was at first delighted to see that someone had cut a path through the trees, which would make it easier to get into the site. Then he realized the same person, driving a wide-tired vehicle with rotating blades called a HydroAxe, had also cut a swath up to 12 feet wide that extended about 300 feet into a hardwood swamp.

"It was kicking up a mound of mud on either side, ripping up trees," Evans told us. In some places big cypress trees had been run over and remained bent over. "Other areas," he said, "rather than bending trees, he actually ripped the trees up, roots and all."

Evans decided to drive around the property "and see what else this idiot has done." Turned out that, to help surveyors who were running east–west transects on 100- to 200-foot intervals all through the property, the HydroAxe driver "just put 'due east' on the compass heading and just drove," Evans said. "He went right through a series of wetlands."

Although all this extensive damage was done without a permit, Nocatee's developers were not fined or prosecuted. Instead they were required to restore the wetlands—but only the ones that were in areas that weren't slated for development. In the sections where they had planned to get rid of wetlands anyway, the HydroAxe driver simply speeded up the process. The 404 permit was quietly approved with none of the public uproar that the state permit caused.

❧

So long as the public doesn't object, approving permits can be relatively easy, say Corps employees. It's usually just a matter of doing some cut-and-paste work on their computers and then signing it. Because they're trying to process the permits as fast as possible, they would prefer not to deal with public objections.

"A couple of years ago the Corps of Engineers' attorney called me and asked me to call them before I sent any comments, because I was slowing things down," said Lesley Blackner, a West Palm Beach attorney who has repeatedly sued the Corps over permits.

The Corps faces constant pressure from developers to keep the flow of permits going. "Every place I go, I'm popular not because people like me but they want to talk to me about why can't we get the permits out," Col. Carpenter told us. "Every workday 60 permits come in the door. If they don't put out 60, then they've lost ground."

Some developers have figured out that the key to getting permits faster may be hiring ex-Corps personnel to help. Terry Rice and Don Wisdom both work as environmental consultants now. When Col. Carpenter retired from the Army in 2006, he landed a job as president of Grubbs Emergency Services, run by a former Corps employee named John "Gary" Grubbs. Grubbs had plans to develop a marina project on about 2,000 acres of marshy land in Pasco County owned by Grubbs Emergency Services. The development, called Sunwest Harbor Towne, would feature 2,400 homes, a 167-acre golf course, a hotel and convention center, and 33 acres of stores. To speed things up even more, Grubbs lined up the newly retired John Hall as the project's environmental consultant.

While saying yes to a 404 permit may be a quick decision that keeps the production line running, denying a permit can take months of negotiations and a lot of paperwork. Among other requirements is a legal analysis of whether the denial effectively takes the property away from the owner, which would be a big no-no.

Denying a permit requires a decision from the highest official in Jacksonville. "All denials go before the colonel," Schnepel said. "First you give him a full briefing, then he brings in the applicant and talks with them. The colonel is acutely aware of any denial packages that are ready to come up to him."

In 30 years with the Corps, Schnepel said, he has recommended denying a permit four times. Only once has it gone through.

Another longtime Corps biologist reviewing permits is Steve Brooker, a shaggy-haired surfer, cave-diver, and sometime guitarist with a band called One Street Over. The band plays "acoustic eclectic," which he said means "bluegrass, newgrass, folk, acoustic rock, blues, Irish music, mountain music, pop, country, and just about anything else you can think of."

When we met Brooker, he was driving a maroon pickup with a bumper sticker that said, "We all live downstream." He was dressed for work in the Corps' Brevard County office in sandals, worn blue jeans, and a T-shirt advertising a music festival in the town of Lacoochee. His eyes looked red and tired.

An ex-teacher from Jacksonville, Brooker has degrees in both botany and construction management. He has worked for the Corps since 1990. "I'll probably get in trouble for talking to you," he said. "I don't care."

The 404 permitting system is broken, Brooker told us. "It's a huge scam . . . a system with good people working in it who can't do what people think they're doing."

In 15 years with the Corps, Brooker said, he had denied just one 404 permit. Writing a recommendation for a permit denial is usually too much of a hassle, he said, because the recommendation "has to be 30 or 40 pages long and has to be well written." One denial recommendation done in his office took a month and a half of manpower for just the writing—and even then there's no guarantee the colonel will sign it.

Instead of spending all that time on a denial that might not go through, he said, "it's best to take the best compromise you can get and move on to the next one. If you put in the effort it takes to deny every one you needed to, we'd be buried."

Even Hall agreed with that assessment. If the staff had more time to fully assess each permit, he said, there probably would be more denials.

When we asked, the Corps staff in Jacksonville couldn't tell us exactly how many 404 permits had been approved and how many denied. That was fine with Col. Carpenter.

"I guarantee you I don't keep a scoreboard," he told us.

But we found out that every three months, the Jacksonville office files a paper report with its headquarters in Washington detailing the number of permit applications, the acreage requested, the acreage permitted, and how quickly the permits were approved.

The only thing the Pentagon really cared about—because it was the only thing that Congress cared about—was how fast the permits were approved, Hall told us. But we saw a way to use the quarterly reports for another purpose. We requested those reports, all of which turned out to be stuffed into the desk of one employee.

Using those paper reports, we built a spreadsheet and then used simple math to come up with some disturbing numbers.

We found that from 1999 to 2003 the Corps approved about 12,000 permits in Florida, allowing wetlands to be destroyed.

Denials totaled exactly one.

The lone denial was for a hotel and marina called Ecotour Lodge that had been proposed for a piece of private property next door to one of the ranger stations at Everglades National Park. The developer had proposed dumping fill into slightly more than an acre of mangroves in the ecologically sensitive area. In 2002, a permit reviewer named Mike Nowicki successfully persuaded his bosses to turn the project down because less environmentally damaging alternatives were available, and a hotel did not need to be built in wetlands.

When we first interviewed Col. Carpenter in May 2005, we brought up the Jacksonville district's incredibly low number of permit denials. Within the next two weeks after the interview, Carpenter denied four permits—three of them in a single day, something Hall said he could not remember ever happening before. The grounds for denial? They all flunked that same "alternatives" test.

"When they require outright denial, they get denied," Carpenter explained. Asked if being faced with reporters' inquiries had anything to do with this sudden flurry of denials, the colonel said, "Absolutely, categorically no."

And anyway, Hall contended that we were using the wrong yardstick to measure his staff's performance.

"Nobody could convince me that straight denials are a very good measure of what the program does," he said. "I think the best indication of what the program does, and we have done an abysmal job of trying to collect the information, and that is how much the permit, the application review process results in modifications to the project. And we simply don't capture that very well."

In other words, if a developer who wanted to wipe out 100 acres of wetlands was persuaded by the Corps to knock his request down to 50 acres instead, that would be a big success in Hall's view.

But as Hall observed, nobody from the Corps had ever calculated how much they had succeeded in trimming down projects. If we wanted the answer, we'd have to get it ourselves. Once again, we turned to the quarterly reports and our spreadsheet.

When we did the math, we found that the Corps did little to stand in the way of wiping out Florida's wetlands.

Nationally the Corps boasts that about 20 percent of the wetlands targeted for destruction are saved by its permitting program. In 2003, for instance, it approved destroying 79 percent of the 27,154 acres of wetlands that developers and others requested permits to wipe out. That meant the Corps saved 21 percent, or 5,824 acres of wetlands nationwide.

Yet we found that in Florida in 2003, the Corps saved a mere 6 percent. Permit applicants sought to wipe out 3,282 acres of Florida wetlands and the Corps approved all but 185 acres of that.

Carpenter refused to believe the numbers we came up with, even though they came from the Corps' own paper trail. He even defended his staff's failure to keep tabs on its own performance.

"We don't spend a lot of time tracking what we do," he growled. "We spend most of our time producing."

We interviewed the Corps' top officials in Washington about the numbers we found. They insisted the Jacksonville office had done nothing wrong by saying yes to virtually everyone wanting to wipe out the state's swamps and marshes. Contrary to what Gen. Gribble said about Deltona, they told us that the Corps just goes along with what state and local officials want, and they want lots of development.

"Our role is not to be an impediment to the development process," Lt. Gen. Carl Strock, then the Army's chief of engineers, told us. "We're not the ones making decisions about where growth occurs."

Hall agreed. He said Floridians expect too much from the Corps. People who see a pristine cypress swamp that's been targeted for destruction may think that surely, somehow, the government should protect it.

"But if you look at the state of Florida over the past 20 years," he said without any apparent irony, "that may not be the best way to protect important wetland areas."

Twenty years ago, at a time when the Reagan-era Corps had started saying yes to everything, Floridians tried to pass their own law to protect the state's wetlands. But it didn't work out the way they expected.

6

"The Joy of Life"

On April 25, 1984, Florida state senator Warren Henderson rose to his feet and delivered the most important speech of his political career.

He apologized.

While trying to drum up support for the state's first comprehensive wetlands protection bill, Henderson, a heavyset man with a face like an old basset hound, had instead created a major political scandal.

Henderson, then 56, was a prominent coin collector and bank director from Venice. For 20 years his Sarasota-area district reelected him to the legislature every time he ran.

He was a Republican in the tradition of Teddy Roosevelt. He was a Shriner and an Elk, a fiscal conservative, but he also belonged to the National Wildlife Federation and the Audubon Society.

In the 1960s, when people who were concerned about the decline of Florida's water and air started one of the state's first environmental groups, Conservation '70s, Henderson served on its board. When the state finally began requiring permits before developers could fill bay bottom to create new land, Henderson sponsored the bill. At one point in the late 1970s, he pulled off a feat that today seems impossible: he was honored as the year's best legislator by both the Sierra Club and the Florida Home Builders Association.

Henderson was known as a quick wit and a bit of a clown, someone willing to do just about anything to get a laugh. When the legislature was in session, after the official business had ended for the day, fellow lawmakers Frank Mann and Tom McPherson often set up an open bar in their suite of offices, calling themselves "the M&Ms." They offered free food and drink from a pantry eagerly stocked by lobbyists. Environmental advocates knew they could always find Henderson at the M&Ms' place, holding court, cracking everyone up.

In the months prior to the 1984 legislative session, the Senate committee that handled environmental issues held a series of hearings on the wetlands bill. Henderson "was a member of the committee, but he never was actively involved," said former state environmental lawyer David Gluckman, who by the 1980s was working as a lobbyist for the Sierra Club.

Actually, the politician most responsible for pushing the controversial wetlands protection bill through the legislature was a wry, sandy-haired law school professor from Gainesville named Jon Mills. Mills chaired the House Natural Resources Committee, which gave him control over any environmental legislation in that chamber. More importantly, he had locked up enough pledges from his fellow House Democrats to guarantee his election as Speaker of the House for the 1986–88 session. The prospect of his future ascension made Mills a man whose every wish became the House's command.

With his tremendous clout, Mills was able to take on some of the toughest issues facing the state. In 1983, the legislature passed a Mills bill setting water quality standards. In 1984, he took on wetlands protection. In 1985, he pushed through a bill that required local governments to start planning for how to handle Florida's explosive growth.

"It was kind of a glorious time," recalled former House Natural Resources Committee director Fred McCormack.

To Mills, protecting the state's wetlands was a natural outgrowth of the water quality legislation.

"Wetlands, it was persuasively argued both by our staff people and environmentalists were diminishing fast," Mills said. Thus this wetlands bill "was a recognition of scientific reality in a political way. Florida was growing rapidly, and dredge and fill was the norm."

Conservation groups had tried since the 1970s to persuade the state to protect its wetlands, to no avail. The state didn't even claim regulatory jurisdiction over its most famous marsh, the Everglades.

Mills knew that any effort by the state to restrict dredge and fill would be seen as an assault on private property rights.

"This is a gut-level issue," he said. "We faced opposition from developers and farmers—overwhelmingly from developers."

Mills and McCormack knew they needed to build public support for saving wetlands, so they launched a campaign to alert the public to the terrible damage dredge and fill was doing to Florida. They held a seminar in Tallahassee in August 1983 with speakers from around the country talking about the importance of wetlands.

"If Florida's ground water is the state's lifeline then I would say our wetlands deserve to be called the 'soul,'" said the state Department of Environmental Regulation secretary, Victoria Tschinkel, at the seminar kickoff.

The goal of the seminar was not really to educate lawmakers but to produce favorable headlines that would give a wetlands bill some popular support. "We carefully orchestrated the coverage—all the major papers had it on their front pages," McCormack said.

By fall, McCormack and his staff had put together what they believed was a strong wetlands bill. But Gluckman and other environmental advocates contended it wasn't strong enough, McCormack said, "so we flew down this guy from New York named Jim Tripp."

Tripp had degrees in both law and philosophy from Yale and had worked as a federal prosecutor for five years. Since 1973 he had worked for a group called Environmental Defense, becoming its chief attorney in 1983. Despite his background as a prosecutor, Tripp did not look like the other pinstripe-and-wingtip lawyers writing legislation in Tallahassee.

"He wore a pigtail and a gold earring," McCormack said, and chuckled. "Goddamn, that was something in those days!"

Tripp helped Mills' staff draft a new, tighter version of the bill, and just after the New Year, Mills unveiled it. The bill would expand the state's jurisdiction over wetlands, requiring developers to get a permit if they wanted to make any alteration. Before approving a permit, state regulators would be required to consider whether the project would adversely affect fish or other wildlife.

Among the biggest wrangles was defining what would count as a wetland where permits were required. The bill called for basing those jurisdictional decisions on looking for certain plants that grow in swamps and marshes. State biologists drew up a list, which ran to about 300 species and became known as the "vegetation index." The index drew intense attacks from developers who wanted to make sure their plans would not be derailed by the new law.

"The special interests had hired every botanist in Florida and half of them in Georgia," McCormack said.

During hearings, Mills said, "People would bring in plants—'You think this is a wetland plant? This grows everywhere! You can't use this as an indicator!'"

There was some talk among the bill's supporters of mapping where the remaining wetlands were located, the better to protect them. However, Mills said that mapping the wetlands "is one of the things we avoided assiduously." Creating such a map would show who would be affected by the bill, likely stirring up even greater opposition, he explained.

"Everybody's goal was not to be inside the line" of regulation, Mills said.

The bill's supporters and opponents also struggled with whether to require regulators to gauge the cumulative impact of permitting decisions. How do you add up all the wetlands that have been wiped out and decide no more permits can be issued? Developers didn't like the idea that someone who showed up after an area had nearly been built out might be told he or she would not get a permit because everyone else had already got one, Mills said.

So he suggested taking out the term "cumulative impact" and instead calling for an "equitable distribution," which Mills said is basically the same thing. Nobody objected to that change.

The bill's opponents were so opposed to anything that might harm private property rights, Gluckman said, that they even opposed the use of the word "wetland" anywhere in the bill.

"To them 'wetland' meant any land that got wet," Gluckman told us. "So everywhere in the act where it should say 'wetlands,' they substituted 'plants designated in the vegetative index.'"

Despite the opposition, Mills' support for the bill virtually guaranteed that some version of it would pass the House. But in the Senate it lacked a highly placed supporter. The Senate president, a Lakeland nurseryman named Curtis Peterson, took the side of the state's agricultural interests, and they saw no advantage in passing a law that would only cause them headaches.

This was where Senator Henderson tried to help. To persuade some of his colleagues to vote for the bill in spite of Peterson's reservations, Henderson invited his fellow senators, some lobbyists, and a handful of Tallahassee reporters to join him on a field trip to view some actual wetlands.

They called it a fact-finding trip. It was a trip all right.

On that fateful spring morning, Henderson and five other senators piled onto a bus bound for the St. Marks National Wildlife Refuge south of Tallahassee. As the bus rolled down the road, Henderson started drinking. By the time the bus pulled into the parking lot at St. Marks, he was obviously drunk.

Henderson wasn't the only senator who imbibed that day, but he was the one who opened his mouth and stuck in his foot up to the knee.

In the bus, reporters overheard Henderson referring to black people with the "N" word. Then, at the wildlife refuge, the reporters overheard Henderson joking that one of the alligators resembled a black senator.

To top it all off, he made some sexist comments about women in general and then grabbed a female reporter for the *Orlando Sentinel*, 27-year-old Donna Blanton, who stood only five feet and weighed just 100 pounds. She said Hen-

Figure 6. Florida's law protecting wetlands was named for state senator Warren S. Henderson after the scandal over this fateful 1984 field trip to St. Marks National Wildlife Refuge. Henderson is holding a drink in one hand and some litter in the other. (Photograph courtesy of Florida Legislative Research Center and Museum.)

derson "grabbed me by the waist and put me on his hip and slung me around like a sack of potatoes. I think he meant it good-naturedly, but it was offensive."

When the bus returned to Tallahassee, nothing happened at first. This was three years before the *Miami Herald* uncovered presidential candidate Gary Hart's extramarital affair, making politicians' personal lives fair game for the press. Back then, Tallahassee reporters routinely ignored lawmakers' carousing. So for several days, none of the reporters on the field trip wrote about what happened.

The press corps covering the legislature was housed in a single poorly ventilated three-story building about a block from the Capitol. The place was like a small town: everybody knew everybody else's business. Rumors spread throughout the Capitol Press Center about what Henderson had done to Blanton.

Soon the story of Henderson's antics reached the ears of a journalist who realized it was news. *Palm Beach Post* reporter Brian Crowley began racing up and down the stairs interviewing the reporters who had been on the field trip, making it clear he planned to write something about what had happened. Rather than let themselves be scooped, other reporters jumped in too. Stories began appearing across the state about the senator's behavior.

Initially when another *Sentinel* reporter questioned Henderson about what he had done, the senator claimed, "If I did it, it was out of the joy of life." But by the time the Associated Press caught up with him, Henderson recognized that the "joy of life" excuse wasn't going to work. This time he explained, "I had a few drinks and I was a little loose."

"A little loose" wasn't sufficient for the NAACP, which called for Henderson's resignation over his use of racial slurs.

And so Henderson stood before the rest of the Senate and apologized for making them all look bad.

"Unfortunately for everybody involved, in what began as a worthy environmental mission, I had the bad judgment to have a few drinks and shoot off my mouth," Henderson said, adding with bitter self-reproach, "What a surprise."

Then he announced his retirement from politics. His colleagues responded with wild applause, followed by a series of speeches of their own. They not only praised his public service but also blasted the media for daring to expose his behavior. One senator even compared Henderson to Christ on the cross, because Henderson might have pointed a finger at colleagues who had made similar comments, but instead he "laid down his career for his friends."

Then, to stick a thumb in the eye of the press and demonstrate political unity in a time of scandal, when the senators passed the wetlands bill, they named it after their fallen comrade.

That was fine with Mills. "I was able to pass several bills over the years by naming it for (other) people," he told us. "The funny thing is, at the beginning nobody wanted their name attached to it."

In the heat of the moment, Henderson's colleagues also slipped up and called the bill what it really was, naming it the "Warren S. Henderson Wetlands Protection Act of 1984." At first the development and farming lobbyists who had opposed even mentioning the word "wetland" in the bill didn't catch what was happening, Gluckman said.

"Then I remember somebody in the gallery started jumping up and down and saying 'NO!' But it was too late. It passed—unanimously," Gluckman said, chuckling.

Now enshrined as Sections 403.91–403.929 of the Florida Statutes, the Henderson Act marked a turning point in how Florida treated its wetlands—both for good and for ill.

Lurking in the language of the new law was a loophole called "mitigation." Mitigation meant that it was okay to wipe out a wetland as long as you made up for the damage somehow.

During the extensive debate on the bill, there was precious little discussion of what Mills now calls "the 'M' word." The subject rated only a passing mention in a five-page analysis of the bill by the legislative staff. But the inclusion of mitigation was vital to the passage of the bill, according to the woman who became state government's preeminent wetlands expert during the 1990s, Ann Redmond.

"Before the Henderson Act, only a very small subset of Florida wetlands were protected by state regulations," said Redmond, who worked for the Department of Environmental Regulation and later its successor, the Department of Environmental Protection. "The Warren Henderson Act encompassed virtually all true wetlands. That meant a whole lot more regulations. In a state as flat and wet as Florida, that could cause problems for development. There had to be some kind of a give. The give was, we had to allow for the mitigation of wetlands, so you could get through the regulations."

The law specified that the developer was in charge of picking what kind of mitigation to use: creating new wetlands, restoring old ones, enhancing the quality of existing wetlands, or simply preserving another swamp somewhere. Regulators would have no say in which one wound up in the permit.

"The bill language provides for 'mitigation acceptable to the applicant.' That was a weakness we accepted to get it passed," Gluckman said.

Mitigation to make up for wetlands destruction was not a new idea. As far back as 1974, the then chief of the Corps of Engineers, Lt. Gen. Gribble, had called for a study of the concept. In the late 1970s, when Disney applied for a 404 permit to build EPCOT next to the Magic Kingdom, Col. Adams said he sent Disney a letter saying he intended to deny the application. He relented after Disney agreed to balance out the destruction with mitigation—"primarily land placed in conservation forever," Adams told us.

But the Henderson Act marked the first time that a Florida law had codified the practice. It turned out to be the law's Achilles heel.

"People had a naive concept of what mitigation was," Redmond told us. "It was like, 'Oh gee, we can go out and create some wetlands and everything's going to be fine and dandy.'"

From the day the Henderson Act took effect on January 1, 1985, through December 6, 1990, the DER issued 1,262 permits for destroying wetlands that required mitigation to make up for the damage. Those permits authorized the destruction of 3,305 acres of wetlands.

As mitigation, the DER required developers to create 3,345 acres of man-made wetlands. Developers were also required by the DER to "enhance"—a term which usually just meant "tear out melaleuca and other exotic vegetation that's bad for native wetlands plants"—another 7,301 acres of existing wetlands. And the state required them to preserve another 7,588 acres of wetlands.

Often the DER, in issuing permits, used a ratio of two acres of mitigation to one acre of wetlands destroyed. By requiring a 2:1 ratio, DER officials figured they would easily cover any potential failures or the time lag required to replace the wetlands that were wiped out.

But was that really enough to replace what had been destroyed?

About four years after the Henderson Act passed, a retired newspaper publisher living in the Sarasota area became suspicious about mitigation. The ex-publisher was a big contributor to a small but influential environmental group called ManaSota-88, and he urged the group to launch a study. So ManaSota-88's attorney, Tom Reese, arranged for a state biologist named David Crewz to spend his weekends checking mitigation wetlands in Manatee and Sarasota counties at ManaSota-88's expense.

Reese personally dug through the state permitting files, and Crewz picked 17 projects to review.

"One Saturday I went with him and we visited the first two on the list," Reese recalled. The first one required creating about three acres of man-made wetlands. "It was amazing," Reese said. "They'd basically dug a hole with a berm. The thing was just full of exotics. The thing was just a mess. The file showed no one had ever gone out and looked at it."

Crewz found that the man-made "wetland" had other problems too—the elevations were wrong and the base was too hard, creating problems for its intended water flow. When it did flow, the new wetland drained into a different creek from the one the natural wetland had supplied with water.

Every single one of the 17 projects Crewz checked had problems. Nuisance plants had not been removed, native plants had not been planted, the hydrology was wrong, and on and on. In two cases, Crewz discovered that the man-made wetlands had been created by digging deep holes in the middle of natural wetlands, "thus decreasing the trade-off value," he noted dryly in his Mana-Sota-88 report.

Lawyer Reese took a close look at the permitting files and found them sorely lacking as well. The developers were supposed to file conservation easements on their mitigation property, in effect giving up their right to develop that part of the property. The easements were missing and clearly no one from the state had checked.

Mitigation was an illusion designed to fool the public, Reese concluded. "The whole thing is just smoke and mirrors," he said.

Armed with the preliminary findings of the Crewz study, ManaSota-88 persuaded a friendly legislator to pass a bill in 1990 ordering a statewide study. The assignment fell to Redmond, a sharp-eyed biologist with a knack for organization and detail. She also had some firsthand experience with mitigation. At a prior job she had tried to create a wetland—and failed.

"It's more complex than just scrape things down, add water and stir," she said.

Redmond pulled 63 of the permits the state had issued, then traveled Florida checking on 119 sites where those permits said wetlands were supposed to be created. They were, of course, a wide variety of types: salt marshes, mangrove forests, freshwater herbaceous wetlands.

Redmond checked each site for two things: Was it built the way the permit required? And did it successfully mimic the natural wetland it was supposed to replace?

Her findings, announced in March 1991, stunned state officials. Of the 119 sites, Redmond found only 17 that could be called a success. Of those, most were in tidal areas where the ebb and flow of water was easy to predict. The rest were failures.

"If you go back and look at the projects in the 1991 report I did that flunked, you'll see that they all had soils data, engineering analyses, all of it saying yes, this will work," Redmond said. But nobody had ever bothered to check on whether those assurances were right.

She singled out the attempts to create freshwater wetlands. There had been

Figure 7. A bulldozer tries to turn a shell mine near the shore of Tampa Bay into a man-made wetland for the Tampa Bay Mitigation Bank. Studies done by Florida biologists in the early 1990s found that creating wetlands often fails, resulting in a loss of wetland acres. (Photograph by Lara Cerri, *St. Petersburg Times*.)

57 of those. All but four flopped. The would-be creators had picked sites lacking the proper soils, or water didn't flow through the areas properly, or the elevations were wrong, or one of the other million things that could go wrong had gone wrong.

"They're trying to create a wetland where Mother Nature never intended one to be," Redmond told us.

Her study also highlighted problems with DER's own oversight. She found that only four of the 63 permittees were fully complying with the state's mitigation requirements.

"Most permitted projects examined had one or more major deviations from the permitted plans," Redmond wrote in a 1992 *National Wetlands Newsletter* article on her study. "These included deviations in the approved site topography, configuration, vegetation plans and wetland outfall elevation."

Some permittees—about a third of them, in fact—hadn't bothered to do any of the required work, she found. And if it hadn't been for her digging through the permits, the scofflaws might never have been caught, because no one at DER checked on compliance.

After completing her study, Redmond drew a logical conclusion from her findings that angered her bosses at the state agency.

"What I did, and what I got in trouble for, was that I wrote a memo throwing cold water on the idea that the 2 to 1 ratio would work," Redmond said. "That wasn't what they wanted to hear."

But to Redmond, the problem seemed clear: requiring two acres of man-made wetlands to make up for destroying one acre of real wetlands won't work if the two acres are built to fail. Instead, the developer has wasted a lot of time and money and the public has still lost an acre of wetlands.

Then Redmond got an amen from another scientist. The South Florida Water Management District had hired a biologist named Kevin Erwin—who had some 15 years of experience with dredge-and-fill projects—to do a similar wetland mitigation study. Erwin's study was to focus on developments permitted by that agency, which covers an area stretching from the Kissimmee River southward to the Keys.

In his July 1991 report, Erwin wrote that out of 100 projects that required mitigation, only 40 were listed as completed. In those 40, he noted, 1,058 acres of wetlands were supposed to have been built—but he found only 530 acres had actually been constructed. The other half existed only on paper. And only four of the 40 "completed" mitigation projects actually met the criteria for success listed in their permits.

The biggest problem: water. Most, he found, had either too much or too little to work.

Redmond had a fairly simple recommendation to her bosses on how to deal with the mitigation problem: stop requiring developers to try to create new wetlands. Since creation often didn't work, why bother trying?

Instead, she told her colleagues to require developers to restore old, drained wetlands. There were plenty of those around the state that were being used as pastures or farms. Restoration, all the scientists agreed, seemed far more likely to succeed than creation.

But Redmond's solution was never adopted because of the language of the Henderson Act.

"The law says mitigation requirements have to be acceptable to the applicant," Redmond said. And restoration was "not what the consultants were bringing us." Instead they kept bringing in more wetland creation proposals, and state regulators had to keep rubber-stamping them.

Besides, by that time it was too late to stop people from thinking that mitigation was the solution. Mitigation had been formally adopted as a national policy, as part of a presidential promise called "no net loss."

7

The Promise, Plus

My position on wetlands is straightforward. All existing wetlands, no matter how small, should be preserved.

—Presidential candidate George H. W. Bush, *Sports Afield*, October 1988

∾

In 1988, George H. W. Bush had been Ronald Reagan's vice president for eight years and a loyal soldier for Reagan's policies.

Now it was time to break free.

As a congressman, Bush had developed a reputation as someone concerned about the environment. But as Reagan's vice president he had overseen the Task Force on Regulatory Relief, telling the Corps to stop saying no to so many permits. The Bush task force also sought to roll back fuel economy standards and relax federal regulation of toxic wastes.

So when Bush ran to succeed Reagan, the League of Conservation Voters gave him a grade of D+, mostly because of his task force work. Meanwhile his Democratic opponent, Massachusetts governor Michael Dukakis, got a B.

Bush knew he had to convince voters he would do a better job on environmental issues. To figure out which ones he should emphasize, the vice president called a luncheon meeting of some top environmental leaders at his official home in the Naval Observatory. The invitation list did not include any scruffy tree huggers from the Sierra Club or Greenpeace. Instead he invited the leaders of the Audubon Society, "people he would be comfortable with and [who] would be comfortable with him," recalled Nat Reed, then Audubon's vice chairman.

These were people unlikely to criticize Bush for putting loyalty to Reagan ahead of his concern for the environment.

"The issues he got stuck with in the Reagan years on the environment—he was sick in his heart that he had any part of it," Reed told us.

The lunch with Bush occurred on "a beautiful day, a glorious, glorious day," Reed recalled. "We went from the dining room to the living room as these marvelous Filipino mess boys removed the dishes. We talked and it was all very civilized."

Reed and his cohorts urged Bush to offer "more thrust on clean water, more concern for national parks." The issue of wetlands strongly resonated with Bush, an avid duck hunter.

"Poppy was looking for a green conservation issue," said Reed, using Bush's nickname. "What could be better? Let's limit the loss of wetlands!"

As a result, when *Sports Afield* magazine questioned the presidential candidates, Bush took a stand that was 180 degrees opposite the one he held as vice president: "My position on wetlands is straightforward. All existing wetlands, no matter how small, should be preserved."

But soon he found a more nuanced position, one that both business and environmentalists could support—one that, ironically, Dukakis had helped to set up.

In 1986, the EPA vetoed a Corps of Engineers permit for dumping 850,000 cubic yards of fill into 39 acres of Sweeden's Swamp to build a new shopping mall in Attleboro, Massachusetts.

Governor Dukakis and his administration had approved the new mall. In fact, Massachusetts politicians at every level lined up to support the developer and sneer that Sweeden's Swamp was just a trash dump.

But the EPA pointed out that a 700,000-square-foot mall is not a water-dependent property use and there were other, less environmentally damaging, places to build. The courts upheld the EPA's decision to veto the permit, but the ensuing controversy proved so nasty that in Congress there was talk—again—of shutting down the entire 404 program.

So in 1987 EPA Administrator Lee Thomas asked an environmental think tank called the Conservation Foundation to convene a forum on wetlands issues in hopes of finding common ground. The foundation—an arm of the World Wildlife Fund—called itself "a nonprofit research and communications organization dedicated to encouraging human conduct to sustain and enrich life on earth."

The foundation's staff had first developed an expertise in wetland issues during a mid-1970s study of Sanibel, an island community off Fort Myers. Sanibel had become a retirement haven for ex-CIA agents who had first visited the area during training for the Bay of Pigs invasion. A building boom there had spurred a cadre of the retired agents to lead a drive to incorporate a city. An ex-agent named Porter Goss became Sanibel's first mayor.

The new city's officials wanted to lasso development before it destroyed Sanibel's natural beauty. Among the foundation's recommendations to Sanibel's new leaders: "Generally there should be no filling of wetlands."

The foundation's handsome and articulate president, William K. Reilly—a Yale graduate with a law degree from Harvard and a master's in urban planning from Columbia University—was known as a thoughtful man skilled at helping competing interests build consensus, exactly the person to thrash out some agreement on the 404 program.

In the summer of 1987 the foundation "put together a task force that was supposed to be very inclusive," Reilly recalled. The head of the National Wildlife Federation was on it, and so was a representative from the building industry. There were farmers, ranchers, academic experts, and a town supervisor. Chairing the 20-member group was New Jersey governor Thomas Kean. Sitting in as advisers were senior officials from the Corps, EPA, and other federal agencies.

But at the first meeting of the newly formed National Wetlands Policy Forum, the future of Section 404 still looked bleak.

"We asked them: do you see any margin of compromise possible, or should we just overturn 404?" Reilly said. A lot of them just wanted to toss out the 404 program and start over.

Gradually, though, over the course of nearly a year of meetings and public workshops, they came up with more than 100 recommendations on how to improve the nation's wetland protection without junking 404. They recommended offering tax incentives to owners of wetland properties to sell the development rights to the government. They told Congress to boost funding for Corps and EPA regulatory efforts and to allow the Corps to charge what 404 permits actually cost to process. They urged the president to report to Congress every five years on what progress was being made on saving wetlands.

Their chief recommendation, the one that led the whole report, was something borrowed from Kean's home state, a concept called "no net loss."

In 1986 New Jersey's Division of Coastal Resources had adopted a policy intended to "assure no net loss of aquatic habitat productivity, including flora and fauna." New Jersey then passed its Freshwater Protection Act, which allowed for mitigation of wetland damage. The preferred mitigation would be the creation or restoration of wetlands on the same site as a development, where the man-made wetlands had an ecological value equal to that of the natural wetlands being destroyed. The notion of copying New Jersey's idea appealed to the forum members.

"What we needed to do was arrest the decline" of the nation's wetlands, Reilly recalled. "So we came up with the idea: any taking of wetlands would be replaced by the addition of wetlands somewhere else."

The forum's final report put it this way: "Without a clear goal, wetlands programs and policies will continue to lack consistency and focus. Therefore the National Wetlands Policy Forum recommends that the nation establish a national wetlands protection policy to achieve no overall net loss of the nation's remaining wetlands base, as defined by acreage and function, and to restore and create wetlands, where feasible, to increase the quality and quantity of the nation's wetlands resource base."

Then, to underline its recommendation, the report stated: "Interim goal: To achieve no overall net loss of the nation's remaining wetlands base. Long-term goal: To increase the quantity and quality of the nation's wetlands resource base."

As stated, these goals weren't meant to "imply that individual wetlands will in every instance be untouchable or that the no-net-loss standards should be applied on an individual permit basis," the report added. Instead, they intended "that the nation's overall wetlands base reach equilibrium between losses and gains in the short term and increase in the long term."

It's easy to see why the forum members jumped on the New Jersey idea. The concept of no net loss of wetlands was easy to grasp, and it offered something for everyone. Rather than forbid any wetlands destruction, it offered some leeway to developers and farmers to still wipe out some wetlands. And rather than let developers and farmers have free reign, it reassured environmentalists that any losses would be mitigated and nature kept from ultimate harm.

The report, entitled *Protecting America's Wetlands: An Action Agenda*, wasn't published until shortly after the 1988 election. But Governor Kean was not only the forum's chairman, he also happened to be one of Bush's advisers. So was the chairman of the Conservation Foundation's board of directors, ex-EPA director Russell Train, who was already talking up Reilly for the job of EPA chief if Bush won.

As a result, several months before the report was published "we caucused with the Bush campaign" about what the forum was going to recommend, Reilly said. They found a receptive audience, too: "The Bush campaign was just hungry for environmental ideas."

Reilly said they tried to pass the same information along to Dukakis too, but "it was not a very well organized campaign." He said he never found anyone in the Dukakis camp who understood the wetlands issue and what the forum was proposing, so by default Bush got the advantage.

Reilly said they leaked the report's recommendations to Bush "because we were interested in influencing policy. We didn't just do the report to have it sit on the shelf."

They certainly got their wish. Going into the Labor Day weekend, Bush and Dukakis were in a dead heat in the polls. Bush wanted to hit Dukakis hard with something unexpected and put him on the defensive. He picked his setting carefully.

On August 31, 1988, Bush cast a fishing line into Lake Erie for the benefit of the photographers following his campaign. Then he made a speech in a lakefront park in which he cast himself as an environmentalist. Between talking about everything from global warming to recycling, he called for a new approach to protecting wetlands.

"I don't have to tell those of you who are hunters and fishermen how important wetlands are as a habitat for fish, ducks, geese, and other waterfowl," Bush said, also noting their importance in controlling floods and filtering pollution. "Wetlands are a vital environmental and recreational resource—and they are at risk. We have been losing wetlands at a rate of almost a half-million acres per year. . . . Much of the loss comes from inevitable pressure for development, and many of our wetlands are on private property. But I believe we must act. We must bring the private and public sectors together, at the local and state levels, to find ways to conserve wetlands."

Then, in an apparent reference to Kean's New Jersey experiment, he first invoked the three-word promise that would shape federal policy for the next 20 years: "One state has a policy of 'no net loss' of wetlands, and it has worked—through mitigating the effects of development, preserving wetlands where possible, and sometimes even creating new wetlands. And that state is not a no-growth, no-development state. I believe this should be our national goal—no net loss of wetlands. We can't afford to lose the half of America's wetlands that still remains."

Bush carefully never mentioned Reagan's name or in any way criticized his soon-to-be-ex-boss. When reporters prodded him about it, he told them, "These are George Bush policies—this is what I will do when I'm elected president."

But Train, traveling with Bush to brief reporters on the details (such as they were), crowed that the Reagan era's hands-off approach to environmental regulation was over. "It's a whole new ballgame," he said.

Dukakis scoffed at what he called Bush's "election-year conversion" to environmental awareness, saying: "Coming from somebody who was a charter member of the environmental wrecking crew which went to Washington in 1981, that's very strange indeed."

But the next day Bush showed up in his rival's own backyard, boarding a boat for a tour of Boston Harbor to slam Dukakis' record by pointing out the pollution there. He also brought up no net loss of wetlands again.

In subsequent stump speeches, Bush repeated his call for a no-net-loss approach to protecting wetlands. His hard-line no-loss stance, quoted in *Sports Afield*, fell by the wayside as he took pains to remind everyone that he was not proposing an end to development in wetlands. Two weeks after Bush won, he told a gathering of governors in Alabama that while he would pursue no net loss of wetlands, "I'm not proposing 'no-growth.'"

Still, he did name Reilly head of the EPA. Bush pointed to Reilly's work on wetlands policy as the reason why: "He brought together 25 people who, as the *Washington Post* put it, would normally have difficulty agreeing even on a place for dinner. Environmentalists, developers, industrialists, state and federal regulators all were there. And the result: Well, by the time he was through with them, which took more than a year, they put aside differences and called for no net loss of wetlands."

Given that history, Reilly said, "when I took office I figured I had a charter to make good on all this." Stiffening his resolve was a luncheon speech Bush gave on June 8, 1989, to the members of the hunting group Ducks Unlimited—tireless advocates for saving wetlands since, of course, that's where the ducks live.

Reilly hadn't seen a draft of the speech in advance and was startled to hear his new boss say: "Wherever wetlands must give way to farming or development, they will be replaced or expanded elsewhere. It's time to stand the history of wetlands destruction on its head. From this year forward, anyone who tries to drain the swamp is going to be up to his ears in alligators. . . . You may remember my pledge, that our national goal would be no net loss of wetlands. And together, we are going to deliver on the promise of renewal, and I plan to keep that pledge."

"I remember hearing him and thinking: 'That's beyond where I am on this. Whoa, I hope you haven't gone too far,'" Reilly said.

It was, in fact, beyond what the other members of Bush's administration would put up with.

In 1990, the EPA and the Corps of Engineers signed an agreement on implementing a policy of no net loss, but the agreement differed in two small but crucial ways from the recommendation of the National Wetlands Policy Forum. It called for achieving no net loss of wetland "functions and values," period—not acres. Just what those wetland "functions and values" would be, and how they would be measured, were left undefined.

While the forum had called that only an interim goal, the EPA-Corps agreement made no net loss sound like it was the only goal. There was no mention of trying to add to the nation's wetland base. And there was no attempt to put the new policy into a law. It would remain a policy only, with no enforcement provision.

Soon, though, the Bush Administration became mired in an even more basic debate—a fight over what constitutes a wetland.

Reilly said the definition debacle grew out of conservative outrage over what was perceived as a Corps attempt to broaden the definition of a wetland. At the time the definition was based on well-accepted scientific principles calling for a three-part test to determine what was and was not a wetland. The three-part test would look at plants, soils, and the flow of water to make the determination.

At one point, Reilly recalled, he met with Vice President Dan Quayle and Office of Management and Budget Director Richard Darman—both advocates of freeing business from the oppression of government regulation—to talk about how to define wetlands. As he explained about how scientists recommended looking for characteristics of hydrology, plant species, and hydric soils, Quayle grew impatient.

"The Vice President looked over at me and said, 'Everything you bring over here is so complicated. Can't we just say if it's wet, it's wet?'" Reilly recalled. "And Darman, his face lit up like he'd just made a connection, and he said, 'And if it's not, it's NOT!' And I said, 'It's a good thing we're doing all this behind closed doors and nobody knows how these issues get worked out.'"

In August 1991, the Corps produced a new manual on delineating wetlands that tossed out the three-part test and instead said a wetland is land that has standing water for 15 or more days in a row or is saturated for 21 days. In other words, if it's wet, it's wet.

When Bush announced the new definition, he presented it as a way to streamline a cumbersome permitting process and help the economy.

"I think we're going to have no net loss, but we're not going to screech this country to a halt and throw everyone out of work in the process," he explained.

But the attempt to redefine wetlands became a political disaster for the man who had declared himself "the environmental president." As it turned out, the new Quayle-approved definition excluded millions of acres of what had been wetlands just days before the policy came out—including about half of South Florida's most famous marsh.

"I had a congressional delegation that came out and I walked them through the east Everglades and I told them, by this language none of this would be jurisdictional" wetlands anymore, Corps biologist Chuck Schnepel told us.

The prospect of losing federal protection for half of the remaining Everglades garnered nasty headlines for Bush, who was portrayed as a hypocrite who claimed to love wetlands while trying to wipe them out. In the ensuing uproar, Congress held hearings that featured testimony from Florida's top environmental regulator, a Miami native named Carol Browner. She warned that using the new definition for wetlands would be "a huge step backwards." In addition to putting the Everglades at risk, she said, it would also leave 30,000 to 35,000 acres along the Apalachicola River in the Panhandle vulnerable to development. In the end, Congress forbade the Corps to use the new manual, and the EPA and the Corps dropped it.

After the blowup over trying to redefine wetlands, the Bush Administration never got around to taking the second step after setting its no-net-loss interim goal of trying to increase the nation's stock of swamps, bogs, and marshes.

"People got so traumatized by the continual fighting that it sobered them into just playing defense," Reilly told us.

Reilly spent the remainder of his term at EPA feeling abandoned by Bush and under attack by his pro-business colleagues. Bush "came to accept the . . . view that there was no constituency for the environment that offered him anything politically, and no public incentive or encouragement to stay on the issue," Reilly said.

During Bush's 1992 reelection campaign, his opponents used his no-net-loss pledge as a stick to beat him over the head. Arkansas governor Bill Clinton, the Democratic nominee, gave an Earth Day speech in Pennsylvania that said Bush "promised 'no net loss' of America's precious wetlands, then tried to hand half of them over to developers. . . . As President, I will protect our old growth forests and other vital habitats, and make the 'no net loss' promise on wetlands a reality."

Shortly after beating Bush, Clinton convened a group from across several federal agencies to look at the wetlands issue. Among the participants: Carol Browner, whom Clinton had selected as the new head of the EPA. By the end of the summer the group had come up with a package of principles, recommendations, and reforms. The first step, the group said, would be to "establish an interim goal of no overall net loss and a long-term goal of increasing the quality and quantity of the nation's wetlands."

Of course with Clinton, one of the canniest operators ever to occupy the Oval Office, there was always a loophole. The details of that long-term wetland goal (not unveiled until his second term) included a pledge to begin adding 100,000 acres of new wetlands a year. But the fine print said that that additional wetlands acreage wouldn't begin showing up until 2005—four years after he left office, which meant keeping that promise would be someone else's problem.

Clinton's wetlands plan also called for giving the Corps a 90-day deadline for acting on 404 permits, allowing the Corps to employ less rigorous reviews of projects with minor environmental impacts and establishing a process for landowners to appeal Corps permitting decisions—all steps designed to placate the opponents of the 404 program.

Neither environmentalists nor developers were thrilled with the Clinton proposals. White House spokeswoman Dee Dee Myers told reporters: "The fact that we're being criticized from both sides is, I think, a mark that we landed somewhere in the middle."

But the middle of the road was not a politically safe spot to seek refuge during the Clinton years. In 1994 a new Republican majority swept to power in Congress, and they weren't inclined to support any regulatory program that might rein in private enterprise.

In 1997, when Army and EPA officials testified before a congressional committee on the progress they were making in carrying out the Clinton wetlands agenda, they were raked over the coals. Representative Don Young, R-Alaska, seemed particularly peeved at the Army for not establishing the appeals process for 404 permits that were denied.

Deputy Assistant Secretary of the Army Michael Davis explained that the process was ready to go, but for two years Congress had refused to approve any money for it.

"If we don't fund it, you're not going to do it," Young snapped.

"We don't know how we can do it, sir," Davis replied. "We're already running a very stretched program."

"What if we direct you to do it?" Young demanded.

"I'm sorry?"

"What if we direct you do it?" the congressman asked again.

"We would certainly comply with any direction," Davis said.

"Then that shall happen," Young told him. (Actually the appeals process didn't get started until 2000—after Congress finally appropriated $15 million to pay for it.)

In a less contentious part of the hearing, Davis testified that the nation was still losing up to 90,000 acres of wetlands every year, but compared to the losses of the 1950s "we kind of have the patient, I guess, stabilized." However, Davis conceded, "I don't think that anybody in the administration would suggest we're at no net loss at this point."

In the grand saga of Clinton's rise and fall, highlighted by his impeachment for lying under oath about adultery, the debate over wetlands protection that consumed so much time and ink during the first Bush Administration became a mere footnote. Yet still the promise of no net loss, and the pledge to go beyond that, would survive.

In 2000, Texas governor George W. Bush was appointed president by the U.S. Supreme Court after a contentious election with Clinton's vice president, Al Gore. Four years later, George W. Bush, son of the man who first promised no net loss of wetlands, was locked in a tight reelection race. Like his father, he faced a Democratic opponent with a far greener reputation than his own, Senator John Kerry of Massachusetts. Like his father, he turned to wetlands as a way to connect with green voters.

On Earth Day 2004, the second President Bush and his white-haired mother Barbara traipsed through a nature preserve in Wells, Maine, where he and his father used to fish. Then the 43rd president unveiled the latest version of no net loss.

"The old policy of wetlands was to limit the loss of wetlands," Bush said. "Today I'm going to announce a new policy and a new goal for our country: Instead of just limiting our losses, we will expand the wetlands of America. . . .We will move beyond the no net loss of wetlands in America to having an overall increase of Americans' wetlands over the next five years. . . . We can achieve this goal. It is a realistic goal."

Bush vowed to add three million acres of wetlands a year—an area roughly twice the size of Everglades National Park—to the nation's stockpile of swamps and marshes. Those acres would come from one million acres created out of land that was not already wet, one million acres of former wetlands that would be restored, and one million acres preserved through various government programs.

A day later, Bush flew to Florida and put in a brief appearance at the Rookery Bay Estuarine Research Preserve, where he used a big set of shears to help volunteers clear away some exotic Brazilian pepper trees and then playfully threatened the gaggle of reporters with them. He made a speech again reiterating his love for wetlands and no net loss. Then he went to a fundraiser in Naples where some of the larger checks were written by developers busy wiping out Florida wetlands as if the Deltona case had never happened.

As each president embraced the no-net-loss policy, Republican and Democrat, one big question remained unaddressed: Did it really work? Were wetlands really being replaced?

The report that Gale Norton so proudly unveiled in 2006 said yes, the nation's wetlands were bouncing back. But the figures Norton cited were based on shaky data used to score political points. The truth turned out to be more elusive.

In 2001, a panel appointed by the National Research Council, an arm of the National Academies of Science, spent months studying the issue of wetlands mitigation. The panel finally concluded there was no evidence that no net loss was even being pursued by the Corps of Engineers, much less being achieved.

Still, the Pentagon civilian appointed by the second Bush Administration to oversee the Corps told us he's convinced that no net loss is being carried out—but he admitted that that's based on guesswork.

"The flaw is we cannot demonstrate or document we have achieved it," Assistant Secretary of the Army John Paul Woodley Jr. told us, explaining that the Corps is just too busy to check. "Right now our guys are working so hard on permits that it's very challenging for them to find time to go back, reach back in the file and grab something from the last two years of files and . . . see whether that is working."

So we figured if we were going to get an answer to this question, we would have to get it ourselves.

8

Images of Loss

When we wanted to check on whether the policy of no net loss was really being carried out in Florida, one of the places we tried to get the answer was the National Wetlands Inventory, an arm of the U.S. Fish and Wildlife Service. NWI seemed like the ideal source—after all, the maps on its Web site are usually treated by planning and regulatory agencies as if they were gospel.

Launched in 1976, this obscure federal agency took on a job of almost breathtaking ambition: map every fetid marsh and bug-infested swamp in the United States.

NWI started its inventory because "Congress decided they needed to know how many wetlands there were and where they were," recalled Blake Parker, one of the agency's first employees. "They wanted to get a trend of what was happening."

NWI's leaders thought they might be done in a couple of years. They were wrong. Thirty years later they were still working on it.

Every 10 years, NWI publishes a "status and trends" report, based not on their maps but on a complex set of sample plots from around the country. It's an attempt to estimate how many acres of wetlands, and what kinds, the nation has lost. Its first report, handed to Congress in 1982 and published for the general public in 1984, made a huge splash. In it, NWI announced that since the 1950s the nation had wiped out more than half of its remaining swamps and marshes, a startling revelation to anyone who wasn't a biologist.

That initial NWI report gave advocates like Ducks Unlimited and the National Wildlife Federation a scientific-sounding number they could cite in lobbying for greater protections for the remaining wetlands—a crucial tool in the antiregulation Reagan era. It "created a sense of urgency regarding the loss of wetlands," historian Ann Vileisis wrote.

To our surprise, we learned that the current nerve center of the NWI staff was only a 20-minute drive away from us. Most of NWI's staff worked in a building in the back corner of a sprawling office park in northern St. Petersburg, a stone's throw from where glum-faced taxpayers line up at the Internal Revenue Service building.

At NWI's fusty, dimly lit office, we found about a dozen biologists toiling away in small cubicles, putting in eight-hour days peering at color-coded aerial photos and drawing lines on a computer. Sometimes they went out in the field to make sure what they thought was a wetland really was one. Years after they started a mapping project for a certain area, they posted the results on their Web site.

We learned that NWI's maps—the ones every regulator treats as Holy Writ—are usually outdated. Three decades after its inception, NWI had mapped an estimated 90 percent the nation's swamps, marshes, and bogs, including all of Florida's. But Florida had been one of the first states NWI had mapped, and so most of its maps are so old they predate the announcement of the no-net-loss policy in the 1988 presidential campaign.

"I wish we had a staff," Norm Mangrum, a bearded, easygoing biologist who had worked there for 24 years, told us. "We could update the whole state. Most of it desperately needs updating."

Back when NWI first started, the federal officials from different regions defined wetlands differently, leading to inconsistencies that could pose legal problems. So first a group of biologists got together and put together a list of standard definitions for the various kinds of wetlands.

Back then, in addition to mapping wetlands, NWI was supposed to train federal employees from various federal agencies in how to use those definitions so their findings would all be uniform, Parker said. Leaders of the Fish and Wildlife Service picked St. Petersburg for the main location for the NWI because it suited the training part of its mission. It was close to a major airport in Tampa and offered easy access to a wide variety of wetlands for trainings, which because of the climate could go on year round. Parker said in his four years with NWI he conducted 30 classes a year.

Early on, Parker said, NWI officials had high hopes of completing all their mapping duties quickly. They expected to use high-resolution satellite imagery of the United States, gathered by the government itself, primarily the military and intelligence services. But when Parker and another NWI official asked for satellite images they could use, they were turned down.

"We were told, 'Sorry, that's classified information,'" Parker said.

Instead, NWI had to compile its swampy inventory by piecing together and analyzing aerial photos. That slowed the process down to a crawl and quadrupled the cost, Parker said.

In its glory days in the 1980s, the NWI staff in St. Petersburg numbered more than 30. A contractor did much of the actual mapping, while the staff provided quality control and training. But the training part of its mission soon dried up as NWI's budget was repeatedly cut.

In the mid-1990s, the heyday of the antiregulation Contract with America, when a budget battle between President Clinton and House Speaker Newt Gingrich led to a brief shutdown of the entire government, Congress slashed NWI's funding in half. The agency has never fully recovered, staffers said. Meanwhile the contractor they depended on, and that depended on their business, went bankrupt.

Still, the remaining staff of about 14 tried to do their jobs. In 2003 they started an update of the Southwest Florida area. As NWI's biologists toured Lee and Collier counties to double-check their work, they were shocked.

Everywhere they looked, wetlands they had mapped 20 years ago were gone, wiped out by shopping centers, roads, and schools. Cypress swamps had been replaced by expensive homes perched atop grass-covered mounds of fill. So many trucks were bringing in more dirt to fill even more wetlands that it was like watching a particularly depressing parade.

"We'd pull over to do soil borings," said longtime NWI biologist Dave Lindsey, "and we were about getting run over by dump trucks."

The bottom line, we found, was that NWI was just as flummoxed by the question of what had happened to all of Florida's wetlands as everyone else.

Meanwhile we were trying to get an answer from the Corps, or rather from the Corps' permitting data. The ever-smiling Bob Barron had told us that each 404 permit is supposed to include a latitude and longitude coordinate for locating the project. We figured we could get a database of all the 404 permits in Florida and then use all those points to create a map showing the wetlands that were wiped out.

Barron said getting the database shouldn't be a problem—just file a Freedom of Information Act request. We did, and more than a year passed, during which we had repeated (and sometimes heated) discussions with the Corps' attorneys. They worried there would be information in the permits that we weren't supposed to see—the names of neighbors contacted about the proposed development, for instance. Finally, after we flew to Jacksonville and met with them in person to talk about the law's requirements, they sent us the database.

It turned out to be useless. Most of the fields in the database that were supposed to be filled out by the permit reviewers were left blank.

When we asked about the blank records, we were told the permit reviewers were too busy processing the permits to spend time entering data for record keeping. Of the records that did have a coordinate point, hundreds of them were in the Atlantic Ocean, the Gulf of Mexico, or scattered around the continental United States, far from their real location inside the state of Florida.

The only sections reviewers filled out regularly were the dates when the application was filed and when it was granted. Hall explained that that's the only statistic Congress or the Corps headquarters really care about: how fast the permits are approved.

Out of options with the federal government, we turned to the state government. We obtained the Florida Department of Environmental Protection's central permitting database. But it suffered from similar gaps. Information was missing. Whole parts of the state weren't covered.

That's when we decided that if we were going to find out if no net loss was really working, we would need an eye in the sky.

We got our answer by carefully analyzing satellite imagery for the entire state—the same approach NWI had tried back in the 1970s, only to be rebuffed for national security reasons.

A few things have changed since the 1970s when it comes to satellite imagery. Back then, scientists needed a room full of mainframe computers to process a single image, a setup costing tens of thousands of dollars. Today, Google will show you a satellite image of anywhere on the globe on your cell phone. With little trouble, we obtained a complete set of images for the entire state of Florida taken in the late 1980s and again in 2003.

Viewing imagery is one thing. Analyzing it is quite another, however.

To understand how we analyzed the imagery, it helps to review a little high school science.

There's more to sunlight than what you can see. Visible light is made up of three bands of color—red, green, and blue. If you've ever taken a picture with a digital camera, you might have heard it called an RGB image. RGB means red, green, and blue. To find Florida's wetlands in an image, we used Landsat data, a kind of satellite imagery that contains seven slices of sunlight—electromagnetic energy for the science-minded. There are the three slices you can see: red, green, and blue. And there are four that you can't see with your eye, but that Landsat satellite sensors record. They are slices of the infrared spectrum—in other words, heat.

Each slice of the spectrum in a satellite image is called a band. Each band is sensitive to different things. By mixing the bands together, the image changes colors and highlights different things in the image. Mix red, green, and blue, and the image looks like what you'd see staring down from the sky. Mix blue, green, and infrared, and areas that have plants with a high moisture content glow. When you're looking for wetlands, areas with lots of plants holding lots of water is where you want to be.

All of this information is recorded in a unit of the image, called a pixel. Each pixel represents a spot on the ground, and it is in the pixel where a significant trade-off in satellite imagery analysis occurs.

Extremely high resolution imagery is now commercially available, at a significant price. The resolution is at such a level that, if so inclined, you could inventory the type of backyard swing sets people use (Do they have a slide? Do they have one swing or two?). But that would take years of analysis to cover just one city or metro area.

To be able to identify wetlands on a statewide level, Landsat offers a moderate resolution—30 meters—and wide coverage areas. The entire state is covered in 14 images.

It's important to understand that no satellite image analysis is ever 100 percent accurate. It's impossible to be perfect with images taken from space. To accurately measure the area of Florida's wetlands, survey crews would have to visit each and every one of them. So all imagery analyses—even ones using far higher resolution imagery than Landsat—are estimates. They contain errors. It's important to understand how those errors occur and how reliable the estimates are.

For all the power in computers now, one thing they can't do very well is look at an image and tell you what is in it. The human brain, when it comes to analyzing an image, is more powerful than any image-analyzing computer in the world. It's not even close. At least for now.

To find Florida's wetlands, we told the computer to group each pixel—each data unit in a picture, of which there are millions in every image—into one of 100 groups based on what data was in that pixel. After the computer did that, it was up to us to decide what each of the groups, from one through 100, really represented.

This is where the difference between the computer and the brain comes in. Highlighting group one, a human can look at it and immediately realize that group one is in the middle of a lake or the Gulf of Mexico. A computer doesn't know what a lake is, let alone what the middle of the lake looks like. Humans know context. Computers don't.

Using soil maps, NWI's old wetlands maps, and other data, we renamed each group as one of two things: wetlands or not wetlands. It takes 14 Landsat images to cover the state of Florida. We did this analysis for each of the 14 images it takes to cover the state, first for the late 1980s and again for 2003. And then we did it again, trying to capitalize on all we learned doing it all the first time.

After that was done, we compared the results to areas of urbanization, also taken from satellite imagery. Urban uses show up very clearly in satellite imagery, and they're permanent alterations to the landscape. Wetlands destroyed for those uses are unlikely to ever be restored.

By comparing where wetlands were with where they remained, we were able to see where wetlands had been wiped off the map by houses, strip malls, parking lots, warehouses, highways, and other urban uses.

Vital in any satellite imagery analysis is a process called an accuracy assessment. You have to know how accurate your analysis is. So we created a random sample of 385 places on the resulting maps and checked our analysis of those locations. Many places, it was obvious we were right—there aren't any wetlands in downtown Miami, for instance. And there are lots of them in the middle of the Everglades. Where we could, we went to the place in the field. Where we couldn't, because it was private property, we checked our analysis against other data through property records, aerial images, and other data sources.

As we said, no satellite image analysis is ever 100 percent accurate. A good rule of thumb is one used by the U.S. Geological Survey. The USGS requires that any map that agency creates with satellite imagery be 85 percent accurate. Our analysis exceeded that standard. We also had our work reviewed by three experts in the field, and they all agreed that our approach was sound.

Our conclusion, after 10 months of study and analysis: during the time when the official federal policy called for no net loss of wetlands, between 1990 and 2003, 84,000 acres of Florida wetlands had been covered over by pavement, rooftops, and other features of urban development.

Our analysis did not include mining and farming, two of the other main contributors to wetlands loss in Florida. Phosphate and rock miners rip up thousands of acres of wetlands over the course of decades. Agriculture takes a more subtle approach. For instance, in 2007 the St. Johns River Water Management District accused a powerful family-owned agricultural company called A. Duda & Sons of illegally digging ditches on its property in Brevard County that drained two square miles of wetlands. Duda contends the drainage work is exempt from state rules because it's for agricultural purposes (although it's part of an area the company now plans to develop).

Unfortunately, both mining and farming present complex imagery analysis challenges we were unable to overcome given the time involved and the pressures of publishing a newspaper investigation. Therefore, wetlands losses in Florida during the no-net-loss era are undoubtedly much larger, perhaps as high as 100,000 acres total between 1990 and 2003, according to the information we gathered.

The greatest losses were in areas of the state where the population grew by more than three million people: South Florida, Southwest Florida, Orlando, and Jacksonville.

When we showed our results to John Hall, he said he was not surprised. In fact, he said it was obvious.

"We know, through the years, we have not hidden it from anybody, that unless you want to go out and create a lot of wetlands out of uplands, you're going to have some spatial change, some spatial decrease in the location and acreage of wetlands," he said, avoiding the use of the word "loss." "We haven't tried to hide that from anybody."

But he contended that the wetlands that were lost weren't all that pristine. The Corps had made sure that only the least valuable swamps, marshes, and bogs were wiped out. At least, that's what Hall hoped was true.

"Through the years, maybe the more marginal, marginally valuable wetlands have been the first to attract attention of developers," he said. "These kinds of pieces of property I think are getting harder to find in Florida."

The ever-cynical Vic Anderson had another theory: the agency where he had worked for 30 years has been merely pretending to follow the no-net-loss policy, conning the public into thinking that wetlands were being saved when they weren't.

"It's all just a big shell game," Anderson said. "Who's kidding whom? The only conclusion you can draw is we're losing it on purpose."

9

The Myth of Mitigation

This is how no net loss really works:

Florida's Panhandle is known for its sugar-white beaches and its picturesque dunes. But amid the dunes on Pensacola Beach lie scattered marshlands, lush with saltmeadow cordgrass and pennywort. These marshes are vital to the purity and health of the emerald green waters of nearby Santa Rosa Sound, home to a plethora of sea trout, redfish, ladyfish, and jack crevalle.

In 1997, a development company with control of 28 acres of the beach proposed building a $250-million luxury condominium project called Portofino. The plans called for building five towers, each with 150 units, each 21 stories tall. The Portofino condos would be the tallest buildings between Tallahassee and New Orleans.

The two main partners in the company building Portofino were lawyer Fred Levin, a leading Democratic Party fundraiser with close friends at all levels of government, and his brother Allen, one of the Panhandle's most successful developers. Fred Levin's name carried a lot of weight in Florida. He used his political contacts to score a multimillion-dollar fee from a major tobacco case, then made such a hefty donation to the University of Florida that the law school was named in his honor. He gained further fame by helping to manage the career of boxing champion Roy Jones Jr.

Fred and Allen Levin grew up on Pensacola Beach, where their father once held the exclusive concession contract for selling snacks and souvenirs to the tourists. Back then Pensacola Beach was a sleepy little resort village with scattered mom-and-pop motels and lots of one-story concrete-block homes available for rent by the week or month.

But the Levins' minds were not fogged by nostalgia. They saw the beach as a resource to be exploited. Still, they appreciated the role nature played in making the property attractive to buyers. So they planned to preserve several of the picturesque dunes as part of their project—but not the marshes that were so important to the sound. Those did not fit the Levins' aesthetic vision.

"When we did our development, we could not do a development on this acreage without impacting some wetlands," Allen Levin told us. They did not want to shift their buildings around to keep the marshes intact, he said, "because then the buildings would be right on top of each other, and we liked the distance."

Of the 11 acres of marsh on the site, the Levins asked the Corps for a permit to dump fill into 6.5 acres—in other words, more than half.

Other federal agencies lined up to oppose the Levins' plans. The U.S. Fish and Wildlife Service strongly objected to wiping out the marshes. So did the EPA and the National Marine Fisheries Service. They all said those wetlands were too important to keeping Santa Rosa Sound clean and full of fish.

Beach residents opposed the Levins' project too. It was too big, too gaudy, too vulnerable to hurricanes, they said. It didn't fit their low-profile neighborhood and would cause all kinds of traffic problems, they warned. A residents' group even sued the developers over whether they could alter the land. Shortly after the Corps published a public notice in 1998 about Portofino's 404 application, the residents petitioned the Corps to hold a public hearing.

"We kept writing, we kept calling," recalled beach resident Jean Kuttina, who led the neighborhood opposition. "We had several letters of objection, we had the lawsuit going. None of it did any good."

In 1999 an environmental activist named Linda Young, a Panhandle native who headed up the Florida chapter of the Clean Water Network, persuaded a top Pentagon official in the Clinton Administration to tour the site. She was hoping to persuade him to block the project. She recalls Deputy Assistant Secretary of the Army Michael Davis walking around the beach as she talked to him. Then, she said, Davis told her, "This project does not need to happen."

"He was adamantly opposed to it," Young recalled. "But then he went back to D.C. A few weeks went by, and I called him. And he said, 'I can't stop this project. These people are too powerful.'"

Davis remembers the tour and remembers thinking Portofino was a bad idea. But he denies telling Young the well-connected Levins were too powerful to stop. "I would've never said those words," he insisted. Instead, he said, he probably made some comment about the permitting process being too far along for even the Pentagon to halt it.

Allen Levin told the *Pensacola News Journal* that the last thing he wanted to leave behind was a legacy of environmental destruction.

"Somebody would have to be a total jerk to want to hurt the environment," he said. "It doesn't make sense. Good developers won't do that. I really believe in this project we are putting more back in than we are taking out."

The Levins promised to build new man-made wetlands to replace the ones they were destroying. The mitigation would make it all okay, they said. However the wildlife service predicted the beach wetlands were just too delicate to be duplicated. That's why the agency urged the Corps to say no to the permit.

"We told them it would be almost impossible to mitigate," said Hildreth Cooper, a Fish and Wildlife Service biologist. "We told them they should either deny the permit or admit they can't mitigate for it."

Even trying to preserve some of the wetlands on the site wouldn't work, the wildlife agency predicted. Past attempts by beach developers to save a few marshes while destroying others had cut off the flow of water, starving the marshes that remained.

The Corps permit reviewer in the Pensacola office, a dutiful bureaucrat named Lyal "Clif" Payne, spent two years struggling to save the wetlands and still make the developers happy. He didn't want to approve the permit the way it was, but he didn't want to deny it either. So he kept suggesting changes that might make the Levins' project more palatable: Cut the number of buildings back to three? Add even more mitigation? Nothing worked.

The developers weren't too thrilled with preserving even some of the marsh in its natural state, telling Payne at one point that the wetlands "would be managed to remove the unsightly effect they have on (their) surroundings."

Finally, frustrated with what he saw as Payne's hemming and hawing, Allen Levin had a heart-to-heart conversation with Payne's bosses in Jacksonville.

"When it finally got to the very higher-ups, we were finally able to get some relief," he said.

Corps officials decided the agencies objecting to the project were off base, and so in August 2000 they approved the permit. The Corps did order two small marshes on the project site to be preserved. They allowed the rest to be wiped out by the Levins' condo project.

For mitigation, the Corps approved the creation of man-made wetlands on county-owned land, along with a little something extra. In October 1995, when Hurricane Opal made landfall at Pensacola Beach, the storm had knocked down most of the big dunes and washed them across the island, leaving a thick layer of sand across the property next door to Portofino. Requiring the Levins to build their mitigation there would not only replace the natural marshes, the Corps concluded. It would also result in all that sand being dug up and used to rebuild the destroyed dunes, thus benefiting the whole island.

On the same day the Corps issued the permit, its top official in Florida, Col. Joe Miller, notified all the residents who had asked for a public hearing that there wouldn't be one. The next day, Miller retired from the Army.

The Corps' behavior left a bad taste in Kuttina's mouth.

"They're destructive people," she said. "They're not really going to save anything."

By July 2004, when we toured the site with Linda Young, three of the towers had been built and occupied and the other two were under construction. They loomed above one-story houses next door. Sales were brisk, with some units selling for more than $500,000.

But the man-made wetlands that the Levins had built looked nothing like the lush natural ones they had wiped out. Most of the year they were bone dry, until heavy rains hit. Then stagnant water puddled up two inches deep, the surface broken every foot or so by a few strands of thin brown grass.

"There's no way that mitigates for the adverse impacts that project is having,"

Figure 8. Clean Water Network activist Linda Young walks through sparsely vegetated man-made marshes on Pensacola Beach that were supposed to mitigate the destruction of wetlands to build the Portofino condominiums, seen in the background. (Photograph by Lara Cerri, *St. Petersburg Times*.)

grumbled Young. She slipped off her shoes and splashed through the standing water, then giggled and pointed out that the straggly sprigs of grass looked like a bald man's hair implants.

"It's not exactly what you'd call thriving," she said.

Two months later, something entirely predictable happened.

On September 16, 2004, Hurricane Ivan roared through the Panhandle. The storm knocked down the dunes that Portofino had recreated, sweeping the sand across the highway and deep into the lobby of the condos. The sand also spread across the same areas of the beach that Opal had covered a decade before. The thick layer of sand that Ivan dumped on the man-made marshes smothered them. It was as if they had never been built.

Since the man-made wetlands were destroyed through a natural disaster, the Corps would not make the Levins rebuild them, Payne told us. The failure was not the Levins' fault, he said. Actually, he explained, the Corps considered it an act of God.

So to sum up: wetlands that were crucial to the health of Santa Rosa Sound and its sea life were filled in and paved over because saving them didn't fit the plans of some powerful people. The federal agency that was supposed to save them instead bent over backwards to aid their destruction. The developers' attempt to make up for the damage failed, and their failure carried no consequences.

Yet in the Corps' recordkeeping, the Portofino project was a success. There was no net loss of wetlands.

What happened at Portofino illustrates both the myth of mitigation and its consequences.

On paper, filled-in wetlands are being replaced and everything balances out. In reality, they are swept aside by the works of man and nothing makes up for them. Development races across the land with all the speed and power of a hurricane hitting a beach, and the attempts to replace what it destroys usually result in expensive failures.

"Mitigation," Vic Anderson said with his usual bluntness, "is a fraud."

In the case of Portofino, the loss of wetlands was on a small scale. Many man-made wetlands are what are commonly called "postage stamp wetlands"— small mitigation sites, often built in a new subdivision near the site where the natural wetlands were destroyed. Those used to be the standard requirement for 404 permits, but not any more.

"A lot of the postage-stamp wetlands have not proven viable," veteran Corps biologist Chuck Schnepel told us. Ultimately, he said, "they're used as a playground, or as dumping grounds. Or they become invaded by noxious or exotic vegetation."

Usually the developer dumps the job of maintaining them on a homeowners association, which has no idea that it's responsible or what to do about it. Eventually the man-made marsh becomes a cattail-choked mud puddle.

When the panel from the National Research Council reviewed the sorry state of mitigation in America, the panel declared in its 2001 report: "In many cases this approach has resulted in the creation of open water areas as compensation for loss of intermittently inundated or saturated wetlands. . . . The stable-water pond has come to typify mitigation efforts in many parts of the country."

Such ponds—the same ones that Gale Norton insisted were being given a bad rap—"will not replace the functions provided" by natural wetlands, the NRC concluded. According to the flawed survey produced for Gale Norton's announcement, quite a few of those ponds started off as Florida mitigation wetlands.

Those are the small mitigation projects. But now look what happens when phosphate mining companies spend 30 years digging up thousands of acres of Central Florida land to get the ingredients for fertilizer—and then try to make up for such vast destruction.

First discovered by a Corps of Engineers captain in 1881, Florida's phosphate deposits today form the basis of an $85-billion industry that supplies three-fourths of the phosphate used in the United States.

To get at the underground deposits, the miners use a dragline with a bucket the size of a truck. It scoops up the top 30 feet of earth and dumps it to the side of the mine pit. Then the dragline scoops out the underlying section of earth, which contains phosphate rocks mixed with clay and sand. The bucket dumps this in a pit where high-pressure water guns create a slurry that can then be pumped to a plant up to 10 miles away.

At the plant, the phosphate is separated from the sand and clay. The clay slurry is pumped to a settling pond, and the phosphate is sent to a chemical processing plant where it is processed for use in fertilizer and other products. The sand is sent back to the mine site to fill in the hole after all the phosphate is dug out.

A byproduct of the processing, called phosphogypsum, is slightly radioactive so it cannot be disposed of easily. The only thing the miners can do with it is stack it into mountainous piles next to the plant. Florida is such a flat state that the 150-foot-tall "gyp stacks" are usually the highest point in the landscape for miles around.

When phosphate miners destroy a wetland, they promise to replace it a few decades later when they're finished—a seemingly impossible task. After all, as Florida wetlands expert Kevin Erwin told us, "You're really talking about creating wetlands after 60 to 80 feet of earth have been souffléed."

The odds against success are higher than any gyp stack. Forty percent of the land that's left behind after mining is covered by the clay settling ponds. Within five years a crust forms on top of the ponds, but the stuff under the crust remains about as hard as a bowl of chocolate pudding. That means the old clay settling areas are too unstable for building or for anything else. Meanwhile the sand-filled pits drain too fast to hold water—a serious problem for any would-be wetland.

The idea of requiring the miners to try to re-create wetlands seemed reasonable in the late 1970s. Col. James W. R. Adams, the district engineer in Jacksonville from 1978 to 1981, told us he had denied 404 permits for several phosphate mining companies and was catching a lot of heat for it because phosphate was viewed as important to maintaining the nation's balance of trade.

"I had all kinds of people calling me saying, 'Jim, be reasonable,'" Adams recalled. So he proposed that, in exchange for getting their permits, the phosphate miners restore the wetlands they destroyed. After all, they had the money to do it right. "We worked out something very concrete, and we had a historic and great agreement. Everybody was really happy about it," Adams said.

Since then, Florida phosphate companies have spent millions of dollars recreating thousands of acres of wetlands wiped out by mining in Polk, Hillsborough, and Manatee counties—or rather, attempting to re-create them. One of the earliest phosphate mitigation sites in Florida was Hooker's Prairie, the mine site in Hillsborough County that Vic Anderson tried to save by suggesting the miners get their phosphate from Morocco instead.

"It was like Payne's Prairie near Gainesville—before W. R. Grace proposed mining it," Anderson told us. "It was a sawgrass prairie . . . I said, 'We ought to deny this permit.' . . . Instead we decided to mitigate."

Anderson urged his bosses at the Corps to monitor the mitigation closely, in a rigorous scientific fashion, to see if it really worked. But Anderson's boss, John Adams (no relation to the colonel), told him the Corps had no time for that.

"John Adams said no, you've got to process these permits," Anderson said. As a result, "we're making these same mistakes 30 years hence."

Anderson didn't get the chance to check on what happened to Hooker's Prairie until years later. When he drove out there, what he found was not a sawgrass prairie but something far less complex, a broom sedge marsh—and thus not something that truly replaces what the miners destroyed.

The track record for phosphate mitigation hasn't improved since Hooker's Prairie was mined. In 2002, in preparation for a lawsuit in which he was listed as an expert witness, consultant Kevin Erwin toured several wetland mitigation sites built by IMC-Agrico, then the largest phosphate company in the world (it has since merged with another company, Cargill, to form an even larger company called Mosaic). Erwin found that virtually all the wetlands the company built were deep marshes, with standing water two to four feet deep.

"We didn't see an acre, let alone the hundreds of thousands of acres, of pine flatwoods that they had mined," Erwin said.

Erwin said he asked his IMC tour guides to show him how the company had recreated a wet prairie. That particular type is extremely difficult to rebuild, he said, but the site the mining officials showed him surprised him. The vegetation looked perfect, as if it had been growing there for decades. But then Erwin looked a little closer and discovered that this wet prairie had no roots.

"What they'd done is gone out in a wet prairie before it was mined and used a sod cutter," Erwin said.

After slicing a swath of vegetation from one location, he said, the company brought the swath out to its mitigation site and rolled it out like a section of carpet. But the miners forgot something important.

"I took some borings and the water table was several feet below the surface," Erwin said. Since wetlands need water flowing through them to survive, these were unlikely to last long.

Erwin's testimony helped convince a judge to rule against IMC, which had sought a permit to mine 2,300 acres in Manatee County. Mining the IMC property would destroy 600 acres of wetlands that form the headwaters of Horse Creek, one of the cleanest streams in the state. Horse Creek is also a major tributary of the Peace River, which supplies drinking water for 100,000 people and ultimately gushes into the state's most productive estuary, Charlotte Harbor, itself the center of a billion-dollar tourism and recreation industry.

Although IMC had promised to build new wetlands to replace the ones it had destroyed, the judge found that those man-made wetlands would differ too much from the ones there now. The mine site boasts a variety of wetlands, some shallow, some deeper, but IMC planned to build just one big, deep wetland, the judge found.

The company tried to show the judge that it has rebuilt other wetlands it damaged by mining. But the evidence Erwin presented showed those mitigation wetlands are not working as well as natural swamps, "despite the fact that most of them have been in existence for more than 15 years," the judge wrote in his decision.

∾

Although the phosphate miners had destroyed thousands of acres of wetlands, they did it over three decades. According to John Hall and Bob Barron, year in and year out the greatest destroyer of wetlands in Florida is the state itself—or rather, one agency: the Department of Transportation, commonly known as the DOT.

With a $7-billion budget, the DOT is Florida's most powerful state agency. Its nearly 7,500 employees oversee more than 12,000 miles of highways. It can condemn property and force the owners to move. And every year it kills lots of wetlands.

The DOT doesn't just kill wetlands by paving them over. When a new road is built, then-DOT Secretary Denver Stutler told us in 2005, "it's going to open up corridors for potential growth." In other words, development follows the roads, wiping out still more wetlands all along the route.

Stutler, who previously worked in a mitigation-related business, said destroying wetlands for roads is the price Florida pays for continued growth.

"To me, transportation is the backbone of our economy," Stutler told DOT employees in a 2005 speech in Sarasota. "And it takes a strong economy to afford the environmentalism we ascribe to here in Florida."

We discovered that DOT officials did not keep track of all the wetlands they destroyed each year. They were too busy building new roads. But agency records we reviewed showed the DOT wiped out more than 1,000 acres of swamps, bogs, and marshes between 1997 and 2005.

The DOT has to go through the same permitting process as the average developer and thus has repeatedly tried to make up for the damage it does through mitigation. DOT officials also didn't know exactly how much of the taxpayers' money they had spent on mitigation, but agency records showed it was more than $62 million during that same eight-year period. How much more we simply could not determine, because the documentation did not exist.

We spent months digging through boxes and boxes of DOT mitigation records, squirreled away in places like Bartow and Palatka and Brooksville. We pored over monitoring reports and interviewed DOT staffers and visited mitigation sites. We found that whenever the DOT has built its own wetlands, they failed, over and over.

"It's not easy to re-create what God put here," said Sue Moore, who oversees the maintenance of dozens of the DOT-built wetlands in the Tampa Bay region.

Yet the DOT kept trying. One seven-acre wetland the DOT built off State Road 44 in Crystal River in 1990 was planted with trees that an expert later found were doomed by root problems. Water management officials warned the DOT in 1992 that the site was too dry—in fact, the wetland was built on sand, with the water table some four feet down. The DOT nevertheless planted 3,000 more trees. Still, no wetland. Finally, in 1998, the DOT abandoned the effort and the site is now overgrown with upland vegetation.

Then there was the man-made wetland in Polk County that got too wet.

In 1994, the DOT planned to widen U.S. 17 where it crosses the Polk-Hardee county line. Because that would destroy about 2.5 acres of wetlands adjacent to the road, the DOT proposed as mitigation turning five acres of pasture by the Peace River into new wetlands. A consultant hired by the state predicted that the new, man-made wetland would be better than the destroyed one.

By July 1995, the DOT had planted cypress, sweetgum, red maple, and other wetland trees, grasses, and shrubs. In the next three months, though, the river overflowed, killing them. So the DOT replanted.

But in late 1997, a storm put the man-made wetland under six feet of water, wiping out hundreds of the new trees. When consultants checked the site in April 1998, they reported finding "no living vegetation." The water was so deep that they found fish jumping as if it were part of the river. When the DOT's consultants checked in again in August 2004, they found it underwater again. Dead trees were sticking out of the water, they reported, "and many more were detected below the water surface."

So after spending 10 years and $242,000, the DOT had not only failed to build a wetland that was superior to the one destroyed—it had failed to replace the natural wetland at all. Rob Dwyer, the DOT employee who oversees the Peace River mitigation area, calls the site "problematic."

"I would think we would have to throw in the towel at some point," he said, though he wasn't sure when that point would be reached.

This sort of thing happened all over the state. Down in the Keys, the DOT spent $66,000 planting thousands of mangroves on a half-acre site in Whale Harbor. They kept dying. The agency replanted the mangroves four times. It even dug out the soil and put in fresh muck. Nothing worked.

At one point, the DOT dropped the ball for a while, failing to plant more mangroves or report on its progress. The Florida Department of Environmental Protection (which had replaced the old DER) didn't notice. Then, in 1995, a DOT employee reviewing the files discovered the problem and asked the DEP what to do.

The response: forget it. The regulators asked, "If FDEP isn't asking for it to be fixed, why is FDOT pursuing it?"

Yet the DOT persisted for another four years, spending even more taxpayer dollars on planting more mangroves. In 1999, after 11 years of trying, the DOT finally gave up and declared Whale Harbor a failure.

We found numerous examples of DOT mitigation failures, but our favorite by far was the one connected to the bridge over the Withlacoochee River in Citrus County in 1990. The new State Road 44 bridge destroyed less than an acre of wetlands. The DOT's efforts to build a new wetland to replace it ran into repeated problems. Then, after nine years of trying, it began at last to flourish.

That's when the DOT widened the road, destroying the man-made wetland it had worked so hard to create.

A DOT employee asked if the agency needed to build new wetlands to replace the man-made wetlands that replaced the natural wetland—in other words, should they mitigate for the mitigation?

In response, a Southwest Florida Water Management District wetlands expert named Mark Brown fired off an e-mail that said: "STOP THE MADNESS!!!"

∾

That mitigation fails should come as no surprise to anyone involved in wetlands regulation. The failures have been obvious to wetland scientists for 30 years.

The practice of requiring mitigation for wetland impacts began in the late 1970s. At the time, it seemed to federal regulators like a way to hold the destroyers of the environment to a higher standard, forcing them to give something back to nature in exchange for getting their permits.

By 1981, the Corps was requiring 5,000 acres of new wetlands to be created or old wetlands to be restored nationwide—though that fell far short of the

50,000 acres of wetlands the Corps allowed to be wiped out. But soon scientists were questioning whether mitigation could really replace what was being destroyed.

In 1987, when the National Wetlands Policy Forum was coming up with the no-net-loss policy, wetland experts handed the committee members briefing papers on various issues they ought to consider. Among the briefing papers was a prescient warning against relying too heavily on mitigation to save the day.

The warning, written by Jon Kusler, chairman of the Association of State Wetland Managers, noted the need for more research but pointed out that the limited surveys of mitigation wetlands done so far had found that that "about half of the projects failed in one or more respects."

In fact, Kusler wrote, "wetlands scientists seem to agree that no wetland can be duplicated or replicated exactly. Most natural systems are far too complex, and represent thousands of years of geologic and hydrologic processes with resulting accumulations of soil profiles and ecologic niches of plant and animal species."

Kusler told us that as early as 1977 wetland experts from around the nation were aware that man-made wetlands often failed. "Even back then, people were saying hey, some of this works, some doesn't," he said.

The members of the wetlands forum saw Kusler's report and knew what it meant, he said. But "remember, there were lots of people on there, homebuilders and everybody else was on that forum," he explained. "The feeling was: better to get half a pie than no pie at all."

In other words, they felt it would be better to get lots of mitigation, even if much of it fails, than to get little or none. The reason, Kusler explained, is simple: while scientists may know that reproducing natural wetlands is virtually impossible, and thus wiping them out causes damage that can't be repaired, "it's one thing to know, and another to have a political will." And there was no political will for declaring all wetlands off-limits.

So the forum's final report still listed mitigation as a way for the nation to hit its no-net-loss target, contending that "achieving the goal will require increased compensation for wetlands alterations through a higher rate of restoration of former and degraded wetlands and, where feasible, creation of new wetlands."

Somehow, though, that call for restoration over creation got lost as the proposal was turned into a policy.

In 1990, when the no-net-loss policy was adopted by the Corps and EPA, the two agencies agreed to follow a three-step process with each 404 permit application: First, try to avoid building anything in wetlands. Second, if wetlands couldn't be avoided, try to minimize the impact on them as much as possible. Third, if the wetlands couldn't be avoided and the impact was as minimal as possible, then and only then could the Corps consider requiring mitigation for the damage.

Today, though, mitigation has gone beyond merely making up for lost wetlands. Now it's used as a justification for wiping out natural wetlands. Mitigation has jumped to the head of the line for the state agencies issuing wetland permits—and that limits what the Corps can do, Corps biologist Steven Brooker told us.

"They've stopped doing avoidance," he said. "Now they're hardly doing minimization. They're going straight to mitigation." Developers submit plans with "ridiculous impacts," he said, and instead of denying the permits "you just throw a lot of mitigation at it."

A prime example of that is a highway project in the Keys known as the 18-Mile Stretch. The two-lane road runs from the southern Everglades to Key Largo, and there have been car crashes at night along its more isolated stretches. In 1988 the DOT proposed widening the road to four lanes, destroying 164 acres of wetlands. It said widening the road would ease hurricane evacuation, improve safety, and accommodate growth.

But Keys residents feared it also could pave the way for a population boom in the fragile Keys. Brooker was the permit reviewer at the time, and he passed along those concerns to Col. Terry Rice, then in charge of the Corps in Florida.

"I was half a week in the Keys with Col. Rice—he saw what was going on. I had his support after that," Brooker said. "It would've been a better highway, but the secondary and cumulative impacts—a term everybody was afraid of then—were really huge."

Rice said he kept asking state officials, "What are you doing to make sure this is not going to inspire more growth in the Keys that's going to outrun your hurricane evacuation plans?" He never got a satisfactory answer, he said. So Rice told state officials he was going to deny their federal wetlands permit. Instead the DOT withdrew its application and revamped its plans.

By then, though, the DOT already had begun building 385 acres of wetlands to make up for the damage it expected to cause by widening the road. In 1995 it filled in more than 6 miles of an old canal, making it more like the Everglades, and tried to create 12 tree islands like the ones dotting the River of Grass. The DOT also filled in an area that had been illegally dredged and planted thousands of mangroves there.

In 2003 the DOT scaled back the highway project and asked for a new 404 permit—and now Brooker was no longer the permit reviewer. Instead of four lanes, the DOT application called for a wider paved shoulder and a three-foot concrete barrier between the two lanes.

But the new highway plan still called for destroying 103 acres of wetlands. So DOT promised even more mitigation to make up for the damage. It pledged to build another 41 acres of wetlands, although some of that would be at the U.S. Navy base in Key West, 100 miles away.

The Corps approved the permit in 2004, even though Corps officials wrote that the project "does not increase hurricane evacuation." Although Keys activists had suggested several ways to improve traffic safety while avoiding destroying so many wetlands, the Corps did not even consider those alternatives, noting only that the agency "typically defers to the FDOT . . . in highway safety issues."

In the official record of decision, the Corps wrote that its staff was particularly impressed with the DOT's mitigation, which it said would "outweigh the minimal detrimental impacts" of destroying wetlands in the Everglades and the Keys. The mitigation became the justification for issuing the permit.

However, when we looked at the DOT's monitoring reports on the mitigation it had already built, here's what we found: after struggling for a decade and spending more than $1 million of the taxpayers' money, the DOT's mitigation was a failure any way you looked at it.

"So often the best-laid plans just don't work," said John Palenchar of the DOT's Miami office, who oversaw the mitigation projects.

Many of the mangroves the DOT planted a decade ago are still only two feet high. Mature mangroves should be 30 feet high. These were so short, Vic Anderson called them "bonsai mangroves." They probably will never get any bigger. Because they were planted in fill dirt instead of natural muck, "you get a dwarf-type mangrove," Palenchar said. "They don't die, but they don't really flourish."

As for the dozen tree islands the DOT built—well, the trees aren't there anymore. Palenchar said the tree islands weren't built high enough to keep the trees out of the water: "They were too soggy and most of them died."

～

The problem of mitigation failure might not be so bad if someone were requiring developers, miners, and roadbuilders to start over and do things right.

"We only care about it working if compliance inspections are at such a level that if people screw up, they get caught," said Roy "Robin" Lewis, an environmental consultant in Florida for 30 years. "That's not taking place. The regula-tors need to be on everybody's tail. Instead, developers hire the cheapest land-scaper they can find to do their mitigation, and then the site goes bad. That happens every time."

As a result, Lewis said, "there isn't any significant incentive to make sure the process works."

This is not a new problem. In 1988, the investigative arm of Congress, the General Accounting Office, issued a report pointing out that the Corps was placing little emphasis on making sure mitigation actually occurred. In 1993, the GAO pointed it out again.

But the Corps' attitude remained the same: we're too busy cranking out new permits. That's particularly understandable in Florida, where the permit reviewers are constantly on the verge of drowning in permit applications, Rice told us.

"People are calling and writing every day: 'Where's my permit?' So that's what you focus on," Rice told us. "Meanwhile enforcement is out of sight, out of mind, unless somebody brings something to your attention."

That's fine with the Corps' leaders. In 1999, Maj. Gen. Russell Furman sent a memo to all Corps commanders outlining what their priorities should be. He told them to think of a dividing line separating their most pressing duties from the ones that could be postponed indefinitely. Above the line: making "timely" decisions on permit applications, he said. Below the line—to be done after everything else—he listed compliance inspections for mitigation.

Two years later the National Research Council panel wrote that "the cumu-lative effect of these policy decisions indicates that . . . issuing permits takes priority over careful evaluation of mitigation projects."

When the National Research Council report came out in 2001, the Corps trumpeted its intention to mend its ways and make mitigation meaningful. Corps leaders joined with the EPA and other federal agencies to prepare a "Mitigation Action Plan" that would fix everything the report had pointed out as wrong.

But four years later, in 2005, the GAO issued a new report that said the same old attitude still prevailed.

"The Corps' Section 404 program is crucial to the nation's efforts to pro-tect wetlands and achieve the national goal of no net loss," GAO investigators wrote. "Although Corps officials acknowledge that compensatory mitigation is a key component of this program, the Corps has consistently neglected to ensure that the mitigation it has required as a condition of obtaining a permit has been completed. The Corps' priority has been and continues to be processing permit applications. . . . The Corps continues to provide limited oversight of compensatory mitigation, largely relying on the good faith of permittees to comply with compensatory mitigation requirements."

Unless the Corps starts doing its job, the GAO investigators wrote, "it . . . will be unable to ensure that the section 404 program is contributing to the national goal of no net loss of wetlands."

Think about the cost of all this failure, not just in the loss of wetlands and the broken promises to the voters, but in actual dollars.

Trying to create new mangrove and tidal wetlands costs about $50,000 an acre, Lewis estimated when we talked to him in 2005. Trying to create freshwater wetlands costs a little more "because you're dealing with water control structures," he said, so figure $75,000 to $100,000 an acre for those.

Now add up all the acres of mitigation built all across Florida—by the DOT, by miners, by developers.

"You're in the tens of millions of dollars," Lewis pointed out. "How much tax money goes into attempts to do this stuff that doesn't work? And when it's private developers doing it, that winds up affecting the cost of a house."

But don't count on any effort by the government to stop relying on mitigation to prop up the politicians' promise of no net loss.

In 2005, we talked to James Connaughton, who as chairman of the White House Council on Environmental Quality is President George W. Bush's top environmental adviser. We pointed out all the mitigation failures throughout Florida, and Connaughton acknowledged that "sometimes some of these projects don't work out the way we think they should."

But mitigation remains a crucial part of the permitting process, he said, because it offers a way to balance wetlands protection with continued development.

"People need homes to live in, hospitals to go to when they're sick, and stores to buy food," Connaughton told us. "As long as we support a growing population in America, there will be a need for land. We need to minimize the impact to valuable wetlands, but where we do have impact, mitigation is the answer."

Yet it's hard to see it that way when you've visited the Wal-Mart store in Oldsmar, a small town between Tampa and Clearwater.

In 1999, Wal-Mart proposed building a supercenter on 28 acres near the

Figure 9. Although hemmed in by apartment buildings, this five-acre cypress swamp in the town of Oldsmar, north of Tampa, is thriving in this 1995 aerial image. (Photograph courtesy of Florida Department of Environmental Protection.)

aptly named Cypress Lakes subdivision development in Oldsmar. Smack in the middle of the site was a five-acre cypress dome that Wal-Mart said had to go. As mitigation, Wal-Mart dug out holes around its parking lot to create three new wetlands. One was built on a site that, before Wal-Mart arrived, held some dumpy apartment buildings.

To show its environmental sensitivity, the retail giant didn't just kill off all the plants in the cypress dome. Instead, the company transplanted the vegetation from the natural wetland it was destroying, even 70-foot-tall cypress trees. Wal- Mart's environmental consultant, Kimley-Horn and Associates, promised the mitigation sites would soon become a "mini-ecosystem" with a "dense canopy." As further mitigation, Wal-Mart also promised to preserve 26 acres of wetlands north of the store by donating them to the public.

The Corps approved the permit in 2000. Five years later, we toured the Wal-Mart mitigation site with a former state wetlands expert named Sydney Bacchus

Figure 10. By 2004 Wal-Mart had built a new store in Oldsmar on the site where 70-foot-tall cypress trees once stood. The company transplanted the trees and all the other wetland vegetation into a man-made wetland constructed north of the store, on land the apartments once occupied. (Photograph courtesy of Florida Department of Environmental Protection.)

who does freelance work for environmental groups. As we slogged through the thigh-deep water, we found that many of the transplanted trees were dead. Bacchus pointed out a lot more were showing signs of severe stress.

Every rainstorm sends polluted water from the parking lot flowing into the largest man-made wetland, which doubles as a retention pond. Cypress can tolerate standing in a few inches of water with an occasionally deeper inundation, but Wal-Mart's man-made wetlands always hold three feet or more of water. In other words, these wetland trees were too wet. They were drowning.

To make matters worse, Bacchus pointed out, the transplanting process severed the tangle of roots that bind one cypress to the trees surrounding it. When a high wind hits the dying trees, they topple easily, their root balls popping out of the muck like a giant divot. At one point we scrambled up on top of one such root ball protruding from the water. It was as big as a retail executive's desk.

Figure 11. Wetlands expert Sydney Bacchus examines the root ball of a dead cypress tree in the Oldsmar Wal-Mart store's man-made wetland. Despite promises that the man-made wetland would form a thriving ecosystem with a dense tree canopy, after five years many of the trees were dying or dead. (Photograph by Lara Cerri, *St. Petersburg Times*.)

So many transplanted trees died in one area that biologists at the Southwest Florida Water Management District, after reading the company's monitoring reports, recommended Wal-Mart replace them with new plantings, in the hopes the new trees might do better than the transplants.

And what of the wetland that Wal-Mart was supposed to donate? Instead, the company tried to sell it for development.

The Cypress Lakes Homeowners Association found out about the sale and sent a letter to the Corps protesting that Wal-Mart was violating its permit. Only then did the Corps take action, forcing Wal-Mart to give the undeveloped wetland to Pinellas County.

Yet in 2005, Wal-Mart trumpeted the news that its Oldsmar mitigation work had won an Award of Excellence from the National Arbor Day Foundation.

When we looked at the company's submittal for the award, we found that Wal-Mart had inflated the number of trees that survived the transplant. National Arbor Day Foundation Vice President Dan Lambe said the contest judges—like the Corps—simply took Wal-Mart's word for how well its mitigation worked.

While troubled by the news of the falsified application, he said the foundation could not give the award to anyone else for one simple reason: Wal-Mart was the only entry.

Regardless of whether a mitigation project like Wal-Mart's is successful, the accounting on wetlands creation is simple. There are acres to measure, costs to total up. The concept is easy to grasp: you wipe out a few acres here; you build a few acres there.

But as creation's failures became glaringly obvious, regulatory agencies turned to other forms of mitigation.

And then the accounting got downright creative.

Turning a Minus into a Plus

We set off on our bicycle ride on a blue-sky February morning, headed for the heart of the topsy-turvy world of wetland mitigation. Just after sunup, a light breeze made the air cool enough for a sweater. But as the sun rose so did the temperature, and soon we stowed the sweaters away. The difficulty of making the wheels of our rusty bikes turn was enough to make us sweat anyway.

Leading the way was Dan Rametta, a retired math and science teacher who tends to use words the way Jackson Pollock used paint. Riding along was Richard Sommerville, a soft-spoken surveyor who quit the business to take care of his ailing parents. They were the Penn and Teller of grassroots environmental activism in Pasco County: the big, energetic guy who's constantly yakking and the silent, smiling detail man who makes the act work.

On battered old bikes that Rametta had picked up for a song at a police auction, we rolled along the paved path the Florida DOT had built alongside the Suncoast Parkway, a wide ribbon of road along Florida's west coast that crosses first over the black and burbling Pithlachascotee River and then over a smaller waterway called Five Mile Creek. Our turnoff was just ahead, but part of the reason for this ride was the slab of pavement next to us.

The parkway is a 42-mile toll road from Tampa to Brooksville that the state spent $500 million to build in the late 1990s. The story of its construction is a primer on how to manipulate numbers to yield the desired result—a little trick the cops on the TV show *The Wire* call "juking the stats."

Before the Suncoast was built, developers in Hillsborough, Pasco, and Hernando counties clamored for its construction because they were eager to replace pastures and swamps with new homes, stores, and offices. That's not unusual.

"Developer interest drives a lot of the toll roads in Florida," J. P. Morgan Securities managing director Bob Muller, an expert on financing for toll roads and bridges, explained once. "Roads driven mostly by developer interest tend to be the ones with the most problems, because developers tend to be an optimistic lot."

State law at that time said that before a new toll road could be built using state money, there had to be some demonstration of sufficient demand for the road so it could quickly pay back the money that had been borrowed to pay for its construction. The law said that the projected revenues must be high enough that, by its fifth year of operation, tolls from the new road would equal half the annual payment toward retiring its debt.

The financial test was supposed to protect the toll system from political influence. But as the Suncoast proved, it did not.

To see whether the Suncoast could pass its financial feasibility test, the DOT hired a company called URS Greiner Woodard. In 1992, URS experts said the Suncoast Parkway would be so popular with suburban commuters it would make $70 million in 2002, with revenues rising steadily to $119 million in 2010. That persuaded the state to proceed with planning the highway.

But then URS scaled back its projections. When the Suncoast faced its do-or-die financial feasibility test in 1995, it barely passed. Then, in 2000, URS reduced the Suncoast's numbers even further to a more realistic prediction of $14 million in revenue by 2002 and $31 million by 2010.

Had the company offered those projections in 1995, the road could not have been built. But by the time URS came up with the lower estimates, it was too late. Construction was going full steam ahead, based on the overblown revenue estimates.

The road opened in 2001, and a year later its revenues were a mere $10 million—even lower than the lowest URS prediction and $60 million below the original set of projections. Five years later the road's tolls brought in just $17 million in annual revenue.

When we questioned how the company came up with such wildly off-base numbers to justify building the Suncoast and other Florida toll roads, a URS official conceded, "We were basically guessing."

To construct the Suncoast along the route it had chosen, the DOT dumped fill dirt in some 200 acres of wetlands in Hillsborough, Pasco, and Hernando counties, most of them cypress swamps that fed the Anclote and Pithlachascotee rivers. In approving the destruction of those wetlands, neither the Corps nor the state ever questioned whether this new road was really necessary.

On this clear and clean morning, as dump trucks loaded with fill dirt rumbled up the Suncoast headed toward yet another subdivision being built in virgin territory, we turned our bikes toward the place where DOT was supposed to make up for all that destruction, a nature preserve known as Serenova.

The Corps allowed the DOT to mitigate for the Suncoast by buying Serenova's 10,000 acres from its owner and donating the land to the Southwest Florida Water Management District, better known as Swiftmud, which also happened to be the state agency that had approved the DOT's wetlands permit.

About 3,300 acres of Serenova is made up of wetlands. To the Corps, this seemed like a good deal: destroy 200 acres of wetlands and get 3,300 acres preserved in return, plus more than 6,000 acres of uplands too. To the Corps, this met the requirements of no net loss.

This was not an unusual arrangement. The idea of using preservation to make up for wetland losses dates back at least to the deal that Frank Mackle Jr. made with Governor Askew to donate thousands of acres of beach property to the state in exchange for state permits to destroy thousands of acres of Marco Island mangroves.

There is a certain logic to using preservation as mitigation, a logic that's based on how permissive the 404 permitting program has become since 1980. Royal Gardner, the Corps' top wetlands attorney in the early 1990s and now vice dean at Stetson University's College of Law, explained it this way: "I'm in favor of more preservation. You look at the 404 program—it's a permit program. It's a fallacy to think that because a wetland is a wetland it's protected by the Clean Water Act. It can be filled. A developer just has to ask permission."

Originally, under the 1990 agreement between the EPA and the Corps that established no net loss as federal policy, preservation was supposed to be the last resort for mitigation—just as mitigation itself was supposed to be the last resort after avoiding wetlands and minimizing the damage. Before allowing them to simply preserve existing wetlands, the Corps was supposed to require its permit applicants to try either restoring drained wetlands or creating new ones.

But through the 1990s, as the evidence piled up that created wetlands often fail, the Corps and the state repeatedly turned to preservation as their preferred method of mitigation, since it enjoys a success rate of nearly 100 percent. As a result, the sequencing requirement has been greatly relaxed, and preservation now winds up being included in many permits—sometimes to the exclusion of any other kind of mitigation.

Over and over, as we dug through wetland destruction permit files from across Florida, we saw language that said that this or that development or mine or road would in fact represent a gain for the environment because so many wetlands would be preserved as a mitigation.

However, to make this kind of calculation requires subverting basic math. Think of it as if the wetlands were money. You have $100. You spend $40 and put the other $60 in the bank. If you use "mitigation math," you have not just blown 40 bucks. Instead, you have gained $60, because you didn't spend it.

You have turned a minus into a plus.

By the same token, if you own 100 acres of wetlands and destroy 40 acres while preserving 60, you still wind up with less than the original 100 acres. But that's not the way the Corps or the state of Florida look at it. Using mitigation math, they regard it as a net gain.

We checked the Corps' quarterly reports to see how many acres of Florida wetlands were being counted as a gain when they were only being preserved. But once again, the Corps' records fell short of offering any meaningful data. The quarterlies did not differentiate between creating new wetlands and preserving existing ones.

When we asked Corps biologist Steve Brooker about this, he explained that the Corps' record-keeping procedures are intended mask its failure to achieve no net loss.

"You read 'mitigation 100 acres,' and it looks like we're creating 100 acres and it's actually preservation," he said.

If pressed, Corps officials will admit that, really, math is not on their side. Instead they will fall back on their definition of what they mean by "no net loss."

"You may have a diminution of acreage," John Hall told us, again avoiding the word "loss." "We do it based on functions and values replacement, not on acreage replacement. We in theory are getting a good environmental return. We have a legitimate issue with the spatial extent of wetlands."

By "legitimate issue with the spatial extent," he really meant, "We're losing wetland acres."

∾

Using preservation to make up for destruction has some problems beyond basic math. One is that the permits rarely take into account the full impact of big projects, particularly roads like the Suncoast Parkway.

The Corps' permit reviewer on the parkway was Mike Nowicki, the same guy who said no to the Ecotour Lodge, the only 404 permit denial between 1999 and 2003. Clearly he was no pushover. But in approving the 404 permit for the Suncoast, Nowicki determined that routing the new highway through a previously undeveloped area would not stimulate new development that would wipe out more wetlands. His official findings state that the Suncoast "will not be a major cause for development."

Yet that's exactly what happened. Even before the parkway opened in 2001, it set off a building bonanza with scores of eager developers applying for wetland permits of their own. Over here was the Bexley Ranch, soon to be the site of 7,000 homes, 400,000 square feet of stores, 250,000 square feet of offices. Over there was the Suncoast Mall, with three retail buildings, a restaurant, a carwash, and a gas and convenience station. Then along came a 1.2-million-square-foot office complex and then a 740-acre subdivision with 669 single-family units, 320 multifamily units, and 380 townhomes, and so on and so on. This is how Florida grows now: a toll road slices through virgin land, and then row after row of shiny slate roofs march across the rural countryside like Sherman's army heading for the sea.

"That's the new suburbs," Brad Monroe, president of the Greater Tampa Association of Realtors, said on the toll road's fifth anniversary. "It's not the sticks anymore."

Yet when we asked Nowicki about the "not a cause of development" line in the toll road's 404 permit, he insisted he was right, telling us, "There really isn't any development spurred by the road."

Nowicki said all those new subdivisions and strip centers would have happened eventually anyway without the parkway. "It's not really attributable to the Suncoast," he said.

The other problem with using preservation as mitigation is that saving a piece of land "forever" doesn't really mean it's saved in perpetuity. It just means it won't be wiped out until somebody really needs it.

Often when a developer agrees to preserve land for mitigation, the ownership of the land itself doesn't change. Instead, he or she files a document at the courthouse that says there's now a "conservation easement" over the property. The conservation easement effectively gives away the right to develop the land to some nonprofit group or government agency that will preserve it, while the ownership remains the same. The Corps likes to see conservation easements in a developer's mitigation. "We take those very seriously," Hall told us.

But the Corps doesn't accept the easements itself. And it doesn't keep files on where they all are.

"Since we're not the recipient, we've pretty much been dependent on the DEP and water management districts to keep records," Hall said. "Say it's a 50-

Figure 12. No net loss is "just a big shell game," said retired Corps permit reviewer Vic Anderson. "The only conclusion you can draw is that we're losing it on purpose." (Photograph by Lara Cerri, *St. Petersburg Times*.)

acre development and five acres is preserved with a conservation easement—that's not easy to keep track of."

Because the Corps doesn't keep track of what's preserved, it may not be preserved for long. Steve Brooker told us they have received repeated reports about developers who go back and build on their "preserved" land in spite of the conservation easements. They know no one is likely to check, he explained.

Even if the Corps finds out the easement has been violated, it's not a big deal, Vic Anderson told us. That's because the easements are just window-dressing.

"They're cosmetic," he said. "They're written to allow authorization of the permit. . . . There are violators out there . . . filling in conservation easements and getting away with it."

He cited the case of a racetrack in Homestead, south of Miami. The Homestead Motor Speedway got a 404 permit to fill wetlands for an expansion but balanced it out with a conservation easement on wetlands that would be preserved.

"Then over time," Anderson recounted, the owners said "'Oh we need more parking.'" That meant wiping out some of the land that was supposed to be preserved. The solution? Make up for the new damage by planting more wetland vegetation in what was left.

That's what was happening with Serenova, only on a far grander scale.

∾

One reason the Corps accepted the Serenova preserve as mitigation for the Suncoast was that it was a large, unbroken stretch of undeveloped land. That's why the EPA and other agencies agreed to the permit for the road, too. Serenova had once been slated for development, so getting it off the market seemed like a big plus for the environment.

But as soon as the DOT finished building the Suncoast Parkway, Pasco County officials said they wanted to extend another road right through the middle of Serenova. They wanted to slice that big, unbroken preserve into two pieces.

Pasco officials said they needed to extend Ridge Road eight miles through Serenova to provide a better east-west evacuation route during hurricanes. Oh, and of course, it would stimulate further growth, they said.

The DOT had no objections to the Ridge Road extension. In fact, the DOT was so accommodating that it went ahead and built an otherwise pointless overpass on the Suncoast right where the extension of Ridge Road would need an off-ramp.

On the day we visited, though, the ramp ran out after a few feet, ending in a field full of hip-high palmettos surrounding a borrow pit—the source of the Suncoast's fill dirt. Now idle, the pit had turned into a murky pond ringed by cattails.

Swiftmud, the state agency that now owns Serenova, had no objections to Ridge Road either. It quickly approved a permit for the new road.

Only the Corps' Nowicki seemed reluctant about approving the project—thanks in large part to the efforts of our guides this morning, Rametta and Sommerville.

Off the paved path, we had to walk our bikes through the stiff and rattling fronds of the palmettos on the Serenova property. Our destination was a large cypress dome, looming in the distance like the Emerald City.

When we got to its edge, each step became a small splash, and the mud sucked at our boots. The wind sighed through the cypress trees, 40 to 50 feet tall. We heard birds chirping and saw a tiny brown frog burrowed into the muck, its eyes twitching.

Toward the center of the dome, the water wasn't more than ankle deep. A dark line on the trees showed that not too long ago, probably during the previous hurricane season, the water had risen a good two feet. Soft green lichens encircled the trunks where the dry met the wet. All through the dome were upthrusting cypress knees, knobby and hard. On the far side, fluttering in the breeze, was a blue surveyor's flag, showing that Ridge Road's route would run right through this swamp.

"Here's the attitude: there's so many wetlands in Florida, what's a couple more?" grumbled Rametta.

"I feel sorry for the biologists and consultants who have to do the work," Sommerville murmured.

Sommerville had reason to empathize. Before Sommerville quit doing survey work, he had begun feeling guilty about helping developers destroy things he treasured. Then, using his knowledge of mapping and land records, he joined forces with Rametta to try to stop some of the destruction. He would pull together the evidence, and then Rametta would use it to argue with the bureaucrats.

In seven years of battling the Ridge Road extension, Rametta figures he spent at least $5,000 of his meager retirement savings. His farm isn't near Serenova. This is just his favorite nature preserve. He frequently takes his grandchildren out to snap pictures of the wildlife there.

Because he has plenty of time to spare, Rametta has made repeated drives up to Jacksonville and Atlanta to meet with Corps and EPA officials. He buries them in Sommerville's documents and barrages them with rapid-fire sentences, all aimed at persuading them to reject the Ridge Road permit.

Ask him why he's going to so much trouble and his answer rambles along about how "these out-of-town, carpetbagger developers bring in their already drawn-up plans and try to change the environment to fit their plans. They are like greedy, spoiled children who want what they want, in a certain color, and fully expect to get it, since they usually do. Why can't they adjust their plans to fit the environment, which has been here for 200,000 years?"

Of course, Pasco County officials have offered mitigation for destroying 48 acres of Serenova's wetlands. They have proposed preserving some other wetlands several miles to the north of the current preserve.

They want to mitigate for the mitigation by preserving something else to make up for not preserving something that was supposed to be.

∾

Often when a developer offers to preserve property as mitigation, that offer is combined with something else: enhancement.

The GAO's 2005 report on the Corps' mitigation failures cites a typical case: "In May 2000, the Corps issued a permit authorizing a developer to fill over 430 acres of wetlands to build a residential golf community in Florida. As a condition of issuing this permit, the Corps required the permittee to enhance over 1,000 acres of wetlands and to create 13 acres of wetlands. The Corps also required the permittee to submit annual monitoring reports for 5 years. The file contained no evidence that the Corps had conducted any compliance inspections or received any monitoring reports to determine the status of the required mitigation."

Enhancement sounds good, but in reality what it means is the developer pays someone to go out and strip some wetlands of exotic plants, usually melaleuca and Brazilian pepper. They might also continue going out to spray for exotic plants for the five-year life of their 404 permit.

"It's either removing exotics and maintaining it [the wetland] for a given time, or enhancement may be as simple as providing a more stable water source," veteran Corps biologist Chuck Schnepel told us.

Once again, though, simple math shows that simply uprooting exotics from an existing wetland will not translate into a gain in wetlands. Once again, no net loss winds up being achieved on paper and undermined in reality.

But Corps officials contend that what counts is not replacing wetland acres but, rather, finding a way to replace the "functions and values" of the wetlands that are wiped out.

"When we mitigate, we calculate the quality of the wetlands as a part of the permit," Col. Carpenter told us.

The quality of the calculations, though, leaves something to be desired.

Over the past 30 years the Corps and other agencies have tried repeatedly to come up with a system for measuring the value of a particular wetland and then comparing it to the value of the mitigation. The systems are an alphabet soup of acronyms—HEP and HGM and WRAP and UMAM and CRAM and so forth—all promising to produce a scientifically and legally defensible result.

WRAP stands for Wetlands Rapid Assessment Protocol, and until 2006 that was the method the Corps preferred to use in Florida. Then the Corps switched to the Uniform Mitigation Assessment Method, or UMAM. One wetland biologist told us with a smirk that it would have been the Florida Uniform Mitigation Assessment Method, except then everyone would have called it "F.U., Ma'am."

Another assessment method, HGM, is supposed to be the one the Corps uses nationwide. HGM is short for the "hydrogeomorphic approach." In the mid-1990s wetland scientists said it was the best of the bunch because of its emphasis on water sources, wetland type, and the relative ease or difficulty of establishing certain hydrological regimes. To make HGM work requires comparing the results with "reference sites"—natural wetlands that provide examples of how a marsh or swamp ought to function.

HGM is far from foolproof, though. Jon Kusler of the Association of State Wetlands Managers once asked a group of builder consultants to compare their own favored method of measuring mitigation versus using HGM. "We asked the consultants, 'Could you have come up with these same numbers using HGM?' They said, 'We could've given you any result you wanted,'" Kusler told us. "The problem with HGM is that it's a pseudoscience method."

HGM's other flaw is that it requires too much fieldwork. That's why it won't work in Florida, explained the Corps' grinning engineer, Bob Barron. He explained that doing HGM right takes too long, and the permits just keep piling up.

"It is superior to what's out there," Barron said. "It just takes forever to develop and calibrate, and that part of the program has been cut. So we're using a tool that takes less time."

The bottom line, he said, was simple: "We would rather use an imperfect assessment on a lot of projects than a perfect one but only get to use it on a few big ones."

So the Corps continued to rely on WRAP, knowing it was flawed. Environment consultants dutifully totaled up the WRAP scores for the wetlands that developers wanted to destroy and then showed how the mitigation they were proposing—while falling far short of replacing the acreage—would nevertheless provide WRAP values that were equal to or higher than what was being lost. Thus, they achieved no net loss.

Brooker and Anderson told us that no matter what method the consultants use, it's just more window-dressing designed to make wetlands destruction seem like a boon to the environment when it really is not.

"The applicants give us these big complicated spreadsheets" with the WRAP calculations on them, Brooker told us. "We don't look at them. They give us these lousy numbers so a good wetland system looks bad, and nobody's checking. They never address secondary and cumulative impacts, and nobody's looking at that either."

As we dug through permitting files, we did find several 404 permits where conscientious Corps permit reviewers themselves applied the WRAP test to controversial development projects. But when they came up with numbers that would have required rejecting the permit, they ignored the test results.

One of them was Portofino, the big condo towers on Pensacola Beach. Records in the permit file showed that Clif Payne, the Corps' painstaking permit reviewer, couldn't get the WRAP scores for Portofino's mitigation to add up to an acceptable number that would match the natural wetlands. Instead of using that as a reason to deny the permit, Payne tossed out the test results.

Hall said there was a simple explanation for rejecting WRAP scores if they don't yield an acceptable answer: none of the tests—not WRAP or HEP or UMAM or any of the others—are as good as a biologist's gut. The whole thing was subjective, not objective, he said.

"In my professional opinion, I'm not sure we've got a really good functions and values tool," Hall told us. "They're all basically based on best professional judgment, every last one of them. You're trying to come up with some kind of number that you hope translates your gut into a values system, a measurable value system."

Thus, if the scores don't match what your gut says, you go with your gut and approve the permit anyway. So far though, no denials have ever been based on gut feeling.

So to recap: The Corps bases its pursuit of no net loss not on acres but on replacing the functions and values of the wetlands being destroyed. Yet it has no reliable tool for measuring functions and values, and it doesn't check its own records on what it has allowed to be destroyed.

We began to think of the Corps as a convoy of truckers driving across country with no map or compass. They had no clue where they were going or where they had been. But they would never stop for directions. That might slow them down.

ℭℭ

As bad as preservation and enhancement are at meeting the requirements of no net loss, there is one method of mitigation that's even worse—and it's being used by the state of Florida itself.

Since 1997, the DOT has not handled its own mitigation. Instead it is supposed to pay the state's five water districts to do the job. When we checked DOT records in 2006, we found the DOT had paid them $62 million to cover the costs of mitigating for 542 acres of wetlands destroyed by road projects.

And what did the taxpayers get for that $62 million? Most of it had been spent buying existing wetlands or clearing away exotic vegetation—on preservation and enhancement, in other words. But some of the DOT's money wasn't even being spent to acquire wetlands.

Since 1997 the DOT has paid Swiftmud more than $9 million for wetlands mitigation. But land costs are so high that the money would not have gone very far if it had been spent buying property.

So Swiftmud officials say 70 percent of the projects they spent the money on involved managing or improving land that was already owned by other public agencies. In other words, they helped pay for mowing grass and mending fences on land already owned by the public. Some of it wasn't even classified as wetlands.

That does not directly replace the wetlands the DOT destroyed—but Mark Brown, the "STOP THE MADNESS" wetlands expert, explained that it did have one virtue: it made the taxpayers' money stretch a little further.

At the dry edge of the Serenova cypress dome we stopped for a bite to eat: fresh strawberries, Pop Tarts, bottles of water. The battle over Ridge Road seemed like a distant concern, some minor skirmish of a bygone day.

But back at Rametta's rural farmhouse, in the utility room he has renamed "the war room," there are two long folding tables and a computer. Boxes of documents about Ridge Road and the 404 process are stacked all over the two tables, as well as on top of the refrigerator, the two freezers, and on the floor underneath the folding tables. And there's a closet that's half-filled with more boxes.

In them are things like the reports from Pasco County's environmental consultant, declaring, for instance, that Wetland No. 14 on the Serenova property is "dewatered, of poor quality and never to recover." In other words, it wouldn't be missed if a road ran through it.

Not long after reading those words, Rametta posed for a photo in the middle of that particular wetland. He was standing in water that reached above his knees.

Rametta sent the photo to Nowicki. At that point Nowicki's last visit to the Serenova site was in 1997, when he was reviewing the Suncoast Parkway permit application. But Rametta convinced him to take another tour in 2006, and seeing this photo of the clearly wet wetland prompted Nowicki to demand a new wetland assessment from the county, with all-new WRAP scores. The new round of studies by the consultant will cost Pasco County's taxpayers still more money—which is part of Rametta's real strategy.

Like the Corps itself, Rametta and Sommerville are trying to delay the permit long enough to get what they want. Rametta said they are hoping the price tag will eventually become too high for the county to continue pursuing the project. The catch is that he needs Pasco officials to reach the breaking point before he runs through all of his savings.

He's not really pinning his hopes on the Corps denying the permit. He knows better.

"Federal permit reviewers are programmed not so much as 'reviewers' but as 'facilitators,'" Rametta wrote us in an e-mail while on one of his Jacksonville jaunts. "I wonder sometimes if I will ever be able to communicate to them how much they are 'bound' by the process. Years ago in China women had to wear tiny shoes. It was their role in life—expected of them. Granting permits is the 'tiny shoes' of federal reviewers."

From time to time Rametta and Sommerville have been advised by attorney Lesley Blackner, who on behalf of the Sierra Club had sued to stop construction of the Suncoast but lost. With her toothy smile, blond hair, and pastel suits, Blackner looks like she could be a Hummer-driving Junior Leaguer, but she talks like a Birkenstock-shod rabble-rouser. She refers to the Florida Chamber of Commerce and the legislature as "the evil twins," and her favorite line is: "We have government of the developer, by the developer, and for the developer."

Since 2003 she has been pushing a controversial constitutional amendment called Florida Hometown Democracy, which would give voters the right to say yes or no to changes in their local land-use plans, instead of county and city officials who often get their campaign contributions from homebuilders and real estate interests.

To Blackner, the folly of Ridge Road and mitigating for the mitigation has a parallel in another legal fiction from the civil rights era, the doctrine of "separate but equal" treatment for black citizens.

"Mitigation, like 'separate but equal,' acknowledges that there is a problem with the status quo, but wants to preserve the status quo," she explained in an e-mail.

In the case of Jim Crow, whites could not deny that blacks are human beings, but the white power structure in the South could not imagine a world in which blacks are given equal standing in society. So they came up with the bankrupt moral construct of separate but equal . . .

Now, we know that tearing up Mother Nature has bad consequences. But the power structure just can't envision a world in which development can't go anywhere and everywhere. So they came up with mitigation, to absolve us of our worry and keep everybody copacetic with the status quo. . . . Mitigation allows business to continue as usual.

When we talked to White House CEQ chairman James Connaughton about all this, he acknowledged that because of the 404 program's failures, both in permitting and mitigation, Florida has lost thousands of acres of wetlands all across the state.

Not to worry, though, he told us. The federal government is going to spend billions of dollars fixing the problem, catching up on all those lost acres. Restoring the Everglades down in South Florida "will be a key component" in offsetting those statewide losses, he boasted.

What Connaughton didn't mention is that a key component of the Everglades restoration program requires destroying thousands more acres of wetlands—using dynamite.

11

"A Mine Is a Terrible Thing to Waste"

The dump trucks rumble out of the CSR Rinker mine just west of Miami, swirling a fine gray dust in the air. Just as the dust starts to settle, another truck full of rocks comes barreling past and stirs it up again.

Every day, mining companies like Rinker blast chalky white limestone out of the ground to feed Florida's insatiable appetite for concrete. Every year the mines excavate about 40 million tons of sand and stone. Rinker's mine alone produces 13 million tons of rock a year, more than any other rock mine in the United States. It runs 24 hours a day, seven days a week.

Miami-Dade County's limestone deposits date back to the Pleistocene era, a time when the highest point in Florida was just a sandbar. The rock, made of ancient shells and coral, starts just beneath the land surface and extends down about 100 feet. The miners boast that this prehistoric stone helped build Orlando's theme parks and the Kennedy Space Center, not to mention Florida's major bridges and highways.

The two largest mining companies are Tarmac, owned by a Greek multinational corporation, and Rinker, which is part of an Australian conglomerate. All told, 10 mining companies own or control about 90 square miles of land that borders the eastern edge of Everglades National Park. It's a big-money business. In 2005, the 10 companies mining in this area reported some $500 million in profits.

To get the rock, miners blow up Everglades marshes, some of them the last remnants of their type of wet prairie in the state. When the mining is done, what's left are water-filled pits up to 80 feet deep and as square as a stamp. Because these pits resemble lakes, the area has been dubbed "the Lake Belt."

But they aren't like any natural lake in Florida. Real Florida lakes are seldom deeper than 30 feet. Unless they're sick with pollution, natural lakes teem with life at every level. In the Lake Belt "lakes," though, no life exists below about 10 feet. That's because there's not enough dissolved oxygen in the water for fish or anything else below that level.

Interior Department officials have called the Lake Belt's lakes "biologically unproductive and functionally impaired." John Hall told us they are "not nearly as valuable as the wetland that was there before they dug the hole."

From the 1950s to the 1990s, the miners destroyed about 17,000 acres of wetlands in the Lake Belt by blasting out the limestone rock. That's about 30 percent of the land in the Lake Belt where the wetlands were blown to bits.

The other 70 percent has been altered by mining too. Creating the quarries and building roads to get to them helped spread the seeds of the melaleuca tree, an exotic plant that sucks up water like a sponge on steroids.

Native to Australia, melaleuca was first introduced to Florida at the turn of the century by John Gifford, a forestry expert who was cofounder of a magazine called *Conservation*. He expected melaleuca to dry up the Everglades' marshes so they could be turned into farms. But the plant, also known as the punk tree and the paperbark tree, did its job all too well. Melaleuca now infests wetlands throughout South Florida, spreading by an estimated 15 acres a day. Not only does it slurp the wetlands dry, but it also creates a continuing fire hazard because the oil in its leaves is highly flammable.

When state officials tried to stop its spread, the melaleuca trees turned out to be as hard to kill as James Bond. Any stress to the trees triggered by fire, cutting, spraying them with herbicide—or blowing them up with dynamite—causes millions of little seeds to pop out, fall to the ground, and quickly germinate. Cut the tree down and the stump regenerates. The only way to get rid of them is to use a combination of methods: spray them with herbicide, chop them down, grind up their stumps and release millions of Australian insects into the Florida forests to munch on the leaves.

The state spends millions of dollars a year trying to halt the melaleuca menace. The workers laboring to eradicate it have to wear heavy protective gear, because this is one tree that fights back. The emanations of its flowers and foliage can cause asthma-like symptoms, a burning rash, headaches, and nausea.

The mines laying waste to the wetlands via dynamite and melaleuca also creates problems underground. The limestone walls of the pits are porous. The section of the underground aquifer which supplies Miami's drinking water is about as deep as the bottom of the quarries. When water flowing through the aquifer seeps into the quarries, it is sucked away from the remaining wetlands. The mines that create the biggest underground problems are those closest to the levee and canal designated the L-31N near the border of Everglades National Park. Quarries dug there increase the seepage of precious groundwater away from the already-thirsty park and toward the canal, which carries it off to the Atlantic Ocean.

Because they are so porous, the quarries pose a major threat to the water supply for the teeming Miami-Dade County population. Miami-Dade draws about 40 percent of its drinking water from a wellfield just outside the Lake Belt area. As of 2005 the 15 wells at the Northwest Wellfield produced 150 million gallons of water a day for Miami-Dade residents. The county put the wellfield there back when it was isolated, but over the years the mining crept closer and closer, increasing the risk.

By blasting apart the limestone layers that confined the aquifer, the miners opened the aquifer up to contamination from the surface, county water officials say. Once there is no intervening wetland or rock to filter out dangerous microscopic bacteria spread by cattle and bird dung and other pollutants, the risk of contamination becomes far greater. County officials fretted about the chance of some bacterial infection from the Lake Belt ruining the entire water supply—*Cryptosporidium*, for instance, which in 1993 got into Milwaukee's water supply and killed more than 100 people and sickened more than 400,000.

Despite all of its dangers, the Lake Belt miners want to keep mining. In fact, in 1991 they told the Corps they wanted to extend their existing 404 permits for 50 years and expand their mining to include about 50,000 acres. However, mitigating for so much damage would be tricky because the mining left nothing of the original wetland untouched.

"The only thing that can be done is to mitigate the edge," Chuck Schnepel told us. "All you're going to end up with is a narrow fringe. You're not going to end up with an area you can mitigate."

So the miners offered one of the least effective mitigation programs ever devised. They promised to create 100-foot-wide submerged shelves around the edge of each quarry's "lake." And they agreed to pay a few pennies per ton of rock into a fund to buy some nearby wetlands and eradicate the melaleuca growing there.

The three-foot-deep littoral shelves are supposed to mimic wetlands in attracting wildlife. But according to a 1996 study done for Miami-Dade County, the shelves don't work. The study suggested reconfiguring them to better mimic wetlands, but county officials said in 2001 that the miners had resisted trying those techniques.

"The bottom line is to maximize rock-mining at the expense of any sort of environmental mitigation," said George Dalrymple, the consultant who did the study for the county.

The per-ton fee should make up the difference, the miners said. "That money will be more than sufficient to offset any negative impacts we have," said Albert Townsend, director of real estate and environmental services for Tarmac Florida.

The fee is based on a calculation of the amount of money required to replace each acre of Lake Belt wetland that was destroyed with two and a half acres of new or restored wetlands. But Interior Department officials said that ratio is about half what's required of other developers. The money falls short, too. In practice the fee works out to less than $15,000 an acre, Dalrymple said, about a third what mitigation usually costs per acre.

"Now that's a sweetheart deal if ever there was one," he said.

When the miners made that mitigation offer, what followed was one of the darker episodes in the history of Florida wetlands protection. The Corps ignored public health concerns to kowtow to a powerful industry. Federal biologists let the miners' consultants do their jobs for them. And the Florida legislature repeatedly ran interference for the miners.

In 2002 the Corps approved what it called "bridging" permits for the 10 mining companies to destroy 5,400 acres of wetlands—a prelude to consideration of approving permits for the rest a few years down the road.

"There are no practicable nor less damaging alternatives which would satisfy the project's overall purpose," Corps officials said in their decision document.

The Corps asserted that the mining would actually be good for the Everglades because it would get rid of more than 5,000 acres of melaleuca.

"It's not like we have a lot of virgin native areas out there," said retired Col. James "Greg" May, who as the district engineer in Jacksonville signed the permits.

That's not what the Corps was saying in 1996, though, when a Corps official told the miners that the wetlands they wanted to destroy "do have substantial ecological values." Besides, as officials from the National Park Service pointed out, there are ways to remove melaleuca that do not require blowing up the swamp where it grows—ways that still leave a functioning wetland, not a big hole.

The Lake Belt's lakes were also cited by the Corps as a reason for approving the permits. The Corps said a landscape filled with those deep lakes was ecologically superior to a landscape filled with houses. However, as the Department of the Interior pointed out, because the lakes are biologically dead they can't really offer a no-net-loss replacement for the wetlands that were blasted to bits.

The other justification for approving the permits: the Corps said two of the quarries, once the miners were done with them, could be bought by the taxpayers and then used as reservoirs for the government's Everglades restoration program. Turning the quarries into reservoirs would be one of the most expensive elements of the complex Everglades plan, with the cost estimated in 1999 as $1 billion out of the restoration project's $7.8 billion total price tag.

Yet the Corps' Everglades planners admitted they weren't sure it would work. They didn't know how they could keep the water from seeping through those porous quarry walls. Also, if the quarries were used as reservoirs, EPA experts pointed out, the water would fluctuate so much that the shelves built for wetland mitigation would be left dry so often as to make that part of the mitigation worthless.

By approving the permits, the Corps allowed new mining to occur within 1,000 feet of Everglades National Park, right in the middle of a natural flowway that the Everglades restoration plan called for using to funnel more water into the park.

Why were Corps officials so obliging to such a destructive industry that threatened one of the most famous wetlands in the country? The miners' political clout is one reason. They are generous campaign contributors. Between 1997 and 2001, for instance, Rinker's parent company donated more than $130,000 to candidates in state races, including more than $44,000 to the state GOP and $13,000 to Florida's Democratic Party.

"The power and politics that drive these plans have enormous momentum," one National Park Service official complained in an internal e-mail. "I would suggest that Everglades National Park has more national and international importance (even economic) than depletable limestone mining. . . . Florida is in a state of cannibalism, eating itself to increase its infrastructure."

But to truly understand the Corps' reluctance to stop the miners requires tracking the bizarre zigs and zags of a court case called *Florida Rock Industries v. United States*, which resulted from one of the rare instances in which the Corps told someone no.

ᙁ

Part of the Lake Belt was once owned by the Pennsylvania Sugar Company. Back in the 1930s the company hired a former mining engineer named Ernest "Cap" Graham to supervise the growing of sugar cane and the operation of a mill on its property. The company's plans fizzled, and Graham moved on, running unsuccessfully for governor in 1944 (a position his son Bob attained 40 years later). The sugar company's name remains on maps, though, in abbreviated form: Pennsuco.

The wetlands in the Pennsuco area are remnants of the historic expanse of the River of Grass, which once flowed in a slow-moving sheet that covered nearly everything south of Lake Okeechobee.

In September 1972, just a month before Section 404 became the law of the land, Florida Rock Industries spent about $2.9 million to buy 1,560 acres of Pennsuco. Nearly all of the land was covered by Everglades wet prairies.

"It's pretty wet," John Hall told us. "If you fell down in the middle of dry season and didn't get up, you'd drown."

The Jacksonville-based company, founded in 1929 by Thompson Baker, was run by his two sons, Edward "Ted" Baker and John D. Baker. Together they turned it into a powerhouse of the industry. The Bakers planned to mine all the limestone rock under their Pennsuco land, but an economic slowdown kept them from starting work until 1978. After the company built a road and dragline tower and launched its first cut, the Corps stepped in with a cease-and-desist order because Florida Rock had neglected to get a 404 permit.

Florida Rock applied on October 1, 1979, for a permit to mine just 98 acres of its land, the amount the company figured it could excavate during the three-year life of the 404 permit. The company and the Corps spent a year negotiating the terms of the permit. But then on October 2, 1980, the Corps—motivated to follow the law as never before in that post-Callaway, pre-Gianelli heyday of wetlands protection—turned the company down.

"They sent their CEO down to browbeat me," recalled the colonel then in charge in Jacksonville, James W. R. Adams. "He seemed surprised to see a uniformed colonel waiting for him. I think he expected to see a bureaucrat in a suit. He sat down and started to tell me what I was going to do, and after about 20 minutes I told him he was misinformed as to the law. I said, 'You need to hire better lawyers.'"

Despite the requirements of the Clean Water Act, Col. Adams told us, the company's legal position was: "They owned the land and they could do what they darn well pleased and the government shouldn't be telling them what to do."

A big part of the reason for the denial was the location where Florida Rock wanted to mine. The Corps was trying to keep the rock mining away from Pennsuco and confined to the areas of the Lake Belt where it had already occurred before Section 404 permits were required. But the big problem, Adams explained, was that "they were cracking the surface, so we were worried the mining could contaminate the water table."

Col. Adams said his boss, the general in charge of the Atlanta office, called him after the denial to warn, "Boy, this guy is really going to make trouble." That turned out to be an understatement.

In 1982 Florida Rock sued the Corps. The suit did not claim the Corps was wrong to deny the permit. Instead, the company contended that the permit denial was a de facto taking of its property by the government. If there could be no mining, Florida Rock said, then the company could not use the property at all. In fact, the company's attorneys argued that the denial of a 404 permit for those 98 acres meant the company couldn't use any of its 1,560 acres, and therefore the government ought to pay them for taking all of it.

The case landed in an obscure new venue: the U.S. Claims Court, created by Congress that same year to hear cases in which people tried to show that the federal government owed them damages—say for lost federal contracts or tax refunds.

There had been previous iterations of the claims court, but this new version had become a prime weapon in the Reagan Revolution's assault on Big Government. The plan, cooked up by Attorney General Edwin Meese III and his conservative aides, involved a classic bit of bureaucratic jujitsu: use the weight of government regulation to bring down the regulators.

They "had a specific, aggressive and . . . quite radical project in mind: to use the takings clause of the Fifth Amendment to put a severe brake upon federal and state regulation of business and industry," former U.S. Solicitor General Charles Fried wrote in his memoir of serving under Meese.

The "takings clause" in the Fifth Amendment is short and sweet: "nor shall private property be taken for public use without just compensation." Thus, for example, when the government runs a highway through someone's land, it must pay a fair price for the property. Or, to pick another example, if the government decides to tear down houses around Bonita Springs and convert the land back into swamps, it cannot merely confiscate the homes but must buy them at a reasonable price.

Over the years the U.S. Supreme Court has held that, on rare occasions, the imposition of a government regulation can amount to a taking of property, but only if it takes away 100 percent of the property's future use. More often, though, the imposition of federal regulations like Section 10 of the Rivers and Harbors Act had been considered to be in the public interest, and the court said regulations carried out for the public's benefit would outrank any private profit or loss.

The plan concocted by Meese and his subordinates, Fried said, was to put private property rights ahead of the public interest. If the courts found that regulations were taking away private property rights, then every time the government dared to tie up a business with red tape, the government would have to pay big bucks.

"If the government labored under so severe an obligation," Fried wrote, "there would be, to say the least, much less regulation." The plan made Fried uneasy, though: "I doubted the wisdom of giving the courts a powerful new engine for redistributing to sympathetic plaintiffs possibly vast sums of money at the expense of the public."

Key to the Meese plan was arranging for the bench to be packed with radical libertarians who could be counted on to rule against government regulation and in favor of property owners. The claims court judge assigned to the Florida Rock case was the perfect embodiment of what they wanted.

A witty and ambitious young man, Alex Kozinski was the son of Holocaust survivors who had fled Communist Romania to run a grocery store in California. The puckish Kozinski was a fully committed libertarian who had worked as a White House aide in the heady early days of the Reagan Administration.

"We were gung-ho Reaganites, all very enthused about cutting back government, which we thought was like fungus," a close friend of Kozinski's named Loren Smith told a reporter from *Legal Affairs* 10 years later.

Kozinski was riding on the Washington Metro reading a weekly law report when he spotted a small item about the creation of the new claims court. He read that "the president would be appointing all the judges of that court—fifteen in all—and, most interesting to me, he would also be designating the court's chief judge," Kozinski later recalled. He said to himself: "Shazam! That's my job!"

Kozinski was anything but shy. He was an amateur magician and, despite his thick accent, had appeared twice on the television show *The Dating Game*. After spotting the item about the new court, he spent weeks pestering friends and pulling strings to get the job he wanted. Finally, despite the fact that Kozinski was only 32 and had no prior judicial experience, Reagan appointed him chief judge of the new claims court.

"I can't think of anyone less suited for that position," Kozinski said years later. "In addition to knowing nothing about the court, I knew nothing about trials. My entire career—all seven years of it—had been spent either as an appellate law clerk or as an appellate litigator. I had tried a single criminal case on a pro bono basis and lost."

The *Florida Rock* case was his first big one as chief judge, and Kozinski threw himself into it. He even visited the mining site prior to trial to see it for himself. If the Corps had faced a more experienced judge, or one less weighed down by ideological baggage, it might have stood a chance. There was ample precedent on the Corps' side. Alfred Zabel and the Deltona Corp. had both accused the Corps of taking their property rights by denying their dredge-and-fill permits. Both argued their cases all the way to the U.S. Supreme Court and both lost.

There was a more recent precedent, too. In 1975, a developer called Estuary Properties applied for permits to build a subdivision with 26,000 homes, four marinas, three golf courses, and 28 acres of tennis courts on 6,500 acres of mangrove-lined coast in Lee County. When local officials rejected the project because it would degrade the local waterways, the company sued in state court, saying the value of its property had been destroyed. The Florida Supreme Court ruled in *Graham v. Estuary Properties Inc.* that "the owner of private property is not entitled to the highest and best use of his property if that use will create public harm." The U.S. Supreme Court declined to hear an appeal from the developer, letting the state court ruling stand.

But one of Kozinski's firmest beliefs is that property owners have a right to use their property as they see fit, despite what environmental regulations may say. In 1985, he ruled that by denying the 404 permit, the Corps had taken away virtually all of Florida Rock's use of its property.

"The fact that plaintiff's proposed mining operation would involve wetlands does not by some peculiar alchemy protect the government from the Fifth Amendment's taking clause," he ruled.

To reach that conclusion, though, Kozinski had to leap over some inconvenient facts. For one thing, he ruled that the Corps' denial of the mining permit meant that the land couldn't possibly be used for anything else, ever.

"In reality, if a permit was denied plaintiff for rock mining, there is little possibility that a permit would be issued for other construction activities (such as apartment houses) which alter the character of the land and surrounding environment much more drastically," Kozinski wrote, apparently oblivious to all the new houses and apartments being built in wetlands throughout Florida with the Corps' blessing.

For another, he had to get around the fact that there were other buyers ready to try their luck with the Corps. Florida Rock had originally bought its Pennsuco land for $1,900 an acre. While the case was tied up in court, several potential buyers had offered to buy it. They were willing to pay up to $4,000 an acre for the supposedly useless land—land that wasn't even advertised for sale.

Kozinski said he disregarded those offers, ruling that "the court finds that the market for plaintiff's land is based on speculation, much of it fueled by unscrupulous promoters"—as if that were somehow atypical for Florida real estate.

He ruled that Florida Rock had no duty to track the changes in federal law governing the destruction of wetlands and thus could not be required to know that the Clean Water Act was on the verge of passing Congress when the company bought its Pennsuco property—the exact opposite of the ruling in the *Deltona* case, where a major corporation was held responsible for keeping up with the changing laws governing wetlands.

Kozinski then went on to decide, based on a flawed understanding of how South Florida hydrology and geology work, that the wetlands to be destroyed don't filter out pollution, that the aquifer would actually be improved by the addition of the quarries, and that the mining posed no threat of contamination to Miami's water supply.

In fact, the judge said, as far as he could tell the mining didn't really produce any pollution at all and therefore the Corps could not claim it was a nuisance to the general public.

For denying the mining permit, Kozinski said the Corps owed the company more than $10,000 an acre for the 98 acres, for a total judgment of more than $1 million. Then he tacked on another $500,000 for legal costs.

Kozinski said he did not agree with Florida Rock that by denying one permit the Corps had limited the use of all 1,560 acres. But he added that, if this turned out to be the case, then the cost to the Corps for taking the use of all of Florida Rock's land would be $10 million. Florida Rock's attorney, John A. DeVault III, praised Kozinski's ruling as "one of the clearest enunciations of the law of regulatory taking yet written."

But the Corps appealed and, after reading Kozinski's ruling and comparing it to the evidence, a five-judge panel of the Federal Circuit Court of Appeals said, "We are left with a profound conviction that a mistake has been made."

The only thing Kozinski did right was limit his decision to the 98 acres where the permit was denied, the appeals court said. On every other point, he was wrong—wrong to say the mining didn't pollute, wrong about how he came up with a value for the property, wrong in determining that a taking had occurred.

Kozinski should not have ignored the fact that people were willing to buy Florida Rock's property, the appeals court said. After all, "South Florida has long enjoyed renown as not only a place where the gullible are fleeced, but also one where far-seeing investors realize fortunes. With the proximity of the huge and growing metropolis of Miami, expanding too in that specific direction, there can be no telling what future Miamians will want to use the instant tract for, still less what they will be willing and able to pay."

The appellate judges sent the case back to the claims court to start over from square one, because "if there is found to exist a solid and adequate fair market value which Florida Rock could have obtained from others for that property, that would be a sufficient remaining use of the property to forestall a determination that a taking had occurred or that any just compensation had to be paid by the government."

By then Kozinski had pulled some more strings and persuaded Reagan to appoint him a federal appeals judge in California. His replacement at the claims court, and the judge who now took over the *Florida Rock* case, was his good friend and fellow Reaganite, Loren Smith.

Smith, a burly and bearded native of Skokie, Illinois, had a broader background than Kozinski. Not long after getting his law degree from Northwestern, he had been host of a nightly radio show called *What's Best for America?* That led to a job as an attorney for the Federal Communications Commission, then work as one of President Richard Nixon's defense lawyers during the impeachment proceedings. Smith then worked as a federal prosecutor and a law professor and served as chief counsel for Reagan's first and second presidential campaigns, where he connected with Meese.

Like Kozinski, though, Smith had zero judicial experience before Reagan appointed him as chief judge of the claims court. Like Kozinski, he believed it was time for the courts to reverse the decades-long trend toward big-government regulation of private property rights.

"You can't ever undo history," Smith said during a panel discussion sponsored by the conservative Federalist Society. "But what you can do is rebuild a society based upon economic freedom. . . . Life, liberty, and property are the fundamental aspects of a free humanity."

When the *Florida Rock* case came back to Smith, he ruled almost exactly the same way Kozinski had. He said the permit denial took Florida Rock's property. As for the offers to buy the property—two of them from an Arizona real estate broker—he wrote: "There is no evidence that these offers were made by knowledgeable investors, nor whether the offerers were capable of consummating the purchase." Instead, he ruled, "the court must discount the proposed use of speculation as being neither practicable nor reasonably probable."

The only way the Corps could get away with denying the permit and not paying for the land, Smith said, was if it could show that Florida Rock's mining would constitute a nuisance to the public. But then he ruled that mining couldn't possibly be considered a nuisance, because there was so much of it going on throughout the rest of the Lake Belt. He didn't mention anything about how important the wetlands might be, or what their destruction might mean to the public at large, or whether the other mining had begun prior to the passage of the Clean Water Act.

Smith awarded the company the exact same amount as Kozinski, too—but he came up with a different rationale for the figure. According to Smith, the permit denial didn't take away the entire value of the property, but "the value of the property in fact has been substantially reduced as a result of government action."

He found that the denial knocked the value of the land down by 95 percent, so it was only worth $500 an acre. To get to that figure, Smith not only had to disregard the $4,000-an-acre offer, he also had to ignore testimony of the company chairman, Ted Baker, who thought the land was worth $10,000 an acre even after the permit denial.

Even his fellow conservatives concluded that Smith—like Kozinski, an amateur magician—was conjuring decisions out of thin air and thus upending decades of legal precedent. Lewis & Clark Law School dean James Huffman, in a piece written for the Heritage Foundation, cheered Smith on but conceded that his ruling in *Florida Rock* and other takings cases "were in direct conflict" with the Supreme Court and would probably be overturned as "abridging the law as interpreted by prior judges." Smith himself contended he was simply exploring uncharted territory, because the area of takings "is really the antithesis of law," where "every case is its own law."

However, attorneys for the U.S. Justice Department had noted a trend in Smith's cases, a trend sure to make Ed Meese smile. "Judge Smith is quite inclined to rule for the plaintiffs, so the government is often in the position of having to appeal his rulings," said Lois Schiffer, an assistant U.S. attorney general who oversaw work on the *Florida Rock* case during the mid-1990s.

The Justice Department, on behalf of the Corps, appealed again. The appeals court ruled in 1994 that the claims court judge was wrong.

But this time, things were different. This time, even the win was a loss for the Corps.

The appeals court opinion was written by a judge named Sheldon Jay Plager, who had been a law professor at, among other places, the University of Florida. More importantly, though, he had been the head of the Office of Information and Regulatory Affairs during the Reagan Administration, a job that entailed conducting cost-benefit reviews of every government regulation before it was enacted—for instance, assessing whether an EPA rule designed to benefit human health was really worth the cost to industry to comply. The *Wall Street Journal* referred to the post as "the administration's main traffic cop for regulation, a sanity check on bureaucrats." Among the bureaucrats, though, Plager was regarded less as a cop and more akin to Darth Vader. His job with the Reagan Administration also carried another duty: executive director of the Task Force on Regulatory Relief, the same organization that had tried to gut the Corps' regulatory operation. Like Kozinski and Smith, he had no judicial experience before being appointed to the appellate bench by the first President Bush.

While Plager overturned Smith's decision, he did so in a way that actually made things worse for the Corps. In an opinion that was joined by another Reagan appointee to the bench with no prior judicial experience, Plager started off by noting that the property clearly still had a value to someone, if not to Florida Rock. He also said the $4,000-an-acre figure seemed a lot more solid than $500 an acre. So maybe it was a taking, but maybe not. The lower court would have to try the case again, he wrote.

But then Plager slipped in something new, something never before seen in any court ruling.

"Nothing in the language of the Fifth Amendment compels a court to find a taking only when the Government divests the total ownership of the property," he wrote, ignoring all the Supreme Court rulings that said otherwise.

Plager told the claims court to go back one more time and find "the difficult line that has to be drawn between a partial regulatory taking and the mere 'diminution in value' that often accompanies otherwise valid regulatory impositions. . . . By taking some portion of Florida Rock's economic use of the property—its power to disturb the overlying wetlands, and with it the common law property right to mine its subsurface minerals—the Government appears to have destroyed part of the value of Florida Rock's holdings. If that proves to be the case, and if the application of the ad hoc tests previously described so warrant, the property interest taken belongs to the Government, and the right to just compensation for the interest taken belongs to Florida Rock."

Plager's opinion marked the first overt appearance in any court ruling of a theory called "partial taking" by regulation. Under that theory, if you buy a car that can go 110 miles per hour and the government limits your speed to 55, then the government should pick up half your car payment. The "partial takings" theory, though contrary to a long line of legal precedents, was popular among conservative lawyers at the time, and Plager was among its advocates. To their way of thinking, a property owner whose 404 permit had been denied should not be required to prove the government had blocked any and all use of the property. Instead the property owner needed to prove only a partial taking in order to get a judgment against the regulators.

Plager, telling the story at a conference a year later, conceded that he had found it difficult "trying to fit the issue you want to write about to the case that is before you." In the *Florida Rock* case, for instance, nobody on either side of the case had argued that it was a partial taking, Plager said. But he didn't let that stop him from shoehorning it into his opinion: "So, we laid out for the trial judge what we saw as the central issue and said: go back and straighten this mess out, and we will review it one more time."

So the case went back once more to Judge Smith at the claims court. Although the name of the court had recently been changed by Congress to the U.S. Court of Federal Claims, the judge's attitude toward the Corps and the Clean Water Act remained the same—and Plager had handed him a new weapon to use against the Corps.

The miners knew that they now had the upper hand. In 1996, an environmental consultant named Paul Larsen who worked for Florida Rock and the other Lake Belt mining companies taunted the Corps about the consequences of denying any more mining permits. He told the regulators that the only question remaining in the *Florida Rock* case was how much the government would have to pay for saying no.

Although the *Florida Rock* case had drawn the attention of the National Association of Home Builders and the National Association of Realtors, who filed friend-of-the-court briefs, it had produced little coverage in the press. Nevertheless, Corps officials nationwide were well aware of its implications, and the 404 program showed the result.

In 1992, the Corps' 38 districts denied a total of 393 individual permit applications, nearly 9 percent of all applications. By 1998 the number of denials had dropped to 158, or about 3 percent of all applications. In 2002, the number of wetland permit denials dropped to 128, less than 1 percent.

A 2000 study by the Congressional Research Service, noting the drop in permit denials, suggested Corps officials had become too scared of the claims court to do their jobs.

Their fears were well founded. A quarter of all the cases filed with the claims court in 1997 stemmed from 404 permit denials. Those wetlands-related suits rarely succeeded—but the winners won big, collecting a total of $350 million from the government.

As study author Robert Meltz wrote, it only takes one or two adverse court decisions "to maintain the hot breath of taking liability on the regulator's neck."

ᘯ

The decision on approving the other Lake Belt permits was in the hands of Col. May, a mild-mannered man with the bland good looks of a local TV anchor. According to Hall, Col. May was "a very cautious person, and reluctant to hurt anyone's feelings. So he was more cautious about denials" than his predecessor, Terry Rice.

May was also wary of getting tangled up in another permitting fight that might cost the government millions in damages. And this time, he wasn't just dealing with one mining company but with 10, all of them working together to bend the Corps to their will.

"You know the *Florida Rock* case had national implications," May told us. "So regulators have to view very carefully the decision they're making. You want to be sensitive that you don't get into a situation where you're making a case with national implications."

Adding to his worries was the intervention of the Florida legislature. Lawmakers had taken a keen interest in the Lake Belt's future as far back as 1991, setting up a committee to plan it, and then larding the committee with pro-mining appointees. When the committee produced its final report in 2000, the only mention in the 529-page document of any opposition was on page 458.

While the miners used the *Florida Rock* case as a threat against the Corps, some federal officials saw it as providing possible leverage for the government. The EPA, in particular, pushed to tie the approval of new mining permits to some settlement of the *Florida Rock* case. However, Rinker and the other miners didn't want their permits in any way tied to the settlement.

When the subject of tying the settlement to permits came up during a March 1998 meeting between the miners and federal officials, the miners stormed out. The miners also did not like a Corps proposal that, to mitigate for the mining damage, they pay a fee of 8 cents per ton of mined rock. In an e-mail, John Hall fretted that if the coalition of miners fragmented and negotiations broke down, the Corps would have to deal with each of the 10 companies individually, which would bog the agency down with 10 times the permitting paperwork.

Soon thereafter the legislature stepped in again to help the miners. It passed a law that imposed a fee of 5—not 8—cents per ton that would go into a mining mitigation fund. The fund, to be administered by the Florida Department of Revenue, would be spent on buying unmined Pennsuco wetlands and eradicating any melaleuca found there. The law said the fee would go into effect in 1999—but it would be suspended "if a long-term permit for mining" was not issued by September 30, 2000.

The state's own permitting agency, the Department of Environmental Protection, fell in line, handing out state permits that said the mining was unlikely to result in a violation of water quality standards. Soon Judge Smith was giving the Corps another reason to cave in as well.

As expected, in 1999 Smith followed Judge Plager's suggestion and ruled that a Corps permit denial had taken part of the value of Florida Rock's 98 acres.

But then Smith took a step that seemed designed to really punish the Corps. He ruled that because the Corps had turned down one permit, it was likely to reject mining anywhere on Florida Rock's 1,560 acres, and therefore the government might owe Florida Rock for the loss of that property as well. According to Smith, the total damage for the 98 acres alone was $752,444, plus compound interest from October 2, 1980, plus $1.3 million for attorneys' fees and costs. He did not set an amount for the rest, because the Corps had already appealed his ruling.

Hall said he urged taking the case all the way to the U.S. Supreme Court, but settlement talks now began in earnest. While the appeal was still pending, the Corps and its lawyers from the Justice Department agreed to a settlement that was not tied to the issuing of new permits for the other miners. Under the settlement, dated September 4, 2001—just short of 20 years after the permit denial—Florida Rock agreed to drop its suit. In exchange, the government handed over $21 million of the taxpayers' money to buy all 1,560 acres of the company's Pennsuco property. Some Corps officials bitterly refer to this land now as the federal government's "strategic lime rock preserve."

The settlement document gives no reason for settling the case and doesn't explain how the parties agreed on such a large sum. The timing seems curious, too, coming just a few months after President George W. Bush appointed a former gravel-pit owner from Mississippi named Michael Parker as the top civilian at the Department of the Army to oversee the Corps.

However, a Department of Justice attorney who worked on the case from start to finish, Fred Disheroon, pointed out that by 2001, with interest and attorneys fees, the cost of the judgment had climbed to more than $25 million, so settling for $21 million seemed fair. Florida Rock didn't object—the company told stockholders the settlement resulted in a pretax gain of $18 million.

By the time of the *Florida Rock* settlement, Miami-Dade County was demanding the Corps deny the new mining permits. County officials said they were concerned about the potential impact to their Northwest Wellfield. The shelves the miners had proposed building around the edges of the quarries as mitigation were sure to attract wildlife—birds and cattle—that carry pathogens. "Quarry lakes have the potential to contain substantially more disease-causing organisms than groundwater," county officials warned. "Mining rock from the Biscayne aquifer in the vicinity of the wellfield decreases the time it takes for a contaminant to travel from the quarry lake to the wells."

Increased mining in the limestone there "will exacerbate the existing footprint of lakes in the vicinity of the wellfield," the county cautioned. As a result, it "has the potential to increase the risk of water quality contamination at the wellheads and result in the necessity for upgrading the water treatment plants to treat for disease-causing organisms at the cost of approximately $250,000,000."

At the very least, county officials said, the Corps should conduct a public hearing on the permits before making a decision. But Corps officials were so focused on negotiating with the miners that they didn't want to hear from the public. The Sierra Club's Barbara Lange, a South Florida stockbroker who had been a persistent critic of what she saw as a rush to approve environmentally damaging permits, got wind of one meeting between the Corps and the miners from a county official. When she showed up at the meeting to try to join in the talks, she was told the meeting was not open to the public. When Lange came back with her attorney, Paul Schweip, they were both kicked out.

Everglades National Park officials also urged the Corps to say no to the miners. They feared the new quarries would cause further diversions of the water flowing into the park's marshes. For a time, the EPA and the U.S. Fish and Wildlife Service were also objecting to the new permits—the EPA based on the potential contamination of the wellfield and the wildlife agency because the wetlands to be destroyed were habitat for the endangered wood stork.

In fact, biologists had documented one wood stork rookery about a mile from the proposed new mines. Despite the melaleuca infestation of the wetlands where the miners wanted to blast, in a single day 53 wood storks had been spotted feeding on apple snails at the site. As one wildlife agency staffer noted in an internal e-mail in 2000, "How could the destruction of so many thousands of acres of the remaining Everglades marshlands not impact the future of this already endangered species?"

But by late 2001 the wildlife service had signaled to the Corps that it would not pursue its objections any further, and soon the EPA did the same. With those hurdles out of the way, seven months after the *Florida Rock* settlement, in April 2002, Col. May approved the mining permits. That included signing off on the miners' mitigation plan, despite internal Corps misgivings that the penny-per-ton fee involved "a pretty large fudge factor."

The official 146-page decision, signed by May, Hall, Bob Barron, and project manager Diane Griffin, noted the county's concerns about wellfield contamination, but that's all. The permits required the miners to monitor water quality in the area without requiring them to do anything else until the Corps reviewed the permits again in three years. Meanwhile, May denied the county's request for a public hearing.

The Corps' decision documents specifically pointed to the court findings in the *Florida Rock* case as reason for saying yes to more mining despite the possibility of wellfield contamination: "While there is a possibility that adverse effects may occur . . . there may be a risk to the Government in denying landowners use of their property based upon such 'possibilities.'"

To May, the end result was a successful balancing of the public interest with private profits. Using the miners' money to rid the area of melaleuca instead of using it for more direct mitigation of the wetland losses suited him just fine.

"From a 404 perspective, that's a very good outcome," he told us.

A coalition of environmental groups—the Sierra Club, the Natural Resources Defense Council, and the National Parks Conservation Association—quickly filed suit, charging that the permit approval had been arbitrary and capricious, violating not only the Clean Water Act but several other federal laws.

Their lawsuit was assigned to a judge so thin and frail he needed help climbing up to his seat on the bench. He had had a hip replaced, undergone heart surgery, survived a massive stroke and the death of his beloved wife. Nevertheless, at age 79, Senior U.S. District Judge William Hoeveler still showed up for work five days a week, overseeing nearly 50 cases. When the stroke paralyzed his right arm, Hoeveler (pronounced HOOV-ler) taught himself to sign his opinions with his left hand, the letters looking crabbed and creaky but still legible.

In Judge Hoeveler's corner office on the ninth floor of the federal courthouse,

Figure 13. Senior U.S. District Court Judge William Hoeveler keeps a painting of an Everglades scene above his desk in the Miami Federal Courthouse. In 2006 he issued a scathing 186-page decision that excoriated the Corps for using "circular reasoning" in approving permits for limestone mining next to Everglades National Park. (Photograph by Bill Cooke, *St. Petersburg Times*.)

his two windows looked out across Miami's ever-boiling downtown hubbub. But on the wall behind his chair hung a painting of a placid Everglades scene by Florida artist Albert "Beanie" Backus.

And on his desk, near the Bible he read every day, Hoeveler kept a ceramic jug labeled "Humble Opinions." The jug contained all the appeals court rulings overturning his decisions since he was appointed to the bench by President Carter in 1977. It was less than half full.

Over the years Hoeveler had handled everything from the drug-smuggling trial of Panamanian general Manuel Noriega to litigation between the state and federal government over the pollution of the Everglades. Not only was he one of Florida's least-reversed judges, but the Miami-Dade Bar Association named its annual award for integrity after him.

Through the next four years, while the mining went full speed ahead under the new permits, Hoeveler heard arguments and read through the extensive evidence. Meanwhile county officials worked with the U.S. Geological Survey to gauge how vulnerable its Northwest Wellfield would be to *Cryptosporidium*, which had been detected in some nearby canals.

A year after the mining permits were approved, USGS scientists drilled a test well near the wellfield and injected red dye into the limestone. They expected traces of the dye to show up in the water supply in two to three days. Instead, four hours later, red water started streaming from the faucets and showerheads of suburban Miami. The edges of the Miami River were stained the color of blood. City officials went on TV to calm residents, reminding everyone the dye was harmless. Still, with the expansion of the mining quarries, it was a poor omen for the future safety of South Florida's water supply. As the USGS scientists drily reported, "Tracer tests indicate that the relative ease of contaminant movement to municipal supply wells is much greater than previously considered."

Sure enough, in January 2005, county officials detected unsafe levels of a cancer-causing chemical called benzene in one of the wells at the Northwest Wellfield. The chemical showed up about 60 feet below the surface. While investigating how it got there, the county shut down five of its wells. A year later a total of seven were shut down—nearly half. The mining companies said the benzene must have come from a gasoline spill, but the county investigation suggested it resulted from the emulsion used in the miners' blasting. The miners, while still not accepting the blame, changed the formula for their emulsion.

Finally, in March 2006, Hoeveler produced a 186-page ruling on the Lake Belt permits. On page after page, he tore into the Corps, the Fish and Wildlife Service, and the mining companies like the Reverend Cotton Mather ripping into a bunch of New England sinners.

Hoeveler found that Corps officials acted from the start as if the mining permits would be approved and treated the application process as a series of negotiations rather than a regulatory action that could have produced a denial. That "sense of inevitability," he wrote, resulted in the Corps bending the rules to give the miners preference over the public interest.

For instance, in defining the project's purpose, the Corps determined that the mining had to take place on the miners' wetlands in the Lake Belt and therefore must be considered water dependent—a ludicrous claim, the judge wrote.

"To permit such circular reasoning would eviscerate the regulatory protections such that any activity, no matter how destructive—and it is difficult to conceive of something more destructive to wetlands than their complete removal by excavating down to 80 feet and leaving a hole in their place—could be justified on wetlands as long as that is where the applicant owned property," Hoeveler wrote.

Over in Lee County, the Corps had taken the opposite stance, classifying a mining application by Florida Rock as not water dependent, Hoeveler pointed out. How could an activity that was classified by the Corps as not water dependent on one side of the state be classified as water dependent on the other side?

"Common sense dictates that if mining (in wetlands) is not inherently water dependent in one situation, it is not inherently water dependent in another," he wrote.

If mining is not water dependent, then the Corps should have looked at less damaging alternatives. But when he looked through the Corps' records for some analysis of such alternatives, Hoeveler wrote, he found only one. The alternatives report was done by Paul Larsen, the miners' own consultant, and the judge said it was laced with suppositions and unsupported statements.

In fact, Hoeveler noted, there were ample alternative sources of limestone: some elsewhere in Florida, some in other states, some in other countries. But because the miners' own consultant pooh-poohed those possibilities, the Corps never bothered to consider them, Hoeveler said.

He found that the Fish and Wildlife Service shirked its duties just as much as the Corps did. Instead of preparing a formal assessment of the impact the mining would have on wood storks, Hoeveler wrote, the Corps and the wildlife agency both relied on a report prepared by a Tampa company called Biological Research Associates, which was working for the miners. That report contended the mining wouldn't affect wood storks at all because, as habitat, the wetlands had already been compromised by melaleuca infestation, a conclusion Hoeveler labeled "patently absurd" because the wood storks still used the melaleuca-infested wetlands. Even sillier, he pointed out, was the Corps' claim that the mining would actually be good for wood storks. The miners' mitigation plan to pay to remove melaleuca from the Pennsuco wetlands, the Corps contended, would make the area more hospitable to the endangered wading birds—even though they would be losing all that other habitat to the mining.

The thing that really bugged Hoeveler, though, was the Corps' cavalier attitude toward the risk to the county's wellfield. While Corps officials could not have foreseen the dramatic results of the dye test, he wrote, they certainly could have done more to deal with the concerns the county had been voicing for years. Instead, the Corps approved the permits before the county could complete its own studies and without the Corps' conducting any studies of its own. He also did not like how the Corps shut out the public, denying the county's request for a public hearing.

The bottom line, Hoeveler said, was that the Corps officials were too afraid to do their jobs. The Corps "gave too much weight to the pressure from the state legislature not to lose a mitigation funding mechanism. They also were swayed by the momentum of decades of mining having taken place in the area—despite the obvious destruction of wetlands that it had caused, as well as the menacing threat of takings litigation being raised very effectively by the permit applicants."

The judge found "a multitude of defects evidenced in the issuance of these permits," which, taken together, constituted "a maze of human failures" that thwarted the protection of the environment:

> The Court cannot ignore the dangers presented by this case. The Corps' apparent disregard for those seeking answers to questions—including the Corps' failure to grant, or even to respond timely, to the request for a public hearing submitted by the Miami-Dade County Manager on behalf of the County Commission—is another item which, in connection with the maze of irregularities referred to, is additional impetus for my conclusion that the permits should not have been issued on this record.

In effect, Hoeveler canceled the permits and told both the Corps and the wildlife service to start over at square one by reevaluating everything about the proposed permits. But while the two federal agencies started going over the permit applications a second time, the mining didn't stop. The miners faced off in court against the environmental groups' attorneys to argue to Hoeveler that they had to keep going, permits or no.

While waiting for Hoeveler's final ruling, the miners lined up some powerful allies, including the Florida Chamber of Commerce. With the chamber and other groups, the miners launched a Web site called "Keep Florida Rockin" to spread the word of dire consequences should they be shut down: "A shutdown of so-called Lake Belt mining would cripple the state's ongoing efforts to keep Florida moving, and would risk bringing Florida's booming economy to a screeching halt." Visitors to the site could buy "Keep Florida Rockin" coffee mugs and T-shirts emblazoned with the slogan, "A Mine Is a Terrible Thing to Waste."

The state DOT jumped in, too, filing an analysis with the court that said a shutdown of the Lake Belt mines "will have an immediate, drastic and long-lasting impact on the state highway system." About $1.7 billion in road projects would be delayed in most of Florida, the DOT warned, including a "100 percent interruption" of work in Miami-Dade, Broward, Palm Beach, Monroe, Indian River, and St. Lucie counties

In July 2007, Hoeveler lowered the boom again, ordering a halt to mining in three quarries near the Northwest Wellfield, citing "grave concerns" about contamination risks. By then, though, the Corps had produced the environmental impact study that he had called for in his earlier ruling. The analysis included seven alternatives, only one of which called for limiting mining. Among the other six were plans to allow the major expansion of mining that the companies had originally sought.

Two months later, the Corps finally held a public hearing, and it was packed with what the *Miami Herald* described as a string of speakers ranging from high-priced corporate executives to "hundreds of sign-waving quarry workers, dozens of representatives from trucking, rail and contracting companies, even horn-blowing cement trucks."

The environmental activists who opposed mining were relegated to the end of the lengthy speakers' list, the *Herald* noted. The fans of mining, without exception, all "warned of lost jobs, canceled projects, skyrocketing construction costs and a multibillion-dollar loss" if the Corps were to find that blasting the Lake Belt's wetlands was not in the public interest.

Actually, though, it turned out the mining companies had some backup plans that didn't involve an economic apocalypse.

Hoeveler's ruling had forced them to consider some alternatives. Florida Rock Industries said in filings with the Securities and Exchange Commission, for example, that it was working on a partnership for rock production on 4,300 acres near Brooksville, north of Tampa. It also doubled its capacity at its mine in Newberry, near Gainesville. And Rinker officials conceded that its future wasn't confined to South Florida either. It operates in 29 states and has about 90 rock quarries in the U.S. alone from which it can get rock should its sources in the Lake Belt wetlands dry up. (Rinker also applied for permits to mine for rock on 3,000 acres of sugar-growing land in Palm Beach County. Because the site lies immediately west of the Arthur R. Marshall Loxahatchee National Wildlife Refuge, it has sparked a new round of controversy over the environmental impact of rock mining in the Everglades.)

The legal tussle over mining in the Lake Belt has yet to be resolved. In November 2007, a federal appeals court heard oral arguments on whether to overturn Hoeveler's decision. As of March 2008, the court still had not announced a ruling.

Still, the case made one thing crystal clear. Had the EPA or the wildlife service stuck to their objections against the Lake Belt mines, the Everglades and its wood storks might have been spared widespread destruction. But the agencies that Congress intended to act as watchdogs on the Corps have become all bark and no bite—and lately even the barking has quieted down.

12

Let Sleeping Watchdogs Lie

Ask Carol Browner what it was like growing up in Miami, and she'll tell you: "The Everglades were my back yard." She likes to reminisce about spending her childhood's summer evenings gazing toward the horizon, "marveling at the towering clouds off in the distance, which we called Florida's mountains."

Browner is a dark-haired woman with fierce intelligence and keen political instincts. She speaks with the polish of an accomplished attorney, although she has not made a career in the courtroom. Instead, after earning her law degree, she worked as a congressional staffer—first for the legendary "He-Coon," U.S. Senator Lawton Chiles, then for an up-and-coming Tennessee senator named Al Gore. Then she parlayed that experience into a job heading up Florida's Department of Environmental Regulation. In 1992, when she was 37 years old, her stint working for Gore led to appointment as head of the EPA for the Clinton Administration.

At the time, a *Wall Street Journal* editorial called her the "most troubling Clinton pick," because she "invariably plumps for the most extreme regulatory approach." One reason the *Journal* disliked her so much: while she was head of Florida's DER, Browner had openly opposed the Bush Administration's attempt to loosen the rules on wetlands protection. The effort to change the wetlands definition was officially dropped by the Corps and EPA on the same day the Senate confirmed her appointment as the nation's top environmental regulator.

Browner served as EPA administrator for eight years, longer than anyone else who has held the job. During Browner's term as the head of the EPA from 1993 to 2001, development boomed in Florida, wiping out thousands of acres of wetlands thanks to 404 permits approved by the Corps. One of the areas hardest hit was the western side of the Everglades, where the Corps cranked out permits allowing the destruction of some 4,000 acres of swamps and marshes, even as it drew up plans to spend billions of dollars repairing the damage done by man to the eastern side of the River of Grass.

"Haven't we learned our lesson?" the top EPA official in Florida, Richard Harvey, wrote in an e-mail to John Hall. "Apparently not."

During her eight-year tenure, Browner told us, she often "struggled with the Corps" over those 404 permits. She believes the Corps should issue more denials, explaining, "Permits shouldn't always be about yes. Sometimes they should be about no." If a developer cannot minimize the impact on wetlands, she said, "they should say no."

She is well aware of the perils of relying on mitigation—after all, it was while she ran Florida's DER that Ann Redmond produced her stunning report on the failure of so many state-approved mitigation projects.

"If you destroy too many wetlands you can't just make new ones," Browner said. "It takes nature to create one, over millions of years."

In fact, Browner told us, "if I had my way we'd stop all wetland development and find a way to put all wetlands into public ownership. We should think of wetlands as a public resource."

Throughout the 1990s, Browner had the power to stop the destruction of wetlands by vetoing 404 permits issued by the Corps. But she did not use that veto power even once—not in the Everglades, not in Florida, not anywhere in the country. When we asked her why, her usually smooth and polished delivery faltered.

"You have a real failure in the system when you have a veto," she explained. "We certainly threatened vetoes."

But somehow, she said, the EPA always found a way to work things out with the Corps, negotiating a compromise that allowed the 404 permit to be approved and the wetlands to be destroyed.

In 1972, when Congress passed the original version of what later became known as the Clean Water Act, the EPA was responsible for implementing everything in it except for the part about dredge-and-fill permits in Section 404. That was left to the Corps, but with the EPA looking over its shoulder. In his comments in the Congressional Record, Senator Muskie made it plain that the EPA was supposed to hold the Corps accountable. Muskie thought the EPA would watch out for the environment even when the Corps did not.

But in the 35 years between 1972 and 2007, the EPA has used its veto power only 11 times. The last time the agency wielded the veto was in 1989, during the first Bush Administration. The last man to employ the veto was then EPA administrator William K. Reilly.

"It's a very big deal to use the veto," Reilly told us. "People do everything to avoid it. . . . It's a lightning bolt."

But the veto has gone unused for so long that this lightning bolt has lost all its juice. As a result, the EPA no longer has much influence over the Corps' permitting decisions.

"The Corps knows that we're kind of a paper tiger," said Harvey of the EPA's South Florida office. The 404 permitting program is "absolutely the worst program I've ever dealt with. I'd rather deal with raw shit."

There was a time when the EPA wasn't afraid to use its veto, a time when it stood up for wetlands and challenged the Corps. The first time the EPA did that was in Florida, and it involved one of the strangest dredge-and-fill projects ever attempted—as well as one of the oddest outcomes.

∞

In 1951, the Florida legislature created the Inter-American Center Authority—Interama for short—to plan, build, and operate the Inter-American Cultural and Trade Center in Miami. The center was touted as a "permanent international exposition providing cultural, educational, and trade activities." It was supposed to combine the features of an amusement park, a world's fair, and a trade fair, all with an eye toward attracting Latin American business to Florida.

Throughout the 1960s, Interama was a top priority of Governor Farris Bryant, U.S. senators George A. Smathers and Spessard L. Holland, and U.S. representatives Claude Pepper and Dante Fascell. They even roped President Lyndon Johnson into supporting it.

"I think this is not only going to be a wonderful thing for the United States Government, and all the Western Hemisphere, but I think it will be a great thing for the progressive and forward-looking State of Florida. For some of you, it is a dream that has come true," Johnson said on a visit to Miami in 1964.

Interama bought 1,700 acres of mangrove-covered coastline in the city of North Miami where the Oleta River flows into Biscayne Bay. On this slice of prime waterfront real estate, the authority promised to build a 1,000-foot Tower of the Sun topped with restaurants and an observation platform. Interama promised a whole lot more, too: a marine amphitheater with a floating stage and seating for 12,000, a symphony hall, an opera, a ballet, an art gallery, an international bazaar full of working artisans.

It was all supposed to be ready to open by 1965. Or maybe 1968. Or maybe in time for the nation's bicentennial in 1976. The deadline kept changing, yet the money kept flowing.

When critics of the project mocked the idea of building something so important in a swamp, Senator Holland snapped, "I say to you clearly . . . that the mangrove swamp referred to is the same kind of terrain upon which most of what is now Miami Beach and other important developments of the Gold Coast were created."

But there was a big difference between Carl Fisher's glittering Miami Beach and what was going on at the Interama site, and the difference was in the fill being put in the wetlands. Instead of dirt, Interama was dumping construction debris and municipal garbage in its mangroves. And that was about all it was doing with the site. For more than a decade, Interama officials spent millions of dollars on architects and publicity and travel to various Latin American countries, yet nothing was built except big mounds of garbage.

In the early 1970s, among the authority's big expenses was the $160,000 in annual rent it paid for spacious offices in Miami Lakes in a building owned by the family of state senator Bob Graham, who as late as 1974 was still trying to prop Interama up with taxpayer dollars. Its bonds were handled by the law firm of former Governor Bryant. The authority's chairman, Elton Gissendanner—who a decade later, as head of the state's natural resources department, went to prison for taking a $100,000 bribe to help a drug smuggler caught by the Florida Marine Patrol—collected the then princely sum of $25,000 a year for his work, even though the law said board members weren't supposed to be paid.

Eventually, though, the Interama money machine began to sputter. Latin American countries that were supposed to invest in it didn't. Federal funding came with strings attached that meant the authority couldn't begin using it until construction started. Attempts to borrow large sums of money to start construction failed because no bond buyer trusted Interama to pay its debts.

Still, in 1970, authority officials persuaded the city of North Miami to lend the project $12 million and, as collateral, offered the city the title to 350 acres of its land. Not long after, though, Interama went under, having blown millions of taxpayer dollars and built nothing grander than a dump. Some of the Interama land became Florida International University, and some became Oleta River State Park. The part with the dump now belonged to North Miami.

Trying to recoup its lost millions, North Miami leased 291 acres of its Interama land to another company with big plans to put the city on the map.

Munisport Inc. said it would build a major recreational facility on the site, complete with tennis courts, an 18-hole golf course, and a clubhouse with a view of Biscayne Bay.

To create the rolling contours of a golf course, Munisport officials told the Corps that 103 acres of mangrove wetlands would have to be filled. They promised to preserve eight acres of mangroves and create three shallow tidal pools. For South Florida, it seemed like a routine project, so in 1976 the Corps approved their 404 permit.

But Munisport turned out to be in the same business as Interama, offering pie-in-the-sky promises and creating nothing but big heaps of trash. Although the permit hadn't mentioned anything unusual about the fill, Munisport started using garbage to fill in the wetlands and collecting money for it, just as Interama had.

By now the piles of garbage were 40 feet high. To cover the garbage with layers of limestone, Munisport dug out 35-foot-deep borrow pits that quickly filled with water.

Around the time the Corps approved the Munisport 404 permit, Miami-Dade County officials on a routine inspection of the site discovered a dozen 55-gallon drums labeled as acetone, ethyl cyanoacetate, and tricresyl phosphate—and they were leaking. A city crew came and hauled them away, though rumors circulated that they simply reburied the drums elsewhere on the site. It wouldn't be the last time hazardous waste wound up at Munisport. A subsequent inspection turned up medical waste, including human biopsies.

In 1977 Munisport applied for a modification of its 404 permit. The company wanted to dig up the eight acres of the preserved mangroves and also those pools. And for the first time, its paperwork said the fill would be municipal garbage and the site would operate as a landfill.

Corps officials were not thrilled with their options: either deny the permit and force North Miami officials to somehow clean up the dump or avoid a messy and expensive cleanup by approving the continued use of garbage as wetland fill.

The EPA office in Atlanta immediately registered its opposition to what Munisport had proposed.

"We didn't like it," recalled Howard Marshall, the EPA employee in Atlanta who was in charge of reviewing 404 permits in South Florida. EPA officials were convinced that approving Munisport's permit would set a dangerous precedent for wetlands across the country, he explained. But "that led to a damn set-to between us and the Corps of Engineers in Jacksonville. Their position was 'garbage is fill material.'"

So Marshall flew to Miami and met at the Munisport site with the colonel then in charge in Jacksonville, James W. R. Adams. The colonel was a slender West Point grad with a receding hairline. Although he was Don Wisdom's successor, Adams was "not an environmental missionary in the Wisdom mold" according to an official history of the Jacksonville office of the Corps. Nevertheless, during his tenure the Jacksonville office led the Corps in wetland permit denials, rejecting applications from South Florida rock miners and even Disney World.

Still, in this case Adams was leaning toward approving the permit, just to avoid requiring a cleanup that he believed might cause even greater water pollution risks than continued burial of municipal trash.

Adams had a longtime sideline teaching other Corps personnel about how to deal with stress. Now here came Marshall, an EPA bureaucrat bucking the Corps' permitting decisions and causing Col. Adams some serious stress.

"I was sitting in the operations trailer at Munisport, Col. Adams was there, maybe one other person with me and he had someone with him, and he said, 'we're going to issue,'" Marshall recalled. "I said, 'Colonel, you probably don't want to hear this but if you do that, we're going to invoke our authority under 404(c) and veto it.' He snarled and said, 'Y'all ain't got the balls to do it.'"

Adams was wrong.

The EPA spent a quarter of a million dollars taking water samples around the Munisport site, checking to see if the garbage already buried there had resulted in toxic contamination. While an analysis of the samples turned up quite a wide array of dangerous chemicals, only one registered at levels above the legal limit: ammonia.

Marshall noted that ammonia could eat through the limestone that was supposed to contain any toxic chemicals and prevent their leaching from the garbage into the Oleta River and Biscayne Bay. But the young engineer who had designed the Munisport landfill swore that would not happen.

At this point, the EPA got help from two crucial allies. One was a woman who worked for Miami-Dade County's Department of Environmental Resource Management. Every week she went to the Munisport site and stood at the base of the mounds of garbage to take samples and scan for any leaks.

"You could be down in one of those lakes and look up and it was like looking up at a damn cliff," Marshall recalled. The county employee kept going out to take water samples, day after day after day. Finally, she called Marshall to report she had looked up at one of the hills and spotted a trickle of liquid. An analysis of the sample found it was very high in ammonia.

That's when the EPA turned to its other ally, the U.S. Air Force. Marshall asked Air Force officials to shoot a series of aerial photos of the Munisport site, beginning at treetop level and then continuing at intervals up to 5,000 feet. He told them the EPA wanted both color and infrared photos, and then he asked that the Air Force put its expert analysts to work reviewing the results to see if they could spot more leaks.

After the review, Marshall said, "they called us and said, 'We can see the ripples on the water as it flows down these things. It looks like a mountain stream.' There was like 40 of them."

At that point, Marshall wrote up all the findings and on June 25, 1980, officially notified the Corps that the EPA was launching its first-ever veto of a 404 permit. As soon as Col. Adams heard the news, he called the Atlanta EPA office "and cussed me," Marshall said.

A month later, though, Munisport stopped accepting garbage, and the city of North Miami soon filed suit against the company to try to find out what had happened to $10 million the company had collected for running the dump.

The next step was an October 1980 public hearing in North Miami. About 20 people from EPA showed up and spent hours detailing exactly what was wrong with the Munisport project. By the time they finished showing their photos and water samples, the clock had struck midnight. Then it was Munisport's turn, but there wasn't much to be said.

According to Marshall, the engineer who had designed the project stood up to say that he had followed what the law and standard industry practice required. Then he added a personal note: "'All I can say is, my mother wanted me to be an engineer. I must've picked the wrong profession.' And then he started to cry and he sat down," Marshall recalled.

Around Thanksgiving, the head of the Atlanta office of the EPA, a woman named Rebecca Hanmer, sent a seven-page recommendation for the veto to headquarters in Washington. Two decades later, the idea of using garbage for wetlands fill seems like "a foolish mistake," she told us. But at the time she treated it as if were as serious as a ticking nuclear warhead that needed to be defused, laying out a carefully reasoned explanation for why the permit needed to be vetoed.

The warhead that was Munisport would keep ticking for a while. Reagan had beaten Carter in the presidential race, and in the turmoil of regime change the Munisport denial sat on someone's desk for several months, Marshall said. On January 19, 1981, the day before Reagan was inaugurated, outgoing EPA administrator Doug Costle signed the final order.

"That was how it got signed, by damn perseverance and happenstance," Marshall said, chuckling.

The EPA didn't stop there, though. In 1983 the agency put Munisport on the national list of sites so contaminated by pollution that they needed help from the federal Superfund. Instead of being a big boon to North Miami, said former mayor Howard Neu, Munisport turned into catastrophic mess.

"It ended up costing the taxpayers a lot of money," Neu told us. "Property taxes went up."

In 1990, while city officials quarreled with Munisport and its contractors about who was responsible for cleaning up the mess, the garbage caught fire underground, sending billows of heavy, black smoke into a nearby mobile home park.

Nevertheless, in 1997, despite complaints from environmental groups and mobile home park residents, the EPA dropped the Munisport dump off its Superfund list, declaring it no longer a hazard to human health. In 2002, North Miami cut a deal with a developer to build condominiums there. Despite the site's checkered past, the developer said he didn't see it as much of a challenge to build something marketable. The Tropical Audubon Society tried to stop the condo project because of continuing concerns about the toxic waste, but failed.

"It was an unregulated dump for a long time," said Cynthia Guerra, executive director of the Tropical Audubon Society in Miami, who failed to halt the construction of the condos atop the Munisport landfill. "Nobody knows what was getting dumped there. . . . There's just been a boatload of bad decisions made along the way."

The Munisport veto marked the last time a Democratic administration vetoed anything. Remarkably, for all the Reagan Administration's antiregulation rhetoric, it was the Reagan-era EPA that issued the most vetoes—most of them in the Southeast and thus signed by Rebecca Hanmer. Marshall explained that the burgeoning scandals in the EPA during Reagan's first term resulted in the firing or jailing of all the appointees who had been ideologically opposed to wetland regulations, and thus in the second term the segments of EPA's professional bureaucracy that had survived enjoyed more of a free hand. The Southeastern EPA offices, because they operated farther from the media spotlight than the agency's Northern branches, took advantage of that freedom to exercise their veto power to an unprecedented degree, he said.

Beginning in 1984, EPA vetoes killed a recycling plant permit in Alabama, an aquaculture impoundment in South Carolina, a flood control project in Louisiana, and dams in Georgia and Virginia. There were a couple of Northern vetoes too, most notably the one that killed a 404 permit for a shopping mall in Attleboro, Massachusetts. The Attleboro veto led to a court fight that validated the EPA's veto authority and indirectly to the creation of the no net loss policy.

Reagan's EPA even vetoed a second 404 permit in the Miami area, earning Florida the dubious distinction of being the only state where the EPA vetoed more than one permit.

The second Florida veto concerned three permits for wetlands destruction in an area of Miami-Dade County where the surface contains a layer of limestone dotted with wetlands. Farmers who want to grow crops there must drag a plow-like implement across their property, over and over, to break up the rock and crush it. Then they slide the broken rock over to the wetlands to fill in the holes in their land, a process that usually obliterates any wetland plants growing there. Because rockplowing deposits the rock in the wetlands, killing the plants growing there and effectively snuffing out the marsh, the Corps requires the farmers to get 404 permits.

In 1987, families and corporations that owned land requiring rockplowing before farming could take place sought a trio of 404 permits from the Corps. All told, about 432 acres of wetlands just outside Everglades National Park would be wiped out. The EPA staff in Atlanta objected to all three. They contended that losing a total of 432 acres of wetlands would result in too great an impact on the area's natural resources, especially on the declining population of wading birds and Florida panthers. And they pointed out that the eastern Everglades had already lost thousands of acres of prairie wetlands, which had caused severe problems for wildlife. But the Corps issued the permits anyway.

The final decision to veto the rockplowing permits was signed in June 1988 in Washington by Hanmer, recently promoted to acting assistant EPA administrator. Not only would wildlife habitat be destroyed, she noted, but the cumulative impact of past wetlands destruction in the area meant that it had reached a point where no further degradation could be allowed.

"It is also contrary to ongoing efforts to improve and restore the Everglades' ecological functions which include support of a rich and diverse wildlife population," Hanmer wrote.

In other words, the impact on the environment trumped the private property rights of the farmers—a decision at odds with the most dearly held beliefs of the Reagan Revolution and certainly at odds with the claims court decisions being made at that time regarding the *Florida Rock* case.

∿

The last time the EPA vetoed a 404 permit was halfway through the first Bush Administration. Reilly used the veto to kill a controversial dam project in Colorado in November 1990. Before he took that drastic step, he recalled, he asked a friendly senator, "If I make a controversial use of 404, will it put the whole program at risk?"

The senator told him that if he planned to veto something big to wait until Congress was out of town. "So I did it on Good Friday," Reilly recalled.

Even so, a huge political firestorm erupted. Reilly became the target of blistering criticism from his own party, led by Vice President Quayle and National Republican Party Chairman Lee Atwater. Even the president's son, Colorado savings and loan executive Neil Bush, jumped on Reilly for blocking the dam. Reilly survived, but the uproar showed the political risks of vetoing a permit.

"You spend capital on a veto," Reilly explained. "You've decided the Corps of Engineers is wrong and you're second-guessing them." And there's always a fear that the subsequent controversy will lead Congress to shut down the whole 404 permitting program or take away EPA's veto power, he said, adding, "Nobody likes that veto authority in Congress."

Besides, it's always easier to find a way to give in and say yes, Reilly said. Politicians all say they love the environment, he said, but when presented with a specific development that might harm wetlands, "they show you a bunch of pretty pictures, and people find a way to think it's not the worst thing in the world."

For the remaining two years of his tenure, Reilly issued no more vetoes. Still, because Reilly's EPA had shown a willingness to use the veto, even the threat of one could change the course of a project. That's what happened with a Miami development called Old Cutler Bay Estates.

In July 1987, a developer named Raul Planas, doing business as Old Cutler Bay Associates, asked the Corps for a permit to destroy 197 acres of wetlands adjacent to Biscayne National Park. He wanted to build a 428-home subdivision featuring a championship golf course designed by Jack Nicklaus.

Reilly joked that "there is something irresistible about a wetland to a golf course developer: it's flat, it's cheap, and it typically has good views of the water." But under Reilly the EPA constantly fought against allowing golf courses to be built atop wetlands—to the point that, according to Reilly, a golf magazine "listed the 25 most important people in the world of golf and I was ranked fourteenth. I don't play golf. My ranking was said to be attributed to the fact that I had personally intervened to block the location of more new golf courses in the United States than anyone else."

Planas told the Corps there was no way he could avoid destroying some mangroves for his new subdivision and golf course. The official project purpose, included in the Corps' official "statement of findings," said so: "to construct an upscale residential/(Jack Nicklaus) designed championship golf course community in South Dade County. The project's basic purpose is to realize a reasonable profit by providing luxury country club type housing to an affluent segment of the Miami area population." It was a classic case of tailoring the purpose so tightly that no alternative site could fit the requirements.

"They said we can have a Jack Nicklaus course or a championship course, but if we're going to have both it's got to be built on this site," said David White, an attorney who represented the National Wildlife Federation in battling the project.

While the Corps reviewed Old Cutler Bay's permit, a team of biologists from the EPA and the Corps inspected the site and flagged a line between the viable, productive wetlands on the east side of the property and some degraded wetlands infested with Brazilian pepper trees on the west. The EPA's position was that any plans by Planas to destroy wetlands on the east side of the line would be unacceptable. Planas revised his plans repeatedly, eventually reducing the wetland impact to just 11.5 acres east of the line—or so he said.

Among the people looking over all the Old Cutler Bay maps and aerial photos was a former mining engineer named Karsten Rist, a German immigrant with a thick accent who owned a plastics manufacturing firm. Rist was an avid member of the Tropical Audubon Society, and he took a strong personal interest in what happened around Biscayne Bay.

"As I studied the maps and aerial photographs it appeared to me that there was a significant discrepancy between the remaining area east of the development line as seen by the EPA and the same area as seen on our own maps," Rist recalled.

With the help of another Audubon Society member, Rist trespassed on the Old Cutler Bay site with a measuring tape and checked the lay of the land. "Our measurement showed that the developer's map, produced by Post, Buckley, Schuh and Jernigan, the largest and most prestigious engineering firm in Dade County, misrepresented the location of the development line by 100 to 150 feet," Rist said. "We shared our discovery immediately with the EPA, the Corps, and the *Miami Herald*."

Nevertheless, the Corps announced it was going to issue the permit. So the EPA and two other federal agencies appealed the decision up the line to the top general in charge of the Corps in Washington, D.C., a process known as "elevation."

Maj. Gen. Patrick Kelly reviewed their complaints and in September 1990 agreed that "the definition of project purpose utilized in the analysis of alternatives was too specific to the applicant's proposal and may have inappropriately limited the analysis, especially of potential on-site alternative configurations of the project." The Corps rewrote its decision papers and again announced it would issue the permit.

So on December 3, 1990, the EPA notified the Corps that it would veto the permit for Old Cutler Bay Estates. It was an easy call, Reilly said.

"I was horrified by the thought of taking that many more mangroves in Biscayne Bay," Reilly told us. "The lawyer for the developer said I needed to realize that this was the way things were done in Florida, they had always been done this way. And I issued a public statement that said, 'Yes, and it was once lawful to eat horsemeat.'"

Less than two weeks after the EPA launched veto proceedings, Planas produced a new development plan showing zero impact on wetlands east of the development line. The EPA dropped its objections and the Corps issued the permit on New Year's Eve 1990.

It was, Rist said, "a great victory for Audubon and wetland protection." But for Planas, the delay and bad publicity proved to be a disaster. Old Cutler Bay Development Associates went under in May 1992 without building anything on its site. Environmental groups had suspected that all the development plans and grand promises of wetland mitigation were built on speculation and shaky loans. The threat of the veto slowed down the project's progress sufficiently to expose the truth, White said.

"We got the EPA to initiate a veto action, and the whole thing came down like a house of cards," White said. "They didn't have the wherewithal to do everything they were promising to do."

While that might have been good for the environment, it wasn't for Reilly. "I lost some friends," Reilly said, explaining, "Republicans play golf."

That was the last time the EPA invoked its authority under Section 404(c) to initiate a veto in Florida.

ᖇ

When Bill Clinton took over the White House for eight years, putting Carol Browner in charge of the EPA, her regional EPA administrator in Atlanta was a man named John Henry Hankinson Jr. Like Browner, Hankinson was a lawyer who had been a Florida environmental official. A heavyset man with a folksy manner and a thick mop of hair, Hankinson had worked for the St. Johns River Water Management District—buying environmentally sensitive land, not enforcing regulations—before Browner named him to the run the EPA in the Southeast.

Hankinson threatened some vetoes in Florida, including one over the permit for the state DOT's plans to widen the 18-Mile Stretch in the Keys. But he never went beyond threatening. After he left office, he told us he regretted not having vetoed some of the things that were built on his watch. He said it was easy to be lulled into a sense that everything is negotiable and the goal is to get to yes.

"As long as the [EPA] wetland guys were talking to the Corps guys, there was a strong presumption that we would work through all of the issues," Hankinson said. "The process is set up to discourage you from getting to the point of saying the hell with it, I'm vetoing this thing. . . . A veto is a strong declaration that everything has broken down in this process."

The pressure to say yes comes from the top, said Haynes Johnson, who retired from the Atlanta EPA office in late 2006. "I would say there are certain people in Washington who want to avoid any sort of a confrontation. They'll tell you, 'Oh it'll create bad press for the EPA! If you elevate this, it's the end of the program! Congress will do away with 404!' They'll give you any excuse."

Johnson compared the EPA to Deputy Barney Fife on the *Andy Griffith Show*, toting an unloaded gun while carrying a single bullet in his shirt pocket. Every time a 404 permit came up that deserved a veto, he said, the EPA staff held off, arguing that they needed to save the veto for something really bad. And so the bullet forever remained in the deputy's pocket, unused.

Although Hankinson failed to veto anything during his tenure in Atlanta, he was sufficiently concerned about the loss of wetlands in the western Everglades that he approved hiring someone to review 404 permits for just Lee and Collier counties, where figures showed the Corps was issuing more permits than in the rest of the Southeast combined.

Hankinson's new hire was a state water quality expert named Bruce Boler, a Pensacola native in his 50s who had taught school before getting a bachelor's degree in biology and a master's in ecology. Despite spending years working for the state reviewing water pollution problems, Boler still had the tone and manner of a persnickety English teacher, a stickler for following rules that everyone else blithely ignores.

Hankinson told Boler he should "get tougher on Southwest Florida." Boler took that instruction to heart.

In his first year he reviewed permits that proposed wiping out more than 2,500 acres of wetlands, and he questioned nearly every large development project that came through the new Fort Myers EPA office. He took great pains to challenge developers' assertions that wiping out wetlands would do no harm to water quality. He frequently questioned why the Corps did so little to slow the loss of wetlands and even prepared an eight-page memo for his bosses blasting the Corps for failing to follow its own rules on water dependency and alternatives analysis.

"I had the biggest fights with the Corps and the developers over avoidance," Boler recalled. "I was writing letters left and right, and the Corps was just rubber-stamping everything. I said: 'Where's the alternatives?' They looked at me like I was crazy."

But the regulations "clearly state the least environmentally damaging alternative must be chosen," Boler pointed out. "If it's not water dependent then there's an assumption that there is an alternative. Then we get these applications for projects on 1,500 acres of wetlands. . . . It didn't matter how sensitive a site they chose, the Corps wasn't going to say no."

Boler ruffled a lot of feathers. Developers and state officials complained about him to EPA higher-ups. Well-connected Washington lobbyists complained too. So did Corps officials, particularly Hall, who labeled him "a loose cannon."

Red-headed civic activist Ann Hauck was convinced Boler was on the right track and said so to Hall. Hall snapped back that if the Corps were to follow Boler in Southwest Florida, then the result would be inconsistent with the rest of the state—and to him, consistency mattered above all other considerations.

"Bruce Boler I am sure is well intentioned but he doesn't know 404 very well," Hall told Hauck via e-mail. "Richard [Harvey] is the same. And so we get these really weird comments/recommendations we don't know what to do with. We CAN use our program to help rectify water quality in basins with impaired waters but we need to do it systematically across the state, and the state and the regulated public need to at least know what we are doing and why. . . . I don't want the Corps to be caught in a squeeze between the EPA and the state."

The job of EPA regional administrator is a political plum, not protected by civil service. After George W. Bush became president in January 2001, Hankinson was replaced as EPA regional administrator by a more conservative bureaucrat named Jimmy Palmer. Palmer, a short, pudgy man with thick eyebrows, holds degrees in both law and engineering. As the former head of Mississippi's environmental protection agency, Palmer believed strongly in deferring to the states on regulatory matters, no matter what the Clean Water Act said about EPA's watchdog role.

"He told us when he came on that if the state wants something, then he doesn't want us to object to it," Boler said. "He wanted us to include in our briefing papers whether the state objected or not. I said, 'Well the state never objects to any project down here!'"

Palmer denied ever issuing a blanket policy that said any project with state blessing would get the EPA's approval too. Still, he told us, "It's not appropriate for the federal government to run roughshod over decisions by the states. . . . If the EPA or the Corps or some other agency chooses to disagree with the state's call, then the burden is on the federal government to articulate why."

When we asked Palmer to name some circumstance where the EPA would be justified in vetoing a permit for a project that had won state approval, he couldn't think of one.

With Palmer in power, Boler said, his recommendations to the Atlanta office for opposing 404 permits were frequently ignored or rejected. For instance, he objected to a permit for a project with the ironic name Winding Cypress that called for building 2,300 homes and a golf course in Collier County, wiping out nearly 200 acres of wetlands. But Palmer and his deputies in Atlanta overruled his objections.

Frustrated, Boler left the EPA in 2003 for a job with the National Park Service working to restore the eastern Everglades. The Southwest Florida office he had opened soon closed.

The decline and fall of the once mighty EPA continued. In 2005, a group of EPA officials, including Haynes Johnson and Richard Harvey, traveled to Jacksonville to talk to the Corps about problems with the way the 404 program was operating. They intended it to be a tough-love meeting to straighten out the Corps, Harvey said.

Leading the delegation was the head of the EPA's wetlands program in Atlanta, Jim Giattina. Before they finished their first cup of coffee, Harvey said, their leader blurted out to the Corps officials that the EPA did not intend to elevate any 404 permit ever again. The Corps officials, Johnson said, "looked suitably thrilled."

But the other EPA employees "looked at each other like: 'Why the fuck did we even show up here?'" Harvey said. "It was like well, we're going into battle, and then the general is telling the enemy, 'Hey, we're shooting blanks!'"

Soon the regional office would have no choice in the matter, anyway. On October 30, 2006—the day before Halloween—EPA Assistant Administrator Benjamin Grumbles sent out a memo to all regional offices telling them they no longer could make decisions about blocking permits. Instead, those decisions would be made in Washington in order to "ensure consistency with national program regulations, policies and goals," Grumbles wrote.

"My understanding is that pretty much Washington dictates that they're not going to elevate anything," Haynes Johnson said.

The end result of the EPA's toothless approach to wetland regulation is what happened with a Collier County development called Mirasol. Developer J. D. Nicewonder, a West Virginia coal mining magnate, proposed building two 18-hole golf courses and nearly 800 homes on 1,766 acres, about 1,000 acres of which was classified as wetlands. Nicewonder's construction plans called for wiping out 587 acres of wetlands in the same area of Bonita Springs where flooding drove 1,000 people from their homes in 1995.

Boler opposed the project because of its huge impact in an area that had already lost too many wetlands. When Boler left, review of the project was handed to Haynes Johnson in the Atlanta office.

"I think they thought I was so old and close to retirement I wouldn't bother to object to it," Johnson said. "Instead I looked at it and said, 'This is the worst project I've ever seen in 35 years!' And I was told, 'You don't understand, the Corps wants to issue this in two weeks.'"

Because of the size of the potential wetlands impact, Johnson took another EPA expert named Tom Wellborn to visit the site.

"We were in the water all day," Johnson said. "We found no high ground. I have pictures of him standing in the road in water up to his knees."

How wet was Mirasol? From May to July of 2002, the EPA found, 25 inches of rain fell in that area—yet none of that water ran off the Mirasol site. It all stayed there, held by the wetlands, and filtered down into the aquifer to recharge the drinking supply, an EPA study found.

The most controversial part of the project was a 3-mile-long drainage ditch, dubbed a "flow-way," that Nicewonder proposed building through his subdivision and several others. Nicewonder's consultants convinced the water management district to count the ditch as part of his mitigation for destroying wetlands—even though the ditch would cut through a small cypress swamp that an earlier development had preserved as part of its mitigation for wetlands destruction.

But because of fears that the Mirasol ditch might prove so effective it would drain Audubon's nearby Corkscrew Swamp Sanctuary, the Nicewonder permit was one of six 404 permits that Col. Carpenter denied the year we wrote our first stories on the Corps.

Nicewonder subsequently submitted revised plans that dropped the ditch but included even greater wetland destruction than before—655 acres now instead of 587. The EPA staff sent the Corps letters in September and October 2006 expressing concerns about the revamped project. They foresaw increased pollution flowing into the area's already-impaired waterways and the loss of habitat for the Florida panther and other endangered species. As with Old Cutler Bay, they pointed out that the Corps should not allow something that is not water dependent to be built in wetlands unless there is no practical alternative—and the Corps' alternatives analysis fell woefully short of being adequate, the EPA staff said.

Then, in April 2007, EPA administrator Palmer signed a letter to the Corps waving the white flag.

Palmer wrote that his staff still opposed giving Mirasol a permit, but the agency would not elevate it to Washington or pursue it any further. Instead, he told Corps officials, "I would welcome the opportunity to discuss the concerns raised by this project with you with the intent of avoiding these same issues on future projects."

This, then, is what the EPA's watchdog duties have dwindled down to: instead of lightning-bolt veto, it has the power to request a phone call.

❧

Another agency that is supposed to have the power to challenge the Corps is the U.S. Fish and Wildlife Service. Unlike the EPA, the wildlife agency lacks the authority to veto a 404 permit. But wildlife service officials can force changes in a project if they believe it will jeopardize the future of any endangered or threatened species, such as the Florida panther, the wood stork, or the manatee. If the Corps' local office doesn't pay attention to such a "jeopardy opinion," then the service, like the EPA, can elevate the argument all the way up to the top echelon of the Corps.

But like the EPA, the Fish and Wildlife Service has seldom used its power to protect wetlands. Since the current elevation process was set up in 1992, the wildlife agency has used it only 16 times. The last time it elevated a permit dispute was at the very end of the Clinton Administration, and the project in question was one in Florida.

A company called the Vineyards Development Corporation wanted to build a new subdivision called Naples Reserve on 691 acres of land in Collier County next to Picayune Strand State Forest. The company, owned by a Pennsylvania family named Procacci that made a fortune in the tomato business, proposed building more than 550 homes and two 18-hole golf courses on its land. That would destroy 109 acres of cypress swamp, freshwater marsh, and wet prairie that formed the headwaters of the primary tributary to Rookery Bay National Estuary Reserve. The Procaccis' land also happened to be prime habitat for the Florida panther, the most endangered mammal in North America.

"It was one of the worst of its class," said Andy Eller, a shy and soft-spoken biologist who wrote the Fish and Wildlife Service's official report on the project. Eller had left a red-headed girlfriend behind in Atlanta in 1993 for the chance to move to Florida and study panthers. But the march of development through panther habitat was starting to get under his skin, and he saw Naples Reserve as a place to take a stand.

The Corps had no problems with the project, though, finding there would be no secondary impacts to the state forest or Rookery Bay, because of the "extensive review of this project that resulted in a mitigation plan that addresses these concerns." In other words, the mitigation justified the destruction.

However, to Eller and the wildlife agency, the Naples Reserve mitigation plan left a lot to be desired. As mitigation, the Vineyards offered to create two acres of wetlands on the site and nine acres elsewhere, as well as preserve hundreds of acres of existing wetlands on the site and on some other land nearby. That meant there would be a net loss of 98 acres of wetlands, which wildlife service officials deemed unacceptable.

So on December 22, 2000, Assistant Secretary of the Interior Kenneth

L. Smith sent the Corps a letter seeking elevation of the permit so the decision would be made by top Pentagon officials. The letter took great pains to outline the wildlife agency's objections. Why not, the wildlife service asked, redesign the project to use some of the site's 512 acres of uplands for development instead of targeting the wetlands? And with 165 other golf courses already operating in the area and dumping fertilizer and pesticides into the waterways, did Naples Reserve really need two of them? Why not just one?

The letter also attacked the Corps for drawing the project purpose too narrowly, just as it did with the Old Cutler Bay project. The Corps defined the purpose as providing "a residential community of approximately 552 dwelling units along with two 18-hole golf courses, lakes for stormwater management purposes and aesthetics and natural preserves." When the Corps reviewed the application, the letter noted, it failed to suggest any changes to the design to save even one acre of wetlands.

By saying the mitigation justified the wetland destruction, Smith's letter pointed out, the Corps was in effect saying that any project that required a 404 permit "would not have adverse impacts nor contribute to cumulative adverse impacts because mitigation is being required."

On January 19, 2001, the day before George W. Bush's inauguration as president, Assistant Secretary of the Army Joseph Westphal wrote back to Smith to say: Forget it. Those wetlands aren't worth saving. They're too full of exotic vegetation to really worry about. The mitigation is fine. And that overly specific project purpose is okay too, right down to the two 18-hole golf courses.

"The Corps must accept basic project principles from the applicant in establishing its project purpose," Westphal wrote. "In this case, these principles included the need in the marketplace for two regulation golf courses, mid-priced dwellings and the location in Collier County, Florida." He didn't explain how this do-what-the-applicant-wants approach meshed with the precedents set by Marco Island and Old Cutler Bay.

Wildlife officials felt stung by Westphal's letter. It "just dismissed our request out of hand," Eller said. "They were like: 'We're the Corps of Engineers. We make the decisions. Have a good day.'"

But the wildlife service didn't give up yet. The agency had a secret weapon: Jeanette Gallihugh, a wildlife service employee who had previously worked for the Corps' regulatory side for four years in Utah and Nevada. Her first job with the wildlife agency's Chicago office was a three-year study of wetland mitigation sites that found lots of problems.

Eller and other biologists griped to Gallihugh that they didn't understand why the Corps was approving so much wetlands destruction in Southwest Florida. "People saw something really systematic that we had a problem with," she said. "Our goal was to bring it to the forefront and talk about it."

Gallihugh dug through the Corps' 404 permitting files in its Fort Myers office looking for the decision documents that would explain why so many acres of the western Everglades were being destroyed. She focused mostly on big residential projects like Naples Reserve and came up with 24 where she believed John Hall and his staff had failed to do their job. She was particularly critical of the Corps' repeated failure to analyze alternatives on non-water-dependent projects, thus ignoring the Marco Island precedent. She wrote it all up in a lengthy and detailed report, which her bosses sent to the Corps as a proposed "policy elevation," indicating they intended to take it all the way to the Pentagon if they did not get some satisfactory answers.

"I am steaming mad," Hall wrote in an e-mail after he saw it. He contended Gallihugh had "distorted the facts," although he conceded that "we did discover some places where we feel we can do better and we are working on those areas."

Gallihugh, along with her boss, a pudgy and garrulous man named Jay Slack, and other wildlife agency employees then traveled to Jacksonville to meet with Hall and his staff and talk about her report. The Corps' response, said Gallihugh, was that she didn't know what she was talking about. The wildlife biologists should stick to their own field and leave the Corps alone. She said Hall told them bluntly: "Stay in your lane."

The whole meeting became caught up in recriminations and finger-pointing. The discussion also revealed a depressing glimpse of the Corps' acquiescence in still more wetland destruction in the future.

When an EPA official at the meeting warned that Florida was becoming "saturated with golf courses," Hall replied, "I don't have a problem with that. I don't think we can say that you can't use that piece of property the way that you want to."

The logical next step would have been for the wildlife service to take the fight straight up the line to the Pentagon. But Slack, then the top wildlife agency official in South Florida, said he didn't see how that would help, given the reception the Naples Reserve elevation had gotten from the Pentagon. Instead, to Gallihugh's surprise and chagrin, he dropped the whole matter.

"At that point it just became something I didn't think we would be able to move forward," Slack told us.

Soon it turned out that the wildlife agency itself was failing to do its job of saving the panther, relying on faulty science that favored development.

The panther—once described by Native Americans as "the lord of the forest" or "the cat of god"—used to roam the Southeastern states but now has been hemmed into the southernmost tip of Florida. About 100 of them remain, and their future depends in large part on whether they will have enough habitat for roaming, eating, and mating. Unfortunately, the panther's habitat happens to be in one of the fastest growing parts of the state.

Between 1992 and 2007, the Fish and Wildlife Service was called in to consult on 57 wetland permits that wiped out more than 40,000 acres of panther habitat. In every case, the wildlife agency officially went along with the destruction of habitat. In at least four cases, field biologists in Florida wrote reports that said development would harm panthers, only to be overruled by their agency superiors in Atlanta.

When Andy Eller looked at the cumulative impact of all the panther habitat that was being wiped out in Southwest Florida, he began having second thoughts about his job. When he told his bosses about his misgivings, he was warned he would get a poor job evaluation if he brought it up again. He says he was told to use inflated panther population estimates in writing his permit reviews. Nothing could stand in the way of development, not even the Endangered Species Act.

In December 2001, Eller said, he was ordered to overstate the panther population to avoid causing permitting problems for an expansion of Southwest Florida International Airport outside Naples. He did. And when he tried to include his concerns about cumulative impacts in a biological opinion on a mining project near Fort Myers, his concerns were edited out. A federal judge subsequently overturned the permit because the wildlife service failed to consider the cumulative impact.

"Essentially, I was a patsy," Eller later told the *Washington Post*. "I lost a lot of innocence."

Beginning in the mid-1990s, the scientific data that the wildlife agency relied on when drawing up its biological opinions came from a single source, a biologist named Dave Maehr. From 1985 to 1994, Maehr had been in charge of the state game commission's panther research in South Florida, where biologists mounted radio-tracking collars on adult panthers and then followed their movements by flying over the swamps in small airplanes. Maehr co-wrote an influential article about the findings of his tracking-collar research, published in 1985 in the journal *Conservation Biology*, it was followed in 1987 by a book for the lay reader called *The Florida Panther: Life and Death of a Vanishing Carnivore*.

Maehr said that panthers preferred forests over every other kind of habitat and wouldn't cross more than 300 feet of nonforested land. To Eller, that seemed wrong. Panthers are known to range 200 square miles, and they had been spotted crossing every kind of land cover, including farms and highways. Other scientists also viewed Maehr's findings with suspicion.

But Maehr was now showing up as a consultant on big development projects, including Florida Gulf Coast University. His job was helping to persuade Eller's bosses to go along with wiping out panther habitat, peddling his expertise while handing out autographed copies of his book.

Because of Maehr, "I went into consultation after consultation arguing with both consultants and the Corps who said that the only habitat that needed to be compensated was forested," Eller said. Any other kind—marshes for instance—didn't matter.

In December 2003, a team of independent, state-hired scientists who had reviewed Maehr's findings reported fatal flaws all through his writings. Maehr's research covered only daytime tracking reports on the panthers, but panthers move around mostly at night. He was looking only at where they slept, not where they traveled. And he had failed to include any of the thousands of radio tracks his team had received from marshy areas in the Everglades. Instead, he only used tracking data from forested areas, which fit better with his theories.

Yet even after the science team review said Maehr was wrong, the wildlife service continued relying on Maehr's science in its review and approval of 404 permits. So in June 2004, with the help of a Washington-based group called Public Employees for Environmental Responsibility, Eller filed a formal complaint that said the agency was knowingly using faulty science in reviewing 404 permits in panther territory.

In November 2004, the day after George W. Bush was reelected president, Eller was fired after 17 years with the agency. The reason given: he took too long reviewing permits and was "unprofessional" in dealing with the public. Meanwhile the boss who fired him, Jay Slack, was promoted.

Yet in March 2005, the wildlife agency had to admit Eller was right about Maehr. Eller was subsequently reinstated, but at his request he was posted to another state where his job had nothing to do with reviewing 404 permits.

As for the wildlife service, its leaders reported that even though Maehr's science had now been discredited, the agency would not be changing any of its biological opinions that led to approved 404 permits based on his data.

And in the meantime, the wildlife service had quit writing the opinions.

In March 2005, around the time Eller was vindicated, another wildlife service biologist sent an e-mail to Lee County's consultant on a road-widening project that said permit applicants were now being asked to write the biological opinions, or BOs, for the agency.

"To speed things up (due to our heavy workload) we are asking the consultant for each project that adversely affects panthers to prepare a BO based on a template BO that we will send you," biologist John Wrublik wrote in the e-mail. He said that adapting the "template" to fit various projects destructive to panther habitat should be "pretty straightforward," requiring only some "deleting and inserting" information "where appropriate."

Paul Souza, who replaced Jay Slack as head of the Fish and Wildlife Service's South Florida office, said no one should think the agency is allowing Florida developers to write the entire biological opinion.

"We prepare all the species analysis," Souza told us. "What we do ask them to provide us are the details of the project—what is the habitat impact? What is the impact on panthers, based on their understanding?"

Souza wasn't sure when the practice started—it might have been with Mirasol. But so far the agency still hasn't produced a single opinion that said a 404 permit might put the panther at risk of extinction. By now it may be too late. In a report issued in January 2006, the wildlife agency noted, "There is insufficient habitat in South Florida to sustain a viable panther population."

∾

The most common natural disaster in America is flooding. Wetlands act as a natural barrier to flooding, stemming the flow by storing the excess. The Corps knows this is true. Corps officials in Massachusetts calculated that losing all the wetlands in the Charles River's watershed would cause $17 million in flood damage every year, so instead of building dams and levees there, they acquired more than 8,000 acres of Charles River wetlands to ensure they would continue to prevent flooding problems naturally.

Wipe out a wetland, though, and all that flood water has to go somewhere. Just ask Melvin Alverson. Just east of Pensacola is a subdivision that flooded so frequently in the 1990s that one resident, Alverson, bought a recreational vehicle so he and his wife would have a place to live during the rainy season.

The flooding started, he said, when another subdivision was built next door to theirs and wiped out the wetlands where the rain once pooled.

"I'm not a scholar or anything, but it don't take a professor to know water runs downhill," Alverson said.

After that subdivision was built, the Alversons and their neighbors filed so many flood insurance claims that finally the Federal Emergency Management Agency decided to buy them out and tear down their homes. Cost to the taxpayers for the buyout: nearly half a million dollars.

Between 2000 and 2002, FEMA repeatedly objected to 404 permits in Florida for projects built in areas likely to flood. They complained that the Corps didn't even bother to worry about flooding or what it might cost the taxpayers in insurance claims and buyouts.

"The Corps appears to make no effort to determine whether proposed projects are located in the floodplain," FEMA officials griped to the Corps in one 2001 letter.

They sent letters objecting to individual permits, and they sent letters complaining about all the permits in general. They repeatedly reminded the Corps that, when Jimmy Carter was president, he signed an executive order that said building in floodplains should be discouraged by federal agencies. Combine that executive order with the requirements of the public interest test for 404 permits, and there's the best reason of all for blocking anyone from building in wetlands, FEMA officials said.

"If one focuses on floodplains instead of wetlands, it may be possible to make a stronger argument," a FEMA employee named Charles Beck told attorney Lesley Blackner in a June 2001 e-mail. Under federal regulations, the key is "whether or not the proposed activity must occur in a floodplain. Unless it must be in a floodplain, it cannot be permitted."

The Corps, of course, saw things differently. An executive order is not as binding as a law, especially an order that was signed by a president who's no longer in office. So the Corps told FEMA to stop griping about all the houses that were being built in areas at risk of flooding.

"They'd like to see the Corps deny all permits in the 100-year floodplain," said John Studt, who at the time FEMA was complaining was chief of the Corps' regulatory division nationwide. "We told them we couldn't do that."

Potential flooding is a problem for the state to handle in its permitting, not the Corps, Studt said. To him, FEMA was barking up the wrong tree.

When the Corps refused to go along with its reading of the regulations and continued approving permits in Florida's floodplains, FEMA officials eventually gave up—just as the EPA and the wildlife service had. There was nothing they could do to stop the Corps, FEMA officials told us.

"They just folded and went away," Hall said with a chuckle. "Sort of like a flash in a pan."

But there's one federal entity the Corps listens to very closely and generally obeys. It's the one that votes on their funding: the United States Congress. And in Florida, the Corps hears from Congress a lot.

13

The Cussing Congressman

In 1991, the Florida legislature voted to build the state's tenth university in Southwest Florida near Fort Myers. A selection committee narrowed the possible sites to three. The one that the state Board of Regents picked turned out to be, at least from an environmental standpoint, the worst of the lot.

"They went to the site where they had the most wetland impacts," grumbled Tom Reese, who as the Florida Wildlife Federation's attorney waged an unsuccessful fight against the choice.

To the Board of Regents this particular site had one big advantage: it was being donated by Ben Hill Griffin III, heir to Florida's preeminent citrus and ranching empire, a major campaign contributor, and a longtime supporter of the state university system. The football stadium at the University of Florida—nicknamed "The Swamp" since it's the home of the Gators—bears his family name.

Griffin said his land was favored over the other campus choices not because of his tremendous clout, but because it was the best: "It had the greatest access to Interstate 75. It had a mile frontage on a 775-acre lake." (Actually the "lake," like the ones in the Lake Belt, was a Griffin-owned rock quarry that he planned to convert into a picturesque real estate amenity.)

What would Griffin gain from donating the university site? Griffin's company, Alico Inc., owned all the land around the new campus—16 square miles of yet-to-be-developed donut surrounding the small hole he was handing over to the state to use as a campus. Once Florida Gulf Coast University was built in the middle of Alico's holdings, Griffin's company could make a substantial profit from developing the countryside around it, as well as by selling land to others to do the same.

However, the site offered a few challenges to be overcome. For one thing, about two-fifths of the campus was swamp. The land was so wet that a university official acknowledged that for anyone to walk the site in the rainy season, "you'd need hip boots." The swamps formed the headwaters of a short river emptying into Estero Bay, classified as an Outstanding Florida Waterway. That means it was supposed to get special protection against any new sources of pollution such as, say, rampant development spurred by the construction of a new state-owned institution.

Another problem arose from the local land-use rules. According to Lee County code, the campus site was part of a large conservation zone that was supposed to be held to low-density development or none at all, so it could recharge the underground drinking supply.

To top it all off, the proposed campus bordered what had been classified as priority habitat for the Florida panther. Three panthers had already been hit by cars driving nearby. Put in a university campus and surround it with new stores and homes and even more roads, and biologists could easily imagine the feline carnage that would follow.

Griffin scoffed at the idea that panthers had ever wandered over his land. "The panther ain't never been there, ain't coming back," he said. "You look close enough, you may find a dinosaur track out there, but I don't think the dinosaur is going to come back again."

University supporters contended that all these concerns about nature were really an argument in favor of building on Griffin's site. University president Roy McTarnaghan said building the campus on such an environmentally sensitive site meant students could more easily focus on environmental studies.

"Instead of saying, 'Come to this university, I'll take you to my field study 50 miles away,' we're going to be right in the middle of it," McTarnaghan boasted.

Because the plan for building on this swampy site required dumping fill dirt into 75 acres of wetlands, state university officials had to apply for the regular permits. The state permit was quickly approved, of course. But months went by without the Corps announcing a decision.

The delay was easy to explain: John Hall told us that the Corps was leaning toward a denial. After all, there were alternate sites which had been favored by several state agencies, and they had smaller wetland impacts. So the Corps staff was taking everything step by step, trying to figure out if a rare permit denial would be the right course of action, he said.

At the time the district engineer in Jacksonville was Col. Terry Rice, regarded by some environmental activists as the second coming of Don Wisdom, the hero of Marco Island. One day when Rice was on an airboat in the Everglades, his cell phone rang. As soon as he answered it, Rice said, the

Figure 14. While on an airboat in the Everglades, Col. Terry Rice got a call on his cell phone. The caller who cursed him out for holding up the permit for Florida's tenth university? A U.S. senator. (Photograph courtesy of U.S. Army Corps of Engineers.)

caller began "cussing me out" for taking so long processing the university's 404 permit.

The caller was Connie Mack, grandson of the legendary baseball manager, a prominent Fort Myers banker, and, most importantly, Florida's Republican U.S. senator. Mack made it plain that he was not happy with Rice or with Rice's staff.

"He used some terms over the telephone that weren't very flattering," Rice told us. "It wasn't a pleasant conversation."

Rice subsequently approved the permit to put FGCU on Griffin's land in 1995 in return for local leaders agreeing to an extensive review of the cumulative impacts of wetland and habitat losses throughout the western Everglades region.

When we asked Hall why his agency changed its mind about the FGCU permit, he said, "I'm not sure I could tell you."

Two months into the construction of FGCU, portions of the site flooded with three feet of water. Wags dubbed it "Mildew U." In the first six years after its opening in 1997, the university was caught three times illegally pumping water off its campus and into adjacent swamps.

Meanwhile FGCU has spawned widespread development in the area around the campus, including new homes and offices and even a shopping mall. Some of the new development lines the university's entrance road, which is named for Griffin.

Mack wasn't the only senator who intervened to help Griffin get what he wanted. Mack's Democratic counterpart, U.S. Senator Bob Graham, helped push another federal agency to roll over.

The U.S. Fish and Wildlife Service office in South Florida had concluded that building FGCU on Griffin's land could jeopardize the panther's chances for survival and had written a biological opinion recommending the Corps deny the permit. But Alico representatives, with help from Graham's staff, arranged a sit-down meeting with the wildlife agency's regional office in Atlanta. Three days later, the regional director overrode the recommendation from his Florida staff and changed the biological opinion to say that FGCU could proceed and the Corps could issue the 404 permit without any harm to panthers.

After the closed-door meeting was uncovered by reporters, Graham's spokesman assured everyone that the senator had not taken a position on the university, despite what appearances seemed to imply. Richard Hannan, one of the Atlanta wildlife officials who had been part of the meeting with Alico, insisted the senator's involvement had no effect on the agency's decision—although biologists in the field, like Andy Eller, were convinced otherwise.

Public interest is supposed to drive the Corps' permitting decisions. That's been the agency's policy since 1967, when Col. Tabb decided that saving what was left of Boca Ciega Bay was more important than helping a trailer park owner make a profit. But politicians often lean on the Corps on behalf of well-connected private interests.

Because the Corps depends on Congress for funding—$180 million for the regulatory program in fiscal year 2008—a call or letter from a member of Congress sends a strong message: approve the permit, or face the consequences. Even a letter asking questions signals an applicant may have political clout and should be treated gently.

"It puts the Corps on the spot," said Rice. "It results in a quick decision, but not necessarily a good decision."

The Corps' Jacksonville office gets so many calls, letters, and e-mails from

Congress that Joe Burns, who served as the Jacksonville district's liaison with Congress until 2005, had to create his own computer database to track them all. The letters were forwarded to the permitting staff along with a garish orange-pink cover sheet that said "CONGRESSIONAL," marking it for urgent attention. When a "congressional" arrived, the permit reviewers had to drop everything and get a response ready for the colonel to sign.

"Generally we try to turn those around in five working days," Burns said.

During a typical three-month period in 2004, Burns' database showed that senators and members of Congress called 34 times and wrote 30 letters about Corps permit applications in Florida. Usually they wanted to complain about how long the Corps was taking to say yes to a permit. Of course, answering the letters slows down the permit review process even more.

"There are times I have gotten incredibly mad at having to answer all these congressional inquiries," John Hall said. "It takes our time away from doing our jobs."

Yet the Corps' top military officer told us he saw nothing wrong with congressional intervention in the regulatory process.

"I think it's absolutely appropriate that they do this," said Lt. Gen. Carl Strock, who was chief engineer when we interviewed him in 2005. "We work for the will of the people as expressed through Congress."

Members of Congress told us that they view contacting the Corps about developers' permits as a routine part of their jobs, a way to help constituents dealing with a confusing federal bureaucracy. Some made no apologies for trying to light a fire under the agency on behalf of a development that will destroy wetlands in the name of economic progress.

"Believe me, I've been after the Army Corps on a number of projects," said U.S. Representative Ginny Brown-Waite, R-Crystal River. For instance, Brown-Waite said she strongly encouraged the Corps to cooperate with Pasco County's plan to extend Ridge Road through the Serenova nature preserve, even though saving it as an unbroken parcel of wilderness was supposed to serve as mitigation for the Suncoast Parkway.

Other politicians contended their correspondence really carries little weight with the Corps, at least in terms of what decision results.

"I think the agencies are experienced in what that means—not to change a decision, but to request them to review it on a professional and timely basis," said Graham, who retired from politics after his failed 2004 presidential campaign.

The jowly and wonkish Graham is a Harvard-trained lawyer notorious for taking meticulous notes about the most mundane events in his day, such as how long it takes him to rewind videotapes. His fortune came from developing his family's farmland in Miami Lakes, but as a politician he built a reputation as an environmentalist. During his two terms as governor he launched the push for Everglades restoration, helped get the Henderson Act passed, and even cofounded the Save the Manatee Club with singer Jimmy Buffett.

Graham's image as an environmental crusader is so entrenched that some fans of Carl Hiaasen's wacky Florida crime novels have suggested he is the basis for the recurring character of Skink, an ex-governor who was driven mad while in office by the corruption around him and who now lives in the wild, exacting vengeance on the despoilers of nature and dining on roadkill. Graham, who is more likely to wear a pinstripe suit than a loincloth, told a reporter, "I do not think I am Skink. But every once in a while I will see a dead possum on the side of the road and wonder if I should pull over."

Despite Graham's green reputation, though, we found repeated instances where he and his senate staff intervened to help developers get their 404 permits to wipe out wetlands. For instance, Graham was a big booster of the Naples Reserve project, the golf course subdivision that the Fish and Wildlife Service fought unsuccessfully all the way to the Pentagon. In March 2000, Graham sent a letter to Jay Slack—biologist Andy Eller's boss in the South Florida office of the wildlife service—that the developers of Naples Reserve, the Procacci family, were frustrated with delays by Eller in giving their project a green light.

"Because of the lengthy period of time which has already expired, I would ask that this process be expedited if at all possible," Graham wrote. "I would appreciate your providing me with a status report of the progress of this opinion."

The president of the company developing Naples Reserve, Michael Saadeh, told us the Procaccis needed Graham's help because Eller "had no positive contributions to the project and actually went out of his way to prevent the (Corps) permit from being issued."

When we questioned Graham, he said his intervention on the Naples Reserve project was no big deal. "That's the sort of standard letter you write on behalf of a constituent who has problems with a federal agency," he said.

But records show Graham didn't just write that one letter to help Naples Reserve. He wrote a similar letter to the Corps on behalf of the developer. And his chief of staff, Mary Chiles, repeatedly asked Fish and Wildlife to speed things up. She noted in one letter to the wildlife service that the developers had decided they didn't like Eller. She asked if the Procaccis and their consultants could meet with Eller's bosses.

Graham said that the letters from him and his staff were not aimed at telling the Corps and the wildlife service what decision to make on the permit, just to get the bureaucrats moving on making a decision. But Eller said everyone in the wildlife service and the Corps understood the senator's message.

"Elected officials always say they just want to facilitate a dialogue, but rest assured, a threat is implied," Eller said.

In another case, Graham and then congressman Porter Goss, R-Sanibel, also sent letters to the Fish and Wildlife Service supporting Florida Rock's efforts to get a permit to mine limestone rock from wetlands near Fort Myers. The letter from Goss—who would later serve a brief, tumultuous term as chief of the Central Intelligence Agency—said that Florida Rock had "a long history of environmental stewardship," which would have been startling news to the Miami-Dade officials worried about what mining in the Lake Belt was doing to their water supply.

Still, the letters from Graham and Goss carefully stopped short of telling the Corps or the wildlife service to give Florida Rock whatever it wanted.

Some congressional letters take a more direct approach. For example, consider the letter that U.S. Representative Alcee Hastings, D-Miami, sent to the Corps on May 3, 2004. Hastings had been Florida's first black federal trial judge until he was impeached by the U.S. Senate in 1989 because of allegations he took a $150,000 bribe from defendants in a racketeering case he was overseeing. However, he bounced back with election to the House in 1992 and has been repeatedly reelected since then.

In his letter to the Corps, Hastings complained that a development company called the Cornerstone Group was growing impatient waiting for a permit to wipe out four acres of wetlands in Riviera Beach so it could build a 302-home development called Sonoma Bay. The message of Hastings' letter was clear: stamp that permit approved, ASAP.

"I strongly urge your office to provide a compelling reason why this referenced permit application hasn't been seriously reviewed by your local permit review office staff after it was submitted months ago," Hastings wrote.

The congressman then set a deadline for the Corps. He said Cornerstone needed the permit no later than May 20, 17 days after the date of the congressman's letter.

When we checked campaign contribution records, we found that Cornerstone and its top executives have donated heavily to the Democratic National Committee and to state and national Democratic candidates. A Hastings staffer, Stephanie Desir-Jean, said no one mentioned the contributions when Cornerstone asked Congressman Hastings for help with the Corps. The congressman was just helping a constituent, she said.

Hastings' attempt to set a deadline for Corps approval didn't work for Cornerstone, but only because it was against the law. Corps officials wrote back to the congressman to tell him that they would probably say yes to Cornerstone's permit very soon, but by law they had to give the public until May 22—two more days than Hastings' deadline allowed—to comment on it.

In politics, timing can be very important. In May 2004, around the same time the Democrat from Miami was pushing the Cornerstone permit, one of his Republican colleagues was sending a similar letter to the Corps regarding another development.

U.S. Representative E. Clay Shaw, R-Fort Lauderdale, sent a letter urging the Corps to approve filling in nearly an acre of mangroves and open water so that a nationally prominent development firm, Toll Brothers, could build a new condominium in Palm Beach County. Campaign records show the company had donated extensively to the GOP and other candidates. There was a more recent contribution too: Representative Shaw sent his letter to the Corps endorsing the Toll Brothers condo just two days after the company vice chairman, Bruce Toll, donated $2,000 to Shaw's reelection campaign.

Shaw's staff insisted there was no connection between the contribution and the congressman's letter to the Corps.

"We've sent many letters like this," Shaw spokeswoman Gail Gitcho told us. "It's a common procedure when people want us to help speed things along.

We had obtained from the Corps a copy of the letter that Col. Carpenter sent back to Shaw, but the Corps either would not or could not provide us with the congressman's original letter. So we asked Gitcho for a copy. She refused to hand it over.

The reason we couldn't have it, she said, was that it "wasn't written for public consumption." (The secretive Shaw lost his bid for reelection in 2006.)

Of course political intervention in permitting isn't limited to Congress. Chuck Schnepel told us about a residential development permit called Turtle Run he reviewed in Broward County in the late 1980s. The developers—Courtelis Corp. and Lennar Homes—strongly disagreed with the Corps over how much of the property was covered in wetlands.

Miami developer Alec Courtelis had personally donated more than $100,000 to the Republican National Committee in 1988 and helped raise millions more for the Bush-Quayle campaign. President Bush, on a 1989 visit to Miami, hailed Courtelis' fundraising prowess: "In my view at least, Alec was a large part in our being boosted to a 40-state victory last November."

As a result of the developers' complaints about his findings on Turtle Run, Schnepel said, someone with the Corps in Washington decided to send in a team of its top wetland experts from its Mississippi laboratory to review Schepel's work. Schnepel said he had spent three hours going over the property, which was covered in cypress and other wetland plants. The Mississippi experts spent a week on the ground and then still more time back in their lab doing computer modeling, he said.

In the end, Schnepel said, the experts told him that he should go by the elevation of the property. Anything above a certain elevation should be classified as upland and anything below it would be wetland, "regardless of what the vegetation showed," Schnepel said. That gave the developer enough "dry" land to build the project: 3,800 multi- and single-family homes, 40 acres parkland, 60 acres of waterways and commercial facilities.

When we asked Schnepel how that approach fit with the no-net-loss policy, he gave us a tight smile and pointed out that if the Corps doesn't classify what's about to be destroyed as a wetland under its jurisdiction, then "it's not a loss."

Corps employees say they are always under fire from developers to move quickly on permit decisions, but pressure mounts when such political intervention occurs. It makes their bosses even more inclined to side with developers against the permit reviewer.

"You find yourself fighting a second front," Steve Brooker told us.

That's what happened with a developer's plans to build an apartment complex in Orlando called College Suites at Orpington. College Suites was proposed for a 21-acre site about a mile from the University of Central Florida. The plans called for wiping out 10 acres of wetlands. The Corps permit reviewer was Brooker. He visited the site and found half of it covered in thigh-deep water flowing into the Econlockhatchee River.

"Is this really where we want to put an apartment complex?" Brooker said, shaking his head. "Knowing you're supposed to avoid impacts to wetlands, and they're half the site?"

As he was reviewing the College Suites permit application, Brooker began asking lots of questions—questions the developer, Udo Garbe of Winter Park, apparently didn't like.

Figure 15. Corps permit reviewer Steven Brooker's bosses got an earful from a Florida congressman when he questioned a development proposed for a site covered in thigh-deep water. (Photograph by Michael R. Brown, *St. Petersburg Times*.)

In March 2003 Garbe contributed $1,000 to the reelection campaign of U.S. Representative Tom Feeney, R-Oviedo. Federal records indicate it was Garbe's first-ever campaign contribution. After Garbe made his contribution, his attorney, Warren E. Williams, then contacted Feeney and asked for help in getting around Brooker. Williams even sent the congressman a letter containing talking points to use in prodding top Corps officials to overrule Brooker's concerns about protecting vital wetlands, concerns the attorney depicted as ridiculous.

"He has completely forgotten about the Corps' obligation to allow development when the community needs outweigh the environmental desires of a few," Williams wrote in the letter, offering a Bizarro-world revision of what the Clean Water Act requires.

This was not the first time Williams' clients had turned to Feeney for help, the attorney noted in his letter.

"We do know it has been successful in the past when congressional leadership has provided some show of interest in a project," the attorney reminded Feeney. "The Corps hierarchy pays more attention, which in turn usually allows for the better evaluation of a particular situation."

Feeney, pink-faced and beefy with a mop of curly hair, is a real estate lawyer from Central Florida who has become a self-described "gladiator" for conservative causes. He idolizes Ronald Reagan, telling the *Washington Post*: "He was our Plato, he was our Moses. He was our Washington and our Churchill, too." The first time Jeb Bush ran for governor, he picked Feeney as his running mate, but incumbent Democratic governor Lawton Chiles called Feeney "the David Duke of Florida politics" and former governor Claude Kirk, despite being a fellow Republican, labeled him a "walking mental paraplegic." Six years after that losing race, Feeney won the job of speaker of the Florida House in 2000 and became nationally known in the postelection debacle for his constitutionally questionable efforts to put the legislature in charge of naming a new slate of electors who would decide the presidential race.

Feeney was quite receptive to the attorney's suggestions for writing to the Corps. In April 2003, Feeney fired off a letter to Col. Carpenter that, when compared to other congressional letters, achieves a quirky rhetorical grandeur.

Feeney's letter to the colonel began by pointing out the importance of the University of Central Florida to the region's economy. Then it noted the dire need for more student housing near campus—say, a new apartment complex a mile away, just like the one Mr. Garbe had proposed. Then Feeney got around to addressing Garbe's irksome wetland woes, making it clear that he regarded the developers' consultants as more qualified to pass judgment on the situation than some government paper pusher.

"Unfortunately, the project seems to have hit an impasse due to [the Corps'] refusal to issue a fill permit based on an assessment that somehow the project will impact wetlands in the area," Feeney wrote. "It is my understanding that a substantial number of experts suggest a difference of opinion on the impact this project would have and, therefore, I would respectfully request a review of the project so that I might clearly understand what issues are preventing the Corps from issuing a permit."

Garbe got his permit. Brooker refused to sign it, so his boss did. As for Feeney, he was reelected without opposition.

Brooker fell victim to a similar end-run when he balked at approving plans for a subdivision called Meadow Pointe, near Orlando. The development company's partners included former Altamonte Springs mayor Hugh Harling.

Harling's company proposed to build houses along the shore of Lake Irma, which like Estero Bay is classified as an Outstanding Florida Water. Because building the houses according to plan would destroy five acres of wetlands flowing into the lake, Brooker suggested changes that would minimize the project's impact.

Instead, Harling and the other partners went over his head. Their attorney was Ken Wright, a member of President Bush's legal team during the disputed 2000 election and Governor Jeb Bush's appointee to chair the state's Environmental Regulation Commission.

Wright put in a call to U.S. Representative Ric Keller, R-Orlando, who represents that district. Keller, like Feeney, is a Central Florida lawyer popular with builders and developers. In his first three campaigns for his congressional seat, he collected more than $179,000 in contributions from the real estate industry, $60,000 of it during his first race in 2000. So he was happy to listen to Wright.

"I expressed to Ric that I was frustrated," said Wright. "Every project it seems you're backed up waiting on the Corps."

Wright also talked to Keller's chief of staff, Mike Miller. "I ran into him at a reception," Miller told us. "Ken came up to me and said, 'Your purview includes correspondence with the Corps of Engineers, right?' I said yes, and he said, 'OK, we'd like to have some circumstances to be addressed.' He said, 'I know you can't advocate, but . . .'"

Miller told us he thought the request was "a little bit outside the box," but he and Representative Keller didn't see any ethical problems. As a result, the congressman fired off a November 2001 letter to Col. Greg May, then the district engineer in Jacksonville, demanding a meeting with Brooker's bosses in Jacksonville to discuss what was happening with Meadow Pointe. Col. May told us he took such letters "very seriously" but "never got the sense that I was being pressured one way or the other to make decisions."

Brooker was not invited to the meeting in Jacksonville between the developers and his bosses. Eleven months later, the Corps approved the permit for Meadow Pointe—without Brooker's requested changes. Brooker, upset at being circumvented, refused to sign the paperwork.

"I just said, I ain't issuing this shit," Brooker said. So once again, his boss signed it instead. Brooker said the next time he came up for promotion, he was passed over. He said he was told he is "too confrontational."

∾

Sometimes the pressure for permits comes from well-connected lobbyists. A prime example of a well-orchestrated lobbying campaign for a wetlands destruction permit is Lee County's effort to extend a road called Daniels Parkway.

In 1997, Lee officials decided to extend the highway three miles, even though it would wipe out 40 acres of wetlands on the western side of the Everglades, not to mention destroying habitat for the Florida panther.

The Corps could not issue the permit without an opinion from the U.S. Fish and Wildlife Service saying how the project would affect the panther. Kim Dryden, a wildlife agency biologist, determined extending the road would not only eliminate about 40 acres of panther habitat, but it would also open 2,000 acres of habitat to further development.

In the previous 10 years, Dryden noted, four panthers died on that road. New development would have an impact by increasing traffic. She wrote a biological opinion that said that Lee County could build the road, but only if it made up for the loss of panther habitat by spending $1.7 million to preserve 252 acres of panther habitat elsewhere.

Lee County officials balked. It wasn't just that the expense was so much greater than they expected. It was also that the developers who hoped to build projects along the new highway were fretting about the precedent this would set for the amount of mitigation they would be expected to contribute, too.

So instead of spending more than $1 million buying land, in 1999 the Lee County Commission spent $156,000 buying the services of a Washington lobbying firm called Dawson & Associates. The firm was founded by Robert Dawson, who had been William Giannelli's deputy and later his successor as assistant secretary of the Army overseeing the Corps under President Reagan. The staff listed by Dawson's firm includes Giannelli himself, as well as retired Corps of Engineers generals, former Fish and Wildlife Service officials, and enough former members of Congress to form a good-sized caucus.

While working on the Daniels Parkway project, Dawson's lobbying staff filed regular reports with Lee County detailing what they did for the taxpayers' money—reports that, thanks to Florida's Sunshine Law, became available for the taxpayers to read. The lobbyists' reports spell out exactly how they put the squeeze on both the Corps and the wildlife service.

First, Dawson himself met with Corps leaders in Atlanta, the people over the ones in Jacksonville. He brought with him a retired general who once oversaw the Corps nationwide.

The lobbyists also met with Florida's two senators, Mack and Graham, and the Republican congressman then representing Lee County, Porter Goss—the same Porter Goss who, back when he was mayor of Sanibel, had sought help from the Conservation Foundation in protecting the island's environment from rampant development. Goss, Mack, and Graham all wrote to the head of the Clinton Administration's wildlife service in Washington about the highway.

The lobbyists also got Goss' chief of staff to call Corps officials in Jacksonville "to urge them to be supportive of the county" in dealing with the wildlife agency.

Dawson's lobbying team even gave the senators and Goss talking points they could use in contacting the Corps and the wildlife service. One was: "It seems to me the project is being subjected to excessive requirements." Another said: "I am confident you share my interest in finding ways of resolving conflicts between economic development activities and ecosystem restoration."

To put a veneer of science on Lee County's position, Dawson's lobbyists trotted out a new method for analyzing the impact of development on panther habitat, a method drawn up by none other than Florida's best-known panther expert, Dave Maehr. At that point, no other scientist had officially poked holes in his data, so the lobbyists could present the Maehr method as a viable alternative.

Using Maehr's new "Panther Habitat Evaluation Model" (PHEM for short) meant that Lee County would have to buy 94 acres of panther habitat, far less than the 252 acres that Kim Dryden recommended. When Dryden and Andy Eller studied PHEM, they could see there were serious flaws in it. By then, though, it didn't matter—politics had superseded science.

In order to "generate broad support of the alternate proposal," Dawson & Associates lobbyists said, they "organized meetings at the Corps headquarters in Washington, D.C., made a series of presentations to appropriate Corps of Engineers field staff and facilitated 13 congressional presentations."

They obtained letters supporting Lee County from, among others, U.S. Representative Ralph Regula, R-Ohio, who chaired the House committee overseeing funding for the Fish and Wildlife Service, and—more importantly—from Senator Slade Gorton, R-Washington, the heir to the frozen fish chain who not only chaired a wildlife service oversight committee but also had become Senate Majority Leader Trent Lott's closest adviser.

Meanwhile the lobbyists were twisting arms at the wildlife service. For this job, Dawson & Associates deployed Jonathan Deason, who had been a top official at the Department of the Interior in the early 1990s and then a lobbyist for the American Road and Transportation Builders Association. He could also boast 30 years of experience as a reserve Army Corps of Engineers officer, as well as a professorship at George Washington University.

On April 2, 1999, Deason met for an hour one-on-one with Jay Slack, the top Fish and Wildlife Service official in South Florida, where, according to the lobbyist's report, he explained "the realities" that Slack "needs to appreciate."

Deason pointed out his firm's access to the Corps' chain of command, the firm's ability to influence Slack's bosses in Washington, and the firm's "involvement with the congressional delegation (Graham, Mack, Goss)." He said Dawson's influence even extended to Florida politics, noting that as a sugar company lobbyist he had been involved in advising Governor Bush on the selection of a new executive director for the South Florida Water Management District.

Once Deason showed how much muscle the lobbying firm wielded, "Slack was very receptive and indicated a strong willingness to work with us to get this problem solved," Deason reported.

After their one-hour session, Deason and Slack convened a larger, three-hour meeting with the wildlife service staff in Vero Beach. Deason brought along Maehr, who explained his new method of judging development impact on panther habitat. The wildlife service officials—all of them supervisors, not panther biologists—"listened very intently," Deason wrote afterward. When Deason handed out copies of Maehr's book, "there was a bit of glee as everyone got Dave to autograph their new books."

Then came the biggest power play of all: Deason persuaded the powerful Senator Gorton to use federal legislation to back the wildlife service into a corner. In July 1999, Deason reported that Gorton had agreed to slip into a budget bill a few lines that said the Fish and Wildlife Service must "ensure that measures designed to minimize the impacts on the Florida panther related to the Daniels Parkway extension are reasonable and conceived properly."

When the Florida staff of the wildlife service saw that budget language, they got the message. "Congress is saying: 'Do this,'" Slack told us.

To Eller, it was even clearer: "We knew it meant accept PHEM or else."

So the wildlife service backed down, producing a revised biological opinion for Daniels Parkway that adopted the Maehr method. As a result, Lee County needed to preserve just 94 acres for panthers, not 252 acres. And once the wildlife service caved, the Corps approved the permit in December 1999.

An even more controversial golf course development in the same area got a boost from Florida's current Democratic U.S. senator, Bill Nelson.

Nelson is a Yale graduate who earned a law degree at the University of Virginia. He had already enjoyed a long career in state politics as state insurance commissioner and a congressman before succeeding Mack in the Senate in 2000. Nelson often likes to reminisce about the time when, as a congressman, he flew on a space shuttle mission. But critics prefer to bring up a 1990 story in the state's premier business magazine, *Florida Trend*, which depicted him on the cover as an empty suit. Nelson gained some national renown in 2006 as the slow-talking incumbent who so easily trounced his erratic challenger, former Florida secretary of state Katherine Harris.

When coal-industry magnate J. D. Nicewonder ran into some problems getting a permit for developing his Mirasol subdivision and its two golf courses near Bonita Springs, Senator Nelson reached across party lines and joined Republican Porter Goss in helping Nicewonder get what he wanted.

It wasn't easy. EPA expert Bruce Boler sharply questioned the project's impact—pointing out, for instance, that as originally designed it would destroy 30 acres of wetlands preserved as compensation for an earlier development in the same area known as Olde Cypress.

"I said, 'How is this the least environmentally damaging site?'" Boler said. Meanwhile Eller with the Fish and Wildlife Service was raising objections to the impact on panther habitat.

But Nelson and Goss had other concerns. Staffers for both called Jimmy Palmer, the EPA's southeast administrator, about the project. They offered to set up a meeting between Palmer and the developers. Nelson's staff also arranged a meeting in the senator's Orlando office—hundreds of miles from the development—between the developer and top South Florida wildlife officials. But not Eller. He wasn't invited.

As a result of that meeting in Nelson's office, Eller said his bosses altered the dates on some paperwork to speed up the production of their report and then threatened to give him a poor job review if he concluded that Mirasol jeopardized panthers.

"They said I needed to be sensitive to the politics of the office," said Eller. Though frustrated, the biologist said he understood why his bosses wanted to help the developer instead of the panthers: "Hey, I would've done the same thing if a senator of the United States was telling me, 'You need to get your ass moving.'"

When we interviewed the senator, Nelson at first said flat-out that any congressional intervention in the permitting process is wrong.

"A constituent has a right to be heard, but we don't want to appear to put pressure on a decision," he said in his measured and resonant baritone. "We don't do that."

But when we pressed him to explain his staff's actions in helping Mirasol wipe out wetlands and panther habitat, Nelson furrowed his brow. He said when developers complain about the Corps and wildlife service bureaucrats taking a long time reviewing a permit, he can see why they want his help getting things moving.

"There's no excuse for somebody putting a file on a desk and not taking any action," he said.

Because the Corps takes so long to say yes to permits, Florida's homebuilders want the feds out of their hair.

"We're sick and tired of it and we're not going to take it anymore," Pensacola homebuilder Dan Gilmore, 2005 president of the Florida Home Builders Association, told us. As far as he was concerned, the Corps "ought to be ashamed of themselves" for making builders wait for months or years to get a 404 permit.

So in early 2005 Gilmore and the homebuilders launched a behind-the-scenes campaign to make it easier to wipe out wetlands. They employed their tremendous political clout to get help from state legislators and members of Congress—including Nelson.

To track down the story of how the developers' campaign came together, we drove to a Florida Chamber of Commerce seminar on environmental permitting that is held every year in, of all places, Marco Island, at the opulent hotel the Mackle brothers built and later had to sell because of their permit denial. The summer seminar draws builders, developers, environmental consultants, lawyers, and local government officials from around the state, plus the occasional Audubon Society official. Cost of attending: about $500 per person, plus $125 a night for the hotel.

We were looking for one of the teachers, an attorney and lobbyist named Frank Matthews. Though he was born in upstate New York, Matthews earned a law degree from the University of Miami and since 1981 has been in the thick of every battle over wetlands protection in Florida. He helped write most of the state laws on the subject. He lobbies for the Florida Home Builders Association and is a member of the Association of Florida Community Developers. He can be witty and wacky, but his clowning masks a sharp legal mind. He's listed in "Best Lawyers in America" under both environmental law and land-use law.

When we located him, Matthews was moderating a panel discussion in one of the hotel's larger ballrooms. He cracked a joke about one of the panelists, a prominent environmental consultant named Steve Godley, being nothing but a mere herpetologist.

Godley—whose firm, Biological Research Associates, had done work for the Lake Belt miners and for Pasco County's intended Ridge Road extension through the Serenova preserve—smiled and calmly retorted, "Frank's just a snake."

"That's why we get along," Matthews said, chuckling.

The seminar subject was the state permitting process, and at one point Matthews said it's "all about negotiation." As for his role in the process, he said, "We're advocates. We advocate for who pays us."

But then, without knowing we were in the audience, Matthews began complaining to the group about how the *St. Petersburg Times*, "the font of all wisdom, published an extensive expose on the Corps of Engineers" and as a result "the Corps denied as many projects in one day as they had in a couple of years. I call it 'Black Thursday.'"

Matthews didn't tell the group that one of those denials affected a client of his, the developer of a shopping and office complex called Freedom Commerce Center which would have wiped out 167 acres of high-quality wetlands near Jacksonville.

As he paced the hotel ballroom with microphone in hand, Matthews was wearing a T-shirt that said, "Pave the World." When we asked him about it afterwards, he assured us the shirt was a gag. He also assured us that builders and developers would much rather deal with state permitting officials than ever try to get a permit from the Corps. He said persuading the Corps to defer most of its work to the state's permitting agencies is "the Holy Grail" for developers. And Matthews was working hard on bringing home the Grail.

When developers want to wipe out a Florida swamp or marsh to make room for homes or a new shopping center, they need a permit from the state under the Warren Henderson Act, as well as their 404 permit from the Corps. They can't get the 404 permit without the state permit. Some of those state permits, such as the ones for mining, are issued by the DEP. But most of them, especially the ones for development projects, are approved by one of the five water management district boards, usually as a routine agenda item.

Though the Corps rarely says no, saying yes can take months or even years, costing builders thousands of dollars. In a 2005 Tampa Bay Builders Association newsletter, vice president Joseph Narkiewicz wrote of the Corps that "the cruelest form of denial is delay."

Unlike the Corps, Florida officials have a deadline. State law allows regulators just 90 days to review a permit or it is automatically issued. When we analyzed state records from 2003, we found that DEP permits were issued in an average of 44 days. That's why developers prefer the state: it says yes even faster than the Corps.

Developers argue the Corps permit is redundant, that it offers no additional environmental protection not already offered by the state permitting program. Actually there are big differences. The state permit certifies that wiping out the wetland will not harm water quality. The Corps permit reviewer is supposed to look at broader issues: whether the project is in the public interest and has a significant environmental impact.

Two more big differences prompt developers to favor state control. The Corps' definition of wetlands includes some plant species on its version of the "vegetative index" that the state does not recognize as wetland species. That may seem like a small thing, but as a result of its broader definition, Corps officials told us they claim jurisdiction over three million acres of wetlands in Florida that the state does not protect.

The other big difference between the two permitting programs is that the Corps, unlike the state, looks at whether a project can be built elsewhere to avoid damage to wetlands. State officials cannot legally look at whether a developer ought to be building on other property. They are limited to only the land shown in the permit application.

Those facts were lost or ignored during the 2005 legislative session, overwhelmed by the lobbying muscle exhibited by the state's development industry. Matthews was just the most prominent of the cadre of professional persuaders working the marble halls of Tallahassee on behalf of the industry. The Florida Home Builders Association had 18 lobbyists watchdogging its issues during 2005, while the Association of Florida Community Developers employed nine. Matthews was one of the few who worked for both organizations. Meanwhile, some lobbyists were employed by individual developers, such as WCI Communities, the largest home builder in Florida with more than 3,000 employees and 40 developments stretching from Jacksonville to Marco Island.

All the lobbyists in the world wouldn't get legislators' attention unless there were campaign contributions pouring in too. Builders and developers have donated millions of dollars to political parties and candidates in recent years. Some were legitimate, some not. For instance, top executives of the Miami-based engineering firm PBS&J (formerly known as Post Buckley Schuh & Jernigan) pleaded guilty in 2007 to making illegal contributions to Florida senator Mel Martinez, the Republican Party of Florida, and other recipients by ordering employees to donate to various campaigns, then reimbursing them.

Some developers gained positions of power with the political parties by bringing contributions from other people. For instance, WCI's multimillionaire CEO through the 1990s, Al Hoffman, chaired the fundraising operation for the National Republican Party, in addition to heading up fundraising for all three of Governor Jeb Bush's campaigns. A polo enthusiast with a mansion overlooking the Caloosahatchee River, Hoffman disdained government regulators who "think the world will end if they can't protect that little tree." He contended that Florida is nowhere near being overbuilt: "Relatively speaking, there aren't that many people in Florida, just about the same as the metro area of New York."

Among the recipients of the builders' campaign contributions was Trudi Williams, the Republican state representative from Fort Myers. Williams, a curly-haired woman in glasses, is an engineer whose clients include Hoffman's WCI. Prior to her election to the Florida House, she served as chairwoman of the South Florida Water Management District, where she routinely voted to approve state permits to wipe out wetlands. Of the $318,000 Williams collected in campaign contributions for her first election in 2004, nearly $54,000 came from developers like Hoffman.

In February 2005, in one of her first actions as an elected lawmaker, Williams filed a bill that would set in motion a possible state takeover of permitting from the Corps for projects that affect 10 acres of wetlands or fewer. Homebuilders' lobbyists estimated that that bill would move as much as 40 percent of the Corps' permitting into the state's hands.

Environmental groups blasted Williams for doing the bidding of big developers. But Williams repeatedly denied that developers played any role in pushing the bill. It was all her own idea, she said.

Then we obtained records showing that the true author of her bill was none other than Frank "Pave the World" Matthews.

Matthews had sent Williams a draft of the bill on January 13, shortly after she was sworn in. A note on top identifies it as "Frank Matthews New 1/13/05 Version." He followed up on February 4 with more refinements, and Williams introduced it as House Bill 759 four days later.

When we told Williams that the records appeared to contradict her claim that the state's developers had nothing to do with her bill, she changed her story. She still insisted the bill was her idea. But she explained that, as a freshman legislator, she just didn't know what it should say, so she sought someone with more experience in writing wetlands laws.

"I'm not an attorney, I'm an engineer, and Frank and I go back 20 years . . . so I called Frank and asked him for help," she explained with a stammer.

She said she could not understand why her bill was stirring up so much opposition.

"I'm a huge environmentalist," insisted Williams. As far as she was concerned, the controversy over her bill was "one of those really innocent things that has taken on a life of its own."

When a Florida voter contacted Williams to complain that she was making it easier for developers to destroy wetlands, she argued that just the opposite would be true: "Please understand that the intent of this bill is NOT to minimize the environmental aspects of wetland permitting, but rather to enhance them by creating a permitting process that has firm guidelines in place to protect wetlands. . . . The DEP is currently the only agency that has established guidelines in place to review such wetland permitting issues"—an apparent reference to DEP's deadline.

Not only would the permitting process be more efficient, she contended, but also it "will save millions of dollars—money better spent on protecting wetlands." She did not explain how saving the home builders money on their permitting would result in them spending the money on saving swamps.

In the 2005 session, the time seemed ripe for the builders to at last attain their Holy Grail. The top three positions in state government were filled by people connected to the development industry. Senate President Tom Lee (R-Brandon) was a home builder, while House Speaker Allen Bense (R-Panama City) made his fortune as a paving contractor; Governor Bush had worked in South Florida real estate and development.

The bill Matthews helped write for Representative Williams, which passed the legislature by a wide margin, called for the state DEP to report to Lee and Bense on how the state could take over the permitting as a first step to actually doing it.

The DEP had proposed cutting out the Corps before, but Corps officials would not give up their power to issue permits. This time, though, in addition to lobbying state legislators, the builders focused on lobbying Congress and the Pentagon to agree to the change.

In April 2005, builders from Jacksonville met with Assistant Secretary of the Army John Paul Woodley, the Pentagon official overseeing the Corps for the Bush Administration. The venue for the meeting: the Washington office of Representative Ander Crenshaw, R-Jacksonville, who made his living in investment banking but who had collected tens of thousands of dollars in campaign contributions from real estate interests.

Since Crenshaw sat on a House Appropriations subcommittee that oversees funding for the Corps, his support for the builders proved invaluable. After the meeting, Assistant Secretary Woodley, a former Virginia state environmental official who often displayed a bubbly optimism about the Corps' performance that environmental activists found disconcerting, told us he didn't see anything wrong with a state takeover of Corps wetland permitting.

"I've always felt that if the state was willing to undertake it, there would be some efficiencies to be gained," Woodley said.

Builders from other parts of Florida pushed the idea of a state takeover with their own congressmen and senators. "We met with everyone whose name we could spell," joked Narkiewicz of the Tampa Bay homebuilders group, which over two years spent $40,000 on the lobbying drive.

The developers worried that Governor Bush might not sign Williams' bill. He had, after all, sent her an e-mail warning her that pushing this issue for the developers was bad for her political reputation.

So they turned to Crenshaw and Senator Mack's son, now a congressman himself and occupying Porter Goss' old seat. In a May 27, 2005, e-mail to Trudi Williams' assistant, home builders' lobbyist Keith Hetrick wrote he had "told Trudi that she should also prompt Congressman Connie Mack . . . to be prepared to sign off on a letter in support of her bill being prepared by Congressman Crenshaw's office next week on behalf of as many of Florida's congressional delegation as we can get."

The result: a June 16, 2005, letter to Governor Bush signed by 15 congressmen—13 Republicans, 2 Democrats—urging him to approve Williams' bill.

"We believe this legislation sends a strong message to the Army Corps of Engineers that Florida is committed to streamlining and eliminating regulatory duplication," the letter said. "The legislation is a timely step in the right direction. . . . There has been considerable discussion with the ACOE to find ways to make the regulatory process more efficient. Passing this legislation into law will assist us in our efforts in working with the Corps to find viable solutions to this growing problem." There was no mention of the developers who were lobbying the congressmen for the changes.

Crenshaw then went a step further. He dispatched his chief of staff to a second meeting involving Assistant Secretary of the Army Woodley. This time they sat down for lunch in Tallahassee at the posh Governor's Club. The sponsor: the Association of Florida Community Developers.

Attending the lunch meeting were representatives from two of the state's major development companies, WCI and the St. Joe Company. Matthews was there, of course, as was Williams, who was flown to Tallahassee by WCI (she later reimbursed the developer, records show). Except for St. Joe, the developers had all donated to Williams' campaign, and St. Joe executives had donated to Crenshaw.

When we tried to question Crenshaw about his efforts on behalf of the developers, he sent us a written statement acknowledging that he had helped them. But he insisted that despite appearances, he still wanted to protect Florida's wetlands.

"I would not support making the permitting process more efficient and less wasteful if that meant Florida's environment would be harmed," Crenshaw wrote. "That would be a hollow victory."

On June 20, 2005, Governor Bush signed the bill. In a letter the charismatic governor explained why, saying the current two-tiered permitting system seemed unwieldy.

"Elimination of unnecessary, duplicative and overburdensome regulations is an excellent goal," Bush wrote, not mentioning the letter from the congressmen that Crenshaw had rounded up.

Now the developers turned to their last hurdle: getting the Corps to give up power, something that it has always loathed to do. Still, the builders knew that Corps officials would be inclined to do whatever Florida's congressional delegation wanted.

"We have worked through our congressmen to get their attention," Gilmore, the Pensacola builder, told us.

Before the legislature approved Williams' bill, Col. Carpenter had been openly skeptical of the proposed takeover. He pointed out that the Corps' definition of a wetland is so much broader than the state's that working out the differences might be impossible. If the builders really wanted faster permits, Carpenter told us, they should lobby Congress to give the Corps more money so it could hire more people to do the work. Just handing off responsibility to the state wouldn't help, since the state wouldn't get any extra funding to do the job.

"If you had a pie, and the pie's too small, cutting the pie in half doesn't make it any bigger," Carpenter explained.

But just a month later, on July 20, 2005, builders met again with Corps officials behind closed doors—this time in Marco Island during the Chamber of Commerce's environmental permitting seminar. We did not realize it at the time, but the meeting took place the day before we showed up to talk to Matthews.

The Marco Island meeting included Col. Carpenter and the replacement for the recently retired Hall, Jacksonville's new regulatory chief, Lawrence Evans. Also there were Representative Williams, Mr. "Pave the World" Matthews, and executives from WCI and other development companies. They talked to Carpenter and Evans about the need for the Corps to hand over its duties to the state. What they heard in response, they liked.

"Col. Carpenter was very gracious," Williams said afterward, "and he said we are going to see what we can do to make it happen."

When we asked Carpenter what changed, all he would say is, "We've reinvigorated the effort." That sounded like bureaucrat for: "We're being forced to look for reasons to do something we disagree with."

None of Florida's many vocal environmental groups were included in any of these closed-door meetings. So six days later, Carpenter and Evans met with a few South Florida environmental activists to talk about Everglades restoration and, while they were there, tried to sell the activists on Frank Matthews' plan for the state to take over some of the wetlands permitting.

"They said if they had fewer smaller wetlands that they had to regulate, then they would be able to focus on larger projects," said Jonathan Ullman of the Sierra Club. "They made it sound like they would be able to protect them. So we asked, 'Would you be able to say no, then?' They didn't answer." The environmental groups remained skeptical.

In October 2005, DEP officials released a 12-page report that said the state could indeed take over issuing wetland permits for projects of 10 acres or less—but only under certain conditions. For one thing, the state would need more money and more people to do the work. How much? It depends on how much of the Corps' permitting work the state has to take over, said the DEP secretary at the time, Colleen Castille.

If the DEP were to take over all of the Corps' wetland permitting duties, she said, then the legislature would have to eliminate the 90-day deadline for processing permits—thus wiping out the main reason behind the proposed state takeover.

Despite those concerns, in March 2006 Representative Williams was back with a new approach. Before the legislative session started, she had asked environmental groups for a bill that she could pass for them as a way of repairing her green reputation.

At the suggestion of the Audubon Society, she filed a bill doubling the amount of money available for the state's popular environmental land-buying program, Florida Forever. But then, to the dismay of the environmental activists, she included a section that called for the state to take over issuing permits to destroy wetlands of 10 acres or smaller. The addition delighted homebuilders.

"This will trim the bureaucratic nightmare," Gilmore crowed. But environmental activists fought the bill, and election year politics played a role as well. It failed to pass. A similar effort by Williams failed again in 2007 after the newly elected governor Charlie Crist said he opposed it.

Still, the push for a state takeover continues. At a U.S. Senate Armed Services Committee hearing in March 2007, the senators were supposed to be questioning Lt. Gen. Robert L. Van Antwerp about his nomination to take over the Corps after the retirement of Gen. Strock in the wake of Hurricane Katrina.

During the questioning, though, Senator Nelson brought up the subject of wetlands permitting in Florida—an odd juxtaposition, given how the loss of wetlands in Louisiana contributed to the disaster in New Orleans that ended Strock's career.

Nelson started off by inaccurately describing the Florida permitting process as "almost exactly a mirror image of the same permitting process of the Army Corps of Engineers." Then he went on to talk about how developers were expressing "a great deal of frustration" at the duplication between the state and the Corps.

Wouldn't it be better, he suggested, if "the two of you administratively can combine the efforts, since that at the end of the day, what we're trying to do is protect the environment, but make that administrative process an easier one. Not a more relaxed one, just a more administratively smooth one."

To make that happen, though, Nelson told the general, "it's going to take somebody like you making sure that the folks down the line are doing it. . . . And if you would give some signals from up high on Mount Olympus, I think that would be very much appreciated."

Even as Nelson was nudging the Corps to do the builders' bidding, the Corps had already worked out its own special deal with Florida's biggest landowner—a deal to cut the public out of having much say on the company's plans to redraw the map of the Panhandle, even though the taxpayers would be footing part of the bill.

14

Loopholes and Sinkholes

On a crisp morning in January 2002, Don Hodges steered his small boat along Burnt Mill Creek, putt-putting around its twists and turns. The day was clear and breezy, with puffy white clouds floating by looking like they were just barely out of reach. The banks of the creek were lined with live oaks and pines. Every one of them belonged to Florida's largest landowner, the St. Joe Company. It owned every square inch of land for miles around. It might as well own the clouds too.

The bustle of the beach town of Panama City lay some 20 miles to the southeast. When Hodges shut off his boat motor, the only sound we could hear was the rippling creek. If St. Joe's corporate executives have their way, that sound will soon be drowned out by the noise of jets landing at a new Panama City airport to be built on this very spot.

The Panama City-Bay County International Airport already sits in the heart of the city. It isn't exactly a thriving concern. As of early 2007 it offered just a dozen outbound commercial flights a day, half the number that took off from there in 2001. When passengers arrive, they walk into a terminal that's so empty it's like a green-roofed ghost town. The control tower shuts down every night at 10 p.m.

Yet at St. Joe's prodding, Panama City's airport authority board wants to build a new airport on 4,000 acres donated by St. Joe—land that until a few years ago was leased to the state as a wildlife management area, where hunters could freely roam around and shoot at deer and turkey without fear of hitting some suburbanite's pet Labradoodle. The nearest neighbor is the 6,900 wooded acres that make up Pine Log State Forest, Florida's oldest state forest, established way back in 1936, two years before the founding of the St. Joe Company.

About half of the proposed airport property, 2,000 acres, consists of wetlands that flow into Burnt Mill Creek and Crooked Creek, tributaries of St. Andrews Bay. So in addition to a green light from the Federal Aviation Admin-

Figure 16. The new $330-million Panama City–Bay County Airport, to be built on 4,000 acres of land along Burnt Mill Creek donated by the St. Joe Company, is expected to wipe out 2,000 acres of wetlands and spur development of surrounding land owned by St. Joe. (Photograph by Doug Clifford, *St. Petersburg Times*.)

istration to move its airport to St. Joe's land, the airport board needed permits from the Florida Department of Environmental Protection and, of course, the Corps of Engineers.

It needed money, too, lots of it. When Panama City airport officials first started talking about moving to St. Joe's land in the late 1990s, the price tag was around $200 million. By 2007 it had climbed to $330 million. The one thing that hadn't changed was the source of the airport's funding: two-thirds of it was supposed to be paid for by state and federal taxpayers.

New airports don't come along every day. Between 1970 and 2007, only four new commercial airports were built: Dallas-Fort Worth, Denver, Fort Myers, and Fayetteville, Arkansas. Each took decades of planning and study. As of 2007, no new airports had been begun since the tragic events of September 11, 2001, sent the airline industry into a tailspin.

Yet here, in a place that's miles from any highways or water lines or sewers, where there is only flora and fauna, Panama City officials want to put an airport that, at buildout, would be bigger than New York's LaGuardia Airport and Newark Liberty International Airport combined.

Panama City and unincorporated Bay County have a population that's less than one 100th of the population of the greater New York metropolitan area. But local officials make no pretense of needing the new airport to serve their current residents or the existing airline traffic, such as it is. Instead, they want a new airport because they hope it will jump-start their local economy and bring thousands of new residents flooding into the Panhandle.

"This new facility will . . . bring improved air service at competitive fares to Bay County," airport executive director Randy Curtis predicted. "It will also be a key factor in attracting more and better-paying jobs."

Hodges, a retired Delta Airlines executive who has been a leading critic of the push for a new airport, is skeptical: "Their idea is that you can put an airport out in a rural area and the airlines will come." He wouldn't object quite so much, he said, except that as a taxpayer he's going to be stuck with the bill for this boondoggle.

St. Joe's motive in donating the land is, of course, not the least bit altruistic. Like Ben Hill Griffin III foreseeing future profits from owning the land around Florida Gulf Coast University, St. Joe sees the new airport as a crucial element in its plans to develop one million acres of land across the Panhandle. In a letter to St. Joe stockholders, CEO Peter Rummell wrote that the new airport is "essential to unlocking the enormous value of our holdings."

"Definitely St. Joe will benefit," Curtis said. "But they're a major part of our community, and this is going to be a major benefit for the whole community."

From the air, this stretch of the Panhandle appears as an unending swath of green. In the rural counties west of Tallahassee, the land is largely untouched by the development that has carved up the rest of Florida. Winding two-lane roads connect a handful of towns too small to have a stoplight. Black bears prowl the thick woods. Along the coast lie miles of glistening white beaches where endangered sea turtles lay their eggs. Offshore, the water is full of crabs, speckled trout, and redfish. In the estuaries and tidal marshes are oysters, some as big as a man's hand.

People who live here call it "the forgotten coast." It has remained forgotten because the man who founded St. Joe, Ed Ball, wanted it that way. He knew a sparsely populated kingdom is easier to govern. People vote. Pine trees don't.

Ball, an eighth-grade dropout, tried his hand at prospecting for gold and ran the concession stand at George Washington's historic Mount Vernon homestead. Although his family in Ball's Neck, Virginia, was distantly related to the Father of Our Country, they were on the shabby side of genteel.

His fortunes changed dramatically when his sister Jessie became the third wife of a rich man named Alfred DuPont. The DuPonts of Delaware had made millions off gunpowder and dynamite. When Jessie and Alfred DuPont moved to Florida to get away from prying tax officials, the best man at their wedding, Ed Ball, came along to help manage their money.

They arrived around the time Florida's big 1920s development boom went bust. Land was dirt cheap, and Ball advised his brother-in-law to buy as much as he could—but not in South Florida, where the prices were higher. DuPont snapped up thousands of square miles of land in the rural Panhandle for mere pennies per acre.

When DuPont died in 1935, Ball became executor of his estate, and he kept on using DuPont's money to acquire things: land, banks, hotels, railroads, telephone companies, sugar plantations, politicians. Though he stood just five foot six, the man everyone called "Mr. Ball" towered over Florida's other would-be powerbrokers. A 1964 FBI memo to J. Edgar Hoover called the gnome-like Ball "the most powerful single individual" in Florida.

Ball maintained a plantation outside Tallahassee called Southwood and a lodge at picturesque Wakulla Springs, and he would invite governors and congressmen to come out and talk things over with him while he sipped a highball. Roads were built at his behest, laws passed for his benefit. Once, when he was tied up in a lawsuit he did not want to lose, Ball arranged for one of his companies to buy the judge's house for far more than it was worth and rent it back to him for a pittance. The judge, to no one's surprise, ruled for Ball. Years later, when a congressional committee questioned him about the purchase, Ball dismissed it as a routine business deal and the inquiry moved on.

Ball didn't like anything that might challenge his iron grip on the quiet Panhandle. Company lore says that in 1959, a well-known California entertainment entrepreneur wanted to buy some of St. Joe's timberland near Wakulla Springs, figuring it was the perfect location for Florida's first major theme park.

The story goes that Ball refused to talk to him. "I don't do business with carnival people," he supposedly snapped. That's how Walt Disney wound up building his Magic Kingdom amid the swamps of Central Florida.

The foundation of Ball's business empire was the firm then known as the St. Joe Paper Company, founded in 1938. The company drew its identity from the town of Port St. Joe. When DuPont bought the town—yes, the whole town—it was just a run-down fishing village, but the new owner had big plans for its transformation. A company history says DuPont envisioned "a model community of tree-lined streets, shops and housing with improved schools and playgrounds for children, and a brighter outlook for adults."

Instead, after DuPont died, Ball built a smoke-belching paper mill.

For decades the mill ran night and day. The first thing tourists cruising along the beachfront highway of U.S. 98 saw as they crossed the bridge into Port St. Joe was a mountain of logs stacked up at the mill waiting to be turned into cardboard boxes. If they made the mistake of rolling down their car windows, the tourists could smell the stomach-turning stench from the smokestacks. Tourists rarely stopped in Port St. Joe. Few even slowed down.

But unlike most of the towns in Florida, Port St. Joe didn't need tourists. The mill paid well enough that there were five car dealerships and three department stores downtown. It was such a company town that the mayor was a St. Joe Paper executive.

St. Joe Paper transformed the countryside around the town, too, ridding the landscape of the native longleaf pine, the kind best for the wildlife of the region. Instead, the company planted tight, orderly rows of slash pine, a species which grows faster and thus can be harvested more often, but which provides far-from-ideal habitat for such dwindling species as red-cockaded woodpeckers and flatwoods salamanders.

When Ball died in 1981, he had amassed a personal fortune worth $200 million, and the conglomeration of companies he had put together was worth more than $1 billion. The company tottered along without him until the mid-1990s, when new investors took over St. Joe Paper and nudged the company in a new direction. St. Joe sold off its paper mill, which then closed, throwing hundreds out of work.

What had attracted the investors was not St. Joe's mill or its trees, but its astonishingly diverse and widespread land holdings. No other private entity in Florida owned so much property free and clear. St. Joe soon dropped the "Paper" from its name, transforming itself into the biggest and most ambitious developer in the state. Its corporate slogan boasted that it was "No Ordinary Joe."

To lead the company in this new direction, the board of directors hired a native of rural upstate New York named Peter Rummell who, irony of ironies, had previously worked for Disney. He was about as far from "carnival people" as you could get, though. A hardheaded businessman with a frosty smile, Rummell had already enjoyed a long career in land development. Among his successes: creating the Disney-owned "New Urbanist" town called Celebration near Orlando. Now he was being handed a far bigger chunk of land to work with, and a chance to replicate Celebration's DNA a dozen times over.

Soon, from the sand dunes of Walton County to the rolling pastures just outside the state capital, bulldozers were rumbling across St. Joe land. In places that had once been considered the middle of nowhere, St. Joe began building homes and hotels, hospitals and schools, golf courses and shopping centers, theaters and restaurants, offices and industrial parks.

"My goal is to create some interesting towns, some interesting places," Rummell told us. He called St. Joe's efforts "regional place-making"—in effect, redrawing the map of Florida, filling in the empty spaces across the Panhandle with something new.

The remaking of the Panhandle began in a beige, four-story building across the St. Johns River from downtown Jacksonville, where St. Joe executives spent five years mapping out how to squeeze what they call "value to the Nth degree" from the company's 39 miles of coastline and an expanse of timberland stretching almost to Alabama. Because St. Joe owns so much land, it can sequence its developments like a line of dominoes, with coastal projects filling up first, leading to the ones further inland, all over the course of the next five decades.

"It's a large, complicated effort to figure out what to do with a million acres," Rummell told us.

There was no comparable effort in the halls of government. No local, state, or federal agency had considered the cumulative impact of St. Joe's plans. State planners—whose offices sit on land St. Joe donated on the outskirts of Tallahassee, land that used to be part of Ed Ball's Southwood plantation—told us state law never anticipated anything as sweeping as what St. Joe is doing. Making the state's job even harder, St. Joe's lobbyists persuaded the legislature to loosen the rules governing big developments in rural areas, arguing that helping St. Joe develop its land more quickly would boost employment in the job-starved region.

So the task of reviewing St. Joe's plans fell to short-handed local planners in small counties. In a land with no stoplights, there has been little to slow St. Joe's steamroller.

"Welcome to the Panhandle, owned and operated by St. Joe," quipped Aubrey Davis, chairman of the Washington County Republican Party.

St. Joe's development machine is oiled by its political influence. Between 1997 and 2002, St. Joe donated the maximum legal amount to more than 100 candidates for state cabinet and legislative posts from both parties, with subsidiaries like Arvida often making an identical donation to the same candidates.

Rummell and his wife gave $20,000 to the Republican National Committee during the 2000 presidential race. From 1997 to 2007, the company contributed more than $750,000 to the Florida GOP. During his 2006 reelection campaign, Senator Nelson collected more than $40,000 from St. Joe and its executives.

Nelson, a Democrat, wrote to the head of the FAA urging approval of the airport move. So did Republican senator Mel Martinez and Republican congressman Allen Boyd. All three elected officials took that pro–St. Joe position despite the clear wishes of a majority of the voters. In a 2004 nonbinding referendum election, Bay County residents voted 54 percent to 46 percent to oppose moving the airport, even if it wouldn't cost them a dime.

The connections between St. Joe and Florida's politicians are not just financial. They are personal, as well. The attorney shepherding St. Joe's development plans in Bay County, William Harrison, cochaired the Bush presidential campaign in the Panhandle. St. Joe bought a one-third interest in Governor Jeb Bush's former real estate company, the Codina Group in Miami. Several of Bush's former aides wound up working for St. Joe.

Rummell said he personally lobbied Governor Bush to support the new airport. Bush also wrote the FAA to urge approval of the project, and during his two terms in office he sunk more than $90 million of the state's highway funds into it. In a 2003 letter to Panama City area residents, Governor Bush explained why: thanks to the airport relocation and St. Joe's development plans "there exists a tremendous opportunity for Bay County to lead as an economic powerhouse."

Yet, in marketing its new developments, St. Joe downplays the company's attempt to give the Panhandle an extreme makeover. Instead the brochures emphasize the area's slow pace and folksy charm. The ads tout the tupelo honey produced nowhere but Wewahitchka and the tasty gumbo at the Indian Pass Raw Bar, a popular restaurant near Cape San Blas that's run out of a turn-of-the-century turpentine company commissary. One brochure describes Port St. Joe as "a place where, if you forgot to put soap on the grocery list, you can call George at the Piggly Wiggly and he'll find your husband on aisle 8 and remind him."

Such homey touches are possible in places like Gulf County, population 13,000, and Franklin County, population 11,000. But if St. Joe succeeds, tens of thousands of newcomers from St. Joe's targeted marketing area, which Rummell calls "the middle South," will pour in from Atlanta, Cleveland, Houston, and points in between. So many rootless transplants will inevitably alter the region's economy, politics, and culture.

"Except for the Piggly Wiggly, there's not going to be any place for a small-town person to be in it," grumbled John Spohrer, fishing columnist for a local weekly called the *Forgotten Coast Line*.

St. Joe's intended customers are more likely to get their hair styled at a salon than get a buzz cut at the barber shop. They will live on Mystic Cobalt Street or Moss Rose Way, not Monument Avenue. They will want full-service marinas for their 60-foot Buddy Davis yachts, not a ramp for their bass boats.

"The type of development that's going on is going to create a rich and a poor community," predicted 59-year-old Port St. Joe native Barbara Eells, a retired schoolteacher. "The prices they're charging, it takes someone from out of town or out of state to buy it."

The company even wants to change the region's nickname from the Panhandle to "Florida's Great Northwest." Company spokesman Jerry Ray said St. Joe executives frown on the word "Panhandle" because a panhandler is someone looking for a handout.

To make their plans work, though, St. Joe executives do have their hands out for a little monetary assistance from the taxpayers. They want new express-ways costing hundreds of millions of dollars. And they really want that new airport.

With the airport in place, St. Joe would be able to proceed with plans for the 70,000 acres immediately around it, building homes, stores, hotels, bars, schools, even a barge port. Without the airport, Rummell said, those plans may never bear fruit.

Normally St. Joe's many projects would require scores of federal permits for wiping out wetlands. Processing all those permits could take years, since each one would require posting a public notice that would invite comments from federal and state agencies, environmental groups, civic activists, and potential neighbors.

Instead, officials from the Corps and the state DEP spent three years holding closed-door meetings with St. Joe executives, then unveiled the result in 2003: a pair of blanket permits—one from the state and one from the Corps, both tailored just for St. Joe and covering the entire region around the airport. Both were officially approved by their respective agencies in mid-2004. The Corps permit covered the filling of wetlands for various projects throughout more than 48,000 acres around the airport. More than three-fourths of the land included in the permit is owned by St. Joe.

This special permit falls under a category known in the Corps as "regional permits." They are supposed to give blanket permission for dredge and fill in a geographic area for one category of activities, provided that the activities are similar in nature and will cause only minimal adverse environmental effects.

At 75 square miles, the Panhandle regional permit is acknowledged by Corps officials to be the largest one they have ever issued. It is also the most sweeping. The regional permit was written to cover dredge and fill for (take a deep breath):

> the construction of residential, commercial, recreation and institutional projects, including building foundations, building pads and attendant features that are necessary for the use and maintenance of the structures. Attendant features may include, but are not limited to, roads, parking lots, garages, yards, utility lines and stormwater management facilities. Residential developments include multiple and single-unit developments. Examples of commercial developments include retail stores, light industrial facilities, restaurants, business parks and shopping centers. Examples of recreational facilities include playgrounds, playing fields, golf courses, hiking trails, bike paths, horse paths, stables, nature centers and campgrounds. Examples of institutional developments include schools, fire stations, government office buildings, judicial buildings, public works buildings, libraries, hospitals and places of worship.

The only type of project that would not be covered by the permit would be the airport itself, which would be handled with its own individual permit.

To Ray, St. Joe's spokesman, this regional permit approach provided far greater environmental benefits than the usual, piecemeal approach to approving development in wetland areas. "This is a very forward-looking approach to managing growth and achieving broad-range environmental protection," Ray told us. "First, you identify what you want to protect, then you decide which areas are appropriate for development."

It's an approach that makes good business sense, Ray said, because "we recognize that the best way to increase the value of our land is to protect its environmentally special qualities, and plan thoughtfully and carefully for the long term. . . . St. Joe believes environmental protection and long-term planning are essential if we are to protect the quality of life in Northwest Florida."

For the Corps, the appeal was far more basic: issuing a single regional permit for the area speeds everything up by shutting out public participation.

Instead of a permit for each project, "the landowner designates where they'll have an impact and we issue a letter of approval," explained Bob Barron, who was part of the Corps' negotiations with St. Joe. That way, he said, "they don't have to go through the whole public notice process. That's really what we want to get to. We want to expand that through the rest of the state."

St. Joe's deal with the Corps had the blessing of Audubon and The Nature Conservancy, which were excited by the permit's mitigation requirements for preserving and restoring more than 13,000 acres of St. Joe land—although, of course, that would mean a net loss of wetland acreage from St. Joe's development. Other environmental groups, including the Sierra Club, the Natural Resources Defense Council, and the Clean Water Network, said the whole thing stunk of back-room dealing to give St. Joe a loophole for getting around the Clean Water Act's requirements. They sued to stop both the state and federal permits.

Ray contended there was no back-room deal. There were, he told us, "multiple opportunities for public input. There were 60 days of public notice and everyone identified as an interested party was notified by mail. There were two public meetings, one in September 2003 and another in January 2004. A briefing was held in August 2003 with eight representatives from local citizen groups."

In addition, he said, "individual briefings were conducted with Bay and Walton county commissioners, the state legislative delegation, and staff from the offices of U.S. representative Allen Boyd and U.S. senators Bill Nelson and Bob Graham."

But Linda Young of the Clean Water Network, the activist who tried and failed to stop the Levin family's Portofino development on Pensacola Beach, said that the environmental groups were shut out of the most important part of the negotiations among the state, the Corps, and St. Joe. By the time the public had a chance to comment on the plans in late 2003, she said, all the big decisions on both permits had already been made. When environmental groups finally were allowed to suggest changes, they were ignored, she said.

The Corps permit was particularly troublesome to the environmental groups. For one thing, the permit divided the wetlands into two classes: high quality and low quality. The low-quality wetlands are the ones planted in slash pine by St. Joe. Those would not require a full acre-for-acre mitigation, the permit said. Instead, they were considered to be worth only 65 percent of the high-quality wetlands. The Clean Water Act, the environmental groups pointed out, makes no such distinctions between types of wetlands.

The regional permit said that no more than 125 acres of the high-quality wetlands could be destroyed throughout the region, and no more than 1,386 acres of low-quality wetlands could be wiped out. The environmental groups questioned how allowing a total of 1,511 acres of wetland impacts could be considered a "minimal" impact on the environment. They also pointed out that there was no requirement for avoiding or minimizing wetland impacts as long as a development did not exceed the cap on the acreage destroyed.

In November 2005, a federal judge slapped a temporary injunction on the Corps to halt use of the regional permit. U.S. District Judge Timothy Corrigan agreed with the environmental groups that regional permits like the kind given to St. Joe are supposed to be issued only when they cover activities "similar in nature" and have only minimal effect on the environment.

The Corps had argued that all the diverse St. Joe projects could be grouped together under the category "suburban development" and thus the agency considered them all to be similar in nature. Corrigan said that made sense only if the phrase were "robbed of all its meaning." Different kinds of development have different kinds of impacts and should be considered individually by the Corps, with the public getting a chance to comment on each one, he ruled.

Corrigan also noted that so many development projects going on in the same area would clearly have more than just a minimal effect on the environment, thus undercutting the whole point of issuing a regional permit.

Ray complained that Corrigan's ruling was "an unfortunate step toward reversing the permanent protection status of these wetlands and other conservation land." But Young, the activist, declared it a huge victory for a public fed up with wetland losses.

In 2006, however, Corrigan reversed himself. He ruled that "by the slimmest of margins" the Corps and St. Joe had now persuaded him that the law and regulations governing Section 404 were so vague that a vaguely defined regional permit was not illegal. Still, Corrigan noted that he was troubled by their argument: "No matter how large or small, the Court just cannot fathom how a golf course is 'similar in nature' to a dry cleaner or a hospital or a horse stable."

The case is still on appeal, but St. Joe has already made use of the regional permit to win Corps approval of several of its developments. The largest, WaterSound North, calls for the destruction of about 60 acres of wetlands for a 1,400-acre golf course subdivision that the environmental groups fear will pollute a rare coastal dune lake nearby.

In August 2007, the Corps approved the 404 permit for the airport, concluding that boosting the Panhandle's economy with a taxpayer-funded construction project was more in the public interest than saving 2,000 acres of wetlands. Corps officials said they were swayed by St. Joe's promise to preserve 9,000 acres of land southeast of the airport site.

"Mother Nature is the best place-maker of all time, and now we will be protecting forever some of her best work," Rummell announced in a news release.

But Linda Young grumbled that the preservation plan would do nothing to protect the upstream wetlands along Burnt Mill Creek. She compared it to saying, "We're going to preserve your arms and legs forever, but we're going to cut out your heart and liver."

The announcement about the airport permit gave St. Joe a badly needed financial boost. With Florida's real estate market in a serious slump, the company's stock price had been trading well below a 52-week high of more than $60 a share in February 2007. After the Corps permit decision was announced, St. Joe's stock closed at $34.56, up $1.08. However, the boost was short-lived. In October, with Florida's real estate industry headed into its worst dive in years, St. Joe announced it would eliminate about 80 percent of its 900-person work force, sell 100,000 acres of land, and scrap its dividend to shareholders.

In the meantime, the Corps pushed ahead with its plans to develop regional permits for other parts of Florida. There's one for the DOT for road projects that wipe out wetlands while widening highways. There's another—for use in Baker, Brevard, Clay, Duval, Flagler, Lake, Marion, Nassau, Orange, Putnam, Seminole, St. Johns, and Volusia counties—that in effect gives homebuilders in some of the state's fastest-growing areas a free pass on the public notice process as long as the project affects only three acres of wetlands or less.

The National Marine Fisheries Service lodged a strong objection to the three-acre threshold for that permit, warning that it would lead to a far from minimal impact on the environment. But the Corps issued the regional permit anyway.

Developers really like those regional permits, Frank Matthews told us when we talked to him in Marco Island. In the various versions of Representative Trudi Williams' bill pushing the state's takeover of some of the Corps' permitting authority—the bills that Matthews helped write—Williams offered a backup idea for speeding up wetlands destruction for development:

a series of regional permits like the one for St. Joe, tailored to different parts of the state.

Even better for the developers, of course, are the areas of the state where the Corps has ceased to require a permit at all.

Every time a hard rain falls on the town of Brooksville, about 50 miles north of Tampa, the water that splashes onto parking lots and driveways and other impervious surfaces in the south end of town flows downhill and washes into a small creek. The creek snakes downhill even further into a wooded area filled with a complex of sinkholes called Peck Sink. From there the water swirls into the Floridan Aquifer, the underground source of water for millions of Tampa Bay area residents.

The rainwater draining into Peck Sink would be loaded with pollution if it were not filtered first by the wetlands scattered around the sinkholes in the creek's 14,000-acre watershed.

Until 2003, anyone who wanted to destroy those wetlands needed a permit from the Corps. But not anymore—and as a result, the Peck Sink watershed is Ground Zero for the biggest development boom in Hernando County. A new hospital and several new subdivisions are under way.

"The big land developers are scrambling," said John Burnett, Hernando County's leading expert on Peck Sink, as he led us on a tour of the sinkhole complex one cool October afternoon.

Peck Sink is typical of what geologists call a karst landscape, a limestone honeycomb of sinkholes, underground caverns, and hidden rivers that gush back to the surface as springs. In a karst landscape, such as the one that covers much of the Florida peninsula, the unstable limestone collapses in spots, making the surface slump. In the resulting depression, rain pools form to create small wetlands that sprout cypress trees and fill up with frogs and other swamp-dwellers.

Florida is covered with these small wetlands, many of which aren't visibly connected to rivers or streams. For years, the Corps justified protecting such isolated wetlands under the Clean Water Act, using a somewhat convoluted line of reasoning. Despite Congress' clear directive that the act was supposed to cover all of "the waters of the United States," the Corps fretted that that was insufficient grounds for invoking its authority. So instead it argued that because migratory birds use isolated wetlands, and because migratory bird protection falls under the rubric of interstate commerce, the Corps should protect isolated wetlands.

But in January 2001, the U.S. Supreme Court said that was too big a stretch. In a case called *Solid Waste Authority of Cook County v. United States* (or SWANCC for short), the high court said the Corps' migratory bird rule was, well, for the birds.

As a result, would-be developers across the country quickly petitioned the Corps to reclassify their wetlands as isolated and therefore "SWANCCed" out from under federal protection. The White Springs Phosphate Company, for example, persuaded the Corps to stop regulating 3,000 acres of wetlands near the historic Suwannee River in North Florida, freeing that land up for mining without a 404 permit.

That's what happened with Peck Sink. In April 2002, Charles Courtenay of King Engineering in Tampa wrote to the Corps on behalf of four development companies with property in Hernando County. He asked the agency to drop its jurisdiction over the area that drains into Peck Sink.

Jake Varn, an attorney for one of the developers, Land Mar of Jacksonville, said it was "just a technical exercise" that was "pretty cut and dried."

Two months after Courtenay sent his letter, two Corps biologists determined that he was right. The wetlands and streams in the 14,000 acres around Peck Sink were not subject to federal regulation.

"All the surface water winds up in the aquifer," explained Richard Legere, who led the Corps team that examined Peck Sink. Because there was no surface connection to a navigable waterway, the Corps could not consider that area to be under its jurisdiction, he said.

The problem is the water that flows into Peck Sink doesn't stay underground, explained Gene Altman of the Southwest Florida Water Management District as we picked our way down the muddy slopes around the sink. He said the water probably gushes back to the surface either eight miles away at Weeki Wachee Springs or 15 miles away at Chassahowitzka Springs.

How much water? Consider this: when we reached the edges of the central depression of the sinkhole complex, we were surrounded by sweet gum trees. On the sweet gums, the lichen line showing where white lichens grow like spots of mold on the tree bark didn't start until at least 25 feet off the ground. The lichens are not water tolerant. They only grow where the bark has remained dry. That means that within the previous five years, the water rose that high on the trees.

Seeing that natural marker of the crest of the flood was a little unnerving because, at the moment John Burnett pointed out how high the water level had been, we were standing about 10 feet below the lichen line.

Most wetlands in a karst landscape only appear to be isolated, according to a study by the U.S. Fish and Wildlife Service. Many, like those in Florida, are actually linked by rivers flowing underground—in other words, by the aquifer that supplies 90 percent of Florida's drinking water.

"There are a lot of areas where what's been classified as an isolated wetland pops up somewhere else," Legere said. But does the corps consider that? "Once it goes underground," he said, "for the most part, not a lot."

Allowing builders to fill in those wetlands has consequences for more than just the aquifer, said Sandy Nettles, a Pinellas County geologist. Think of such wetlands as a funnel that drips down into the underground caverns. Now put fill dirt on top of it and a house on top of that. Slowly, over a decade or more, the plant material under the fill will decay and the fill will begin to settle, sinking into the funnel. As it settles, the foundation of anything built on top will crack, Nettles explained.

In his files are repeated examples of homeowners who took their builder or insurance company to court over the cracking of their home's foundation. In one Pasco County neighborhood, a dozen houses had cracks. Each one had been built atop filled wetlands that years later settled and sank.

"You start looking at what was there and what happened, and you wonder why the hell are we still building in these things," Nettles told us. "You may last 10 years, you may last 20 years—but it's gonna go on you."

In the case of Peck Sink, the Corps should have determined if its flow resurfaces somewhere before deciding to stop regulating its wetlands, said Jim Murphy, an attorney for the National Wildlife Federation. In 2002, Murphy pointed out, a federal court in Idaho ruled that the Clean Water Act protects underground waterways that are connected to waterways on the surface, "particularly under circumstances where the introduction of pollutants into the groundwater adversely affects the adjoining surface waters."

In Tennessee, the Corps decided in 2003 that plans to expand an airport in Sparta across 10 acres of apparently isolated wetlands did not need federal permits. But then the National Wildlife Federation paid for a test to see where the water went. Using dye to trace its path, the test showed that water from the wetlands flowed underground to Falling Water River. As a result, the Corps reversed its decision in 2005.

Also in 2005, a ping pong ball forced the Corps to backtrack on a decision not to protect an apparently isolated wetland near Lysander, New York. A staffer in the New York Attorney General's Office tossed the ping pong ball into the wetland. The ping pong ball then popped out half a mile away in a stream that flowed to the nearby Seneca River, proving that the wetland and the river were connected underground.

No one has done a dye test or tossed a ping pong ball into Peck Sink, but area residents are well aware of how the underground and aboveground flows are connected. In 2004, when four hurricanes belted Florida in short order, so much rain washed down from Brooksville that the sinkholes couldn't absorb it all.

Water backed up across roads and climbed halfway up pasture fences, said cattle rancher George Casey. The flood rose so high that a house built atop an eight-foot mound of fill only narrowly avoided inundation. Slowly, the muddy flow glug-glugged down into the sinkholes—and as it went down, the private water wells in the area all turned brown, Casey said. He wants Brooksville to divert its stormwater runoff away from Peck Sink. If that polluted flow goes down into the sinkhole, he said, "you're talking about drinking water for 1,000 people being polluted."

When Hernando officials let us ride along with them to check the flow into Peck Sink two months after the last hurricane hit, the flow had returned to normal, but mud coated the hillside and the trees several feet up.

To get to the sinkhole complex, we drove through a farmer's gate and then hiked back into the woods. Two weeks later, the farm's owner padlocked the gate and posted a sign that said: "FOR SALE 40 acres. Will divide."

Even Land Mar's attorney could see the problem with using SWANCC to make it easier to wipe out wetlands. "We have to get away from the mentality of out of sight, out of mind, when it comes to the quality of groundwater in this state," said Varn, former secretary of the state Department of Environmental Regulation.

But when it comes to the Corps' most popular wetland permits, they might as well be out of sight, as two retirees in New Smyrna Beach discovered.

∾

Pam Winchester heard the news from her son in March 2001. He'd heard it from friends at his middle school, kids whose parents were local attorneys and city council members. The word was that the world's largest retailer, Wal-Mart, was going to build a new supercenter on 37 acres of land just down the road from her house. A shady wooded area on a creek would be turned into a 225,000-square-foot store surrounded by 1,000 parking spaces.

Winchester lives on State Road 44 in New Smyrna Beach, a family-friendly beach town popular with surfers. SR 44 is a stretch of two-lane blacktop that, in Winchester's neighborhood, has no commercial development on it at all. A Wal-Mart (and not just any Wal-Mart, but a Wal-Mart supercenter) would forever alter everything around her—the amount of traffic, the noise level, even the night sky.

"I took my dog for a walk and I was in tears," Winchester said. "I moved here because I liked the quiet, the woods. I liked to be able to see the stars at night."

Winchester is a retired optical technician. She recruited one of her neighbors, a retired banker named Barbara Herrin, to help her mobilize the neighborhood to fight Wal-Mart.

"I made a flier announcing there was going to be a meeting in my front yard," Winchester said. "Everybody brought their lawn chairs."

They organized a group of 200 people to try stopping Wal-Mart. They did the standard protest stuff: led a march, waved picket signs, showed up at public hearings. But in the end, it was their digging through public records that made a difference.

They knew the site Wal-Mart had picked for its new store usually flooded in the rainy season, with the flow running toward nearby Spruce Creek, which is classified as an Outstanding Florida Waterway. They were convinced that such a soggy site would never get a permit from the state or federal government—until they discovered that the permits had already been issued. The Corps had issued its permit a month before Winchester ever heard about the new Wal-Mart.

"What angered me the most was everybody said it was a done deal," Winchester said. "They keep telling you can't fight Wal-Mart. I'm either extremely stupid or stubborn."

The reason the Corps issued the permit so quickly was that Wal-Mart's environmental consultants, Kimley-Horn and Associates, had put on the 404 application that only a tenth of an acre of wetlands on the site would be destroyed. That qualified Wal-Mart for something called a "nationwide permit."

Nationwide permits are designed to give quick approval for impacts to small wetlands. Developers like nationwides because the Corps approves them rapidly, with minimal review. There was a time when nationwides covered wetland impacts of up to five acres, but during the Clinton Administration they were scaled back to cover impacts of only half an acre.

The Corps approved Wal-Mart's permit without verifying its consultant's information. That's what usually happens with nationwide permits. The impact is so small that the Corps staff spends very little time on an application before saying yes.

But when Herrin and Winchester looked at the information in Wal-Mart's permit, "we knew it couldn't be true," Winchester said.

By then the controversy over the Wal-Mart had reached the ears of Lesley Blackner, the West Palm Beach attorney who had tangled with the Corps over the Suncoast Parkway. Blackner had become concerned about nation-wide permits and was looking for a good case to take the Corps to court. Since Herrin and Winchester were looking for an attorney, Blackner volunteered to help.

What Blackner saw unfold was a cautionary tale about why Florida continues to lose wetlands, regardless of the Clean Water Act and the no-net-loss policy.

"The whole Corps permitting system is based on the assumption that if no citizen objects, then there's nothing wrong with issuing the permits as the Corps sees fit," Blackner said. Instead the permit reviewers take as gospel what's in the application, "which I think is crazy."

Herrin, a former member of Volusia County's land-use planning panel, discovered that the site Wal-Mart wanted to build on had once been considered for a new high school. The school board rejected it because it was too wet. Herrin and Winchester dug through school board records and found a report showing that the site actually contained 18 acres of wetlands—far more than Kimley-Horn had said.

Herrin drove over to the Corps' office in Palatka that had issued the nation-wide permit, where she discovered that most of the paperwork processing was being done by teenagers with after-school jobs. There was no analysis of the information being submitted by the applicant.

"They go strictly on the applicants' word: 'Give us the permit,' bam-bam-bam!" Herrin said bitterly.

Wal-Mart, Kimley-Horn, and the Corps all should have known how extensive the site's wetlands really were, Herrin said, because in the file in the Corps' Palatka office, she found Wal-Mart's purchase contract with the school board report attached to it.

With that documentation in hand, Herrin and Winchester persuaded experts from the St. Johns River Water Management District to visit the site. The water district experts determined that Wal-Mart's plans would wipe out

10 acres of the site's wetlands—100 times what Kimley-Horn had actually reported. (We tried to talk to someone from Kimley-Horn about the discrepancy, but the company spokesman turned us down. When we called Wal-Mart, a spokesman would say only that the company did everything the Corps required, period.)

Because that nationwide permit was based on bogus information, the women urged the Corps to rescind it. Instead, the Corps required Wal-Mart to apply for an additional permit for the extra acreage that had not been covered in the original.

By that point, the two retirees had alerted other federal agencies to the situation. The U.S. Environmental Protection Agency and the National Marine Fisheries Service told the Corps it should deny the new permit and save the wetlands.

Then Blackner, on behalf of her clients, sued the Corps. The suit pointed out that for 15 years the Corps failed to study the cumulative impact of its nationwide permits in Florida.

"There's no review at all, because it's been presumed that they have no impact," Blackner said. "They don't know what kind of impact they have. All they really care about is the efficient issuance of permits. They think it's what their job is. It's outrageous."

The Corps did not want to go trial, so in December 2003 the two sides met for settlement talks.

"There were a lot of suits," at the meeting, Winchester said. "They gave us their version of the dog and pony show." She said Corps officials asked what the women wanted. Winchester said she told them, "We just want you to do your job. We want you to protect us."

In June 2004 the Corps agreed to do a cumulative impact study of all its nationwide permits issued in Florida. Meanwhile, the Corps rejected Wal-Mart's second permit, thus preventing the retail giant from building on the site. The project was not in the public interest said the denial document signed by John Hall and Col. Carpenter. It asserted that "a less environmentally damaging project site may have been located with a more exhaustive search for alternatives."

Hall told us the permit denial—one of just four the Jacksonville office issued that year—had nothing to do with the lawsuit or with the false information in Wal-Mart's prior permit application. He insisted it was turned down strictly because the wetlands on the Wal-Mart site were worth saving and less damaging alternatives existed.

"The area they wanted to fill," Hall said, "was really, really nice."

Building Wal-Marts on wetlands tends to lead to more and more pollution showing up in Florida's waterways. The wetland permitting system is supposed to make sure that doesn't happen. But as the people who live on the St. Johns River found out in 2005, there's a loophole in the system big enough to choke a city.

15

Dirty Water

The green goop first showed up in the St. Johns River in July 2005. At first it was just a little here, a little there.

"Then it just exploded," said Neil Armingeon, the burly, pony-tailed guru of an environmental watchdog group called the St. Johns Riverkeeper.

Soon slimy blue-green algae coated the water's surface everywhere. It clogged the river for miles, producing toxic fumes that left Jacksonville residents coughing and sneezing if they got downwind.

The cause: water polluted with nutrients.

The nutrients come from the nitrogen and phosphorous in fertilizers, poorly treated sewage, and septic tank waste that's washed into the river—from storm drains like the one by John Hall's condo and a million other places along the banks—every time there's a storm.

The St. Johns meanders northward from the marshes around Lake Hell'n Blazes west of Melbourne, but it flows so slowly toward Jacksonville that it may be the laziest waterway in the state. From source to mouth, the drop is only an inch per mile, making the current sluggish at best. This river doesn't run—it walks. Twice a day, when the tide from the Atlantic Ocean pushes into the river's mouth, the St. Johns' current actually flows backwards.

That means the St. Johns cannot flush out pollution as easily as rivers that flow more steadily. Instead, the nutrients from suburban yards, golf courses, shopping center landscaping, sewage plants, and farms pour into the river, piling up. So much nutrient pollution has been dumped into the St. Johns over the years that the river can't absorb any more, state officials say.

The nutrients flowing into the river function just the way you would expect fertilizer to function: they stimulate plant growth. In this case, though, the stimulated plants are microscopic algae. The algae are always there, usually just a few of them. But when conditions are just right, they proliferate and crowd together in what's called an algae bloom, creating a thick mat that blocks sunlight from reaching the grasses growing on the river bottom. As the algae bloom and die, they suck up all the oxygen in the water, which leads to big fish kills.

In the summer of 2005 the conditions were just right for a truly massive algae bloom. The rainfall from the previous year's string of hurricanes had sent a particularly heavy flow of nutrient-laden runoff cascading into the St. Johns, where it washed back and forth with the current. Record high temperatures cooked it all up, and soon the gargantuan bloom painted the river, the riverbanks, the docks, and everything else that touched the water a weird neon green.

Swimmers and anglers who had made the mistake of splashing in the river reported skin rashes. Tests confirmed the bloom was a type of toxic blue-green algae called *Microcystis aeruginosa*. The algae produce a kind of toxin known as mycrocistins, and the sampling also detected a second toxin, cylindrospermopsin. These toxins do more than just irritate the skin. In extreme cases, both can cause liver damage.

And this sure seemed like an extreme case. The World Health Organization says that the maximum concentration for this type of algae that's still safe for human health is 10 parts of algae per one billion parts water. Near Jacksonville Naval Air Station, the river contained more than 1,400 parts per billion.

County health officials warned residents and tourists to refrain from any activities that could lead to exposure or contact with the river. In other words, no swimming, no fishing, no boating, no wading, no riding around on Jet Skis—nothing.

"The algae is the river's way of telling us that it's sick," Armingeon said.

By September the bloom stretched more than 100 miles from downtown Jacksonville to rural Crescent City. It finally faded toward the end of October.

While the bloom in the St. Johns River was making headlines, a similar bloom was going on in Lake Okeechobee. The lake has been a dumping area for nutrients from farm and suburban runoff for decades. Though it covers 730 square miles, Okeechobee is only nine feet deep, and some of the bottom is covered in three feet of nutrient-packed ooze. The hurricanes stirred up the ooze, producing what Col. Carpenter called "a chocolate mess."

When heavy rains pushed the water level in Lake Okeechobee too high, threatening to breach the dike that's supposed to protect the communities around its edge, state and federal officials dumped millions of gallons of lake water into the rivers that are connected to it. That spread the pollution into the

Caloosahatchee River and the St. Lucie River, which suffered their own algae blooms.

Fish in the St. Lucie developed skin lesions and rotting fins, driving away anglers and tourists. The people didn't do too well either. Seventeen-year-old Grayson Kyte waded into a lagoon off the St. Lucie hoping to catch some mullet and caught something no fisherman wants. The next day, he said, "my whole right leg swelled to twice its size." Doctors told him he had developed a staph infection from the algae bloom.

"It's an ecological disaster for both estuaries," said Kevin Henderson of an environmental restoration group called the St. Lucie River Initiative.

The ecological disaster became an economic one. Tourists took one look at the sickly green water and the dead fish and canceled their hotel rooms. Lee County officials figured their tourism-related businesses lost $4 million. The fishing industry lost income too as their catch either died or fled the polluted area.

"There's no fish, no crabs, no nothing," complained Sanibel bait shop owner Ralph Woodring. "It's the worst I've ever seen. It makes me want to cry."

What happened in the St. Johns, Lake Okeechobee, the St. Lucie, and the Caloosahatchee that summer was simply the most visible manifestation so far of a growing epidemic among most of Florida's waterways. All over the state are rivers, lakes, creeks, bays, and estuaries beset by similar pollution problems. Even the state's famous springs have not been immune. Swimmers have reported skin rashes, nausea, swelling, dizziness, breathing problems, and stomach pains. State officials are investigating whether the cause could be pollution-fueled algae blooms. Their prime suspect: a type of toxic blue-green algae called *Lyngbya wollei*.

In 1998 state officials drew up a list of 1,200 Florida waterways impaired by various kinds of pollution. About 80 percent had problems with high levels of nutrients and low levels of dissolved oxygen. Both are manifestations of fertilizer-heavy runoff.

When we compared the list of waterways in Florida suffering from too many nutrients or too little dissolved oxygen with our satellite imagery analysis of the state, we found those waterways were all in areas where Florida has lost the most wetlands to urbanization since 1990.

That's no big surprise. Wetlands soak up rain and filter out pollution. Paving them over means the runoff and pollutants have to go somewhere else.

But when Florida officials issue a permit for destroying a wetland, they certify that the project will not result in a violation of water quality standards. So how is it that these areas where the state has permitted the loss of wetlands wind up experiencing such severe water pollution problems?

Because, we discovered, that's the way the state's permitting process works.

Everything hinges on a document called the "Basis of Review for Environmental Resource Permits." Clark Hull, who heads up environmental permitting for the Southwest Florida Water Management District, calls it "the Bible."

In the Basis of Review—which is used by all of the state's water districts in processing permits—state officials outline the criteria that developers must meet when they wipe out wetlands. The criteria spell out what steps they must take to deal with flooding and rain runoff. For instance, the Basis of Review gives specifics for how retention ponds must be constructed, using language such as, "Wet detention volume shall be provided for the first inch of runoff from the developed project, or the total runoff of 2.5 inches times the percentage of imperviousness, whichever is greater."

If a developer meets the criteria in the Basis of Review, Hull said, then the developer has given the regulators a reasonable assurance that his or her development project won't cause flooding or water pollution and they issue the permit.

In 2002, a developer proposed building a new shopping mall and apartment complex called Cypress Creek Town Center that would destroy 56 acres of Pasco County cypress swamps. The swamps feed Cypress Creek, which flows into the Hillsborough River, which supplies drinking water for Tampa. The Sierra Club and other opponents of the new $200 million mall rounded up lots of people to sign postcards urging Hull's bosses at the water district to deny the permit because they feared its stormwater runoff would taint Tampa's water supply.

But it was a wasted effort. The mall's planners, the Richard E. Jacobs Group of Cleveland, made sure they followed the requirements of the Basis of Review. Since the plans followed the rules, the agency commonly known as "Swiftmud" approved the project. And once the state said it wouldn't cause water quality violations, the Corps found little reason to oppose it either. The Corps approved the mall's Section 404 permit in May 2007.

One reason state officials rely so heavily on their Basis of Review to help them make their decisions is that the clock is ticking. State regulators have just 90 days to say yes or no. If they take no action, the permit is automatically issued, so state officials move as fast as they can to say yes.

During a DEP internal investigation of permitting in the Pensacola office in 2005, state employees painted a portrait of an office so focused on cranking out permits that nothing else mattered. So many permit reviewers burn out and quit, or get higher-paying jobs as consultants, that at the time, half the staff was turning over in six months. Two weeks after being hired right out of college, a 23-year-old employee was named a senior permit reviewer.

Because they're so focused on shuffling papers, DEP employees told investigators, they didn't have time to see if the projects are built the way they're supposed to be or if there are things being built without permits.

A year after a permit is approved, a DEP inspector is supposed to check compliance. But one DEP permit reviewer told investigators that she hadn't done any inspections in three years, and that was the norm.

Developers know that they can get away with building in wetlands without permits, DEP employees told the investigators.

"They know there is nobody out there checking, they know," one DEP employee testified.

"So they are wreaking havoc?" an investigator asked.

"Absolutely," she replied.

When a grand jury investigated the DEP's permitting operation in the Panhandle in 1999, it found the same lack of oversight hampering protection of the environment:

> Builders frequently fill wetlands with impunity because permitting authority over stormwater controls and dredge and fill activity is uncoordinated. . . . For example, a few years ago, a large tract home builder filled wetlands to build a subdivision in southwest Escambia County. The construction, however, caused flooding on property in and adjacent to the subdivision. To mitigate the wetland losses, the builder "designated" a certain parcel of land as "mitigation." Later, it was discovered by building officials and regulators that the parcel designated for mitigation was, in fact, a pre-existing county holding pond.

Like the Corps, state permit reviewers don't have much of a chance to get out of the office to visit the wetlands they're allowing to be destroyed. Like the Corps, they end up trusting the applicant to tell them the truth.

"We issue a lot of permits to 7-Elevens, Burger Kings, Subway shops," Hull told us. "We've got lots of tools available in the office—U.S. [Geological Survey] maps, soil maps, NWI maps—so we can get a pretty good feel for what a site is like. We're generally not out inspecting the site."

Sometimes they're in such a rush to approve a permit they don't even look at where the runoff will end up. In 1999 a company called HBJ Investments got a permit from Swiftmud to build a health spa in St. Petersburg. A critic of the proposal took Swiftmud to court, where a judge determined that Swiftmud officials never bothered to see what would become of the runoff or what effect it would have on the waterway where it was headed. Turned out the runoff, full of oil, grease, and other contaminants, was going to flow into a storm drain, go two blocks, and then dump into Tampa Bay, which was already suffering from too much pollution.

The larger problem is with what's in the Basis of Review itself. Its criteria for water quality haven't been updated in 20 years. As a result, those criteria are entirely focused on a type of pollutant known as suspended solids or particulates.

"The general criteria is to provide one inch of detention, usually in a lake system," explained Damon Meiers, deputy director of environmental regulation for the South Florida Water Management District. "The first inch of runoff is to be detained. When the rain first starts to run off, that's the dirtiest water. If you detain that in the lakes, the water sits in there and bleeds back down, which allows the particulates to settle out. That catches most of the pollutants coming off the site."

But the criteria don't require developers to do anything to deal with what has become Florida's most common water pollution problem.

"There isn't anything for nutrients," Tony Janicki, a St. Petersburg environmental consultant, told us. "There's no required level of treatment."

So when state agencies say yes to destroying a wetland, they do not tell developers to clean up nutrients from runoff, which flows into waterways already polluted with nutrients. Meanwhile the Corps does not double-check the state's work.

Individual developments may not cause much harm by themselves, but "when you add them all up, they still contribute to the impaired water bodies," said Meiers.

Development after development destroys wetlands that could filter out pollutants, then suburban homeowners fertilizing their lawns and golf courses fertilizing the greens put still more nutrients into the stormwater stream. The pollution load quickly snowballs, said Wayne Daltry, Lee County's "Smart Growth" coordinator and former director of the Southwest Florida Regional Planning Council.

"We've got an area where development has increased and water quality declined," Daltry said. "It's the cumulative impact of all these projects that individually weren't supposed to cause water quality problems."

State officials have known for years that their permitting criteria were obsolete, said former South Florida water district attorney Marcy LaHart. They failed to update the requirements because they feared developers, she told us.

"The political reality is that complying with more stringent stormwater criteria will make development more expensive," LaHart explained.

Thus, even when the St. Johns River was so full of toxic algae that residents couldn't touch the water, the St. Johns River Water Management District continued approving permits for new developments that would add still more nutrients to the river. One of them was Freedom Commerce Center, Frank Matthews' client. The shopping center project was going to wipe out 130 acres of wetlands that form the headwaters of a pair of creeks flowing into the St. Johns, until the Corps issued a rare permit denial—something Matthews in his talk at Marco Island blamed on our reporting.

Kraig McLane of the St. Johns water district told us the state agency had been working on reducing the river's nutrients since 1993, but so far had made "no linkage" to permitting decisions.

"We're looking into it," he said in the winter of 2005.

The problem was, the one man in Florida who had tried to do something about nutrient pollution and wetland preservation had the whole thing blow up in his face.

❧

To stem the controversy over issuing the 404 permit for Florida Gulf Coast University, Col. Terry Rice cut a deal. The Corps would do a full-fledged environmental impact statement on all the wetland losses in Lee and Collier counties, and it would then be used to guide future wetland permitting decisions.

One of the findings of the EIS: water quality in the major estuaries was declining as a result of the filling of wetlands by development.

So when the EPA's John Hankinson dispatched Bruce Boler to Southwest Florida to "get tougher" on wetlands permits there, Boler took aim at the region's water quality problems. He quickly spotted the flaw in the state's permitting.

"The state has a presumptive criteria: 'If you build it a certain way, then we assume you've gotten rid of 80 percent of the pollutants,'" Boler explained. However, the state rules are focused exclusively on fixing what were considered the big pollution problems back in the 1980s, such as pesticides. They don't deal with the chemicals that are causing nutrient pollution problems, namely nitrogen and phosphorous.

The whole point of the Clean Water Act is to clean up water pollution, not cause it to get worse, he figured. The EPA's rules for reviewing wetland permits "say if you contribute to significant degradation of water resources, you can be rejected," he said. "I interpreted that to mean that if you increase nitrogen and phosphorous, then that can be significant degradation."

Boler looked for some scientific backing and found it in the work of an Orlando engineer named Harvey H. Harper III, who ran a consulting firm called Environmental Research and Design. The son of a Baptist minister, Harper grew up playing in creeks in rural Tennessee and Kentucky. The family moved to Orlando when Harper was a teenager, but he hadn't lost his interest in flowing water. He had earned a Ph.D. in environmental engineering from the University of Central Florida, where his dissertation was on heavy metals in stormwater runoff, and he had continued studying that subject and publishing papers on what he learned. The Harper paper that caught Boler's eye was a compilation of other people's scientific studies.

"Harvey Harper had collected work done by scientists all over Florida, and that showed that the nutrients were being removed only by 35 to 50 percent," Boler recalled. "That's not good. . . . I said, 'That's significant degradation. These projects should be stopped. The state's criteria is not adequate.'"

Boler called up Harper and talked about the permit reviews he was facing. "We spoke for many, many hours over the phone about how to calculate loadings," Harper told us.

Bolstered by Harper's findings, Boler began opposing every large development project that would add nutrients to the western Everglades—a position that not even Harper agreed with.

"He was trying to stop development in Southwest Florida," Harper contended. "He felt like a project should have no discharge of any kind, which is a lofty goal, but there's no statutory authority to support that."

It also made Boler extremely unpopular.

"Everyone was being upset with the EPA," Boler said. "They thought we were being heavy handed." Many developers and the Corps were angry because he was holding up permits. State regulators were upset, Boler said, "arguing that EPA was picking on them, since other states have even less protective regulations."

But the smart developers, instead of complaining, asked what Boler wanted them to do. He told them if they could set up stormwater treatment systems that would eliminate enough nutrients to guarantee no increase in pollution flowing into the bays and estuaries, he would not object to their permits. He worked out deals with Lee County on its road projects and with the port authority on an expansion of its airport.

While Boler was negotiating what sort of techniques would work best for each development, the developers and environmental consultants formed a group called the Water Enhancement and Restoration Coalition to take on the Boler problem through another route.

When WERC asked Boler to name his scientific expert on nutrients, he cited the work of Harper. WERC then turned around and hired Harper to produce a report for the developers.

The report Harper unveiled in August 2003 pulled the rug out from under Boler by proposing far less stringent stormwater treatment techniques to deal with nutrient pollution. Harper concluded that wetlands don't just filter out nutrients—they also produce them. Therefore, filling them in and replacing them with a parking lot or a golf course may not produce such a huge increase in nutrient pollution for local waterways. He recommended taking certain steps that he said would cut nutrients by 80 to 90 percent.

Boler said he found when he read the report that Harper's conclusions were based on water samples provided by the developers themselves.

"They gave him the data, and he used it to determine that wetlands had a (nutrient) loading rate," Boler said, shaking his head. "It's really the silliest thing I've ever seen."

One of the flaws in Harper's study, according to Jim Beever of the Southwest Florida Regional Planning Council, is that his report takes samples from polluted lakes and streams and canals "and says this is the water quality of a natural stream in Florida."

As a result, Beever told us, when regulators use Harper's data to compare predevelopment and postdevelopment water quality on a site with wetlands, the pollution problem that would result from developing the property doesn't seem all that bad. In some cases, Beever said, the Harper method yielded clearly absurd results: developments that claimed that by wiping out wetlands they could actually produce less pollution.

"He reaches the inaccurate conclusion that a developed landscape is less polluting than a natural wetland," Beever said. Thanks to Harper, he said, developers "came up with a way to increase the impervious surface and decrease environmental protection and call it good."

Yet, before Harper's study had been subjected to peer review by other water-quality experts, it was immediately accepted for use in permit reviews by the South Florida Water Management District, the DEP, the Corps, even by Boler's bosses at the EPA.

"While it may not be the end-all, be-all, it's a step in the right direction," explained Jim Giattina of the EPA's Atlanta office. "We felt it gave us the best opportunity to access the impacts of runoff and stormwater from developments."

Eric Livingston, the head of stormwater management for the DEP, dismissed complaints that Harper's report could make things worse: "What is being missed is that it provides for higher levels of protection than the current regulations of the district. . . . Do we have a perfect tool? No. It is a step in the right direction."

If the DEP were to wait until the peer review of Harper's study to find out if he was right, Livingston contended, "then all these projects would have to go through current requirements, which we know do not provide as high a level of stormwater treatment as the alternative methodology."

Just like that, all the permits that Boler had held up began getting approved. For instance, Boler had objected to a development called Winding Cypress that called for wiping out 200 acres of wetlands to make room for 2,300 homes and a golf course in Collier County. But thanks to the Harper report, EPA officials in Atlanta signed off on the project's plans and the Corps approved the permit.

In disgust, Boler quit. But a local environmental group, the Conservancy of Southwest Florida, battled on without him, filing a legal challenge to the South Florida Water Management District's wetland permitting criteria. When the Conservancy questioned Harper under oath, the Orlando consultant conceded that his 80 to 90 percent nutrient removal claim wasn't based on any scientific studies.

Still, the Corps stuck with the Harper method of dealing with water pollution in runoff. In 2004, when John Hall and Bob Barron visited the Estero Bay Agency on Bay Management, a Conservancy official named Gary Davis took dead aim at the Harper method in his segment of the program. As part of his PowerPoint presentation, Davis included a slide that said: "Harper methodology should be repudiated by EPA and Corps as methodology for assuming water quality in 404 permitting."

"Or at least suspend its use until peer review is complete," Davis pleaded. "Whatever we do here may have implications statewide."

"Let's say we repudiate it—OK, so what do I do in the meantime?" Barron asked.

In other words, as with the problematic WRAP method for evaluating the worth of wetlands, the Corps would rather use a bad method than hold up development permits while waiting for scientific data that might offer true environmental protection.

But the Conservancy's lawsuit turned the tables on the state. In the testimony prior to trial, state water district officials acknowledged the permitting criteria in the water district's Basis of Review hadn't been updated since 1988, and the criteria didn't say anything about nutrients.

Rather than fight the battle in court, water district officials voted in 2005 to update their criteria to require developers in Lee and Collier counties to deal with nutrients—though developers in other parts of South Florida would not be held to those same requirements.

"We've begun telling developers you cannot add any additional nutrients to the system" through their drainage, South Florida Water Management District executive director Carol Wehle told us in early 2006. "We're going to be more aggressive about new development."

Following South Florida's lead, the DEP commissioned a study that, in June 2007, confirmed exactly what Boler had said: the state's stormwater treatment standards were failing to stop the runoff from development from polluting Florida's waterways. So the DEP set to work on developing a new statewide standard for runoff that would specifically target nitrogen and phosphorous.

But to the Conservancy's dismay, the expert the DEP paid $50,000 for a study to lay the groundwork for the new standard was none other than Harvey H. Harper III.

There is another statewide problem with the dirty water running off all the new development built atop wetlands. When the problem was brought to the attention of the state legislature, instead of fixing it, they made it worse.

One of the biggest debates in passing the Warren Henderson Act concerned cumulative impact. Developers did not want the state permit reviewers to add up all the previous wetland impacts in an area and conclude that one more permit would be too many.

Nevertheless, in a 1993 revision to the state law, the legislature said explicitly that cumulative impact should be considered. However, the law did not spell out just how regulators were supposed to calculate cumulative impact or how to gauge when the breaking point was reached. Left to their own devices, the regulators came up with some fairly broad guidelines.

One South Florida Water Management District official testified that, as far as he was concerned, the definition of "unacceptable cumulative impact" from wetlands permitting meant that the entire wading bird population in the region would go extinct. Since no single development permit was likely to ever cause such an event, none would ever be denied.

But then along came some state auditors asking uncomfortable questions.

Just as Congress has an investigative arm called the Government Accountability Office, so the Florida legislature enjoys the services of an obscure auditing agency with an unwieldy and somewhat misleading name: the Office of Program Policy Analysis and Government Accountability, or OPPAGA for short. Created in 1994, the agency's mission is to support the legislature by "providing evaluative research and objective analyses to promote government accountability and the efficient and effective use of public resources."

In 1999, the legislature asked OPPAGA's investigators to look into the state's wetland permitting process. What was being lost? What about mitigation? Was it working?

"They looked at our records and the water management districts' and they said, 'You can't tell,'" said Connie Bersok of the state DEP. "They couldn't figure out what we were really doing."

The state agencies had approved a total of nearly 18,000 permits to destroy wetlands between 1995 and 1999, the OPPAGA auditors found. But because they weren't tracking what and where those individual permit impacts might be, OPPAGA's investigators reported, state officials had no idea of the cumulative impact of allowing developers to wipe out so many thousands of acres of wetlands.

The auditors from OPPAGA recommended the legislature order a full-fledged study of cumulative impacts of wetland losses throughout the state: "The study would examine the cumulative impact review in concert with larger environmental permitting and growth management issues. Elements of this study may be incorporated into current legislative . . . efforts to review aspects of the growth management and planning laws."

In a follow-up report in 2001, the OPPAGA investigators went a step further. They said the state should tie wetlands permitting into land-use maps. They recommended the state begin "identifying priority conservation areas and cooperatively developing strategies to protect and restore those areas, while encouraging economic development in more appropriate areas."

State agencies could map out the most important areas to save from development in order to ensure flood protection, a continuing supply of clean water, and habitat for valuable wildlife. Then, the OPPAGA auditors wrote, "local communities would evaluate the potential effects of future development on these priority resource areas. Local communities would also work with stakeholders to develop strategies that protect and restore priority conservation areas, while encouraging economic development in more appropriate areas."

The legislature made no such sweeping change. Instead, it passed a law that discourages regulators from making any attempt at assessing the cumulative impact of wetland permitting decisions.

Around the time OPPAGA was digging into the question of cumulative impact, the Sierra Club was suing the St. Johns River Water Management District over its failure to ever consider the cumulative impact of its permitting decisions. The suit focused on overturning a St. Johns' rule that said so long as a developer's mitigation was in the same watershed as the wetlands being wiped out, there could never be any impact from it and there was thus no need to consider cumulative impact.

Of course, since the mitigation often entailed preservation of existing wetlands or fumbling attempts at creating manmade wetlands, wetland acreage disappeared with nearly every permit. The Sierra Club's attorneys, Deborah Andrews and Peter Belmont, pointed out that by taking that approach, the St. Johns water district was skipping over the steps of avoidance and minimization and considering developers' mitigation as justification for approving a permit.

While the case was still unresolved, the legislature stepped in and passed a new law that said St. Johns was right. That maneuver not only killed the lawsuit, it also spread the St. Johns approach statewide. So now, as long as the mitigation for wetland impacts is carried out somewhere in the same watershed area as the development that's wiping out the wetlands, state regulators must say the development has no adverse impact.

There was no mention in the new law of the many scientific studies showing that mitigation fails to really replace wetlands. It was as if Ann Redmond and Kevin Erwin had never written their reports.

Since the law discourages regulators from ever calculating a cumulative impact, they don't. Thus, for instance, when the St. Johns River was coated in toxic green slime fueled by polluted runoff, the St. Johns River Water Management District board could approve a permit for a Jacksonville subdivision development called Longleaf Plantation to wipe out about 14 acres of wetlands. In exchange, the developer promised to preserve 145 acres of wetlands on the site, remove bedding rows for a pine plantation from another 46 acres of wetlands, and create 7.5 acres of manmade wetlands.

"The proposed mitigation offsets the project's adverse impacts and is in the same drainage basin," the August 2005 permit states. Therefore the development would have no adverse cumulative impact—even if the color of the river water said different.

Here's the bottom line. The state's permitting program isn't really focused on trying to stop the loss of wetlands, the OPPAGA auditors found. Instead, they said, the state's wetland regulators try to balance the desires of developers with what's required to protect the environment.

But that approach, the auditors wrote, "acknowledges that growth will entail some loss of environmental and wetland function." The state's actual goal, the auditors wrote, is simply "to prevent these losses from reaching a critical threshold."

In the 1990s a new savior of the swamps appeared, promising to rescue Florida's wetlands from that "critical threshold," while still allowing development to proceed unabated. State lawmakers fell in love with it, as did Congress.

But when we looked at it closely we discovered that, like everything else in the world of wetlands protection, it depended on playing a cynical game with the numbers.

16

Banking on Phony Numbers

On a broiling August morning in 1993, two would-be development magnates, D. Miller McCarthy and Alan Fickett, turned themselves in at the Polk County Jail in the small Central Florida town of Bartow. Jail deputies rolled their prints, snapped their mug shots, and, after they promised to show up in court, turned them loose.

The crime they were accused of: illegally filling wetlands.

Neighbors saw construction going on at a piece of land the two were managing and reported it to the authorities. State investigators found new roads plowed through the swamps. McCarthy blamed a frontloader driver who got carried away.

When investigators asked McCarthy and Fickett if they had finished the work in the swamps, both answered at once—but one said "yes" and the other said "no."

McCarthy stood six foot six and weighed more than 300 pounds, a mountain of a man with an outsized personality to match. He had plenty of friends, but even they said he could be abrasive and difficult to deal with. St. Johns River Water Management District executive director Henry Dean, for instance, called him "a little gruff." He made money in the 1980s cell phone boom, dabbled in real estate, and ran a sand mine and logging operation. His main asset was his soaring imagination.

Fickett, a smooth talker with a doctorate in finance and a strong interest in politics, had been McCarthy's friend and business partner for years. Before joining forces with him in the development business, Fickett had put his folksy charm to work as a lobbyist for the University of Central Florida. That's where he ran across McCarthy, who was an enthusiastic supporter of the college's athletic programs.

Because of constant complaints from neighbors of the Polk County land the pair managed, state officials had been warning McCarthy and Fickett for two years that they needed permits for any work in wetlands or they might face charges. Finally, investigators raided the offices of ScanAmerican Holdings, as well as the construction site in the Green Swamp, and carted off several boxes of evidence. They found documents showing McCarthy and Fickett had told their Swedish investors that the new roads were built to enhance the property's development potential. In the documents were complaints about "the crusading bunny-huggers" who wanted to save the swamps.

The state charged McCarthy, Fickett, and ScanAmerican with seven felonies and nine misdemeanors for destroying wetlands at the edge of the Green Swamp, the headwaters of most of the major rivers in Central Florida. The state filed charges "because it was so serious and blatant," explained one investigator. "They knew where the wetlands were and they did it anyway."

Because it was the first time a corporation had been charged with a felony for illegally destroying wetlands, their arrest made news around the state. But the case never went to trial. A judge declared that the search warrant used to collect all the evidence had not been properly carried out. Without the evidence, the case fizzled and prosecutors dropped all the charges.

Some men might breathe a sigh of relief and go right back to land development. Not McCarthy and Fickett. Instead, they discovered a way to turn themselves into bunny-hugger heroes and make some money. They decided to enter the fledgling industry of wetland mitigation banking.

Over the next 10 years, as more than 40 banks sprung up in Florida, they became known as the leaders of the business—before everything fell apart.

But while it worked, they got lots of help, and money, from the same state government that had charged them with a crime.

By the mid-1990s, everyone involved in wetlands regulation realized the 404 permitting system was broken. Developers complained bitterly that a permit to wipe out even small wetlands took too long to get, driving up their overhead costs. Environmentalists complained that permits came too easy, and what was offered in replacement offered too little and usually failed. The regulators themselves realized they were overwhelmed by the number of applications and that they could do little beyond checking to make sure the forms were filled out correctly.

A potential solution came from an unlikely source: the oil industry.

A decade before, the Fina Oil Company had taken a 7,000-acre parcel of degraded wetlands in Terrebonne Parish, Louisiana, and built levees and weirs to fix the flow of water across the property. The company then persuaded regulators to calculate how much that restoration was worth in mitigation and banked the mitigation value to use later. That way, as Fina destroyed wetlands elsewhere during its oilfield operations, it could then draw those mitigation credits from the bank to make up for the damage.

The idea of banking mitigation credits for future use caught on quickly, with county governments and state highway departments jumping in to build their own mitigation banks. In 1993 the Corps declared that mitigation banking could be used to make up for the destruction approved in 404 permits, giving the practice the imprimatur of official approval. Then, with the EPA, the Corps produced a formal set of rules for permitting the banks in 1995.

McCarthy and Fickett had started thinking about mitigation banking even before their arrest. McCarthy's reports to Sweden talked of starting a mitigation bank on the Green Swamp property to quiet environmentalists' complaints about the road construction.

"This 'bank' of wetlands would compensate for all the planned improvement activities," McCarthy wrote. But this was still a bank built just for the benefit of its owner.

Then along came a Florida company that further refined the idea, and made a big success of it—thanks to a hurricane.

George Platt, a former Broward County commissioner and state treasurer of the Democratic Party, joined forces with a New Zealand–born engineer named David Johns to launch a company called Florida Wetlandsbank Inc. Platt and Johns cut a deal with the city of Pembroke Pines in Broward County for use of a weed-choked garbage pit that a developer had donated to the city. Then they set to work turning the property into a 450-acre marsh on the eastern edge of the Everglades.

Florida Wetlandsbank, like the mitigation banks that came after it, first put together a permit application that spelled out what the bankers were going to do to restore the pit to a marsh. In that document are reams of facts and figures attempting to put a number on the amount of good the bank will do for the environment.

Typically, bankers and regulators then go back and forth over what each believes the bank is worth, arguing over what the WRAP or UMAM calculations may show. Bankers and regulators told us these negotiations are fierce because the more credits the bank gets, the more money it can make.

Out of all the discussion and debate come two things: a final number of credits that the bank is worth and a schedule showing how many credits the bankers will get at each stage of completion. For instance, each bank usually gets a certain number of credits just for putting a conservation easement on the property, then more credits at each stage of progress.

Florida Wetlandsbank counted on using a successful restoration project—not creation, not enhancement, not preservation—to generate mitigation credits. The difference was that, instead of keeping the credits for its own use or for use by the city, Florida Wetlandsbank would sell them to developers who were destroying wetlands elsewhere.

Because of the devastation wrought in Miami-Dade County by Hurricane Andrew in 1992, some 100,000 Miami-Dade residents forced out by the hurricane had decided to move away. But most of them moved just one county north. The demand for new housing led to lots of builders wiping out wetlands in Broward County.

"Of course the whole south end of Broward is a flood plain, practically, so everything needed to be mitigated," Platt said.

Thanks to Platt and Johns, the quick and easy way for the builders of the new Broward houses to make up for their wetland destruction was to buy credits from Florida Wetlandsbank. The company started out with two employees sharing a single desk. In six years they managed to sell every credit the Pembroke Pines bank had generated. Total take: $20 million.

However, the wave of development that made Florida Wetlandsbank such a success left its restored swamp an island of green surrounded by Broward's wetland-destroying sprawl.

"We're adjacent on three sides to areas that were either developed or were going to be developed," Platt told us. "One is called The Preserve, and the developer charges an extra $10,000 a lot to look out on our swamp."

Soon Platt and Johns' success spawned other entrepreneurial banks. For instance, real estate investor Dennis Benbow bought 1,650 acres of drained ranchland near Kissimmee and turned it back into a swamp. His Florida Mitigation Bank takes all the stormwater runoff from the nearby Disney theme parks and runs it through the bank's restored wetlands, which filter out pollutants before the runoff reaches a creek.

Like Platt and Johns, Benbow kept his operation simple, aiming to keep his overhead low until he could finally begin selling credits. He recouped his investment with his first sale—60 credits, purchased by the Orlando-Sanford Airport Authority.

Mitigation banking as practiced by Platt and Johns caught on quickly nationwide because it seemed to offer something for everyone. For developers, the entrepreneurial bankers offered a way to make up for wiping out wetlands that was far easier and cheaper than any other alternative. For environmentalists, the bankers promised to do mitigation right for a change and to have the mitigation in place before the developers did the damage. For the government, the banks offered a sort of one-stop shopping. Instead of Corps permit reviewers having to check on hundreds of small mitigation projects scattered all over the countryside, they could go to one mitigation bank and sign off on everything at once. For the bankers, of course, the profits—when they finally arrived—could be substantial. In Florida in 2006, for instance, some banks were selling credits for up to $150,000 each.

The possibility of turning a piece of pasture into a business worth tens of millions of dollars attracted people to the business who were more interested in profits than environmental protection.

"A lot of banks are square pegs pounded into round holes," said Chuck Olson, a longtime environmental consultant who runs the 2,693-acre Bluefield Ranch Mitigation Bank in St. Lucie and Martin counties on Florida's east coast. "A lot of them are people looking to cash out on bad pieces of property by turning them into mitigation banks."

As often happens, though, the concept sounded good enough to blind government officials to any potential downfalls. The new industry gained fans on both sides of the political aisle. Republicans loved mitigation banking as a free-market solution to a regulatory problem. Democrats loved the banking industry's promise of large-scale environmental restoration.

The first Bush Administration endorsed the concept of mitigation banking, as did the Clinton Administration a few years later. Meanwhile Congress passed a series of transportation bills that dictated the use of mitigation bank credits to make up for federally funded road projects, thus steering millions of dollars of taxpayer money into the pockets of a business that had yet to post any consistent, scientifically approved successes.

In 1996, when a Senate subcommittee wanted testimony on the wonders of mitigation banking, Senator Bob Graham introduced a baby-faced young engineer from St. Petersburg named Denver Stutler Jr., who identified himself as a partner in a company called Ecobank.

Graham said Stutler could tell the senators all about "this important initiative in wetlands protection," because "his is one of the older of those programs and, therefore, we will have the benefit of his extensive experience."

"To be successful, conservation has got to be good business," Stutler earnestly explained to the senators. "Only then can the highest and best land use be conservation."

The "older" company that Stutler was touting had been incorporated for just a year—and it was already on shaky ground. But you would not have known that from the size of the staff assembled by Ecobank's founder and primary stockholder, D. Miller McCarthy.

The company's actual name was Ecosystems Land Mitigation Bank, but everyone simply called it Ecobank. Not long after McCarthy and Fickett launched the company, George Platt and David Johns from Florida Wetlandsbank visited Ecobank's offices in the Orlando suburb of Winter Park. They were amazed at what they found there.

"In their office, they had 12 people and all this rented furniture," said Platt, who was used to his own shoestring operation. "When we left I looked at David and said, 'That's got to be $100,000 a month!'"

Fickett and McCarthy disagree on when Ecobank officially started—Fickett says late 1993, McCarthy 1994—but this much is clear: it was McCarthy's baby. When they incorporated in 1995, McCarthy listed himself as holding 98.6 percent ownership of the company.

McCarthy, dreaming big, immediately hired a large staff of engineers like Stutler who started putting together permit applications for big, new mitigation banks throughout rapidly growing Central Florida.

"Ecobank is currently permitting more than 16,000 acres in four separate banks in Florida," Stutler bragged to the senators in 1996. "We've invested significant amounts of capital and have dedicated 100 percent of our resources because we think it can work."

He didn't mention that, at that point, Ecobank hadn't gotten any federal permits or sold a single credit. Despite all that overhead, the company had no income. In fact, just a month after boasting about Ecobank's "extensive experience" to the senators, Stutler sent a letter to a Florida congressman named Bill McCollum pleading for help in getting the company's first 404 permit. Even then, getting that permit from the Corps took Ecobank another six months.

Meanwhile, Ecobank donated more than $5,000 to a foundation started by Jeb Bush, the former president's son who had recently lost his first bid for governor. The Foundation for Florida's Future, Bush's organization that kept him in the public eye until the next governor's race, published a newsletter. When Ecobank made its contribution, the newsletter published an essay by Stutler that read like a lengthy paid advertisement. The subject: how terrific Ecobank's free-market approach to environmental protection was.

In the Bush foundation newsletter, Stutler wrote that "completing ecologically successful projects is critical to the future of private mitigation banking," adding that the company's strategy is to "establish 'megabanks' to support complete ecosystem restoration and maintenance, while allowing credits to be produced quickly and economically."

In an effort to create those "megabanks," Ecobank deployed seven registered lobbyists in Tallahassee that spring during the legislative session. In addition to Fickett and Stutler, they hired former Florida Department of Environmental Regulation secretary Vicki Tschinkel and former legislative aide Fred McCormack, who had helped write the Warren Henderson Act.

McCarthy dispatched this army of paid persuaders to change a state law that could limit Ecobank's sales. The law said that because wetlands benefits are local, a mitigation bank could only sell credits to developers destroying wetlands in the same watershed. But the bigger the service area where a bank can sell its credits, the more potential customers there will be and thus the higher a bank's profits.

Because they were looking for big profits, McCarthy and Fickett wanted the largest service areas possible for Ecobank so customers could buy credits miles away from where wetlands were being destroyed. Although the legislature did expand the service areas, it did not expand them as much as Ecobank wanted.

But when we looked at how far away other bankers were selling credits, we found that the new rules weren't exactly restrictive either. One block of credits sold from a bank in southern Miami-Dade County were used as mitigation for wetlands destroyed up at the northern end of Palm Beach County, some 80 miles and an eternity of gridlock on I-95 to the north.

Then there's the Little Pine Island Mitigation Bank, where developer Raymond Pavelka has restored 1,600 acres of wetlands on a spit of state-owned land a mile off the coast of Southwest Florida. Pavelka's customers are wiping out wetlands on the mainland in booming Lee and Collier counties. One customer bought credits from the island bank to make up for destroying wetlands more than 30 miles inland, near the Hendry County line.

"Admittedly it is somewhat removed from the majority of impacts," said Ron Silver, who oversees mitigation banks for the Corps in Florida.

When we told him that the island bank sells credits as far inland as the edge of the Everglades, Silver said, "That's not the kind of thing I like to hear."

Pavelka defended his bank, saying his restoration of the island's ecosystems helps improve the entire coast. But an EPA-funded study found that the Little Pine Island bank did a poor job of replacing wetlands destroyed on the mainland. Because of its location, the bank could not protect the mainland areas from flooding, recharge the drinking supply, or filter pollution the way the natural wetlands could.

For McCarthy and Fickett, the expanded sales areas they were seeking were designed to accommodate one potential customer: the Florida DOT. Ecobank was keenly interested in lining up government agencies like the DOT as customers. Early on they hired a former head of the DOT, Kaye Henderson, to help convince the DOT to buy Ecobank credits for its road projects.

On December 30, 1996, Ecobank at last made its first sale—2.7 credits, their first income in more than two years of existence. The buyer: the DOT.

But the wetland mitigation bank that supplied those credits had an odd problem: It wasn't particularly wet.

∾

About 15 minutes outside the Central Florida town of Clermont is a rolling hillside covered with wildflowers and stunted oak trees. Although this sandy hill rises 140 feet above sea level, the Lake Louisa-Green Swamp Mitigation Bank has been allowed by both the Corps and the St. Johns River Water Management District to claim it's the equivalent of a muddy swamp.

Fickett told us that state regulators steered them toward the Lake Louisa site because it was land the state had been trying in vain to buy. To get it done, the state was willing to make a deal with onetime wetland violators.

"Basically they asked us to work as, in essence, their partner on a private basis, to see if we couldn't acquire those lands that they wanted and put them in conservation," Fickett said.

In all, Lake Louisa got 280 credits from state and federal regulators. Of those, 257 credits—each one, under state law, equivalent to an acre of pristine swamp—were for land so dry it provided ideal habitat for the rare and threatened sand skink, not for frogs and alligators.

"It really had very little to do with wetland restoration," said Benbow, a competitor.

For 11 years, Todd Gipe reviewed bank permits for the St. Johns River Water

Figure 17. Workers spray herbicides to kill invasive plants at the Lake Louisa Mitigation Bank in Central Florida. Although state and federal regulators gave its owner, Ecobank, credits for restoring wetlands, Lake Louisa is nearly all dry land. (Photograph by Lara Cerri, *St. Petersburg Times*.)

Management District, and he's the one who recommended approval of Lake Louisa. He told us the reason Lake Louisa got most of its credits for dry land is that, otherwise, there wouldn't have been much of a bank.

"More credits were given for uplands because the wetlands themselves were not greatly improved directly," said Gipe, who in 2005 quit his state job to become a consultant for the mitigation banking industry.

In the decade after Ecobank started selling credits at Lake Louisa, its biggest customer was the government. The state spent $2 million buying credits from the bank to make up for 102 acres of wetlands it had destroyed building an expressway around Orlando.

In effect, the state wiped out swamps vital to the water supply and spent tax dollars replacing them with dry land.

Corps regulations say the whole point of wetland mitigation banks is "to provide for the replacement of the chemical, physical and biological functions of wetlands." Saving dry land is not the goal.

The nonpartisan Environmental Law Institute, based in Washington, surveyed the entire mitigation banking industry in 2002. In its report, the institute recommended that dry land "should not be directly counted as mitigation credits."

It hardly takes a math genius to see why. Said Jessica Wilkinson, who led the ELI survey team, "It's a net loss if you're permitting 5 acres of wetland losses and you're only doing 2 acres of wetland restoration and 3 acres of uplands. That's a net loss of acres."

Some banks constitute a complete loss of wetland acres. When state regulators approved the Peace River Mitigation Bank in Hardee County in 2006, the bank not only got more credits for saving dry land than for doing anything for wetlands, it got all 138.82 credits for doing little beyond merely preserving the land.

Because nothing is being restored, each credit sold from that bank will equal a lost acre of wetland in the Peace River area—at a time when the river, which supplies drinking water to Sarasota and Charlotte counties, has been drying up.

The Peace River Mitigation Bank is owned by EarthBalance, a company headed by Don Ross, a former Charlotte County commissioner and a gubernatorial appointee to the state Environmental Regulation Commission. Ross said it makes perfect sense to give the Peace River bank more credits for dry land than for wet: "If you develop those uplands, you would degrade those wetlands without putting a foot in them."

EarthBalance vice president Allison DeFoor—vice chairman of the Florida Republican Party and a onetime candidate for lieutenant governor—is a big booster of the industry to everyone he meets, in Tallahassee and everywhere else.

"It's a great way to make a living," said the dapper and diminutive DeFoor, an ex-judge from the Keys who briefly served as Governor Bush's top adviser on Everglades restoration. "We're doing the Lord's work and getting paid for it."

Peace River is one of 10 mitigation banks in Florida that claimed a third or more of their credits for saving dry land instead of restoring real swamps. Those 10 banks—nearly a quarter of the 45 banks operating in Florida as of 2007—were granted a total of 5,386 wetland credits for preserving and restoring dry land. Those credits can be sold as if they were the equivalent of

Booming banks

Banking on mitigation: Wetland mitigation banking has become a billion-dollar business fueled by lots of government contracts. But several of Florida's 45 mitigation banks fall short of the goal of no net loss of wetlands.

Sundew Mitigation Bank
County: Clay
Size: 3,104 acres
Potential credits: 698
Permitted: 2001
Notes: Given credits for paperwork and sold them before any work done.

Farmton Mitigation Bank
County: Volusia
Size: 23,922 acres
Potential credits: 4,585
Permitted: 2000
Notes: Largest mitigation bank in the country.

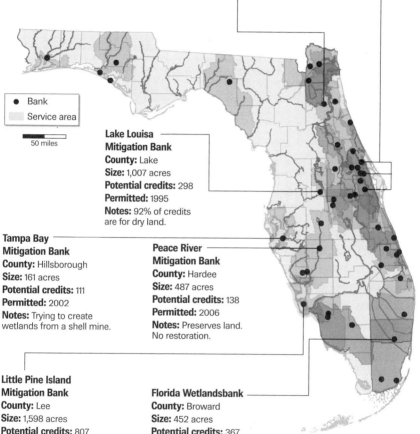

● Bank
▨ Service area

50 miles

Lake Louisa Mitigation Bank
County: Lake
Size: 1,007 acres
Potential credits: 298
Permitted: 1995
Notes: 92% of credits are for dry land.

Tampa Bay Mitigation Bank
County: Hillsborough
Size: 161 acres
Potential credits: 111
Permitted: 2002
Notes: Trying to create wetlands from a shell mine.

Peace River Mitigation Bank
County: Hardee
Size: 487 acres
Potential credits: 138
Permitted: 2006
Notes: Preserves land. No restoration.

Little Pine Island Mitigation Bank
County: Lee
Size: 1,598 acres
Potential credits: 807
Permitted: 1996
Notes: Restoration done on island for impacts miles away on mainland.

Florida Wetlandsbank
County: Broward
Size: 452 acres
Potential credits: 367
Permitted: 1995
Notes: Florida's first commercial bank, now hemmed by sprawl.

Source: Florida DEP

MATTHEW WAITE, DANA OPPENHEIM | St. Petersburg Times

Map 2. Booming banks. Wetland mitigation has become a billion-dollar business fueled by lots of government contracts. But several of Florida's 45 mitigation banks fall short of the goal of no net loss of wetlands. (Map created by Matthew Waite and Dana Oppenheim, *St. Petersburg Times*.)

saving 5,386 acres of pristine swamps and marshes, even though they clearly are not.

Some banks are drier than others. At the Lake Monroe Mitigation Bank, 75 percent of the credits are for dry land. At the Barberville Mitigation Bank, it's 80 percent. Drier yet is Colbert-Cameron Mitigation Bank at 88 percent. The driest of them all: Ecobank's Lake Louisa, with 92 percent of its credits for uplands.

The designs of Barberville and Lake Monroe were overseen by environmental consultant Stuart Bradow, who, like Don Ross, contended the dry land is as essential as the wet to protecting the ecosystem. Scientists agree that wetlands benefit from a small upland buffer. But does the dry land deserve more wetland credit than the wetlands?

Conceded Bradow, "It's a little bit of a convoluted logic."

When we asked him how giving wetland credits for dry land fits with the national policy of no net loss of wetlands, Bradow laughed and then said, "Yeah, well, good luck with that."

∾

McCarthy and Fickett's second bank, the East Central Florida Mitigation Bank in Volusia County, was little better than Lake Louisa. Nearly half of its state-approved wetland credits are for saving dry land.

It got more credits than it should have because of a project that never existed anywhere but in McCarthy's vivid imagination.

In applying for its state and federal permits, Ecobank argued that its allotment of credits should be higher because East Central Florida would be a vital link among other conservation lands, including what was to become their third Florida bank. Ecobank was granted its extra credit, but the third bank never got off the ground.

For its third bank, Ecobank promised to restore wetlands on a sprawling piece of old Florida called the Lee Ranch in Seminole County. Ecobank's plan called for tearing down levees along the St. Johns River and flooding the property, restoring its wetlands.

But the state claims ownership of any submerged land that's navigable. So if Lee Ranch was inundated by the river, the land would belong to the state. That would mean Ecobank couldn't claim ownership to sell mitigation credits.

Ecobank tried repeatedly to persuade state officials to make an exception or cut a deal with them so they could turn Lee Ranch into a mitigation bank, but the talks always stumbled over some detail.

The closest they ever came was in 1997, when Fickett and McCarthy's friend Henry Dean stood before Governor Lawton Chiles and the cabinet to try to cut a deal: let Ecobank make Lee Ranch a mitigation bank, and the state would share in the credit-sale profits. Not mentioned was the fact that McCarthy and Fickett were hoping to sell most of the credits on the state-owned land to a state agency, the DOT. Still, they faced a skeptical audience.

Fickett told Chiles and the cabinet that Ecobank had grown weary of the lengthy negotiations: "I have to tell you, Governor, this is the gol-darned-est, most frustrating process I have ever been through. We're trying to help you. . . . You've got a program like this, it doesn't take anybody with an IQ much above room temperature to understand how good it is."

"You're right, maybe, on your argument of the temperature of the brain capacity of most of us up here," drawled Chiles, clearly insulted. "It's pretty cold today, and I'm a little frozen up myself."

After that, Chiles and the cabinet refused to go along with Ecobank's proposal on Lee Ranch. McCarthy tried for years to revive it, but it remained the deal that got away. By then Ecobank's big overhead was beginning to take its toll on the company's finances, with only two mitigation banks selling credits to bring in an income.

"They hired the best and the brightest team," Benbow said. "The payroll was $100,000 a month. They dug this giant freaking hole." But when it came to filling the hole, Benbow said, Ecobank used tactics reminiscent of the disgraced energy giant Enron: "They had a sort of a Ken Lay idea about what you do."

Most mitigation bankers say they have to make a lot of small sales to keep the lights on, though the big ones are where they make their profits.

Ecobank's original business plan, the one that they sold to outside investors when they hit a cash crunch and sought outside capital, followed that same strategy. The Lake Louisa land was technically owned not by Ecobank but by a trust set up to benefit McCarthy's children. Now, to avoid a cash crunch, he sold it to a New York investment firm called Da Capo Al Fine Ltd. for $2 million. As part of the deal, Ecobank could continue selling the credits at Lake Louisa but would split the profits with Da Capo.

Howard Seitz, the attorney who represented Da Capo, said that at first he liked Ecobank's strategy: "You pursue small deals to cover the overhead while you were hunting elephants." But McCarthy became fixated on landing the big sale with state and local government agencies to the exclusion of all the smaller potential customers, Seitz said, and that proved Ecobank's undoing.

One such "elephant" came along in 1998, when the Orlando-Sanford Airport needed to extend a runway through a swamp. Their need for credits would start a series of business deals between Ecobank and a group of Central Florida politicians that shows how Ecobank did business, how banks compete with each other, and how much money there is floating around the industry.

The chairman of the airport authority was Ken Wright, an influential Orlando land-use attorney who was also a prominent Republican activist—the same lawyer who persuaded U.S. Representative Ric Keller to help the developers of the Meadow Pointe subdivision get around Steve Brooker's objections to its wetland impacts.

Wright told the board they should buy their credits from the Colbert-Cameron Wetland Mitigation Bank, a bank run by two brothers on family-owned farmland. Wright said he had checked out Ecobank, but recommended against doing business with them. Wright had met McCarthy before and did not think much of him.

"He had a natural aversion to doing business with Ecobank because he also thought that Mr. McCarthy was a jerk," one of Wright's friends later said.

Colbert-Cameron mitigation bank co-owner William Colbert, on the other hand, happened to be Sanford's city attorney. As a local resident and a city employee, he had offered to sell the airport the credits it needed, worth $20,000 each, for a discount price of $18,000 per credit. Thrilled at the savings, board members voted June 2, 1998, to buy the credits they needed from Colbert's bank.

But then Ecobank found a way to take the sale away from him: pay some politicians for their help.

McCarthy and Fickett hired the chairman of the Seminole County Commission, Randy Morris, and the chairman of the Seminole Republican Party, Jim Stelling, to sell wetlands credits for them. Fickett would later testify in a lawsuit filed between Ecobank and the politicians that the two men were hired because of "their ability to deal with political entities."

Their first target: the airport project Colbert thought he had all sewn up.

"They were very well acquainted with the chairman of that authority, attorney Kenneth Wright. And they indicated they could assist us in getting these credits," Fickett later testified. "And they made contact with Mr. Wright, and we had a number of discussions back and forth with him and with Commissioner Morris and Mr. Stelling."

Morris and Stelling, who were in the real estate business together, had been friends with Wright for a decade. They were close enough to him that in 2000, when Governor Bush appointed Wright chairman of the state's Environmental Regulation Commission—the board that approves the state's rules for limiting air and water pollution—the lawyer listed Stelling as a character reference.

Stelling was a widely known figure among Florida GOP activists. In 2003, he even ran for chairman of the state party. After he lost, he sued another GOP leader whom he accused of sabotaging his candidacy by mailing out a flier full of false information. The false information was that he had been married six times, he said. The truth was he had been married only five times.

Morris, too, was well known in Central Florida politics. When we interviewed him, we met him at the Seminole County building, which was an old hospital. The commissioners' offices were the old maternity ward. Morris was a pudgy middle-aged man with a droopy lock of graying hair and a hoarse voice that sometimes trailed off toward the end of a sentence. Behind his desk was a sign that—like Frank Matthews' T-shirt—read, "Pave the World." He said the county engineering department gave it to him.

Morris told us that he and Stelling had been informed by a local developer that McCarthy had "some market needs, he needs some help." Morris said he remembered thinking, "So, I'll have a consulting job for me."

Instead, it was more of a sales position, with one special customer as the target. Four days after Morris and Stelling were hired, the airport contract swung away from Colbert-Cameron and over to Ecobank.

On June 8, 1998, Ecobank sold 17.3 credits to the airport authority for more than $300,000 in public money. The price: $17,500 per credit, undercutting Colbert's discount by $500.

Airport authority records show that Wright alone made the decision to switch to Ecobank, with his board ratifying the purchase after the fact. Stelling later testified that despite Wright's distaste for McCarthy and his bluster, "we were able to induce Mr. Wright, due to our friendship with him, to do business with Ecobank."

When we asked Morris about the airport deal, the commissioner told a somewhat different tale. He said Wright had called them to alert them to the possible sale, thus pulling the rug out from under the city attorney.

No matter who called whom, friendship certainly proved lucrative for Ecobank's new supersalesmen. On the airport deal, Fickett testified, Morris and Stelling split a $37,844 commission. Although Morris was a public official and the money came from a public agency, his role in the sale was not made public and was not listed in the financial disclosure forms he filed with the state.

While Wright agreed to do business with Ecobank because he was friends with its new salesmen, friendship only went so far, according to sworn testimony from Fickett and McCarthy.

"Morris and Stelling, one or the other or both—I can't remember—called me late one night and asked if I would pay a commission to Ken Wright if we got the order for the mitigation for the runway," McCarthy testified. So the airport chairman "was given 25 percent commission on sales for the taxiway," McCarthy said. Fickett gave similar testimony.

When we talked to McCarthy and Fickett, they insisted they had become "confused" by an attorney's questions and didn't mean to say Wright was paid for his help in landing the airport contract. Commissioner Morris said he didn't know anything about the financial arrangement, if any, Wright had with Ecobank.

Testifying in a lawsuit that Morris and Stelling later filed against Ecobank, Wright denied getting any commission for the airport deal, and there is no evidence that he did.

We wanted to hear from Wright himself, but Wright was extremely reluctant to talk to us about Ecobank. For months he didn't return our calls or respond to our e-mails. When we finally got an interview with him, he insisted he got no personal benefit from the airport sale he engineered.

"I'm a straight guy," Wright told us, sounding exasperated. He said that taking such a deal from Ecobank would have endangered his law practice, adding that "if you don't think I'm an honest guy, then I hope you deal with me enough to know that I'm not a stupid guy."

But someone else remembered a discussion about Wright getting a payment back in 1998. Da Capo al Fine's attorney, Howard Seitz, said that at the time of the airport deal, McCarthy told him Wright "would be entitled to a commission" if Ecobank got the contract. Seitz said he questioned the propriety of that arrangement.

"My concern was whether that was fully disclosed to everyone," said Seitz. "I didn't want anyone to come back and say they didn't know about it. I was assured by Miller that everything had been done properly."

Though Wright denied getting a commission on the public airport deal, his work on behalf of his private development clients was another story. Wright had a thriving side business buying environmentally sensitive land and then selling it to his clients who needed to show regulators that they were preserving something as mitigation for their developments. But writing a check to Ecobank might be even easier for them—so long as Wright made money too.

Wright told Stelling that before he would agree to send any of his development clients over to Ecobank to buy credits, "I would have to receive some kind of discount or commission," he later testified.

That's how Ecobank gained a third salesman. Wright testified that over the next two years he received thousands of dollars in commissions "marketing" Ecobank credits at the East Central Florida Mitigation Bank to clients who were wiping out wetlands.

A month after the airport deal, Wright said he landed his first customer for Ecobank: Seminole County. For $48,000, the county bought 2.4 credits at the East Central Florida bank to make up for wetlands destroyed by a road widened for a new development.

The check to Ecobank was signed by none other than Wright's fellow Ecobank salesman, the chairman of the Seminole County Commission, Randy Morris. Wright's commission on the sale: $6,000.

A few months after Wright collected his money from the sale to Seminole County, Morris and Stelling sent Ecobank an invoice that said they, too, were owed money for helping nail down the sale to Seminole County.

Stelling testified that they later realized that because Morris was on the county commission, they probably shouldn't claim any money from that sale. But Morris told us that the money for the road really came not from the county but from a developer who needed the road widened, so "technically I could have been paid."

However, Morris said he decided to let it go "because it wouldn't have been right."

While they worked for Ecobank, Morris and Stelling set off on one big elephant hunt after another. "We were looking for 100 to 200 credits," Commissioner Morris told us. "We were looking for large deals."

To try to find a big sale for Ecobank, Stelling testified, "we traveled to Tallahassee. . . . We met with the assistant secretary of transportation. We met with the chairman in Tallahassee of the Transportation Committee. We met with the chairman—no, the counsel—of the (Orange-Orlando) Expressway Authority. . . . We met with a lot of people and a lot of developers, which we both came in contact with on a daily basis."

At one point they also tried to help McCarthy organize all of the mitigation bankers in Florida into a single organization—a cartel that could handle bulk credit sales and work together in lobbying the legislature.

"Miller's a big thinker," Morris told us. "He's an extremely bright guy and a big thinker, and really, he had some big ideas in terms of trying to, if you will, have a more stable, a more level playing field."

The only trouble with trying to form a cartel of mitigation bankers was the bankers didn't want to work together.

"It was chaos," Morris recalled. "It didn't work. These guys didn't like each other. . . . I got everybody to sit down in the same room, which was remarkable, but we couldn't reach agreement. And it really was because of personalities."

Over two years, Ecobank paid Morris and Stelling more than $48,000 for helping sell credits for its East Central Florida bank—but it wasn't enough. Thanks to a tip from Wright, the two politicos discovered they had not been paid for some sales they believed they helped land.

Furious, they sued Ecobank. Five years later, they settled. Their final payout: $92,000.

∾

Ecobank's one big success was a bank started in North Carolina in the late 1990s by George Howard. Howard had been a congressional aide, "the Senate staffer in charge of the small corner of federal policy called wetlands policy," he told us. Denver Stutler, in one of his last acts before leaving Ecobank, had recruited Howard to go back to his home state and use his connections to get approval for a mitigation bank there.

Howard landed one deep-pocketed customer for Ecobank, but it was a good one. The North Carolina DOT bought all the bank's credits.

But Howard didn't stay with Ecobank very long. "I could already see that Ecobank had overspent, that their business plan was not going to be successful," he told us. He quit to start his own mitigation banking business and now is one of the industry's leaders.

The end for Ecobank that Howard foresaw had been coming for a while. Because mitigation banks are supposed to be preserved as undeveloped forever, Florida law requires bank owners to set up a fund for their long-term maintenance. Ecobank had been putting aside thousands of dollars from each credit sale to build its maintenance fund. Once Da Capo came on board and bought the land under Lake Louisa, McCarthy persuaded Seitz to put up a letter of credit for the full amount, more than $600,000. All the money that Ecobank had set aside was plowed back into paying the bills, McCarthy said later, including his annual salary of more than $300,000.

Still, it wasn't enough. To keep the money flowing in from credit sales and to stay competitive against other banks, Ecobank sometimes slashed its credit prices so low that they were below what would bring in a profit.

"Miller and Fickett sold credits for $12,000 when the market was $22,000," Seitz told us. "They combined arrogance and . . ." Clearly agitated, Seitz caught himself before he completed the thought. He paused for a few seconds, then finished in a calmer tone: "It was just mind-boggling."

By 2003, the credit sales at Ecobank's two Florida mitigation banks had slowed to the point that Ecobank stopped sending Da Capo its share of the take. The checks would be signed but not mailed, so the books looked fine, but the money stayed in Florida.

"Nothing in this whole transaction is not a mess," Seitz said.

Meanwhile, McCarthy had a disagreement with the people who owned the land under the East Central Florida bank, and they sued. Then McCarthy and Da Capo, which owned Lake Louisa, got into a legal wrangle. Ecobank was now feuding with both of its landowners, jeopardizing the continued sale of credits from its two Florida banks.

The last straw came when the North Carolina DOT sent Ecobank a $175,000 check for credits at the mitigation bank that George Howard had launched—and McCarthy didn't pass any of it along to Da Capo.

"He took that dough and he paid 50 grand to his bankruptcy counsel," Seitz said. "The rest, I guess they used it for operations, paid the rent and so forth. And then he filed for bankruptcy."

On June 25, 2004, Ecobank filed for Chapter 11 bankruptcy protection. McCarthy followed it into bankruptcy court in October, listing among his assets a $2.8 million home, a $200,000 villa, a 20-foot Regal Destiny boat, a 2001 Chevrolet Tahoe, and a Jet Ski. McCarthy reported loaning Ecobank $956,000 and said he was owed $116,000 in back salary.

Though Ecobank's Chapter 11 filing jeopardized the operation of both mitigation banks, no one notified state and federal regulators, even though their permits required them to do so.

The regulators, even though they were supposed to be staying on top of what the mitigation banks did, somehow failed to notice anything amiss. St. Johns water district officials figured out Ecobank was circling the drain two months after it filed for Chapter 11. But the Corps remained in the dark for more than a year.

"We're all busy people," said Silver of the Corps, shrugging. "We've got a lot to do. Do I wish they had told us? Yes, absolutely."

That the Corps dropped the ball on Ecobank is not surprising. It took the

Corps even longer to notice anything was wrong at the Sundew Mitigation Bank in Clay County. Silver calls Sundew "the poster child" for his agency's failure to play its watchdog role.

The Sundew bank received its state and federal permits in 2001. The 2,104-acre property was mostly pine plantation, which owner Ernest Hale promised to convert back to wetlands. He put a conservation easement on the property, received 60 credits to get started, and then everything ground to a halt.

Five years passed, during which time Hale sold his 60 credits to people destroying wetlands, including 36 credits that went toward making up for the eradication of a swamp to build a Lowe's home improvement store in Palatka.

But Hale didn't do any of the restoration work he had promised. In 2005, just as his permits were about to expire, he asked for an extension so he could finally get started restoring the property. As of September 2007, the extension was still under consideration.

Hale said he stalled because he didn't have demand for more than the 60 credits he was given up front. So on paper, the credits from the Sundew bank made up for paving over a swamp to build a Lowe's. But because Hale hadn't done the work, in reality those wetlands were a net loss.

No state or federal government agency checked on Sundew, even though their offices are all of 16 miles from the mitigation bank.

Sundew wasn't the only bank the Corps ignored. In 2005, investigators from the GAO searched through 15 mitigation bank files in Jacksonville and found that 10 contained no evidence the Corps had ever inspected them.

That's because the regulators don't really concern themselves with whether the banks succeed or not. If they did, they would not have issued permits for the Tampa Bay Mitigation Bank.

For 34 years, the site near Ruskin was a shell mine. Dump trucks roared through the gates and hauled millions of pounds of ancient sea shells to be crushed and turned into road base. Then, in September 2006, the 161-acre mine went out of business, and owner William Casey set to work converting his land into 42 acres of mangrove swamps and 90 acres of freshwater wetlands to be connected via a creek with nearby Cockroach Bay.

It's hardly an ideal spot for a new wetland, hemmed in by a road, a mobile home park, and a commercial farm. Yet Casey, a stocky, white-haired man in khakis and a Hawaiian shirt, told us he was convinced it would work.

Of course, creating wetlands where they don't exist is frequently an exercise in futility. Creating wetlands out of a shell mine poses a particularly strong challenge. Casey, who proudly showed us around the site and talked of all the prehistoric fossils that had been found there, told us that mining shell from the site had required excavating the land to a depth of 12 feet. But now he had an employee on a Caterpillar hydraulic excavator putting most of that back, sculpting the landscape to contour it properly. Casey said his Caterpillar guy was an artist, despite having only one good eye. He joked that his employee was so adept at contouring the ground because "he has a plumb bob in his butt."

State and federal regulators decided to let Casey try to turn a mine into a wetland because they were so eager to accommodate developers clamoring for a mitigation bank in the fast-growing Tampa Bay region. One of Casey's partners, Tampa environmental consultant Beverly Birkett, told us the regulators "have been very supportive" because of what she called "a high demand in the region." Even though the bank was years from completion, she said would-be customers were already bombarding her with requests to buy credits, priced at $100,000 each.

"Consultants and developers are calling me: 'Is the bank ready to go yet?,'" said Birkett, who gamely joined us in trudging through the thick sand and scattered shells despite wearing open-toed high heeled sandals.

Whether the Tampa Bay Mitigation Bank succeeds or fails is up to Casey and his partners, said Clark Hull of the Southwest Florida Water Management District, which issued the state permit for the bank.

"If it doesn't work, it's really their neck," Hull told us. "They're taking the risk to get it done."

Except that, before anyone knows if the wetlands Casey is building will really work, his bank is allowed to sell 60 percent of its 111 credits. If Casey's wetlands fail, so much for no net loss.

That's why "it kind of sets off bells in my mind of whether it would be appropriate" to approve a bank like that, Silver told us. But the Corps issued Casey's group a permit anyway, Silver said, because "the Corps isn't judging them on whether they're financially stable or not."

As Casey started working on creating his wetlands in late 2006, he told us he expected to declare them a success in 2009, after just three years.

"I would not hesitate to say that's optimistic," said a skeptical Silver.

❧

Even when the state and Corps did find out about Ecobank's financial collapse, they didn't stop the company from selling credits. The state still needed mitigation for its road projects, and while East Central Florida had lots of competitors, Lake Louisa was the only bank in its region.

Meanwhile, the Chapter 11 proceedings grew heated. Seitz called Ecobank's plans to get out of debt a "fantasy" that only a child visiting Disney World might buy. During McCarthy's deposition, McCarthy swore at an attorney and threatened to walk out.

When the case settled in January 2005, Da Capo took possession of everything Ecobank once owned, including the two Florida mitigation banks and the name of the company. East Central Florida Mitigation Bank has since been sold to the state for preservation. As for Ecobank's first project, Lake Louisa, it still hasn't been completely restored after 10 years of effort. But it's still in business. Da Capo hired Ecobank's rival, Benbow, to help sell its credits.

McCarthy told us that Ecobank was the best mitigation banker ever in Florida, with environmental results he called "unequaled." The last time we talked to the pair, in 2006, he and Fickett were mulling their next big project.

"We're still looking at other mitigation options here in the state of Florida," Fickett said. Asked if that included starting another mitigation bank, he replied, "You never can tell."

To Denver Stutler, who became head of the DOT under Governor Bush, Ecobank failed only because it was ahead of its time. "When you're really changing the way people view mitigation and you're shifting the paradigm, you have to give it time to shift," he told us.

But Stutler seems to be the only person with anything nice to say about McCarthy and Fickett. Other mitigation bankers don't enjoy talking about Ecobank. Its failure shows everything that can go wrong with mitigation banks, including financial mismanagement, lax regulatory oversight, and relying on political influence rather than providing environmental benefits. But when the subject came up, they were quick to tell us that Ecobank was an aberration.

"They are the real bad apple of the bunch," said Sheri Lewin of the National Mitigation Banking Association, an Orlando-based organization that was founded to help the bankers work together and lobby for legislation to help their industry—sort of like the one McCarthy tried to start years before.

∾

Despite failures like Ecobank, the mitigation banking industry has convinced Congress that it's the wave of the future

Congress has spent more than a decade steering federal dollars the industry's way by writing preferences into key legislation, including pork-heavy highway projects. It also has required the Corps itself—the banks' regulators—to use the banks to make up for wetlands destroyed by its dams, canals, and levees.

The bankers say their biggest congressional champion has been Representative Walter Jones. The North Carolina Republican has attended their conventions and they have attended his fundraisers.

"He's just always been quite a champion for it," George Howard told us.

Sometimes his championship of the banking industry has carried some caveats that environmentalists found objectionable. For instance, one bill he proposed in 1996 said that developers wouldn't need a 404 permit to destroy a wetland if they made up for the destruction by buying credits from a Corps-approved mitigation bank. (It didn't pass.)

In November 2003, Congress passed a 400-page defense-spending bill, the 2004 National Defense Authorization Act, which dealt with such weighty matters as the reconstruction of Iraq and medical assistance for injured Iraqi children. Amid such grave concerns, Jones tucked in some language that required the Corps to establish new rules for wetland mitigation—rules that would boost the mitigation banking industry even further. In a news release, Jones predicted these rules would result in "greatly enhancing the quantity and quality of wetlands in the future."

The new rules would encourage private developers to make bank credits their preferred mitigation alternative—ahead of creating new wetlands, restoring drained swamps, or preserving existing bogs. If they go through, the demand created is expected to double the number of banks across the country, which as of 2007 had already topped 400.

The new regulations would also change how regulators define the areas where a bank can sell its credits. Until now the primary concern has been the impact on the environment. But the new rules say, "The service area should be large enough to support an economically viable mitigation bank."

An economic viability test, as Ecobank's principals knew, would lead to far larger service areas. Credits will be sold to developers who destroy wetlands even farther away.

There is one more wrinkle in the new regulations. They would allow district engineers the leeway to grant new banks some credits for dry land, as Florida did at Lake Louisa and so many other banks.

The proposed regulations drew more than 12,000 comments, so many that it forced the Corps and EPA to extend the comment period. A revised version of the rules was due to go to the White House Office of Management and Budget by the fall of 2007, with final issuance slated for early 2008.

Jessica Wilkinson, who led the Environmental Law Institute's nonpartisan survey of the nation's mitigation banks, said Congress and the regulators are treating the industry as if it has proven to be the best option for dealing with wetland losses, even though the jury is still out.

"If the agencies are building in preferences for one type of mitigation over the other, I believe it should be based on some empirical, field-based research," Wilkinson said.

The first such research was published in 2006, and it reads a lot like Ann Redmond's report on mitigation in general. Ohio's Environmental Protection Agency studied 12 mitigation banks and found that only three could be called successful. The other nine were partial failures or total flops.

Yet the report noted that "half of all credits were released before a demonstration of any ability . . . to meet even the limited performance standards in the agreements." The study concluded: "Too often, mitigation banks have simply meant more acres of poor quality wetland restoration than a comparable, small individual mitigation site. This is clearly not acceptable nor what was intended."

But that's beside the point for investors, who just want in on the banking bonanza. George Platt, the Florida Wetlandsbank founder, said he had been contacted four times in just two months by investors wanting to jump on the mitigation banking bandwagon.

Platt said he understands why they're so interested: "The idea is to make money."

17

Toward a More Honest System

In May 2007, Florida was trapped in a terrible drought. The rain had dried up as surely as if God Himself had turned off the faucet.

Homeowners throughout the state were told to all but stop watering their grass, even if their lawns turned as brown and crunchy as toast. Lake Okeechobee dropped to a record low and the muck in the lake bed caught fire. Blazes in the Okefenokee Swamp near the Georgia border sent smoke and ash drifting southward, turning a normally sunny day in St. Petersburg an eerie shade of Apocalyptic Yellow.

And that's when the Corps decided to approve the revamped permit for the Mirasol golf-course development in Collier County, allowing the developer to wipe out 655 acres of swamps in the western Everglades. The mitigation: preserving and "enhancing" other wetlands, meaning there would actually be nothing to balance out the loss of wetland acreage. The South Florida Water Management District—the same agency in charge of enforcing the region's restrictions on lawn watering—had already signed off on the project.

Despite Florida's desperate need for water recharge areas, like the one the Mirasol development would destroy, despite the strong objections expressed by the EPA and environmental groups, the Corps concluded that allowing this development to wipe out such a huge swath of wetlands was "not contrary to the public interest," Jacksonville's new regulatory boss David Hobbie told us.

Two weeks later, the Corps put out a public notice about another development in the same region. It promised a new town, with lots of residential and commercial construction, plus police and fire stations and everything else, to be built on the century-old Babcock Ranch straddling the Lee County–Charlotte County line. That one, if approved with no changes, would destroy more than 300 acres of wetlands.

Only three months had passed since the 40-year-old Hobbie, a pudgy Midwesterner who had spent 17 years working for the Corps, assumed John Hall's old job of heading up the regulatory division of the Corps in Florida, picking it up after the brief tenure of Lawrence Evans.

But Hobbie, whose father was once a construction company executive, already had the same approach to the work. Like Hall, Hobbie readily acknowledged that there might seem to be a conflict between the state and federal agencies approving wetlands destruction in the Everglades while asking the taxpayers to spend billions of dollars to restore the Everglades. And like Hall, he shrugged and blamed someone else.

"All we do is enforce the rules and regulations given to us by Congress," Hobbie told us.

That the policy of no net loss is a failure is obvious. It relies on discredited science and accounting tricks to create the illusion of environmental protection while doing little to stem the destruction.

"It's a huge scam," Steve Brooker had told us toward the beginning of our investigation, and everything we learned proved him right.

The blame for the broken promise of no net loss falls on every level of government in Florida, said Estus Whitfield, who served as chief environmental adviser to former governors Reubin Askew, Bob Graham, Bob Martinez, and Lawton Chiles.

"My bottom line is that the failure to protect wetlands goes much further than the Corps; it starts right here in Florida," Whitfield told us. Counties won't protect them, leaving the job to the state. State officials won't do it, leaving the job to the Corps. But the Corps won't say no.

If Florida is to avoid an ecological and economic disaster, the system needs to change. Yes—economic. When wetlands are destroyed to make room for subdivisions and stores and limestone mines, we taxpayers wind up footing the bill. We pay for government-subsidized flood insurance for homes built in what used to be swamps. We pay for the government to spend millions buying homes that are repeatedly inundated just to tear them down. We pay to clean up the water pollution that the wetlands once filtered naturally. We pay to find new sources of water to replace the ones we've paved over.

And right now, we're paying for a government wetlands protection program that doesn't work.

In 2006, Congress budgeted $158 million for the Corps' wetland permitting program nationwide. The Jacksonville office got $12.5 million. Yet wetlands continue disappearing.

Corps officials say Congress never asks anything about the program other than how fast they can issue more permits. But that's not true. In 1988, 1993, and 2005, Congress asked the Government Accountability Office to look into how well the Corps was doing its job under the Clean Water Act.

The GAO's answer, in every single report, has been the same: awful. The title of the most recent report says it all: "Wetlands Protection: Corps of Engineers Does Not Have an Effective Oversight Approach to Ensure That Compensatory Mitigation Is Occurring."

"Until the Corps takes its oversight responsibilities more seriously, it will not know if thousands of acres of compensatory mitigation have been performed and will be unable to ensure that the section 404 program is contributing to the national goal of no net loss of wetlands," GAO investigators wrote in the September 2005 report.

The problem is, Congress has never acted on the GAO's findings. And it didn't do anything about the 2001 report from the National Research Council that said no net loss didn't work and the Corps wasn't doing its job.

But now, add the GAO reports and the NRC report to the recent string of federal court reversals for Corps decisions in Florida, especially Judge Hoeveler in the Lake Belt case. In those decisions—by Hoeveler, by Judge Middlebrooks in the Scripps case, by Judge James Robertson who invalidated a 404 permit for Florida Rock to mine in panther habitat near Fort Myers—the judges all said the Corps wasn't following the law and doing its job of protecting wetlands.

All those reports and rulings combined should give Congress enough reason to make changes. They should certainly give the taxpayers a strong reason to demand Congress do something to fix this broken system.

We've spent four years researching the state of wetlands protection in Florida. We are reporters, not biologists or lawyers or policy experts. Still, after doing hundreds of interviews, reading thousands of pages of documents, and spending more time on a single subject than most reporters ever get a chance to, we can offer this thought: if nothing else, the government would do well to be honest about how things really work.

Think of this, then, as a 12-step program toward making a more honest system:

1) **No more "no net loss."** As with any 12-step program, the first step is acknowledging that there's a problem. Congress and the Florida legislature (and every other government entity in the United States) should stop passing laws that allow the rampant destruction of wetlands and depend on mitigation to make it all better. They should acknowledge that mitigation cannot replace what is lost when wetlands are destroyed.

They should focus on policies that would encourage developers, road-builders, miners, and everyone else to avoid dredging or filling swamps and marshes—especially the road-builders, who are using tax dollars to destroy public assets and then spending tax dollars on poorly conceived efforts to replace them.

If lawmakers don't make a change, then they're going to have to keep spending millions in tax dollars trying to fix the problems that result: flooding, water pollution, and so on. Isn't it more conservative to conserve the natural processes that are already there rather than spend government money on a man-made fix?

2) **Stop the Enron-like accounting tricks.** Don't preserve a wetland and count it as if it were new acreage that never existed before. Don't claim a melaleuca infestation justifies destroying the wetland where it grows—after all, it's still a wetland. Don't say removing melaleuca from one wetland justifies destroying a wetland elsewhere. Don't say uplands equal wetlands, especially when it comes to selling wetland credits. None of those things help Florida or any other state regain any of its lost wetlands. They're just a way to cook the books and allow for continued destruction.

3)**Emphasize restoration.** All over Florida are pastures and farmlands that once were wetlands but were drained for cultivation or to make room for cattle. A wetland that's been filled in and paved may never be a wetland again, but one that's been converted by agriculture can be restored. Restoration appears to offer a far better chance of success than any other form of mitigation. It should be the only kind of mitigation allowed in the mitigation banking program. And if a development must destroy a wetland, then the developer should be required to restore—not create, not enhance, but restore—wetlands elsewhere. Preservation is nice—an admirable goal outside of no net loss—but it should not count toward any sort of ratio that allegedly makes up for destruction, because it doesn't.

4) **Institute a pay-as-you-go system**. One way to encourage avoidance of wetlands is to make the federal permitting program pay for itself. When the Corps approved the Lake Belt miners' wiping out more than 5,000 acres of wetlands in the Everglades, it charged just $100 for each permit. That's the same amount the Corps charged the developer of a subdivision called Grand Hampton in Tampa, which in its first phase managed to avoid touching all but one acre of the 189 acres of wetlands

on its site. That's unfair to the developer who spares more wetlands, and it's unfair to the taxpayers, because the fee does not cover the cost of reviewing the permits.

By contrast, Florida's water management districts charge for permits on a sliding scale that's tied to the size of the project, and the money stays with the permitting agency. Congress should put the cost of a federal permit on a sliding scale based on the size of the impact to wetlands, with the cost escalating rapidly as the acreage increases. That would provide developers, miners, and everyone else with more of an economic incentive to avoid them. And if the money generated went to funding the Corps' regulatory program, the Corps could hire enough employees to give permits a more rapid yet more thorough review.

5) **Set a deadline for the Corps.** Developers' biggest objection to the Corps is how long it takes to review permits. An official of the National Home Builders Association told us unofficially that his group would be happy to pay more for permits if the Corps had to meet a deadline for processing them. So Congress should tie those two issues together, raising the cost of a permit much higher while telling the Corps that the time for reviewing permits is limited. The deadline could vary by the size of the project and whether it involves wiping out the habitat of any endangered species—another way to encourage a smaller impact. But the penalty for the Corps' missing its deadline should not be automatic issuance of the permit (and the state should drop that provision as well). Instead, to borrow an idea from the field of pizza delivery, the penalty for late arrival should be a full refund of the fee. That would give the permit reviewing agency an incentive to keep the process moving without making wetlands protection the victim of an agency failure.

6) **Tell the public what's happening.** Currently the Corps makes all of its decisions in secret. The state's water management districts are nearly as secretive, waiting until all the details of a permit are worked out before putting it to a routine vote that usually lumps a dozen or more permits together in a "consent agenda" that's passed all at once. Since the public is paying the bills, and suffering the consequences of bad decisions, the public should be given better access to information about how each agency is doing its job. The Corps already posts public notices about individual applications on its Web site, but it's not in a user-friendly format.

A better way to handle this would be to copy what the St. Johns River Water Management District does: it posts on its Web site a copy of every scrap of paper—every map and letter and memo—involved in each of its wetland permits. That information stays on the Web site even after a permit has been approved. Even better for the public would be the Corps' and the state agencies' linking those permits to locator points on an interactive map of the area—all permits, both the approved ones and the new applications. That way, the public could see just exactly how many wetlands are being wiped out in their region, their city, their neighborhood.

Permit reviewers need to stop looking at the public as a nuisance that slows down their process and instead use the public to fact-check their work. After all, one permit the Corps denied resulted from alert neighbors spotting false information in an application to build a new Wal-Mart in New Smyrna Beach. The Corps was fooled, but the neighbors knew where the wetlands really were.

7) **Map the swamps.** The Florida Fish and Wildlife Conservation Commission has already launched a project to map important wildlife habitat across the state, using its own analysis of satellite imagery. The state wildlife agency should team with the National Wetlands Inventory and the state's water management districts to produce an updated map of where Florida's remaining swamps, bogs, and marshes exist, while rating their worth as wildlife habitat, for water pollution cleanup, and for flood prevention. They should post the results on a publicly available Web site, as NWI does now, and with a way for the public to correct any bad information. The two agencies should also produce annual updates charting where the greatest losses have occurred and analyzing why.

8) **Find the tipping point.** There is a line that must not be crossed, a line beyond which too many Florida wetlands will have been destroyed, and with their destruction, our water supplies ruined, our flood protections gone, and commercially viable wildlife like fish and shrimp vanished. State and federal officials should define that line and then use it to establish how much needs to be saved. (Of course, we may have already crossed it.) When state biologists study the habitat of certain endangered species, like panthers and gopher tortoises, they try to figure out what an area's "carrying capacity" is—how many of that kind of animal the area can support before there are too many of them and they run out of food or fall prey to illness. Does Florida have a carrying capacity for people?

9) **Save the priority areas.** Once the maps are in hand, then the state Department of Environmental Protection and the Department of Community Affairs should work with the Corps, EPA, and FEMA to identify the wetland areas that should never be destroyed. This goes back to the recommendation that OPPAGA made to the legislature to begin "identifying priority conservation areas and cooperatively developing strategies to protect and restore those areas, while encouraging economic development in more appropriate areas."

In early 2007 a new group set up by the legislature, the Century Commission for a Sustainable Florida, chaired by St. Petersburg mayor Rick Baker—a staunch Republican and a strong ally of Governor Charlie Crist—issued its first report. One of its recommendations called for the state to "identify Florida's most precious natural resources and develop a comprehensive Conservation Blueprint for the state." That recommendation received praise from Department of Community Affairs secretary Tom Pelham, who said it's essential to map out what natural resources the state wants to save, so growth can be directed elsewhere. "Mapping always scares people to death," he said, noting that there could be private property rights concerns that run counter to what might be best for the broader public interest. "For that reason no one has really done it." But when private citizens and businesses wipe out wetlands, dry out springs, and damage other vital resources, he said, the public as a whole winds up paying the price—both in environmental degradation and in the price of restoring what was lost.

The state has already collected a lot of the data necessary for just such a map, and the next step should be collating it and—admittedly, the hard part—deciding what's most important to preserve. That part should be done in the open, so the public can see what the data says. Quipped Century Commission executive director Steve Seibert, "Wouldn't it be something if data actually drove government policy?"

10) **Consider the Canadian variation.** In Ontario, the government has mapped all the wetlands, labeled some of them a priority to preserve, and banned development from those areas. Then, to give landowners an incentive to leave wetlands alone, it offers tax breaks for property that keeps its marshes and swamps in a natural state. After all, saving wetlands is a public service, and the private entities who do the work should be rewarded. A good starting point would be with the list of people who have asked the Corps for a "jurisdictional determination" so the Corps can

tell where the wetlands are on their property. Usually that information has been used to mark what needs to be destroyed, but giving tax breaks could turn it into a way to prevent destruction.

11) **Put a price on failure and dishonesty.** The Corps can't say which permits were carried out properly or which mitigation projects have failed because it has only seven employees assigned to monitor thousands of projects all across Florida. In their best years, they manage to check on less than a quarter of all the permits issued. And when consultants file false reports—as happened with the Wal-Mart in New Smyrna Beach, where the consultants claimed a smaller wetlands acreage than was actually at stake—or when applicants break promises about mitigation—as happened with the Wal-Mart in Oldsmar, which was going to sell its "preserved" wetlands until the neighbors blew the whistle—there are no consequences. There are no fines, no ban on doing business with government agencies, no requirement that a project cease, no threat that future permits will be denied or at least delayed.

Where there is no consequence for failure or dishonesty, there is no incentive to do things right. As Roy "Robin" Lewis, a Tampa Bay area environmental consultant who has spent 30 years working on wetland restoration projects around Florida, told us: "We only care about it working if compliance inspections are at such a level that if people screw up, they get caught. That's not taking place." At the very least, the Corps should require permit applicants to post a bond to pay for inspections of the mitigation site by Corps employees. If they find it's not working, the permit holder should be required to fix it or face stiff administrative fines. Other consequences could follow if it recurs, including a refusal to process future permits until the work on the previous ones is completed. That's the way a private business would handle a contractor slow to follow through on promised work, and that's the way government should handle it too.

12) **Give more people the power to say no.** Some of the most stringent wetland regulations in Florida have been imposed by county governments. For instance, in 2007, Hillsborough County's Environmental Protection Commission had a $2 million annual budget and employed 27 people to review permits and check whether the rules are being followed. Homebuilders tried in vain to get the legislature to override county rules by arguing they duplicate what the state and federal agencies do. The homebuilders dislike them not because their requirements

are the same as the other agencies, but because the county's rules are tougher.

The state does not protect wetlands of a half-acre or less, but Hillsborough County does. For 20 years, Hillsborough has said no wetlands can be destroyed unless there is a documented need to do so to use the property, say, for a road for access to the land. Only then can county officials consider mitigation. State officials take the opposite approach, EPC attorney Rick Tschantz said, allowing developers to propose mitigation up front, which then becomes the justification for approving the permit. The result: Hillsborough has lost little wetland acreage to development. Clearly, the stringent local approach has done what the Corps and state could not.

On the federal level, the "elevation" policy needs to be ditched, since it discourages the agencies from objecting to Corps decisions. Instead, in addition to EPA having the veto power, FEMA should have the power to shoot down wetland permits too. Then, perhaps, it could stem the tide of building in flood-prone areas, thus decreasing the number of properties that must be covered by taxpayer-subsidized flood insurance. Each agency that gets to veto projects should be held accountable for their use or misuse of that power. They should be required to submit an annual report to Congress on how often they have vetoed permits and explaining why they did so—or why they failed to do anything to protect the public.

Changing the way we protect wetlands won't be easy. It will require making some hard choices between private property rights, which benefit the owners of wetlands only when those wetlands can be developed, and the rights of the population at large to flood protection and clean water and abundant fishing and duck-hunting, things that are available only when we leave wetlands alone. It will require action by Congress and the legislature, two bodies that so far have shown more interest in making it easier to wipe out wetlands than in trying to save them.

But remember, wetlands protection affects more than just our quality of life and our survival on the planet. As taxpayers, we're footing the multi-million-dollar bill for this program.

Shouldn't we get what we're paying for?

Appendix A. Satellite Imagery Methodology

This document is substantially the same methodology we sent to experts for review prior to the publication of our May 2005 newspaper series. A few editing changes have been made for publication.

In 1989, then president George H. W. Bush told a Ducks Unlimited convention that the federal government's policy toward wetlands would be "no net loss." For every wetlands destroyed by man, the damage would be mitigated. In 1990, through a memorandum of agreement between the U.S. Army Corps of Engineers and the Environmental Protection Agency, the "no net loss" policy was put into place.

Getting an accurate picture of wetlands losses through agency permits during that time period, however, is all but impossible because information is incomplete, insufficient, or systematically flawed. And, agency records by themselves would give an incomplete picture of wetlands destruction through urbanization.

After a lengthy Freedom of Information Act fight, the *St. Petersburg Times* found that the Army Corps of Engineers permitting database contains records that are largely incomplete. Corps officials said that the only reliable information contained in their RAMS permitting database is the date a permit was applied for and the date the permit was issued. Quarterly reports generated from the RAMS system have to be screened by hand against paper records to ensure accuracy. For the first four years of "no net loss," the Corps didn't track permitted acreage. Until 2003, the Corps didn't track one of their permit types at all.

A database of Florida Department of Environmental Protection Environmental Resource Permit records are more reliably filled out but contain a similar systematic problem that the Corps data contain: geographic locations are generalized to the mile-square section, township, and range area. Exact location information at the regional, state, and federal level is by and large unavailable for wetlands destruction.

No agency that regulates wetlands destruction in Florida maintains data on the location of wetlands destruction mitigation.

Regulatory agency data in Florida is largely based on the word of the applicant the *Times* found in dozens of interviews with regulators. State and federal permit reviewers rarely ever go to the site of the wetlands destruction, and it is equally rare that any kind of independent verification of the applicant's information is done. There are examples of permit applicants claiming far smaller wetlands losses than would occur in the actual construction. Only a small fraction of permits are reviewed for compliance. Lone compliance officers at the Corps of Engineers must cover areas of more than a dozen counties.

Not included in the data are losses for which no permit was sought. Illegal wetlands filling occurs, the regulatory agencies told the *Times*, and no one knows the extent of such destruction. Thus, remote sensing and satellite analysis becomes an ideal—and perhaps the only—solution to determining the loss of wetlands to urbanization.

The process of acquiring data for this project was driven by limitations.

The first source of data found was the National Wetlands Inventory. However, that data was static and hadn't been updated in some parts of Florida for nearly 20 years. It was, and remains, the only systematic effort at mapping the state's wetlands through high resolution aerial imagery to achieve statewide coverage. The National Wetlands Inventory is also one of the most widely used geographic datasets in computerized mapping.

The State of Florida, through the Office of Environmental Services in the Florida Fish and Wildlife Conservation Commission's GAP Analysis Program, has performed remotely sensed assessments of Florida's landscape for the time periods the *Times* studied. However, their methods and land cover classifications changed between the late 1980s and 2003, as did their data source, making comparisons troublesome. From the state, the *Times* could acquire the statewide Landsat 7 ETM+ data used in the 2003 GAP analysis, but the agency no longer had the data used for the late 1980s, which was Landsat 5 TM data. Instead, the *Times* acquired statewide Landsat 5 TM coverage for dates between 1988 and 1990 from the Global Land Cover Facility at the University of Maryland.

The first step in the analysis was the creation of the *Times'* own statewide wetlands map, using the University of Maryland data and the state's Landsat

7 ETM+ data. The analysis was done in ESRI's ArcGIS software, using Leica Geosystems' Image Analyst for ArcGIS extension. Because of known variations in water levels and seasons in Florida, the *Times* selected a method that focused more on wetlands vegetation than water levels.

For both the Landsat TM and ETM data, the *Times* used unsupervised classifications of bands 2, 3, and 4, resulting in 100 pixel classes. Bands 2 and 3 were selected because of their sensitivity to green, healthy vegetation, as well as band 3's usefulness in determining soil or geologic boundaries. Band 4 was selected because it is sensitive to the amount of vegetation biomass in a scene and is useful in identifying contrasts between land and water (Lunetta and Balogh 1999, Jensen 2000). Lunetta and Balogh highlighted band 5's usefulness in identifying soil and vegetations moisture content, and others have pointed to band 5's usefulness in wetlands identification. However, given single date imagery and the understanding that Florida's climate means highly variable water levels throughout the year, the *Times* chose not to use band 5.

Each Landsat scene—28 in all, 14 for each image set—was classified, and then each pixel class was analyzed, using multiple ancillary datasets to aid in identification, including elevation, soils, wetlands and, on occasion, property or land use maps. Each pixel class was then grouped into one of two classifications—Wetlands or Not Wetlands. No attempt was made to separate wetlands types, because that kind of analysis was beyond the *Times*' abilities and the scope of the analysis.

After the classification of both image years was completed, they were set aside and the classifications were done again. This was done to take advantage of the increased experience of the analyst and to only use the most accurate classifications in the final analysis. Each image year was then merged together into one raster file, with particular attention paid to ensuring seamless melding of the two image scenes.

The accuracy of the *Times* analysis was then formally assessed, using a random set of 385 points—enough for a 95 percent confidence level with a +/- 5 percent confidence interval where the distribution of the data is unknown—generated in ArcGIS through Hawth's Analysis Tools. The points were visually inspected to ensure spatial randomness, and further tested using spatial density analysis. Overall accuracy of the *Times* analysis was around 80 percent for both image years. However, wetlands accuracy for both years was around 66 percent, and errors were largely of commission—calling something a wetland that wasn't. Errors were primarily misclassifications of certain kinds of agriculture—for example, sugar—and misclassifications of wetlands forest types that share similar spectral characteristics of non-wetlands forest types.

Relying on only the *Times* analysis would be a mistake for several reasons. Using single-date imagery for wetlands change detection has been found many times over to be less accurate than using multi-date imagery, owing partly to seasonal changes in wetlands (Lunetta and Balogh 1999, Ozesmi and Bauer 2002, Reese et al. 2002). Moreover, the two image years use different sensors—Landsat TM for one, ETM for another—which creates some sensor-based differences that can't be extracted or accounted for.

Each taken alone, the state's GAP analysis, the *Times* analysis, and the National Wetlands Inventory had weaknesses that made change detection difficult or impossible. So a simple method to screen misclassifications was created out of three raster layers in ArcGIS' Spatial Analyst extension.

The first layer was a rasterized version of the National Wetlands Inventory maps for Florida. The vector data was converted to a raster map with two values: Wetlands and Not Wetlands. This raster layer served as the base, as the vast majority of wetland areas in Florida don't change—for instance, the three-million-acre Everglades National Park, representing nearly one third of the wetlands acreage in Florida. And, in areas that did change, the two other analyses would be relied on to detect such change.

The second layer was a distilled version of the state's GAP analysis. The multiple land cover classes used in their analysis were collapsed into Wetlands and Not Wetlands for both the late 1980s and 2003. The weaknesses of these layers were that their methods and sensors changed between analyses, and according to their metadata they did no formal accuracy assessment, relying only on anecdotal information and aerial videos of certain areas to check accuracy. The analysts estimate an 85 percent overall accuracy but have no assessment to verify that claim (Cox et al. 1994).

The third layer was the *Times* analysis, detailed above.

Our method combined the three layers so that if two of three pixels agreed that the individual pixel was a wetland, it was classified Wetlands. If only one of the three classified that pixel as a wetland, the pixel was classified Not Wetlands. The three-layer combination resulted in eight possible responses. A majority of pixels—over 60 percent in both image years—agreed 100 percent with each other.

This two-of-three method overcame two weaknesses inherent to the layers used. First, the National Wetlands Inventory layer is static—the maps were the same for the 1980s analysis and the 2003 analysis. Second, as the Pearlstine study (2002) notes, using converted vector maps as a hard mask in an image would create a classification with hard boundaries that are more part of the original vector map than changes in the image.

Visual inspection of the resulting datasets showed that the screening method removed problems associated with each individual dataset and increased the accuracy of wetlands classification. Formal accuracy assessments bore this out: overall accuracy levels increased to 86 percent for the late 1980s dataset and to 88 percent for 2003. Compared with the lone *Times* analysis, the two-of-three method substantially increased wetlands classification accuracy, giving 88 and 85 percent accuracy—about 20 percentage points higher than the single-date, single-analyst analysis.

A change detection algorithm was then run on the two wetlands maps. Anecdotally, a large amount of change can be directly tied to seasonal variations or tidal influences. Along the coasts, wetlands gains and losses run parallel to each other, indicating the tide was in for one image set and out for another. Other wetlands changes indicate areas where the water levels changed, as, for example, with increases or decreases along lake or stream margins. Given the data we had, and its limitations, it is impossible to isolate these seasonal or tidal changes and classify them in any meaningful way.

To extract meaningful information, the state's 2003 GAP analysis data was brought back. This time, areas were collapsed into two categories: Urbanized and Not Urbanized. Because the accuracy of the state data had not been assessed, the *Times* performed an accuracy assessment on the urbanized area data and found the accuracies quite high—96 percent overall, with urban area accuracy at 87 percent.

Using urbanized areas as a means to identify wetlands change is ideal, because the spectral signatures of all wetlands types and urbanized areas are very different (Pearlstine et al. 2002). In two studies, urban accuracies were well above 90 percent. In Reese et al., a statewide land cover project using Landsat TM data resulted in over 90 percent urban accuracy. Errors in the urban identification were the result of misclassifying high-density urban as low-density urban and vice versa. Similarly, in Lunetta and Balogh, urban area accuracy was above 90 percent in both single-date and multiple-date analyses, and the lone error in the accuracy assessment in the urban area identification came from labeling an area of open water as urban. Neither study resulted in an urban area being misidentified as a wetland or vice versa.

For the sake of computational efficiency, areas of wetlands decrease identified in the change detection analysis were isolated and then compared to areas of urbanization. Where they intersected, those pixels were extracted and labeled "Lost to Urbanization."

In all, statewide, approximately 84,000 acres of wetlands were replaced by urbanized areas—homes, stores, strip malls, parking lots, churches, apartments, and condos. Those changes are not seasonal, are not subject to tides, and are permanent.

By and large, this tracks well with available Army Corps of Engineers records, which show a 61,000-acre loss over 10 years. However, the Corps can't document all permitted losses during the "no net loss" policy period, and some of the Corps-documented loss is attributed to mining and agriculture, two changes that would not be detected by this analysis.

The resulting dataset largely comports to what the regulatory agencies say is occurring—wetlands are being destroyed bits and pieces at a time. Rare are the projects that wipe out large areas of wetlands at once. Far more common are large projects that slice and nibble wetlands a small piece at a time.

Appendix B. Accuracy Assessment Tables

1990 wetlands map accuracy assessment

			Ground points	
Wetlands map	Not wetlands	Wetlands	Grand total	Accuracy
Not wetlands	263	42	305	86%
Wetlands	10	70	80	88%
Grand total	273	112	385	86%

2003 wetlands map accuracy assessment

			Ground points	
Wetlands map	Not wetlands	Wetlands	Grand total	Accuracy
Not wetlands	255	30	285	89%
Wetlands	15	85	100	85%
Grand total	270	115	385	88%

State 2003 GAP analysis urban area accuracy assessment

			Ground points	
Urban map	Not urban	Urban	Grand total	Accuracy
Not urban	332	8	340	98%
Urban	6	39	45	87%
Grand total	338	47	385	96%

Notes

Authors' Note

Unless otherwise indicated, the more than 140 separate interviews cited in the notes that follow were conducted by Craig Pittman between January 2002 and October 2007 as research for the authors' *St. Petersburg Times* "Vanishing Wetlands" series, for other stories published in the *Times*, and for use in *Paving Paradise*. Matthew Waite went along on some interviews to record audio and video clips for the *Times* Web site (http://www.sptimes.com/2006/webspecials06/wetlands) or to search through and scan records for documentary purposes. For readers who want follow up on sources, some of the documents cited below will be available online at *PavingParadise.org*.

Prologue. The Numbers Game

"There is a strong interest . . . ": Peter Reuter, "The (Continued) Vitality of Mythical Numbers," *Public Interest* 75, 135–47, quoted by Jack Shafer in "The (Ongoing) Vitality of Mythical Numbers," *Slate*, June 26, 2006,http://www.slate.com/id/2144508/.

For five tumultuous years . . . : Tim Kenworthy, "Interior Secretary Norton Submits Resignation," *USA Today*, March 10, 2006; "Ethics scandal didn't prompt resignation, Norton says," *Seattle Times*, March 11, 2006; Edmund L. Andrews, "Interior Official Assails Agency for Ethics Slide," *New York Times*, Sept. 14, 2006; Susan Schmidt and James V. Grimaldi, "Ex-Official At Interior Hid His Ties To Abramoff; Griles Pleads Guilty To Lying to Senate," *Washington Post*, March 24, 2007; press release from Defenders of Wildlife, "Interior Secretary Gale Norton Resigns: Statement of Rodger Schlickeisen, President, Defenders of Wildlife," March 10, 2006.

On March 30, 2006, her next-to-last day . . . : Tape of press conference provided by Steve Davies of *Endangered Species & Wetlands Report*.

But now, at last, Norton was ready . . . : Figures from Dahl, *Status and Trends of Wetlands . . . 1998 to 2004*, http://wetlandsfws.er.usgs.gov/status_trends/national_reports/trends_2005_report.pdf.

But then the reporters . . . : National Wildlife Federation press release, "Secretary Norton to Claim False Victory on Wetlands," March 29, 2006; Steve Davies, "Artificial water bodies credited with realizing 'net gain' in wetlands," *Endangered Species & Wetlands Report*, March/April 2006, 1.

Norton's elastic definition of wetlands . . . : Felicity Barringer, "Fewer Marshes + More Man-Made Ponds = Increased Wetlands," *New York Times*, March 31, 2006; Bob Marshall, "Special Report: You Call This a Wetland?" *Field and Stream* online, "Field Notes" blog, April 3, 2006, http://fieldandstream.blogs.com/news/2006/04/you_call_this_a.html; Matthew Waite and Craig Pittman, "Are these both wetlands?" *St. Petersburg Times*, March 31, 2006; Fark.com posting, April 1, 2006, http://forums.fark.com/cgi/fark/comments.pl?IDLink=1992073; *The Colbert Report*, Comedy Central network, April 4, 2006, transcript available at http://www.tv.com/the-colbert-report/rev.-jesse-jackson/episode/694425/summary.html.

One of the reporters who covered . . . : Interview with Steve Davies; Davies, "Estimated 'net gain' of wetlands could be much larger—or smaller," *Endangered Species & Wetlands Report*, March/April 2006, 3.

As reporters for the St. Petersburg Times . . . : Our series, comprising stories published in 2005 and 2006, is available online at http://www.sptimes.com/wetlands.

Nevertheless, Florida's wetlands . . . : Interview with D. Bruce Means, coauthor of *Priceless Florida*, and with Ron Larson, author of *Swamp Song*.

Such a wide array can be overwhelming . . . : Katherine C. Ewel, "Swamps," in Myers and Ewel, eds., *Ecosystems of Florida*, 281.

"You can't do anything in Florida . . . " : Interview with Chandler Morse.

In fact, the flawed report . . . : Dahl, *Status and Trends of Wetlands . . . 1998 to 2004*, 66–67.

In parts of fast-growing Pasco County . . . : Interview with Wesley Chapel resident, Jennifer Seney, and tour of Saddlewood Estates, Quail Hollow, Shenandoah, Forest Park, and Circle Eight Acres subdivisions, December 2004.

After hurricane season arrives . . . : According to the National Climatic Data Center, the Tampa Bay area's average annual rainfall exceeds Seattle's famous drizzle, with 44.77 inches versus 37.07 inches. Miami gets even more than Tampa Bay: 58.53 inches. Pensacola gets the most: 64.28 inches.

Wet or dry, every inch . . . : Federal Bureau of Economic Analysis and Census Bureau statistics; Florida Department of Agriculture and Consumer Services, "Agriculture and Resource Conservation Assessment," December 2001, 3.

So we wondered . . . : Government officials frequently say that the demand for housing is so great that nothing can stop Florida's growth, but a large part of Florida's recent housing boom was based not on actual need but on speculative investment and outright fraud. See Michael Van Sickler, "Investors drive hot housing market," *St. Petersburg Times*, July 17, 2005, http://www.sptimes.com/2005/07/17/Tampabay/Investors_drive_hot_h.shtml; Noel C. Haner, "Mortgage fraud huge in Florida, FBI report says," *Orlando Business Journal*, Aug. 8, 2005, http://www.bizjournals.com/orlando/2005/08/08/story1.html; and Shannon Behnken, "Florida Leads Country in Mortgage Fraud," *Tampa Tribune*, May 18, 2007, http://www.tbo.com/news/metro/MGBZ80N4U1F.html.

Chapter 1. "The National Emblem of Florida"

Back before he was the Father of His Country . . . : Vileisis, *Discovering the Unknown Landscape*, 42; Thomas E. Dahl and Gregory J. Allard, "History of Wetlands in the Conterminous United States" in *National Water Summary on Wetland Resources*, U.S. Geological Survey Water-Supply Paper 2425, http://water.usgs.gov/nwsum/WSP2425/history.html.

Not until halfway through the 20th century . . . : Wright et al., *Direct and Indirect Impacts*, 1–12; Bill Sipple, "Wetland Functions and Values," EPA Watershed Academy Web, http://www.epa.gov/watertrain/wetlands/text.html; "Functions and Values of Wetlands," EPA 843-F-01-002c, Environmental Protection Agency, Office of Wetlands, September 2001, http://www.epa.gov/owow/wetlands/pdf/fun_val.pdf.

And of course no one knew . . . : "Climate Change Mitigation," Ramsar Papers on Wetland Functions and Values, http://www.ramsar.org/info/values_climate_e.htm; Tom Pelton, "Can this muck save the planet?" *Baltimore Sun*, Oct. 9, 2007.

Because wetlands often existed . . . : Vileisis, *Discovering the Unknown Landscape*, 29–50, 111.

Across Florida's 35 million acres . . . : Dahl, *Florida's Wetlands . . . 1985 to 1996*, 7, http://wetlandsfws.er.usgs.gov/status_trends/St_and_Reg_Reports/Florida_1985.pdf.

That was a tad too damp . . . : Proby, *Audubon in Florida*, 25–26.

Because so much of Florida's interior . . . : Marth and Marth, *Florida Almanac 1998–1999*, 53.

Florida became a state . . . : Grunwald, *The Swamp*, 64–69; interview with Joe Knetsch, historian of the Florida Division of State Lands.

So in 1850, in an effort spearheaded . . . : Shaw and Fredine, *Wetlands of the United States*, http://www.npwrc.usgs.gov/resource/wetlands/uswetlan/index.htm. (This document is better known among wetland scientists as Circular 39.)

Florida's government did its best . . . : Rothchild, *Up for Grabs*, 28.

Still, it took a long time . . . : Anonymous tourist's letter to a newspaper quoted by

Harriet Beecher Stowe in her *Palmetto Leaves*, 117. After the Civil War, the author of *Uncle Tom's Cabin* moved to the St. Johns River and became an early promoter of Florida tourism.

The king of dredge-and-fill development . . . : Joe McCarthy, "The Man Who Invented Miami Beach," *American Heritage Magazine* online, December 1975, http://www.americanheritage.com/articles/magazine/ah/1975/1/1975_1_64.shtml; Nolan, *Fifty Feet in Paradise*, 156–57.

Charles Green Rodes refined Fisher's technique . . . : Vileisis, *Discovering the Unknown Landscape*, 128; Allen, Kuder, and Oakes, *Promised Lands*, vol. 2, *Subdivisions*, 125; official Web site of the City of Cape Coral, http://www.capecoral.net/about/abt_history.cfm; Florida Fish and Wildlife Conservation Commission, Fish and Wildlife Research Institute, "A Special Study of the Caloosahatchee River Eastward to the Edison Bridge and of Mullock Creek," November 2002, http://research.myfwc.com/features/view_article.asp?id=18833.

Developers had a strong incentive . . . : F. L. Allen, *Only Yesterday*, 235–36; Derr, *Some Kind of Paradise*, 181–93; Doug Stewart, "The Madness That Swept Miami," *Smithsonian*, January 2001, 63; Groucho Marx quotation from *The Cocoanuts* (1929), Internet Movie Database, http://www.imdb.com/title/tt0019777/quotes.

The Florida fantasy reached its apotheosis . . . : Foglesong, *Married to the Mouse*, 60, 80; Fjellman, *Vinyl Leaves*, 187; Martin Reuss, "Engineer Memoirs: Maj. Gen. William E. Potter," U.S. Army Corps of Engineers publication, EP 870-1-12, 1983, 191–94.

In St. Petersburg, for instance . . . : Bruce Stephenson, "A Monstrous Desecration: Dredge and Fill in Boca Ciega Bay," in Davis and Arsenault, eds., *Paradise Lost?* 326–49.

Floridians got the federal government's help . . . : U.S. Army Corps of Engineers, "Kissimmee River Restoration Study," March 17, 1992, 67, 112.

Somehow the forces of progress . . . : Blake, *Land into Water*, 216–22; Grunwald, *The Swamp*, 253–59; Vileisis, *Discovering the Unknown Landscape*, 205.

"By the year 2000 . . . *"*: John G. Mitchell, "The Bitter Struggle for a National Park," *American Heritage Magazine* online, April 1970, http://www.americanheritage.com/articles/magazine/ah/1970/3/1970_3_97.shtml.

In rounding up allies, Browder . . .: Douglas, *Voice of the River*, 224–26.

Before long the jetport fight . . .: Blake, *Land into Water*, 216–22.

Browder, with the help . . .: Grunwald, *The Swamp*, 257–58.

What killed the jetport . . . : Luna B. Leopold et al., "Environmental Impact of the

Big Cypress Swamp Jetport," U.S. Department of the Interior, 1969, http://sflwww.
er.usgs.gov/publications/reports/jetportimpact/jetportimpact_mag/index.html.

Chapter 2. A Reasonable Curb

In the 200 years it took to transform . . . : Dahl, *Wetlands Losses . . . 1780s to
1980s*, http://www.npwrc.usgs.gov/resource/wetlands/wetloss/.

By the end of the 1960s . . . : Adler, Cameron, and Landman, *The Clean Water Act*,
5–6.

Congress had tried before . . . : Andreen, "The Evolution of Water Pollution Control," 235–38.

Another law that Congress passed . . . : Cowdrey, "Pioneering Environmental Law,"
331–49; Andreen, "The Evolution of Water Pollution Control," 220–22; Milazzo, *Unlikely Environmentalists*, 166–71.

"No modern environmental law . . . ": Milazzo, *Unlikely Environmentalists*, 166.

Six decades after Frye's law passed . . . : Cowdrey, "Pioneering Environmental
Law," 344–45.

In one nationally publicized case . . . : Milazzo, *Unlikely Environmentalists*, 168–69.

While the Corps was slow to employ . . . : Stine, "Regulating Wetlands in the 1970s,"
62–63; Bruce Stephenson, "A Monstrous Desecration," in Davis and Arsenault, eds.,
Paradise Lost? 343–44.

Far larger dredge-and-fill projects . . . : Douglas Doubleday, "Submerged Land Low
Cost Leads to Many Fills," *St. Petersburg Times*, March 24, 1957; unsigned editorial,
no headline, *St. Petersburg Times*, March 26, 1957 (located in the *Times'* clip files).

Zabel was a town councilman . . . : No byline, "Obituaries: Alfred Zabel," *St. Petersburg Times*, Sept. 15, 1970; No byline, "Obituaries: David H. Russell," *St. Petersburg
Times*, Feb. 9, 1970.

But by the time Zabel and Russell . . . : No byline, "Slides Used in Protest Against
Fill," *St. Petersburg Times*, Jan. 29, 1959; "Commission Turns Down Trailer 'Isle,'" *St.
Petersburg Times*, Nov. 13, 1959; Associated Press story on Florida Supreme Court's
4–3 decision (headline missing), Jan. 20, 1965.

That's how the permit application . . . : Interview with Tom Jorling.

Col. Tabb, a West Point grad . . . : "Soldiers' Stories: Col. Robert P. Tabb III,"
at "*Military.com* Remembers D-Day," http://www.military.com/Content/
MoreContent1/?file=dday_0015p1; Ann Weldon, "Residents Flock to Hearing on
Zabel-Russell Permit," *St. Petersburg Times*, Nov. 30, 1966; no byline, "Fill Decision
Expected Early in 1967," *St. Petersburg Evening Independent*, Nov. 30, 1966.

To the developers' surprise . . . : James Lewis, "Boca Ciega Fill Plan is Rejected," *St. Petersburg Times*, March 16, 1967.

The case was heard by . . . : Craig Basse, "U.S. District Judge Ben Krentzman dies," *St. Petersburg Times*, March 31, 1998; undated "Man in the News" profile, *New York Times* News Service, April 1970; Ronald Hutchison, no headline, *St. Petersburg Times*, Feb. 20, 1969.

When the Justice Department appealed . . . : Associated Press, "Zabel-Russell Case: Dredge, Fill Appeal Is Heard," *St. Petersburg Times*, Dec. 6, 1969.

The judges were not swayed . . . : Unsigned editorial, "Ruling Opens Corps' Eyes," *St. Petersburg Times*, July 23, 1970; Douglas R. Williams and Kim Diana Connolly, "Federal Wetlands Regulation: An Overview," in Connolly, Johnson, and Williams, eds., *Wetlands Law*, 5.

When the ruling was announced . . . : Hedeman, "The Evolution of Federal Legislation," 174.

In February 1971, the high court . . . : Charles Stafford, "Saving Our Ecology—With an 1899 Law," *St. Petersburg Times*, Feb. 28, 1971.

Pete Seeger even wrote a song . . . : Albert E. Cowdrey, "Pioneering Environmental Law," 332, footnote.

With the public demanding the government . . . : Stine, "Regulating Wetlands," 63–64; Milazzo, *Unlikely Environmentalists*, 172–75.

By then, though, another senator from Maine . . . : Milazzo, *Unlikely Environmentalists*, 63–66; "Remembering Ed Muskie," *McNeil-Lehrer News Hour*, March, 26, 1996, transcript at http://www.pbs.org/newshour/bb/remember/muskie_3-26.html; Leon Billings, speech at the 75th annual meeting of the Missouri Water Environment Association, Osage Beach, Mo., March 22, 2004, http://www.muskiefoundation.org/leon.missouri.html.

By 1971, Muskie was widely considered . . . : *Time* cover, Sept. 13, 1971, http://www.time.com/time/covers/0,16641,19710913,00.html.

About a month after that . . . : "Amendment of Federal Water Pollution Control Act," from the Online Legislative Record of Senator Edmund S. Muskie (*Congressional Record*, 33692–33694), Edmund S. Muskie Archives and Special Collections Library, Bates College, http://abacus.bates.edu/Library/aboutladd/departments/special/ajcr/1972/CWA%20Conference%20opening.shtml#33692-72-T; interviews with Leon Billings and Tom Jorling.

By then Muskie's presidential campaign . . . : Jamieson, *Packaging the Presidency*, 278–79; Crouse, *The Boys on the Bus*, 122, 332.

That second phrase was intended . . . : Dingell cited in *U.S. v. Holland*, 373 F.Supp. 665 (M.D. Fla. 1974). In 2007, in response to a pair of U.S. Supreme Court rulings regarding the Corps' regulatory authority, Representative Dingell—now the House's longest serving member—cosponsored a bill called the Clean Water Restoration Act intended to clarify that Congress intended the Clean Water Act to cover all the waters of the United States, period. Dingell said the bill, if passed, "will . . . prevent any further mess made of a wonderful law." The two cases that Dingell called a "bungle" are *Solid Waste Agency of Northern Cook County v. Corps of Engineers* in 2001 and *Rapanos et ux., et al. v. United States* in 2006.

The authors of the new law . . . : Interviews with Leon Billings and Tom Jorling.

The ambiguity meant that regulators . . . : Interview with Vance Hughes; *U.S. v. Holland*, 373 F.Supp. 665 (M.D. Fla. 1974).

Wray, the son of a former city attorney . . . : Eleanor Randolph, no headline, *St. Petersburg Times*, July 21, 1972; Christopher Cubbison, no headline, *St. Petersburg Times*, Aug. 15, 1973, and Dec. 2, 1973; Laurie Mayers, "As always, Wray positive about his latest big project," *St. Petersburg Evening Independent*, June 7, 1985; no byline, "Gigantic Dredging Project Approved," *St. Petersburg Times*, Jan. 9, 1973.

State biologists reported . . . : "Florida's Cabinet" column, *St. Petersburg Times*, July 18, 1973.

Hughes said Krentzman quickly grasped . . . : At the time he issued his ruling, Krentzman was also picking a jury for the trial of U.S. Senator Edward "Ted" Gurney on charges of accepting bribes from builders and thus he may have developed a less than favorable view of the construction industry.

With Krentzman's ruling in hand . . . : Interviews with Vance Hughes and Jim Range. Hughes worried that Krentzman might be overturned on appeal so he agreed to settle with Wray, allowing a less destructive development plan to proceed so the EPA could continue using Krentzman's ruling as a precedent.

Somehow they got the new version through . . . : President Jimmy Carter, "Clean Water Act of 1977 Statement on Signing HR 3199 Into Law," December 28, 1977, *American Presidency Project*, online archive compiled by John Woolley and Gerhard Peters, University of California, Santa Barbara, http://www.presidency.ucsb.edu/ws/?pid=7063.

"Federal regulation of wetlands . . . ": Committee on Characterization of Wetlands, *Wetlands*, 13.

Chapter 3. "Let Us Try"

Since its inception . . . : Lt. Gen. J. W. Morris, "The Corps of Engineers and the American Environment: Past, Present, and Future," EP 360-1-15, U.S. Department of the Army, Office of the Chief of Engineers, Washington, D.C., 1978, 3–5.

"The Corps is in a strange position . . . ": Interview with Chuck Hummer.

Carl Fisher would have made . . . : U.S. Army Corps of Engineers online, Historical Vignettes, Vignette 48: "Did you know the Corps Connection to the Washington, D.C., Tidal Basin and its Beloved Cherry Trees?" http://www.hq.usace.army.mil/history/Vignettes/Vignette_48.htm.

That such a first-class destroyer . . . : Michael Grunwald, "An Agency of Unchecked Clout," *Washington Post*, Sept. 10, 2000, http://www.washingtonpost.com/wp-dyn/content/article/2006/05/12/AR2006051201550.html; interview with Terry Rice.

A good example of how the Corps . . . : Craig Pittman, "Digging ourselves into a hole," *St. Petersburg Times*, Oct. 31, 1999; Blake, *Land Into Water*, 199–215.

By the late 1960s, people were beginning . . . : Douglas quoted in Heuvelmans, *River Killers*, 43; Udall quoted in Heuvelmans, 179; *Field and Stream* quotation from Mighetto and Ebel, *Saving the Salmon*, 175.

Even other federal agencies complained . . . : Interview with Bill Lake; Reed quoted in Heuvelmans, *River Killers*, 204.

"The Corps is everywhere . . . " : Heuvelmans, *River Killers*, 95.

The Corps leaders' reaction . . . : Mighetto and Ebel, *Saving the Salmon*, 177; interview with Leon Billings.

On paper, at least, this move . . . : Interview with Tom Jorling.

Still, the first time someone proposed . . . : Muskie quoted in Andreen, "Evolution of Water Pollution," 272.

But the long summer of conference committee . . . : "Amendment of Federal Water Pollution Control Act," from the Online Legislative Record of Senator Edmund S. Muskie (*Congressional Record*, 33692–33694), Edmund S. Muskie Archives and Special Collections Library, Bates College, http://abacus.bates.edu/Library/aboutladd/departments/special/ajcr/1972/CWA%20Conference%20opening.shtml#33692-72-T.

Unlike their reaction to NEPA . . . : Interview with Leon Billings; Stine, "Regulating Wetlands," 65.

When Congress passes a new law . . . : Stine, "Regulating Wetlands," 65.

But the case that Vance Hughes . . . : Interview with Vance Hughes; Krentzman's *U.S. v. Holland* ruling.

Krentzman's ruling in March 1974 . . . : Train letter, Justice, and House committee correspondence, as well as the Corps' response, quoted in Finnell, "Federal Regulatory Role in Coastal Land Management," 192–98.

On August 16, 1974, the NRDC . . . : *NRDC v. Callaway*, 392F.Supp. 685; Stine, "Regulating Wetlands," 65–66; interviews with Gus Speth and Bill Lake; Timothy S.

Robinson, "Judge Widens Army Corps' Jurisdiction," *Washington Post*, March 28, 1975. The environmental groups considered the case such a slam dunk that they let their oral argument be handled by an eager young attorney who had never before argued in court: Lake, formerly of Nixon's Council on Environmental Quality.

Intervening on behalf of the plaintiff . . . : Interviews with David Gluckman and Reubin Askew; Virginia Ellis, no headline, *St. Petersburg Times*, Jan. 21, 1975.

At the time Askew was elected . . . : "Statement to Gov. Reubin O'D. Askew from the Governor's Conference on Water Management in South Florida," 1971, 1, in Everglades Digital Library, Arthur R. Marshall Jr. Collection, http://everglades.fiu.edu/marshall/FI06011112/FI06011112.pdf; Blake, *Land Into Water*, 229.

Askew and the cabinet had some practical . . . : Transcript of Jan. 21, 1975, Florida Cabinet meeting, Florida State Archives.

The case went to U.S. District Judge . . . : Robinson's ruling in *NRDC v. Callaway*, 392 F.Supp. 685; interview with Gus Speth. Some conservative and libertarian groups contend Congress did not intend for the Clean Water Act to protect wetlands, but an activist judiciary stretched the law to allow the government to infringe on property rights. Yet even a cursory reading of *U.S. v. Holland* and *NRDC v. Callaway* shows that this is a misstatement of congressional intent and of these two rulings.

Instead, disgruntled Corps leaders decided . . .: Stine, "Regulating Wetlands," 67–70; Hedeman (the former Corps attorney), "The Evolution of Federal Legislation," 175–76; interview with Gus Speth. The Corps' reputation as a gang of jackbooted thugs has been boosted by a handful of criminal cases filed over illegal filling of wetlands, such as *U.S. v. Ocie and Carey Mills*. The defendants are a father and son from the Florida Panhandle community of Navarre who in 1988 were indicted and ultimately sent to prison for 21 months for violating Section 404. Although groups such as the John Birch Society depicted the pair as martyrs, Washington University professor Kathleen Brickey notes that "the previous land owners received a cease and desist order from the Corps, the Mills purchased the property with full knowledge of its designation as wetlands and of the resulting implications for unrestricted development, and they continued to fill in the site without a permit in defiance of two additional cease and desist orders issued to them." See Brickey, "Wetlands Reform and the Criminal Enforcement Record," 71.

Gen. Gribble, the chief of engineers . . . : Gribble quoted in Finnell, "Federal Regulatory Role in Coastal Land Management," 196; Askew reply dated May 13, 1975, from Florida State Archives.

In the late 1970s, Florida developers . . . : Frank DeLoache, "Land rush: Critics say U.S. agency acts hastily on proposals to develop wetlands," *St. Petersburg Times*, May 13, 1984; interview with Haynes Johnson.

Onetime California governor Ronald Reagan . . . : Johnson, *Sleepwalking Through History*, 170–71 (the author is not related to the former Corps permit reviewer); Patricia Sullivan, "Anne Gorsuch Burford, 62, Dies; Reagan EPA Director," *Washington Post*, July 22, 2004; Greg Hanscom, "Watt turns history on its head," *High Country News*, March 1, 2004; Cocke et al., *Army Historical Summary, Fiscal Year 1982*, chapter 11, http://www.army.mil/cmh/books/DAHSUM/1982/ch11.htm; interview with Jim Range.

Still, the 404 program could be hamstrung . . . : Pete Weissner, "DWR's 50th Anniversary—Former Directors: William R. Gianelli," California Department of Water Resources Public Affairs Web site, http://www.publicaffairs.water.ca.gov/dwr50th-anniversary/directors/gianelli.cfm; Reuss, "Interview with William R. Gianelli," 1, 25–36.

Dawson, in testifying . . . : Philip Shabecoff, "Wetlands to Lose Some Protection," *New York Times*, July 17, 1982.

In fact, Gianelli made . . . : Interviews with Haynes Johnson and James W. R. Adams.

To critics who complained . . . : Reuss, Gianelli interview, 32. In 1985, during his confirmation hearing to replace Gianelli, Dawson handed a Senate subcommittee the same argument. He met with what the *New York Times* called "strong disagreement from both the chairman of the subcommittee, Senator John H. Chafee of Rhode Island, and the chairman of the full Senate Environment and Public Works Committee, Robert T. Stafford of Vermont, both Republicans and both authors of the Clean Water Act." See Philip Shabecoff, "Conservationists and Others Battle a Reagan Nominee," *New York Times*, Sept. 19, 1985.

The Corps, like good soldiers . . . : Statistics and quotations all from Frank De-Loache, "Land rush: Critics say U.S. agency acts hastily on proposals to develop wetlands," *St. Petersburg Times*, May 13, 1984. The current NMFS staff was unable to locate a copy of this study for us.

"The Army's regulatory program . . . " : Philip Shabecoff, "Conservationists and Others Battle a Reagan Nominee," *New York Times*, Sept. 19, 1985.

Justice Department lawyers explained . . . : Plaintiffs' brief in *United States v. Riverside Bayview Homes*, 474 U.S. 121 (1985), http://www.usdoj.gov/osg/briefs/1984/sg840106.txt. The Supreme Court decision in this case upheld the Corps' post-Callaway definition of wetlands under its jurisdiction.

Section 404, designed to save wetlands . . . : Interview with Vic Anderson, who provided internal Corps memos.

That mindset has not changed . . . : University of South Carolina law professor Kim Diana Connolly collected customer satisfaction surveys from nine different Corps districts (including Jacksonville) and discovered that "an impressive percentage of applicants give the Corps perfect marks in their overall ranking of the permitting experience." See "Can Happy Subjects Have an Enlightened Despot? Customer Satisfaction Among Army Corps Permit Applicants," *National Wetlands Newsletter*, vol. 29, no. 3, May–June 2007. Such high approval ratings, she wrote, "likely demonstrate that too many permits are being issued too frequently by the Corps."

Chapter 4. Marco Island & Bonita Springs

In the early 1960s, Marco Island . . . : Antonini, Fann, and Roat, *Placida Harbor to Marco Island*, 58, http://nsgl.gso.uri.edu/flsgp/flsgpmo2003/flsgpmo2003_full. pdf; interview with Frank Mackle III; description of inhabitants of predevelopment Marco Island from Frank Mackle III's tribute to his father, http://www.themackle-company.com/femjrstorypublic/oo-index.htm.

"Marco Island is the last . . . " : No byline, "$500 Million Development Planned for Marco Island," *Daytona Beach Journal*, Jan. 31, 1965.

In 1975, a 44-year-old Army veteran . . . : Interviews with Don Wisdom and his successor, James W. R. Adams; quotations about and by Wisdom from Moser, "Mangrove Island," 72; Stine, "Regulating Wetlands," 71–75; Buker, *Environment—The Third E*, 1–5.

However, Deltona assured the Corps . . . : Letter from Robert M. White, administrator, National Oceanic and Atmospheric Administration, to Brig. Gen. Kenneth E. McIntyre, Department of the Army, April 14, 1976, and attached National Marine Fisheries Service report dated April 1, 1976. These documents are among several attachments to the deposition of Bernard N. Goode, housed in the Environmental Defense Collection at Stonybrook University's Frank Melville Jr. Memorial Library.

Still, Deltona had a reputation . . . : Stine, Oral history of Bernard Goode, 45–46. As curator of Engineering and Environmental History at the Smithsonian's National Museum of American History, Jeffrey Stine has conducted a number of interviews with top officials at the Army Corps of Engineering, including Bernard Goode.

A year later, when the Mackles . . . : Mormino, *Land of Sunshine, State of Dreams*, 57; Moser, "Mangrove Island," 71.

The governor, despite . . . : Interview with Reubin Askew.

Every big environmental group . . . : Mike Toner, "Marco—Ecological Mess or Tax Boon?" *Miami Herald*, July 3, 1975; Moser, "Mangrove Island," 70.

Wisdom flew down to Naples . . . : Interview with Don Wisdom.

Wisdom convened a two-day . . . : Interview with Don Wisdom; "The Marco Permits," on Frank Mackle III's Web site, http://www.themacklecompany.com/

femjrstorypublic/17-deltona-marcopermits.htm; no byline, "Deltona Buses Stack the Deck," *Naples Star*, Sept. 5, 1975, http://www.themacklecompany.com/femjr-storypublic/images2/09-05-75deltonabusses-p1&2-1080.jpg; Moser, "Mangrove Island," 75.

Thousands of people wrote . . . : Stine, Oral history of Bernard Goode, 50–53; Moser, "Mangrove Island," 76; interview with Don Wisdom.

Because of the project's importance . . . : Grathwol and Moorhus, *Building for Peace*, 163–64; Carroll N. Letellier, "Report on Application for Department of the Army Permits to Dredge and Fill at Marco Island, Collier County, Florida," Jan. 10, 1976. The Letellier report is attached to the deposition of Bernard N. Goode.

The final decision rested with . . . : Stine, "Regulating Wetlands," 73; "William Charles Gribble Jr.," Arlington National Cemetery Web site, http://www.arlington-cemetery.net/wcgribble.htm; Stine, Oral history of Bernard Goode, 69; deposition of Bernard Goode in *Deltona Corp. v. Secretary of the Army Martin Hoffman and Col. Donald Wisdom*, U.S District Court, Middle District of Florida, 76-473-CIV-J-T, 98.

On March 17, 1976, Gribble invited . . . : Interview with Don Wisdom; Stine, Oral history of Bernard Goode, 59–63; Goode deposition, in *Deltona Corp. v. Secretary of the Army Martin Hoffman and Col. Donald Wisdom*, U.S District Court, Middle District of Florida, 76-473-CIV-J-T, 98, 182–83; interview with Don Wisdom.

When the general was ready . . . : Stine, Oral history of Bernard Goode, 63–66; interview with Frank Mackle III; William C. Gribble, "Report on Application for Department of the Army Permits to Dredge and Fill at Marco Island, Collier County, Florida," April 15, 1976. The Gribble report is attached to the deposition of Bernard N. Goode.

Gribble told subordinates . . . : Stine, "Regulating Wetlands," 73; Gribble, "Report on Application" (see note *When the general was ready* above).

Deltona president Frank Mackle Jr. . . . : Deltona press release, April 16, 1976; interview with Frank Mackle III (see the Mackle Company Web site, http://www.themacklecompany.com/femjrstorypublic/20-deltona-dealingwiththedenial.htm); Moser, "Mangrove Island," 75; interview with Reubin Askew.

The Mackles had lost . . . : Richard Carelli, "Supreme Court lets Deltona ruling stand," *St. Petersburg Times*, March 23, 1982; Stine, "Regulating Wetlands," 74; Cocke et al., *Army Historical Summary, Fiscal Year 1981*, http://www.army.mil/CMH/books/DAHSUM/1981/ch13.htm; interview with Frank Mackle III.

In public, Frank Mackle Jr. . . . : James Russell, "Mackles in Toughest Fight," *Miami Herald*, April 25, 1976; interview with Frank Mackle III.

Col. Wisdom was acclaimed . . . : Buker, *Environment—The Third E*, 3; the colorful quotation from the Florida Wildlife Federation's Johnny Jones was published in *People Weekly* magazine and reprinted in Stine, "Regulating Wetlands," 74; interviews with Don Wisdom and James W. R. Adams.

The Marco Island decision shocked . . . : Hedeman quoted in Stine, "Regulating Wetlands," 75; Adams quoted in Moser, "Mangrove Island," 76.

But Wisdom's lost promotion . . . : Interviews with Don Wisdom and Chuck Hummer.

Fast-forward 20 years . . . : Thomas C. Tobin, "Livin' Large," *St. Petersburg Times*, June 2, 2002.

"Wetlands get dried up with money . . . " : Interview with Danny Curran and tour of Bonita Springs with him.

Upscale subdivisions—several of them . . . : E-mail from Wayne Daltry, former executive director of the Southwest Florida Regional Planning Council; Craig Pittman, "As Collier builds, so does tension," *St. Petersburg Times*, June 14, 1999; Craig Pittman, "Collier growth had seamy side," *St. Petersburg Times*, Nov. 4, 2001; Monica Davey, "Awash in misery," *St. Petersburg Times*, Oct. 14, 1995.

The Corps and the South Florida . . . : Janel Shoun, "Water managers seek OK for condemnation of flood-prone East Bonita lands," *Naples Daily News*, Nov. 10, 2000; Rebecca Wakefield and Erinn Hutkin, "Buyout: A closer look at the buyout proposal," *Naples Daily News*, Feb. 26, 1999.

Given the Marco Island precedent . . . : Interviews with John Hall and Vic Anderson.

Chapter 5. Six Percent Saviors

The busiest Corps of Engineers . . . : Interviews with John Hall and Terry Rice; Jane Bennett, "750 Army Corps workers will move to new digs," *Jacksonville Business Journal*, July 5, 2002.

His passion could also boil over . . . : Interviews with Bruce Boler and John Hall.

But Hall could also be refreshingly frank . . . : Estero Bay Agency on Bay Management meeting, Fort Myers, May 10, 2004; interview with John Hall.

In the late 1990s a sharp-tongued . . . : Interview with Ann Hauck; e-mail from John Hall to Ann Hauck, Aug. 21, 2004. A tireless researcher, Mrs. Hauck has amassed a trove of government documents, which she generously shared with us.

With reporters, Hall tended to be . . . : We interviewed Hall seven times between 2003 and 2005 and exchanged numerous e-mails with him. Some of what he told us he asked we keep off the record. Although he stopped responding to our questions after our first stories appeared in May 2005, we have kept that promise.

The first time we encountered Barron . . . : CLE (Continuing Legal Education International) Florida Water Law conference in Tampa, March 30, 2004.

The first biologist the Corp hired . . . : Interview with Vic Anderson.

"A permit will be granted . . . *"*: *Individual Permitting Workbook*, U.S. Army Corps of Engineers, Jacksonville Regulatory Division, 1995, 14.

Experts on wetlands law . . . : Interviews with Royal Gardner, Margaret Strand, Kim Diana Connolly, and John Hall; see section 320.4(b)(1) of the General Regulatory Policies of the U.S. Army Corps of Engineers.

"If it's a flawed reading . . . *"* : During the Reagan era, one new regulation the Corps proposed to speed up permit approval called for reversing the presumption that wetlands were worth preserving; instead "a permit will be granted unless its issuance is found to be contrary to the public interest." The National Wildlife Federation sued, and in a 1984 settlement the Corps agreed to go back to presuming wetlands are worth saving. In spite of that settlement, the training manual appears to still contain the 1983 regulatory language.

Still, before approving a permit . . . : U.S. Army Corps of Engineers Regulations, 33 CFR 320.4(a) explains the public interest review; interview with Vic Anderson.

The grind of churning out . . . : Ryan Burr, "Corps of Engineers says message was not official," *Panama City News Herald*, June 1, 2005; John Hall e-mail contained in *Sierra Club, Natural Resources Defense Council, and National Parks and Conservation Association v. Robert B. Flowers, Chief of Engineers, et al.*, U.S. District Court, Southern District of Florida, case no.case no. 03-23427-CIV-HOEVELER.

In contrast to Col. Wisdom's . . . : Interview with Charles "Chuck" Schnepel; interview with John Hall; list of regulatory offices in Florida, http://www.saj.usace.army. mil/regulatory/where/office_map.htm.

A prime example is the Scripps . . . : Stacey Singer, "Lawyer defends official's role in wooing Scripps," *Palm Beach Post*, Tuesday, Jan. 2, 2007; editorial, "Dishonest Scripps search: Truth finally comes out," *Palm Beach Post*, Jan. 7, 2007.

The Florida Wildlife Federation . . . : Reed quotation from "Major Victory for Smart Growth Advocates: Scripps Moved to Abacoa/Briger Site!" 1000 Friends of Florida press release, April 12, 2006, http://www.1000friendsofflorida.org/palmmartin/scrippsoverview.asp; order on cross-motions for summary judgment, *Florida Wildlife Federation and Sierra Club v. U.S. Army Corps of Engineers and Col. Robert Carpenter*, U.S. District Court, Southern District of Florida, case no.case no. 05-80339-CIV-Middlebrooks/Johnson.

"There's no job out there . . . " : Interviews with Robert Carpenter and Vic Anderson.

The other way to find out . . . . : We picked July 1, 2004, at random to pull every notice posted on the Web site and see who was applying for 404 permits. We then requested information from the Corps on the outcome of each one. The URL for the Corps' Web site for public notices in Florida is http://www.saj.usace.army.mil/regulatory/publicNotice/publicNotice.htm.

The applicants listed . . . . : St. Joe Company: Corps permit no. SAJ-2003-3744; backyard builder: permit no. SAJ-2004-1824; U.S. Homes: SAJ-2004-50; Flagler Beach developer: SAJ-2004-4894; Naples developer, SAJ-2004-1689; Collier County Airport Authority, SAJ-1997-02362; Ormond Beach church, SAJ-1995-5787; Seminole Tribe limestone mine: SAJ-2004-5312.

That's not unusual . . . . : Interview with Mark Evans; Corps permit no. SAJ-2003-01267.

So long as the public . . . . : Interviews with Lesley Blackner, Charles Schnepel, and Steve Brooker.

The Corps faces constant pressure . . . . : Interviews with John Hall, Charles Schnepel, Steve Brooker, Mike Nowicki, Terry Rice, and Robert Carpenter.

Some developers have figured out . . . . : Dan DeWitt, "Developer taps into ex-corps leader," *St. Petersburg Times*, July 23, 2006; Chuin-Wei Yap, "Developer armed with experts," *St. Petersburg Times*, Jan. 16, 2007.

Denying a permit requires . . . . : Interviews with Charles Schnepel, Steve Brooker, and John Hall.

When we asked, the Corps staff . . . . : Interviews with Robert Carpenter, John Hall, and Bob Barron.

The lone denial . . . . : Corps administrative appeal decision, James Johnson, permit no. SAJ-1996-01445. The would-be developer set up a Web site making it appear that the motel exists, but every link goes to a page protesting the denial: http://www.ecotourlodge.com/.

Nationally the Corps boasts . . . . : Robert Brumbaugh and Mark Sudol, "ORM, GORM and WORM: The Future of Wetland Databases," PowerPoint presentation at Mitigation Action Plan Stakeholders Forum, Washington, D.C., May 11, 2006, http://www2.eli.org/pdf/mitigation_forum_2006/brumbaugh.orm.pres.pdf. We had to use 2003 because it's the only year the quarterly reports from Jacksonville included all types of 404 permits. The Corps says its own figures for 2004, 2005, and 2006 are suspect because of computer problems. Interview with Robert Carpenter.

We interviewed the Corps' top officials . . . : Interviews with Lt. Gen. Carl Strock, John Paul Woodley Jr., and John Hall.

Chapter 6. "The Joy of Life"

On April 25, 1984 . . . : Neil Skene, "Senator apologizes; colleagues offer support," *St. Petersburg Times*, April 26, 1984; "Warren S. Henderson," Florida House of Representatives Clerk's Manual, 1982–84, 232–34; interview with David Gluckman.

Actually, the politician . . . : Interviews with David Gluckman, Jon Mills, and Fred McCormack.

Conservation groups had tried . . . : Blake, *Land Into Water*, 229; interviews with Jon Mills and Fred McCormack; Tom Hillstrom, United Press International, "Environmentalists urge wetlands purchases," *St. Petersburg Times*, Sept. 4, 1983; William Cotterill, United Press International, "Campaign begins to sell wetlands protection plan," *St. Petersburg Times*, Feb. 21, 1984.

Tripp had degrees . . . : Tripp background at Environmental Defense Web site, http://www.environmentaldefense.org/page.cfm?tagID=877. Tripp did not respond to our requests for comment. Interview with Fred McCormack.

Tripp helped Mills' staff draft . . . : Interviews with Jon Mills, Fred McCormack, and David Gluckman; unsigned editorial, "Protecting the wetlands," *St. Petersburg Times*, April 29, 1984. The original vegetative index was primarily the work of state game commission biologist Jim Beever.

Despite the opposition, Mills' support . . . : Interviews with Jon Mills and Fred McCormack; John Harwood, no headline, *St. Petersburg Times*, April 29, 1984.

This was where Senator Henderson . . . : Mills and McCormack say they had counted the potential votes, and the bill probably would have passed the Senate without Henderson's field trip.

On that fateful spring morning . . . : Associated Press, "State senator apologizes for slurs, actions on trip," *St. Petersburg Times*, April 22, 1984. Blanton, now a lawyer, had another moment in the limelight representing Florida secretary of state Katherine Harris during the 2000 presidential recount.

The press corps covering . . . : Author's personal recollection from covering the 1984 session for the *Pensacola News Journal*.

Initially when another Sentinel . . . : Associated Press, "State senator apologizes for slurs, actions on trip," *St. Petersburg Times*," April 22, 1984. The AP story quotes the *Sentinel* report and includes Blanton's version of events.

"Unfortunately for everybody . . . " : Neil Skene, "Senator apologizes; colleagues offer support," *St. Petersburg Times*, April 26, 1984.

Then he announced his retirement . . . : Neil Skene, "Senator apologizes; colleagues offer support," *St. Petersburg Times*, April 26, 1984. The senator who compared Henderson to Jesus was Frank Mann, a Democrat from Fort Myers. After Henderson left politics, the ex-senator remained active in environmental causes, serving on the board of organizations such as Nat Reed's 1,000 Friends of Florida.

Then, to stick a thumb . . . : Author's personal recollection.

In the heat of the moment . . . : Interview with David Gluckman.

Lurking in the language . . . : Interviews with Jon Mills, Ann Redmond, David Gluckman, and Fred McCormack.

Mitigation to make up for . . . : Reuss, *Shaping Environmental Awareness*, 34, available online at http://www.usace.army.mil/publications/eng-pamphlets/ep870-1-10/toc.htm; interviews with James W. R. Adams and Ann Redmond.

From the day the Henderson Act . . . : Redmond, "Report on the Effectiveness of Permitted Mitigation," Florida Department of Environmental Regulation, March 5, 1991, executive summary.

About four years after . . . : Interview with Tom Reese. Because the retired publisher requested anonymity, Reese would not name him—even after all this time.

Crewz found that the man-made . . . : Crewz, "Wetlands Mitigation Evaluations." Because Crewz could do his research only on weekends, his final report is dated after the Redmond and Erwin reports, though his preliminary survey was the first to raise questions about mitigation. There have been plenty more since then. For instance, see Schneider, "Guess What! Fake Wetlands Don't Work," *Great Lakes Bulletin* online, http://www.mlui.org/pubs/glb/glb14-01/glb14-16.asp.

Armed with the preliminary . . . : Interviews with Tom Reese and Ann Redmond; Redmond, "Report on the Effectiveness of Permitted Mitigation."

Then Redmond got an amen . . . : Erwin, "An Evaluation of Wetland Mitigation," 2–5, 7–11; interview with Kevin Erwin. In 1994, U.S. Fish and Wildlife Service biologist John Tichy did a similar study, looking at mitigation projects approved by the Corps in South Florida and finding similar problems. "I essentially said there's no follow-up, and wetland mitigation is not appropriate to what's being taken," Tichy told us.

Redmond had a fairly simple . . . : Interview with Ann Redmond.

Chapter 7. The Promise, Plus

As a congressman, Bush . . . : No byline, "Bush, Dukakis and the Environment," *Sacramento Bee*, Oct. 30, 1988; Jon East, "Bush can't gloss over his poor environmental record," *St. Petersburg Times*, June 16, 1988; Philip Shabecoff, "Environmentalists

Say Either Bush or Dukakis Will Be An Improvement," *New York Times*, Sept. 1, 1988.

Bush knew he had to convince . . . : Interview with Nat Reed; Tom Paugh, "*Sports Afield* and the Candidates," *Sports Afield*, October 1988, 15.

In 1986, the EPA vetoed . . . : Blumm and Zaleha, "Federal Wetlands Protection Under the Clean Water Act," 742–44.

So in 1987 EPA Administrator Lee Thomas . . . : Interview with William K. Reilly; Clark, *Sanibel Report*; EPA oral history interview with William K. Reilly, http://www.epa.gov/history/publications/reilly/index.htm; Vileisis, *Discovering the Unknown Landscape*, 317.

Gradually, though, over the course . . . : National Wetlands Policy Forum, *Protecting America's Wetlands*, vii–viii.

In 1986 New Jersey's Division . . . : Bingham et al., *Issues in Wetlands Protection*, 178. A 2006 study by Rutgers University and Rowan University shows no net loss hasn't worked in New Jersey. Because of development pressure, "wetlands lost a total of 12,747 acres statewide between 1995 and 2002, increasing its annualized loss to 1,821 acres per year, a 4% increase over the 1,755 acres lost per year during 1986–1995," the study found. See http://www.crssa.rutgers.edu/projects/lc/urbangrowth95_02/PressRelease_03_22_07_LathropHasse.pdf.

The forum's final report . . . : National Wetlands Policy Forum, *Protecting America's Wetlands*, 18–19.

As a result, several months . . . : Interview with William K. Reilly.

They certainly got their wish . . . : Text of Bush's August 1988 speech from Federal News Service, http://www.fnsg.com/; Christine Chinlund, "Bush Offers Proposals on the Environment," *Boston Globe*, Sept. 1, 1988; Associated Press, "Bush Vows to Set Timetable on Acid Rain," *St. Louis Post-Dispatch*, Sept. 1, 1998; Catherine Woodward, "Bush Courting Conservationists," *Newsday*, Sept. 1, 1988.

But Train, traveling with Bush . . . : Robert Greene, "Bush Courting Conservationists," *Newsday*, Sept. 1, 1988. In his autobiography, Train says he personally drafted the speech for Bush. See Train, *Politics, Pollution, and Pandas*, 169.

Dukakis scoffed at what he called . . . : Robert Greene, "Bush Courting Conservationists," *Newsday*, Sept. 1, 1988; Robert Greene, "Bush, Dukakis Trade Barbs on Environmental Records," *Seattle Times*, Sept. 1, 1988.

Two weeks after Bush won . . . : Associated Press, "Bush gives pep talk to GOP governors," *St. Petersburg Times*, Nov. 23, 1988.

Still, he did name Reilly . . . : Neal Pierce, "Bush's Choice for EPA," *Washington Post* Syndicate column, published in *St. Petersburg Times*, Jan. 3, 1989; President George

Bush, "Remarks at the Swearing-in Ceremony for William K. Reilly as Administrator of the Environmental Protection Agency," Feb. 8, 1989, *American Presidency Project*, http://www.presidency.ucsb.edu/ws/index.php?pid=16657.

Given that history . . . : Interview with William K. Reilly; President George Bush, "Remarks to Members of Ducks Unlimited," June 8, 1989, *American Presidency Project*, http://www.presidency.ucsb.edu/ws/?pid=17125.

In 1990, the EPA and the Corps . . . : "Memorandum of Agreement Between the Environmental Protection Agency and the Department of the Army Concerning the Determination of Mitigation Under the Clean Water Act Section 404(b)(1) Guidelines," Feb. 6, 1990, http://www.swf.usace.army.mil/pubdata/environ/regulatory/permitting/mitigation/epa%20memorandum%20of%20agreement.pdf.

Soon, though, the Bush Administration . . . : Associated Press, "White House to rethink new wetlands definition," *St. Petersburg Times*, Nov. 23, 1991; interview with William K. Reilly.

When Bush announced . . . : Vileisis, *Discovering the Unknown Landscape*, 319–21.

But the attempt to redefine . . . : Interview with Charles Schnepel; David Dahl, "Wetlands need protection, state official tells Congress," *St. Petersburg Times*, Oct. 31, 1991; Glendenning, "Presidential Campaigns and Environmental Policy," 34, http://www.ohiolink.edu/etd/send-pdf.cgi?miami1155570547; interview with William K. Reilly.

Reilly spent the remainder . . . : EPA oral history interview with William K. Reilly, http://www.epa.gov/history/publications/reilly/index.htm; interview with Nat Reed.

During Bush's 1992 reelection . . . : Clinton-Gore campaign press office e-mail, "The Record Bush Can't Hide: Broken Environmental Promises," Oct. 28, 1992; "Remarks of Gov. Bill Clinton, Earth Day," Drexel University, Philadelphia, April 22, 1992; "A Presidential Wetlands Debate," *National Wetlands Newsletter*, May/June 1992, 5–6.

By the end of the summer . . . : Associated Press, "Policy on wetlands changed," *St. Petersburg Times*, Aug. 25, 1993; unsigned editorial, "The importance of wetlands," *St. Petersburg Times*, Aug. 31, 1993; "Protecting America's Wetlands: A Fair, Flexible and Effective Approach," White House Office on Environmental Policy, Aug. 24, 1993, http://www.usace.army.mil/cw/cecwo/reg/aug93wet.htm; Clean Water Action Plan, EPA press release, Feb. 19, 1998, http://www.epa.gov/history/topics/cwa/03.htm.

In 1997, when Army and EPA officials . . . : "Recent Regulatory and Judicial Developments on Wetlands," Hearing Before the Subcommittee on Water Resources and Environment of the Committee on Transportation and Infrastructure, U.S. House of Representatives, April 29, 1997, hearing transcript 27–29.

Four years after Clinton's vice president . . . : "President Announces Wetlands Initiative on Earth Day," White House Press Office, April 22, 2004, http://www.whitehouse.gov/news/releases/2004/04/20040422-4.html; "Fact Sheet: President Announces Wetlands Initiative on Earth Day," White House Press Office, April 22, 2004, http://www.whitehouse.gov/news/releases/2004/04/20040422-1.html.

A day later, Bush flew . . . : Elizabeth Bumiller, "Bush Promotes Wetlands Plan to Counter Kerry's Attack," *New York Times*, April 24, 2004; "President Discusses Earth Day, National Volunteer Week," White House Press Office, April 23, 2004, http://www.whitehouse.gov/news/releases/2004/04/20040423-8.html; Denise Zoldan, Dianna Smith, Alan Scher Zagier, and Eric Staats, "Presidential visit: It was the President's day," *Naples Daily News*, April 24, 2004; unsigned editorial, "President Bush: A clockwork visit, but exhilarating nonetheless," *Naples Daily News*, April 24, 2004.

In 2001, a panel appointed . . . : Committee on Mitigating Wetland Losses, *Compensating for Wetland Losses*, 2–3. The committee found that a lot of mitigation "wetlands" turned into open water ponds—the very thing said to be increasing in the report Gale Norton touted in March 2006.

Still, the Pentagon civilian . . . : Interview with John Paul Woodley Jr. Three years after our interview, on the 35th anniversary of the Clean Water Act, Woodley told a congressional committee: "For the last 10 years, Corps data show an overall no net loss of wetlands for the 404 program . . . " But he cited no specific figures.

Chapter 8. Images of Loss

NWI seemed like the ideal . . . : Over and over we encountered biologists and bureaucrats who cited NWI's Web site maps as authoritative, apparently unaware of how long ago they were created. For our purposes, NWI's maps served as a guide to what once was, as opposed to what now exists.

Launched in 1976, this obscure . . . : Interview with Blake Parker; Vileisis, *Discovering the Unknown Landscape*, 271–74; Jeff Klinkenberg, "Vanishing species," *St. Petersburg Times*, Feb. 8, 1981; Dahl, *Status and Trends of Wetlands . . . 1986 to 1997*, http://www.fws.gov/nwi/statusandtrends.htm; interview with Norm Mangrum.

Still, the remaining staff . . . : Interview with David Lindsey.

Meanwhile we were trying . . . : Between 2003 and 2006, we filed more than 20 Freedom of Information Act (FOIA) requests with the Corps, the EPA, the Fish and Wildlife Service, and the Federal Emergency Management Agency. We also filed dozens of Sunshine Law requests for documents from various state agencies. The FOIA for this database was our first public records request, and it took longer than all the rest.

The only sections reviewers . . . : Interview with John Hall.

To understand how we analyzed . . . : Matthew Waite enrolled in two courses in remote sensing and satellite imagery analysis at the University of South Florida taught by Professor Barnali Dixon. The primary texts for the courses were Jensen's *Introductory Digital Image Processing* and *Remote Sensing of the Environment* (see Selected Sources on Remote Sensing). For a complete recounting of our methodology, see the appendix.

Our analysis did not include . . . : Interviews with John Hall, Bob Barron, and Vic Anderson; Jim Waymer, "City claim wetlands illegally excavated," *Florida Today*, Sept. 10, 2007.

Chapter 9. The Myth of Mitigation

Florida's Panhandle is known . . . : Corps permit no. SAJ-199360817; Interviews with Allen Levin, development partner Robert Rinke, and Jean Kuttina; Ginny Graybiel, "Long fight to build Portofino nears end," *Pensacola News Journal*, Jan. 16, 2000.

In 1999 an environmental activist . . . : Interviews with Linda Young, Michael Davis, Allen Levin, Hildreth Cooper, and Lyal "Clif" Payne.

The developers weren't too thrilled . . . : Lyal Payne, telephone conversation, Jan. 28, 1999, in permit file, Corps Permit SAJ-199360817; interview with Allen Levin.

On the same day the Corps . . . : We tracked down and talked to every colonel who oversaw the Jacksonville office of the Corps dating back to 1975, except one. Joe Miller was the only one who didn't return our calls. Interviews with Jean Kuttina and Linda Young.

On September 16, 2004, Hurricane Ivan . . . : Video and still photos of Pensacola Beach shot before and after Hurricane Ivan were provided to us by M. Dennis Krohn of the U.S. Geological Survey's St. Petersburg office. They show the sand washed across the mitigation areas and into the condos. Interview with Lyal Payne.

On paper, filled-in wetlands . . . : Interview with Vic Anderson and Charles Schnepel; Committee on Mitigating Wetland Losses, *Compensating for Wetland Losses*, 101–6, 109, 122. The problem is not confined to Florida. A recent study by the Corps looked at 60 wetland mitigation sites in New England and found that 40 met their permit conditions but only 10 to 17 percent "were considered to be adequate functional replacements for the impacted wetlands." See Minkin and Ladd, "Success of Corps-Required Wetland Mitigation in New England," http://www.mitigation actionplan.gov/USACE%20New%20England%20District%20Mitigation%20Study. pdf.

But now look what happens . . . : Florida Institute for Phosphate Research, "Phosphate Primer," http://www1.fipr.state.fl.us/PhosphatePrimer; interviews with Kevin Erwin, James W. R. Adams, and Vic Anderson.

Erwin's testimony helped convince . . . : Interview with Kevin Erwin; Florida Department of Administrative Hearings, case number 02-004134.

With a $7-billion budget . . . : Florida Department of Transportation, "Fast Facts," http://www.dot.state.fl.us/publicinformationoffice/moreDOT/mission.htm#fdot; interview with Denver Stutler Jr.

We discovered that DOT officials . . . : Record keeping at the DOT was byzantine and fragmented. To get to these estimates, we requested detailed breakdowns of money spent on something called the "Bronson Bill" or "Senate Bill," a program created by the legislature in 1997 that allows the DOT to pay the water management districts to do its mitigation work. Since then, most of DOT's spending on mitigation has gone through that program. We totaled up spending figures from the water management districts plus any figures DOT officials could give us about their own mitigation projects. Because some costs aren't itemized—for instance, one contract could cover the grading of both the road and the creation of the mitigation—it was impossible to calculate an accurate total cost. Interview with Sue Moore.

Yet the DOT kept trying . . . : Florida DOT files, state permit number 403070.00.

In 1994, the DOT planned . . . : Florida DOT files, federal permit number SAJ-199401102. Interview with Robert Dwyer.

This sort of thing happened . . . : Florida DOT files, project number 90060-3524.

We found numerous examples . . . : Florida DOT files, project number 09-601241279.

In 1987, when the National . . . : Interview with Jon Kusler; Kusler, "Views on Scientific Issues," 217–30.

Today, though, mitigation has . . . : Interviews with Steve Brooker and Vic Anderson.

A prime example of that . . . : Florida DOT files, federal permit number SAJ-1994-2783; interviews with Steve Brooker, Terry Rice, the DOT's John Palenchar, Vic Anderson, and Keys civic activist John Hammerstrom.

The problem of mitigation failure . . . : Interview with Roy "Robin" Lewis.

This is not a new problem . . . : U.S. Government Accountability Office, "Wetlands Protection: Corps of Engineers Does Not Have an Effective Oversight Approach to Ensure That Compensatory Mitigation Is Occurring," GAO-05-898, September

1995, http://www.gao.gov/new.items/d05898.pdf. This 2005 report summarizes GAO findings from 1988 and 1993.

That's fine with the Corps' leaders . . . : Maj. Gen. Russell Furman, "Memorandum for Commanders, Major Subordinate Commands, and District Commands," April 8, 1999, appendix F in Committee on Mitigating Wetland Losses, *Compensating for Wetland Losses.*

Two years later the National . . . : The Corps' Mitigation Action Plan is available at http://www.mitigationactionplan.gov/background.html; see report GAO-05-898, 26–27, http://www.gao.gov/new.items/d05898.pdf.

Think about the cost . . . : Interviews with Roy Lewis and James Connaughton.

Yet it's hard to see . . . : Corps permit number SAJ-1998-06042; Southwest Florida Water Management District permit number 4302661.209; "2005 Award Goes to Wal-Mart for Transplanting Ecosystem," PR Newswire, Sept. 20, 2005; "Wal-Mart Accepts National Arbor Day Award of Excellence for Building With Trees Program," http://www.walmartfacts.com/articles/2051.aspx; interviews with Wal-Mart executive Don Moseley and National Arbor Day Foundation vice president Dan Lambe. We visited the store mitigation site twice more after reading through the permitting files to verify what we had seen with Sydney Bacchus; we also checked aerial photos of the site.

Chapter 10. Turning a Minus into a Plus

The parkway is a 42-mile toll road . . . : Michael Kruse, "Driving Growth," *St. Petersburg Times*, Feb. 5, 2006.

"Developer interest drives . . . " : Interview with Robert Muller.

State law at that time said . . . : Craig Pittman, "Flawed figures leave toll roads running flat," *St. Petersburg Times*, July 16, 2000; Kelly Barron, "The Roads Less Traveled," *Forbes*, Sept. 3, 2001. Another project URS' poor forecasting skills helped get built is the Garcon Point Bridge, nicknamed "Bo's Bridge" because it was a pet project of former Florida House Speaker Bolley "Bo" Johnson (who went to prison for not telling the IRS he was taking "consulting fees" from a road-building company and other interests). The URS projections were so far off that the bridge's owner, the Santa Rosa Bay Bridge Authority, was forced to delay paying back millions of dollars in state loans. Col. Terry Rice told us that the 404 permit for "Bo's Bridge" was the one permit he regretted approving, because the bridge was built only to stimulate development.

When we questioned how the company . . . : Interview with URS Greiner Woodard vice president Hugh Miller.

The Corps allowed the DOT to mitigate . . . : Florida DOT files, Corps permit no. SAJ-RD-W-199604305.

There is a certain logic . . . : Interview with Royal Gardner.

We checked the Corps' quarterly reports . . . : Interviews with Steve Brooker, John Hall, and Vic Anderson.

The Corps' permit reviewer . . .: Florida DOT files, Corps permit number SAJ-RD-W-199604305.

"That's the new suburbs" . . . : Michael Kruse, "Driving Growth," *St. Petersburg Times*, Feb. 5, 2006; interviews with Mike Nowicki, John Hall, Steve Brooker, and Vic Anderson.

One reason the Corps accepted . . . : Interviews with Mike Nowicki, Dan Rametta, Richard Sommerville, Chuck Schnepel, and Robert Carpenter, Haynes Johnson, and Lesley Blackner; GAO-05-898 report, 22, http://www.gao.gov/new.items/d05898.pdf.

Over the past 30 years . . . : Interviews with Jon Kusler, Bob Barron, Steve Brooker, Vic Anderson, John Hall, Royal Gardner, and environmental consultant Tom Odom. A headline in the March 2002 *National Wetlands Newsletter* is telling: "HGM: Hidden, Gone, Missing?"

So Swiftmud officials say . . . : Interview with Mark Brown of Swiftmud.

From time to time Rametta . . . : Interviews with Dan Rametta, Richard Sommerville, Lesley Blackner, and James Connaughton; Mike Vogel, "Who's Lesley Blackner?" *Florida Trend*, March 2007, 56–61.

Chapter 11. "A Mine Is a Terrible Thing to Waste"

The dump trucks rumble . . . : Craig Pittman, "Mining blasts away at Glades' future," *St. Petersburg Times*, May 9, 2001.

Miami-Dade County's limestone . . . : Kindiger, "Lake Belt Study Area," http://sofia.usgs.gov/publications/ofr/02-325/index.html.

But they aren't like any natural . . . : E-mail to John Hall from Melanie Steinkamp, U.S. Fish and Wildlife Service, April 18, 1997; interview with John Hall.

Native to Australia, melaleuca . . . : Grunwald, *The Swamp*, 129–30; Environmental News Service, "Florida Battles Invasive Melaleuca Acre By Acre," Nov. 2, 2004, http://www.ens-newswire.com/ens/nov2004/2004-11-02-01.asp.

The mines' laying waste . . . : Records from *Sierra Club, Natural Resources Defense Council, and National Parks and Conservation Association v. Robert B. Flowers, Chief of Engineers, et al.*, U.S. District Court, Southern District of Florida, case no. 03-23427-CIV-HOEVELER; Dan Rutz, "Milwaukee learned its water lessons, but many other cities haven't," *CNN.com*, Sept. 2, 1996, http://www.cnn.com/HEALTH/9609/02/nfm/water.quality/.

Despite all of its dangers . . . : Record of Decision, Corps Permit Nos. 2000-02284, 2000-02285, 2000-02286, 2000-02346, 2000-02348, 2000-02366, 2000-02367, 2000-02368, and 2000-02373. Through the Freedom of Information Act, RODs on permits may be obtained by contacting USACE's regional offices, in this case the Jacksonville District. *Sierra Club et al. v. Flowers et al.* (see note *The mines' laying waste* above); interview with Chuck Schnepel.

The three-foot-deep littoral . . . : Miami-Dade County Lake Belt Plan Implementation Committee, "Phase II Plan," 2000, 18, Phase I and Phase II plans available at https://my.sfwmd.gov/portal/page?_pageid=1874,4167195,1874_4164189:1874_4166101&_dad=portal&_schema=PORTAL; interviews with George Dalrymple and Albert Townsend.

In 2002 the Corps approved . . . : Record of Decision (see chapter 11 note, *Despite all of its dangers*, above); interview with James "Greg" May.

That's not what the Corps . . . : Letter from John Studt, chief, South Permits Section, Regulatory Branch, Corps of Engineers, to Paul Larsen, Larsen & Associates, Jan. 18, 1996. Studt's letter is part of the administrative record in *Sierra Club et al. v. Flowers et al.*

The other justification . . . : *Comprehensive Everglades Restoration Plan* (CERP) approved by Congress and the Florida legislature in 2000. The entire plan is available in .pdf format at the CERP Web site, http://www.evergladesplan.org/pub/restudy_eis.aspx; also see, "So you want to know more about USACE Lake Belt permits," CERP online, http://www.evergladesplan.org/facts_info/sywtkma_lakebelt.aspx.

Yet the Corps' Everglades planners . . . : Michael Grunwald, "Between Rock and a Hard Place: Wetlands Shrink Before Growing Demands of Industry, Consumers," *Washington Post*, June 24, 2002; "Projects To Improve the Quantity, Quality, Timing, and Distribution of Water: Water Preserve Areas and Seepage Management along the Marsh/Urban Interface," U.S. Geological Survey, http://sofia.usgs.gov/publications/reports/doi-science-plan/waterinter.html.

Why were Corps officials so obliging . . . : Contribution records obtained from Florida secretary of state.

"The power and politics . . . " : E-mail from Phil Cloues, National Park Service, to Karyn Ferro, National Park Service, April 8, 1999. Cloues' e-mail is part of the administrative record in *Sierra Club et al. v. Flowers et al.*

Part of the Lake Belt was once . . . : P. K. Yonge Library of Florida History, Papers of Ernest R. Graham, http://web.uflib.ufl.edu/spec/pkyonge/egraham.htm.

In September 1972 . . . : Records from *Florida Rock Industries v. U.S.*, 791 F.2d 893 and 18 F.3d 1560; interview with John Hall.

The Jacksonville-based company . . . : Securities & Exchange Commission, Florida Rock 8-K, filed Feb. 27, 2007.

"They sent their CEO down . . . " : Interview with James W. R. Adams.

The case landed in an obscure . . . : Federal Circuit Act of 1982, Federal Judicial Center online, History of the Federal Judiciary, http://www.fjc.gov/history/home. nsf/page/22a_bdy.

They "had a specific, aggressive . . . " : Fried, *Order and Law*, 183.

A witty and ambitious young man . . . : Emily Bazelon, "The Big Kozinski," *Legal Affairs*, January–February 2004, http://www.legalaffairs.org/issues/January-February-2004/feature_bazelon_janfeb04.msp; Robert S. Boynton, "Wiseguy," *George*, December 1995–January 1996; Kozinski, "Honoring the Court's Past," 529.

There was ample precedent . . . : *Zabel v. Tabb* is regarded as the first attempt to claim a regulatory taking in a dredge-and-fill case, although it involved a Section 10 permit not a Section 404 permit. In the Deltona case, as with Florida Rock, the company bought its property before the passage of the Clean Water Act, yet it still lost its takings claim over denial of its 404 permits. For details on the Deltona takings case, see *Deltona v. United States*, 657 F. 2d 1210 1184 (Ct. Cl. 1981), cert. denied, 455 U.S. 1017 (1982). For details on *Graham v. Estuary Properties*, see 399 So. 2d 1374 (Fla. 1981), cert. denied, sub. nom., *Taylor v. Graham*, 454 U.S. 1083 (1981). For a look at what a more experienced claims court judge might have done with Florida Rock, see the results in *Good v. United States*, 189 F. 3d 1355, 1362 (Fed. Cir. 1999). The judge in that case, James Merow, had been hearing trials since 1978.

But one of Kozinski's firmest . . . : Emily Bazelon, "The Big Kozinski," *Legal Affairs*, January–February 2004, http://www.legalaffairs.org/issues/January-February-2004/feature_bazelon_janfeb04.msp.

"The fact that plaintiff's . . . " : Ruling in *Florida Rock Industries v. U.S.*, 8 Cl. Ct. 160.

Florida Rock's attorney . . . : John DeVault, "The Saga of Florida Rock: Illegiti Non Carborundum," ALI-ABL/Pacific Legal Foundation Seminar: Inverse Condemnation and Related Governmental Liability, April 30–May 2, 1998, San Francisco. DeVault did not return our calls. In his presentation he estimated that Florida Rock had spent $1 million in legal fees and compared the long-running case to the voyage of Odysseus.

But the Corps appealed . . . : Ruling in *Florida Rock Industries v. U.S.*, 791 F.2d 893.

Smith, a burly and bearded . . . : Tom Castleton, "Claims Court Crusader: Chief

Judge Puts Property Rights Up Front," *Legal Times*, Aug. 17, 1992; Richard Miniter, "The shifting ground of property rights; costs of implementing federal regulations," *Insight on the News*, Aug. 23, 1993, http://www.richardminiter.com/pdf/articles/19930823-art-insight.pdf; no byline, "Property Owners Fight Overzealous Regulations," Cybercast News Service, March 31, 2001, http://archive.newsmax.com/archives/articles/2001/3/30/190802.shtml.

When the Florida Rock case . . . : Ruling in *Florida Rock Industries v. U.S.*, 21 Cl. Ct. 161.

Even his fellow conservatives . . . : James L. Huffman, "A Case for Principled Judicial Activism," Heritage Lecture 456, May 20, 1993, http://www.heritage.org/Research/LegalIssues/HL456.cfm; Miniter, "The shifting ground" (see chapter 11 note, *Smith, a burly and bearded*, above).

However, attorneys for . . . : Interview with Lois Schiffer.

The appeals court opinion . . . : Judicial Biographies, United States Court of Appeals for the Federal Circuit, http://fedcir.gov/judgbios.html; Paul Gigot, "Regulation Cop No Longer Walks His Beat," *Wall Street Journal*, April 13, 1990; *New York Times*, "Washington Talk: Briefing; Regulatory Czar," Feb. 18, 1998, http://query.nytimes.com/gst/fullpage.html?res=940DE7DB1339F93BA25751C0A96E948260; Kendall and Lord, "The Takings Project," 11n, available online at *BNet*, http://findarticles.com/p/articles/mi_qa3816/is_199804/ai_n8783469/pg_1.

While Plager overturned Smith's . . . : Ruling in *Florida Rock Industries v. United States*, 18 F.3d 1560; Blumm, "The End of Environmental Law?" 171.

Plager, telling the story . . . : Plager, "Takings Law and Appellate Decision Making," 161.

The miners knew that they . . . : Quoted by Judge William Hoeveler, "Order on Motions for Summary Judgment," *Sierra Club et al. v. Flowers et al.*, 3n. In his March 2006 decision on this case—the events and proceedings of which spanned more than a decade and in which several mining companies, including Florida Rock, were litigants—Judge Hoeveler thoroughly reviewed the whole history of the Lake Belt and analyzed all the documents and evidence involved at some length.

In 1992, the Corps' 38 districts . . . : Robert Meltz, "Wetlands Regulation and the Law of Property Rights 'Takings,'" Congressional Research Service Report, RL 30423, Feb. 17, 2000, http://ncseonline.org/NLE/CRSreports/Wetlands/wet-6.cfm#28.

The decision on approving . . . : E-mail to us from John Hall, July 22, 2004; interview with James May.

Adding to his worries was . . . : Judge William Hoeveler, "Order on Motions for Summary Judgment," *Sierra Club et al. v. Flowers et al.*, 19, 20n, and 22.

As expected, in 1999 . . . : Ruling on *Florida Rock Industries v. U.S.*, 45 Fed. Cl. 21, 38.

However, a Department of Justice . . . : E-mail from Fred Disheroon, April 24, 2007.

By the time of the Florida Rock . . . : Judge William Hoeveler, "Order on Motions for Summary Judgment," *Sierra Club et al. v. Flowers et al.*, 65; interview with Barbara Lange.

But by late 2001 the wildlife service . . . : Record of Decision, 37 (see chapter 11 note, *Despite all of its dangers*, above); interview with James May.

Their lawsuit was assigned . . . : Interview with Judge William Hoeveler; Craig Pittman, "Everglades judge stands his guard," *St. Petersburg Times*, May 18, 2003.

A year after the mining permits . . . : Steven Dudley, "Beneath the Pink Underwear," *Miami New Times*, June 5, 2003, http://www.miaminewtimes.com/2003-06-05/news/beneath-the-pink-underwear/; Curtis Morgan, "Benzene at core of mining case," *Miami Herald*, Aug. 6, 2006; see R. A. Renken et al., "Assessing the Vulnerability," 319.

Hoeveler found that Corps officials . . . : Judge William Hoeveler, "Order on Motions for Summary Judgment," *Sierra Club et al. v. Flowers et al.*, 19. The entire decision can be accessed at http://www.corkscrewroad.net/Lake%20Belt%20Mining%20Decision%20March%202006.pdf; however, as the .pdf format is different from the one in the actual court file, page numbers will differ from the ones we cite here.

While waiting for Hoeveler's final . . . : Associated Press, "Some say rock mining case threatens road work," *St. Petersburg Times*, June 12, 2006; *Keep Florida Rockin*, Web site sponsored by Floridians for Better Transportation, http://www.keepfloridarockin.org/; Florida DOT online, "Lake Belt/Mining Issue," http://www.dot.state.fl.us/statematerialsoffice/administration/resources/library/issues-trends/lakebelt.htm.

In July 2007, Hoeveler lowered . . . : Curtis Morgan, "Judge curbs mining to shield water," *Miami Herald*, July 14, 2007; Curtis Morgan, "Rock-mining forces turn out to protest proposed restrictions," *Miami Herald*, Sept. 19, 2007. For information about the miners' alternate plans, see Associated Press, "Some say rock mining case threatens road work," *St. Petersburg Times*, June 12, 2006; Cynthia Barnett, "Rock and a Hard Place," *Florida Trend*, September 2007; and Mark Hollis, "County delays zoning change request on rock mines," *South Florida Sun-Sentinel*, Sept. 25, 2007.

Chapter 12. Let Sleeping Watchdogs Lie

Ask Carol Browner what it was like . . . : Interview with Carol Browner; Craig Pittman, "From Florida to D.C., but where next?" *St. Petersburg Times*, Jan. 19, 2001; *Wall Street Journal* complaint about Browner quoted in David Dahl, "EPA may have more clout with Floridian in charge," *St. Petersburg Times*, Dec. 24, 1992.

"Haven't we learned our lesson?" . . . : Michael Grunwald, "Growing Pains in Southwest Fla.," *Washington Post*, June 25, 2002; interviews with Richard Harvey, Carol Browner, and William K. Reilly.

In 1951, the Florida legislature . . . : Interama land use records, State Archives of Florida Online Catalog, http://dlis.dos.state.fl.us/barm/rediscovery/default. asp?IDCFile=/fsa/DETAILSS.IDC,SPECIFIC=484205,DATABASE=SERIES.

"I think this is not only . . . " : President Lyndon Johnson, "Remarks in Miami Upon Receiving a Book Relating to the Interama Cultural and Trade Center," Oct. 25th, 1964, *American Presidency Project*, http://www.presidency.ucsb.edu/ws/?pid=26655.

Interama bought 1,700 acres . . . : Don North, "$20-million spent without real result," *St. Petersburg Times*, Aug. 11, 1974.

When critics of the project . . . : *Miami Herald* Service, "And Right Over Here, Folks, We Have the Interama Swamp," *St. Petersburg Times*, Oct. 13, 1965.

In the early 1970s . . . : Don North, "$20-million spent without real result," *St. Petersburg Times*, Aug. 11, 1974.

Trying to recoup its lost millions . . . : Florida DEP report on Munisport, 2000, www.dep.state.fl.us/waste/quick_topics/publications/wc/sites/summary/019.pdf; Florida Department of Health and Rehabilitative Services, "Public Health Assessment: Munisport Landfill," January 28, 1993, http://www.atsdr.cdc.gov/hac/PHA/munisport/mlf_toc.html.

In 1977 Munisport applied . . . : Interviews with Howard Marshall and Rebecca Hanmer; "City of North Miami, Fla., Corps of Engineers Permit 75-B0869 and Permit Application 77B-0376, Recommended Determinations of the Regional Administrator," Nov. 28, 1980, http://www.epa.gov/owow/wetlands/pdf/NorthMiamiRD.pdf; interview with James W. R. Adams.

So Marshall flew to Miami . . . : Buker, *Environment—The Third E*, 5; interviews with Howard Marshall and James W. R. Adams. Col. Adams said his "balls" comment was not intended to describe Marshall but rather Marshall's boss, Rebecca Hanmer.

The EPA spent a quarter of a million . . . : Interview with Howard Marshall.

The next step was an October . . . : The EPA's public hearing in North Miami convened on Oct. 2, 1980, the same day the Corps denied Florida Rock's permit to mine in Pennsuco; interviews with Howard Marshall and Rebecca Hanmer.

The warhead that was Munisport . . . : "Final Determination of the Administrator Concerning North Miami Landfill Site Pursuant to Section 404(c) of the Clean Water Act," Jan. 19, 1981, http://www.epa.gov/owow/wetlands/pdf/NorthMiamiFD. pdf.

The EPA didn't stop there . . . : "EPA Superfund Record of Decision: Munisport Landfill, North Miami, FL,," July 26, 1990, http://www.epa.gov/superfund/sites/rods/ fulltext/r0490062.pdf; EPA Superfund Record of Decision Amendment: Munisport Landfill North Miami, FL," Sept. 5, 1997, http://www.epa.gov/superfund/sites/rods/ fulltext/a0497187.pdf; interviews with Howard Neu, Cynthia Guerra, and Howard Marshall; Curtis Morgan and Amy Driscoll, "Condo tries to bury its past life as a dump," *Miami Herald*, June 15, 2007; Curtis Morgan, "Plan to treat ammonia lake falls short," *Miami Herald*, June 16, 2007.

Beginning in 1984, EPA vetoes . . . : "EPA's Veto Decisions," in Connolly, Johnson, and Williams, *Wetlands Law and Policy*, 306–14.

Reagan's EPA even vetoed . . . : "Final Determination of the U.S. Environmental Protection Agency's Assistant Administrator for Water, Concerning Three Wetland Properties (sites owned by Henry Rem Estate, Marion Becker et al., and Senior Corporation) for which Rockplowing Is Proposed in East Everglades, Dade County, Fla.," June 15, 1988, http://www.epa.gov/owow/wetlands/pdf/RemFD.pdf.

The last time the EPA . . . : Interview with William Reilly; EPA brochure, "Clean Water Action Section 404(c) 'Veto Authority,'" 2005, 2, http://www.epa.gov/owow/ wetlands/pdf/404c.pdf. In February 2008, the EPA began proceedings for its twelfth veto, this time aimed at one of the Corps' own projects. Known as the Yazoo pumps, this flood-control project would drain or damage at least 67,000 acres of wetlands in Mississippi. For details, see Michael Grunwald, "A Green Day for Bush," *Time*, Feb. 2, 2008, http://www.time.com/time/nation/article/0,8599,1709351,00.html.

For the remaining two years . . . : Interviews with William Reilly, David White, and Karsten Rist; Maj. Gen. Patrick Kelly, "HQUSACE Review and Findings Old Cutler Bay Permit 404(q) Elevation," Sept. 13, 1990, http://www.epa.gov/owow/wetlands/ pdf/CutlerBayGuidance.pdf; EPA oral history interview with William K. Reilly, http://www.epa.gov/history/publications/reilly/index.htm.

When Bill Clinton took over . . . : Interviews with John Henry Hankinson and Haynes Johnson.

Although Hankinson failed to veto . . . : Interviews with John Henry Hankinson and Bruce Boler.

"Bruce Boler I am sure . . . " : John Hall e-mail to Ann Hauck, Nov. 15, 2001.

After George W. Bush . . . : Interviews with Bruce Boler, Haynes Johnson, Richard Harvey, and Jimmy Palmer; Chad Gillis, "EPA water quality expert for Lee, Collier loses his job," *Naples Daily News*, Oct. 19, 2003.

The decline and fall . . . : Interviews with Richard Harvey and Haynes Johnson.

Soon the regional office . . . : Benjamin Grumbles, "Memorandum for the Field: Subject—U.S. Environmental Protection Agency coordination between regional offices and headquarters on Clean Water Act Section 404(q) actions," Oct. 30, 2006.

The end result of the EPA's . . . : Interview and tour of Mirasol with Bruce Boler; interviews with Haynes Johnson, Andy Eller, Ann Hauck, Audubon ornithology expert Jason Lauritsen, Florida Wildlife Federation attorney Tom Reese, Jim Giattina of the EPA, developer attorney Steve Walker, and David Hobbie of the Corps; Corps permit denial, Dec. 7, 2006, and subsequent EPA letters regarding Mirasol permit SAJ-2000-1926: Giattina to Col. Paul Grosskruger, Sept. 22, 2006; Giattina to Grosskruger, Oct. 18, 2006; Palmer to Grosskruger, April 16, 2007, all part of the Mirasol permit file.

Another agency that is supposed . . . : U.S. Fish and Wildlife Service 404(q) Elevation Requests, http://www.fws.gov/habitatconservation/elevations.htm.

A company called the Vineyards . . . : Kenneth Smith, U.S. Fish and Wildlife Service Request for Elevation, Naples Reserve, Dec. 22, 2000, http://www.fws.gov/habitatconservation/404(q)elevations/NAples_Reserve1.pdf; interview with Andy Eller.

On January 19, 2001 . . . : Joseph Westphal, Department of the Army Response, Naples Reserve, Jan. 19, 2001, http://www.fws.gov/habitatconservation/404(q)elevations/Naples_Response.pdf; interview with Andy Eller.

But the wildlife service . . . : Interviews with Andy Eller and Jeanette Gallihugh; "Preliminary Briefing Statement: Proposed Policy Elevation of Corps of Engineers, Jacksonville District's implementation of the 404(b)(1) Guidelines in Southwest Florida," Jan. 3, 2001; "Fish and Wildlife Service Policy Concerns, 404 Permit Program, Army Corps of Engineers/Jacksonville District," February 2001.

"I am steaming mad" . . . : E-mail from John Hall to Ann Hauck, Nov. 15, 2001.

Gallihugh, along with her boss . . . : Interviews with Jeanette Gallihugh, Jay Slack, Haynes Johnson, Richard Harvey, and John Hall; PowerPoint presentation and U.S. Fish and Wildlife Service notes from Southwest Florida Policy Elevation Issue Resolution Meeting, March 14, 2001. Several witnesses verified hearing Hall say, "Stay in your lane," but those words do not appear in the notes, and Hall says he does not remember saying them.

The panther—once described . . . : Bill Updike, "The Fall of the Cat of God," *Defenders of Wildlife Magazine*, Summer 2005, http://www.defenders.org/newsroom/defenders_magazine/summer_2005/the_fall_of_the_cat_of_god.php.

Between 1992 and 2007 . . . : Figures on permit applications and acreage from the March 1, 2007, Fish and Wildlife Service biological opinion on the revised Mirasol permit application. Interviews with Andy Eller and Jeff Ruch of Public Employees for Environmental Responsibility; Warren Richey, "Developers squeeze Florida big cat," *Christian Science Monitor*, Sept. 24, 2004; Manuel Roig-Franzia, "Panther Advocate Fights to Get Job Back," *Washington Post*, March 8, 2005; Gross, "Why Not the Best? How Science Failed the Florida Panther," http://biology.plosjournals.org/perlserv/?request=get-document&doi=10.1371%2Fjournal.pbio.0030333; Bill Updike, "The Fall of the Cat of God" (see preceding note, *The panther—once described*); *Andrew C. Eller and Public Employees for Environmental Responsibility v. Department of the Interior*, http://www.peer.org/campaigns/whistleblower/panther/pantherDQchallenge.pdf; letter from Steve Williams, director of the U.S. Fish and Wildlife Service, to Jeff Ruch, March 16, 2005.

And in the meantime, the wildlife . . . : Interview with Paul Souza; e-mail from John Wrublik of U.S. Fish and Wildlife Service to Lee County consultant RaeAnn Boylan, March 9, 2005; U.S. Fish and Wildlife Service, "Draft of the Third Revision of the Florida Panther Recovery Plan, available online via the *Federal Register*, vol. 71, no. 20, Jan. 31, 2006, http://ecos.fws.gov/docs/federal_register/fr4503.pdf.

The most common natural disaster . . . : National Flood Insurance Program Web site, http://www.floodsmart.gov/floodsmart/pages/events.jsp;jsessionid=4F85C434FCD; "Wetlands, Protecting Life and Property from Flooding," EPA Web site, http://www.epa.gov/owow/wetlands/pdf/Flooding.pdf; interview with Melvin Alverson; Scott Streater, "Stronger protection debated for wetlands in Northwest Florida," *Pensacola News Journal*, March 15, 1999.

Between 2000 and 2002, FEMA . . . : E-mail to Lesley Blackner from Charles Beck, FEMA environmental specialist, June 13, 2001; interviews with John Hall, John Studt, and William Straw of FEMA's Atlanta office. Most of the letters from FEMA objected to a specific 404 permit in the 100-year floodplain. The exception was a scathing three-page letter dated Oct. 23, 2001, about all Corps permitting in the floodplain. That led to a conference between FEMA and the Corps that resulted in Straw acknowledging that his agency has no power over the Corps.

Chapter 13. The Cussing Congressman

In 1991, the Florida legislature . . . : David Olinger, "Free university land could carry steep ecological price," *St. Petersburg Times*, Oct. 31, 1994; David Olinger, "University site swims in muck," *St. Petersburg Times*, Oct. 19, 1995; Pamela Smith

Hayford, "Water district warned FGCU," *Fort Myers News-Press*, July 30, 2003; Maribel Perez Wadsworth, "Water district fines FGCU," *Fort Myers News-Press*, Aug. 19, 2003; Corps of Engineers permit no. 199400807; interviews with Tom Reese, Terry Rice, Connie Mack, and John Hall. Mack, now a Tallahassee lobbyist, confirmed making the call to Rice but said he couldn't recall what words he used.

Rice subsequently approved . . . : John Henry Hankinson, then EPA's regional director, told us in 2004 that the cumulative impact study that Rice pushed for hadn't slowed the loss of wetlands, and he wished he had vetoed the FGCU permit.

Mack wasn't the only senator . . . : David Olinger, "Free university land could carry steep ecological price," *St. Petersburg Times*, Oct. 31, 1994. After the Atlanta office of the Fish and Wildlife Service changed the findings to clear the way for the permit, Florida Field Supervisor David Ferrell and Florida Panther Coordinator Dennis Jordan sent a memo to their boss in Atlanta warning that panthers were going to lose out. The boss sent it back covered with sarcastic handwritten comments, including one that said, "Florida will be developed."

Public interest is supposed to drive . . . : Interviews with Vic Anderson and Terry Rice; "Statement of Deputy Secretary of the Army John Paul Woodley Jr. before the House Committee on Transportation and Infrastructure on the 35th Anniversary of the Clean Water Act: Successes and Future Challenges," Oct. 18, 2007, 6, http://republicans.transportation.house.gov/Media/File/Testimony/Full/10-18-07-Woodley.pdf.

The Corps' Jacksonville office . . . : Interview with Joe Burns. As soon as he mentioned his database, we typed up a Freedom of Information Act request for it. With the database in hand, we were able to file additional FOIA requests for some of those letters. Many of the entries in the database, however, did not mention a specific permit, just the word "regulatory," so our research may have only scratched the surface. Interviews with John Hall, Lt. Gen. Carl Strock, Ginny Brown-Waite, and Bob Graham.

The jowly and wonkish Graham . . . : Jeff Klinkenberg, "Skink and Bob: Florida's guardian alter egos," *St. Petersburg Times*, May 8, 2005; Bill Adair and David Adams, "Buffett adds laid-back air to Graham campaign," *St. Petersburg Times*, May 29, 2003; Michael Grunwald, *The Swamp*, 181, 248.

For instance, Graham was a big booster . . . : Corps permit no. SAJ1999-00619; letter from Michael Saadeh, June 28, 2005.

Graham said that the letters . . . : Interviews with Bob Graham and Andy Eller.

Graham and then congressman Porter Goss . . . : Corps permit no. SAJ1994-02492. Because we were reporting on this during Goss' tenure as CIA director, we were unable to get any response to our questions about why he sent so many letters on behalf of developers given his prior record as Sanibel's conservation-minded mayor.

Some congressional letters take . . . : Hastings' letter did not include a permit number and neither did the Corps response, but we were able to get information from the South Florida Water Management District permitting file; Ruth Marcus, "Senate Removes Hastings," *Washington Post*, Oct. 21, 1989; Andrea Koppel, "Pelosi looks past Hastings for intelligence committee post," *CNN.com*, Nov. 26, 2006, http://www.cnn.com/2006/POLITICS/11/28/hastings.intelligence/.

In politics, timing can be . . . : As with the Hastings letter, Col. Carpenter's response letter contained no permit number, and we couldn't get Shaw's letter. We again obtained information from the South Florida Water Management District; interview with Gail Gitcho.

Of course political intervention . . . : Interviews with Charles Schnepel and Charlie Newling, one of the Mississippi experts; Richard Berke, "Prodded by Lobbying Group, G.O.P. Reveals $100,000 Donors," *New York Times*, Jan. 24, 1989; Vicki Kemper, "With friends like these . . . (fundraisers for Republican presidential candidates)," *Common Cause Magazine*, Summer 1995; Tracy L. Kolody, "Development Speeds Coral Springs' Growth," *South Florida Business Journal*, Sept. 14, 1987; President George Bush, "Remarks at a Campaign Fundraising Luncheon for Ileana Ros-Lehtenin in Miami, Florida," Aug. 16, 1989," *American Presidency Project*, http://www.presidency.ucsb.edu/ws/?pid=17433. We were unable to get Courtelis' side of the story because he died in 1995.

Corps employees say they are . . . : Interviews with Charles Schnepel, Vic Anderson, and Steve Brooker.

That's what happened with . . . : Interview with Steve Brooker; letter from U.S. Representative Tom Feeney to Robert Carpenter, April 21, 2003; letter from Warren Williams to Tom Feeney, April 9, 2004 (obtained from Feeney's office along with fax cover sheet addressed to Burns); Corps permit no. SAJ-2003-03545; Mark Leibovich, "The Reaganest Republican," *Washington Post*, June 11, 2004; contribution records from Federal Elections Commission. Garbe did not return our calls for comment.

Brooker fell victim . . . : Interviews with Steve Brooker, civic activist Marjorie Holt, James "Greg" May, development attorney Ken Wright, and congressional aide Mike Miller; letter from U.S. Representative Ric Keller to Joe Burns, Nov. 28, 2001.

Sometimes the pressure . . . : Corps permit no. SAJ1999-00619; Gross, "Why Not the Best?" (see chapter 12 note, *The panther—once described*, above); interviews with Andy Eller and Jay Slack; Dawson & Associates employee list from company Web site, http://www.dawsonassociates.com; Dawson & Associates reports to Lee County provided to us by activist Ann Hauck (see also the Dawson Web site at http://www.

dawsonassociates.com/images/daniels.pdf); Peggy Noonan, "A Good Man Gets His Due," *Wall Street Journal*, Dec. 8, 2000, http://www.opinionjournal.com/columnists/pnoonan/?id=65000751.

An even more controversial . . . : Interviews with Andy Eller and Bill Nelson; U.S. Fish and Wildlife Service files on Corps permit no. SAJ-2000-01926. J. D. Nicewonder declined to comment.

Because the Corps takes so long . . . : Interviews with Dan Gilmore and Joseph Narkiewicz; Joseph Narkiewicz, "The Cruelest Form of Denial Is Delay," *Building Barometer*, Tampa Bay Builders Association newsletter, July 2005, 4. In the column, Narkiewicz denied that developers use political influence on the Corps, then detailed the builders' trip to Washington to persuade lawmakers to prod the Corps to say yes more quickly.

We were looking for one . . . : Frank Matthews profile posted at Hopping Green & Sams Web site, http://www.hgslaw.com/lawyers/frank-e-matthews.html; 19th Annual Environmental Permitting Summer School at Mariott's Marco Island Resort, July 20–22. After the denial, the Freedom Commerce Center developer retooled his plans to limit wetlands impact to 35 acres. The Corps approved the new plan.

Though the Corps rarely says no . . . : Narkiewicz, "The Cruelest Form of Denial" (see chapter 13 note, *Because the Corps takes*, above).

All the lobbyists in the world . . . : Patrick Danner and Dan Christenson, "Ex-PBS&J chairman pleads guilty" *Miami Herald*, Oct. 10, 2007; Susan Burns, "Tales of Hoffman: WCI's Hoffman's Rise to Success," *Gulfshore Business* online, December 2004, http://www.gulfshorebusiness.com/Articles/2004/12/Tales-of-Hoffman.asp?ht=%22tales%20of%20hoffman%22.

Among the recipients . . . : Records of campaign contributions from the Office of the Florida Secretary of State; interview with Trudi Williams; copies of all correspondence came from a records request to Williams' office.

The bill Matthews helped write . . . : It passed the House 105 to 11 and the Senate 35 to 0 and was signed by Governor Jeb Bush; Ron Milavsky provided us with copies of his e-mail correspondence with Williams.

In April 2005, builders . . . : Interview with John Paul Woodley Jr.; background on Crenshaw comes from his Web site, http://crenshaw.house.gov/; campaign contribution records from *opensecrets.org*, the Web site of the Center for Responsive Politics, http://www.opensecrets.org/.

Builders from other parts of Florida . . . : Interviews with Dan Gilmore and Joseph Narkiewicz; no byline, "FHBA Issues Victories," *Building Barometer*, December 2005, 12.

The developers worried . . . : The DEP opposed the bill because one provision delayed imposing new permitting requirements on the Panhandle. That prompted Wayne Bertsch, FHBA director of political affairs, to warn in an e-mail: "I will lay in the weeds for them, and when I strike, I will kill."

The result: a June 16, 2005, letter . . . : The other signers were Representatives John Mica, Jeff Miller, Katherine Harris, Michael Bilirakis, Adam Putnam, Ileana Ros-Lehtinen, Ginny Brown-Waite, Ric Keller, Allen Boyd, Cliff Stearns, Tom Feeney, Mario Diaz-Balart, and Debbie Wasserman-Schultz.

Crenshaw then went a step further . . . : We obtained a list of attendees from the Corps and by interviewing Robert Carpenter, Lawrence Evans, and Jonathan Ullman. Interview with Dan Gilmore.

In October 2005, DEP officials . . . : Department of Environmental Protection, "Consolidation of State and Federal Wetland Permitting Programs—Implementation of House Bill 759 (chapter 2005-273, *Laws of Florida*)," September 30, 2005; letter from DEP secretary Colleen Castille to Representative Allan Bense, Oct. 3, 2005, both obtained from DEP.

Despite those concerns . . . : Interview with Eric Draper, deputy director for policy, Audubon of Florida; interview with Dan Gilmore.

Still, the push for a state takeover . . . : Transcript of Senate Armed Services Committee hearing, March 8, 2007, http://www.northcom.mil/News/Transcripts/030807. html.

Chapter 14. Loopholes and Sinkholes

Don Hodges steered . . . : Interview with Don Hodges and January 2002 tour of waterways around airport site.

The Panama City-Bay County . . . : Craig Pittman, "Florida's Great Northwest, Brought to You by the St. Joe Co. (with your help)," *St. Petersburg Times*, April 21, 2002; Abby Goodnough, "In a Quiet Part of Florida, a Bid to Bring in the Crowds," *New York Times*, May 9, 2007; Ziewitz and Wiaz, *Green Empire*, 259–61; Alfred I. DuPont Testamentary Trust Financial History, http://www.alfrediduponttrust.org/history/financial.asp.

"This new facility . . . " : Interviews with Randy Curtis and Don Hodges.

St. Joe's motive in donating . . . : Interview with Peter Rummell; Craig Pittman and Kris Hundley, "Panama City Airport okayed; hurdles loom," *St. Petersburg Times*, Sept. 16, 2006.

Ball, an eighth-grade dropout . . . : Ziewitz and Wiaz, *Green Empire*, 35–50; Griffith, *Ed Ball: Confusion to the Enemy*, 19; Nolan, *Fifty Feet in Paradise*, 285–93.

When DuPont died in 1935 . . . : Ziewitz and Wiaz, *Green Empire*, 51–87; Roberts, *Dream State*, 220.

Ball maintained a plantation . . . : Roberts, *Dream State*, 231; "Southwood House and Cottages Garner Awards," *Front Porch News* no. 3, Spring/Summer 2002, Arvida Community newsletter published by St. Joe Company, 4, http://www.joe.com/NR/rdonlyres/750D5548-E836-40EE-A2B9-2718939FF7F5/705/2002_spring_summer.pdf; Griffith, *Ed Ball: Confusion to the Enemy*, 61–64.

Ball didn't like anything . . . : Ziewitz and Wiaz, *Green Empire*, 95. For a story that questions whether this really happened, see Karen Mathis, "Was Duval a Crossroads for Disney?" *Florida Times-Union*, April 7, 2007.

To lead the company . . . : Interview with Peter Rummell.

There was no comparable effort . . . : Interview with Charles Gauthier, Florida Department of Community Affairs; Ziewitz and Wiaz, *Green Empire*, 106–7, 312–13; interview with Aubrey Davis.

St. Joe's development machine . . . : Ziewitz and Wiaz, *Green Empire*, 269–70; contribution records from the Office of the Florida Secretary of State and the Center for Public Integrity; letter from Gov. Bush to Bay County residents, April 7, 2003, announcing a community meeting to unveil economic prospects of area's development plan.

Yet, in marketing its new . . . : Pittman, "Florida's Great Northwest, Brought to You by the St. Joe Co. (with your help)," *St. Petersburg Times*, April 21, 2002; interviews with Peter Rummell, John Spohrer, and Barbara Eells.

The company even wants . . . : Interview with Jerry Ray.

With the airport in place . . . : Interview with Peter Rummell.

Instead, officials from the Corps . . . : Interviews with St. Joe counsel Robert Rhodes, DEP secretary David Struhs, Nature Conservancy executive director Bob Bendick, and St. Joe spokesman Jerry Ray; DEP press release, "Florida and the St. Joe Company Sign Protective Agreement," Feb. 25, 2004, http://www.dep.state.fl.us/secretary/news/2004/feb/0225.htm; Kendall Middlemas, "Feds approve large-scale wetlands permit," *Panama City News Herald*, July 13, 2004; Joan Hughes, "Sheer Magnitude," *Florida Trend*, October 2003; St. Joe Company press release, "The St. Joe Company Reports Second Quarter 2004 Net Income of $22.7 Million, or $0.30 Per Share," July 21, 2004, http://findarticles.com/p/articles/mi_m0EIN/is_2004_July_21/ai_n6115762; Corps regional generalpermit no. SAJ-86, "Memorandum for the Record," CESAJ-RD-NN-P SAJ-2004-1861, June 30, 2004.

For the Corps, the appeal . . . : Barron speech at Continuing Legal Education (CLE) Florida Water Law Conference, Tampa, March 30, 2004.

St. Joe's deal with the Corps . . . : Abby Goodnough, "In a Quiet Part of Florida, a Bid to Bring in the Crowds," *New York Times*, May 9, 2007; interviews with Jerry Ray, Lesley Blackner, and Linda Young; records from *Natural Resources Defense Council v. U.S. Army Corps of Engineers, Gen. Carl Strock and Col. Robert Carpenter*, case no. 3:05-CV-459-TJC-MCR and *Sierra Club v. U.S. Army Corps of Engineers and Col. Robert Carpenter*, case no. 2:05-CV-362-TJC-TEM, both filed in U.S. District Court, Middle District of Florida, Jacksonville Division.

In August 2007, the Corps . . . : Record of Decision, Corps permit no. SAJ-2001-5264, Aug. 15, 2007; Craig Pittman and Kris Hundley, "New Panhandle airport will be first in U.S. since 9/11," *St. Petersburg Times*, Aug. 17, 2007; Kris Hundley, "Fla. developer calls retreat," *St. Petersburg Times*, Oct. 9, 2007. Interviews with Peter Rummell and Linda Young.

Every time a hard rain . . . : October 2004 tour of Peck Sink with John Burnett and Alys Brockaway of Hernando County and Gene Altman of the Southwest Florida Water Management District.

Florida is covered with . . . : *Solid Waste Agency of Northern Cook County v. Army Corps of Engineers*, 531 U.S. 159 (2001) 191 F.3d 845, reversed; Kara K. Baxter and Alfred J. Malefatto, "Supreme Court Ruling Limits Federal Wetlands Jurisdiction," Greenberg Traurig Alert, February 2001, http://www.gtlaw.com/pub/alerts/2001/baxterk_02.asp; Cynthia Barnett, "Unfiltered: The Truth About Water in Florida," *Florida Trend*, August 2005.

But in January 2001 . . . : This case is one of two Supreme Court decisions that Representative John Dingell, one of the original sponsors of the Clean Water Act, says bungled its reading of the law's intent.

That's what happened with Peck Sink . . . : Interviews with interviews with Bob Barron and Richard Legere of the Corps, with developer's attorney Jake Varn, and with Gene Altman of the Southwest Florida Water Management District; letter from Charles Courtenay of King Engineering to Richard Legere, April 15, 2003, and follow-up letter and maps sent by Courtenay to Legere, June 7, 2002 and jurisdictional determination by Corps of Engineers, signed by Legere, July 10, 2002, all obtained from USACE, Jacksonville District, via FOIA.

Allowing builders to fill . . . : Interview with N. S. "Sandy" Nettles and review of his case files; interview with Jim Murphy.

In Tennessee, the Corps . . . : National Wildlife Federation press release, "Army Corps To Protect Tennessee Wetlands," May 6, 2005, http://www.aswm.org/wbn/archive/05/050531a.htm; Michael Gormley, "Army Corps of Engineers submits to Spitzer's wetland argument," Associated Press, Jan. 20, 2005, http://www.geocities.com/ntgreencitizen/nysoag.html.

No one has done a dye test . . . : Interviews with George Casey and attorney Jake Varn.

Pam Winchester heard . . . : Interviews with Pam Winchester and Barbara Herrin.

The reason the Corps issued . . . : Interviews with Pam Winchester, Barbara Herrin, John Hall, and Lesley Blackner; *Floridians for Environmental Accountability and Reform v. United States Army Corps of Engineers*, United States District Court, Middle District of Florida, case no. 6:02-CV-530-ORL-18JGG; letter from Ronald J. Mikulak, chief, Wetlands Regulatory Section of the U.S. Environmental Protection Agency, to Col. James G. May, District Engineer, U.S. Army Corps of Engineers, May 23, 2002; denial contained in Corps Memorandum of Record, permit no. SAJ-2001-1107; letter from Barbara Herrin to David Dewey, St. Johns River Water Management District, Nov. 13, 2001; Corps permit no. 2001-01107. All documents in connection with the New Smyrna Beach case were provided by Barbara Herrin, Pam Winchester, and Lesley Blackner.

In June 2004 the Corps agreed . . . : Interview with John Hall. The story does not end neatly, however. In spring 2007, Herrin told us that she and Winchester expected the study to provide a basis for making future permitting decisions, but it fell far short of that lofty goal. She said she has seen no change in the way the Corps issues nationwide permits in Florida. Meanwhile the owner of the property where Wal-Mart was to be built has now proposed building a conventional shopping center. Herrin says they suggested the developer formulate the plans around the information in the Corps' permit denial.

Chapter 15. Dirty Water

The green goop . . . : Interview with Neil Armingeon; Lower St. Johns River Basin site, http://floridaswater.com/LSJRB/water_quality.html; John Hay Rabb, "St. Johns River struggles against pollution," *ESPN.com*, Jan. 26, 2006, http://sports. espn.go.com/outdoors/bassmaster/conservation/news/story?page=b_con_pollu-tion_StJohns_River_FL.

Swimmers and anglers . . . : Bob Snell, "River Trouble: Growing problems on the St. Johns River set the stage for an environmental showdown," *Florida Trend*, November 1, 2005, http://www.floridatrend.com/article.asp?aID=04559451.82638702.579930.79 44009.73421.137&aID2=44601; Chris Williams, Mark Aubel, Andrew Chapman, Peter D'Aiuto, Dale Casamatta, Andrew Reich, and Sharon Ketchen, "Toxin Producing Blue-Green Algae at Recreational Sites in the St. Johns River, Florida," GreenWater Laboratories/CyanoLab, Palatka, Fla., April 3, 2006, http://www.greenwaterlab.com/ newsite/articles/FDOHSJR2005.pdf; interview with Neil Armingeon.

While the bloom in the St. Johns . . . : Craig Pittman, "Plans abound to fix the ooze of Lake Okeechobee," *St. Petersburg Times*, Feb. 26, 2006; Craig Pittman, "Springs bring mystery illness," *St. Petersburg Times*, Aug. 24, 2006.

Everything hinges on a document . . . : Interviews with Clark Hull and Michael Molligan; South Florida Water Management District, "Basis of Review for Environmental Resource Permit Applications Within the South Florida Water Management District," August 2000, 68, http://www.dep.state.fl.us/water/mines/docs/BOR_08_00.pdf.

In 2002, a developer proposed . . . : Interview with Michael Molligan; Chuin-Wei Yap, "Corps okays mall in Pasco," *St. Petersburg Times*, May 17, 2007.

During a DEP internal investigation . . . : Transcript of interview by investigators in DEP case no. II-01-15-2005-14; interview with Clark Hull.

Sometimes they're in such a rush . . . : *Ahmed Thalji v. Southwest Florida Water Management District and HBJ Investments*, Florida Department of Administrative Hearings case no. 99-1919.

"The general criteria . . . " : Interviews with Damon Meiers, Tony Janicki, Wayne Daltry, Marcy LaHart, and Kraig McLane.

One of the findings . . . : "Environmental Impact Statement on Improving the Regulatory Process in Southwest Florida, Lee and Collier Counties, Florida," U.S. Army Corps of Engineers, U.S. Fish and Wildlife Service, U.S. Environmental Protection Agency, July 2000.

So when the EPA's . . . : Interviews with John Henry Hankinson, Bruce Boler, and Harvey H. Harper III. Boler said the two Harper papers he relied on were "Estimation of stormwater loading rate parameters for central and south Florida," Environmental Research & Design, Inc., Orlando, 1992, and "Stormwater loading rate parameters for central and south Florida," 3rd rev., Environmental Research & Design, Inc., Orlando, 1994.

When WERC asked Boler . . . : Interview with Bruce Boler; Chad Gillis, "EPA water quality expert for Lee, Collier loses his job," *Naples Daily News*, Oct. 19, 2003; Boler resignation statement, http://www.peer.org/docs/epa/Boler_Statement.pdf.

The report Harper unveiled . . . : To Harper, saying that his report says "wetlands pollute" is "a nice sound bit." He says a more accurate statement would be that wetlands do not clean all pollutants out of stormwater. "Wetlands don't discharge distilled water," he told us.

One of the flaws . . . : Interviews with Bruce Boler and Jim Beever; letter on Harper report from Conservancy of Southwest Florida to Eric Livingston of the Department of Environmental Protection, Aug. 23, 2007, provided by Conservancy; Estero Bay Agency on Bay Management meeting, Fort Myers, May 10, 2004; Melora Grattan, "Regulators, activists clash over SW Florida wetlands permitting methodology," *Enviro-Net*, November 2004, http://www.enviro-net.com/main.asp?page=story&id =2&month=11&paper=fl&year=2004. Interview with Carol Wehle.

Following South Florida's lead . . . : Harper and Baker, *Evaluation of Current Stormwater Design Criteria*, http://www.florida-stormwater.org/pdfs/Final%20Report%20 -%20SW%20Design%20Criteria-June07.pdf.

One of the biggest debates . . . : *Broward County v. Arthur Weiss, Trustee, and South Florida Water Management District*, Florida Department of Administrative Hearings case no. 01-3373.

In 1999, the legislature . . . : Interview with Connie Bersok; Office of Program Policy Analysis and Government Accountability (OPPAGA), with assistance from the Department of Environmental Protection and the Water Management Districts, "Policy Review: Wetland Mitigation," Report No. 99-40, March 2000, http://www. oppaga.state.fl.us/reports/pdf/9940rpt.pdf, and "Policy Review: Cumulative Impact Consideration in Environmental Resource Permitting," Report No. 01-40, September 2001, http://www.oppaga.state.fl.us/reports/pdf/0140rpt.pdf.

The legislature made no such . . . : The bill, HB 2365, was sponsored by Representative J. D. Alexander. It changed Florida Statue 373.414 to say, in subsection 8(b): "If an applicant proposes mitigation within the same drainage basin as the adverse impacts to be mitigated, and if the mitigation offsets these adverse impacts, the governing board and department shall consider the regulated activity to meet the cumulative impact requirements."

Around the time OPPAGA was digging . . . : *Sierra Club v. St. Johns River Water Management District*, Florida Division of Administrative Hearings case no. 01-0583RP; Longleaf Plantation, SJRWMD environmental resource permit no. 4-031-87852-2.

Here's the bottom line . . . : OPPAGA, "Policy Review: Wetland Mitigation," Report No. 99-40, 2 (see chapter 15 note, *In 1999, the legislature*, above).

Chapter 16. Banking on Phony Numbers

On a broiling August morning . . . : Florida Department of Environmental Protection file on ScanAmerican Holdings investigation, DEP archives; Tom Palmer, "Green Swamp logging: 2 developers charged in first wetlands felony case," *Ledger of Lakeland*, Aug. 10, 1993; Tom Palmer, "Environmentalists laud felony case," *Ledger of Lakeland*, Aug. 11, 1993; Tom Palmer, "Environmental violations: ScanAmerican charges send out tough message," *Ledger of Lakeland*, Aug. 15, 1993; Maryemma Bachelder and Tom Palmer, "Judge: Records seized illegally," *Ledger of Lakeland*, Dec. 21, 1993; no byline, "Charges against swamp developers dropped," *Ledger of Lakeland*, Jan. 8, 1994.

A potential solution came . . . : Fari Tabatatai and Robert W. Brumbaugh, "The Early Mitigation Banks: A Follow-up Review," working paper, Institute for Water Resources, Alexandria, Va., 1998, 11, http://www.iwr.usace.army.mil/inside/products/pub/iwrreports/98-WMB-WP.pdf.

McCarthy and Fickett had started . . . : Florida DEP files on ScanAmerican investigation.

Then along came a Florida company . . . : Interviews with George Platt and Pembroke Pines City Manager, Charlie Dodge; Corps permit no. SAJ-1993-300370.

Soon Platt and Johns' success . . . : Interviews with Dennis Benbow and Sherri Lewin and tour of Florida Mitigation Bank, August 2006; Corps permit no. SAJ-1996-03573; interview with Chuck Olson.

The first Bush Administration endorsed . . . : White House press release, Aug. 9, 1991. The endorsement of mitigation banking formed a minor part of the Bush Administration's attempt to make a sweeping change in wetlands policy that included changing the definition of wetlands, a move which backfired politically. The first official guidance documents for mitigation banking permits were issued by the Corps and EPA on Nov. 28, 1995, during the Clinton Administration.

In 1996, when a Senate . . . : Transcript of testimony submitted by Senator Bob Graham and Ecobank partner Denver Stutler Jr. before the U.S. Senate Committee on Environment and Public Works, March 14, 1996; interview with George Platt.

Fickett and McCarthy disagree . . . : Testimony in Ecosystems Land Mitigation Bank Corporation Chapter 11, United States Federal Bankruptcy Court, Middle District of Florida, case no. 6:04-BK-07391-KSJ; Stutler testimony (see note *In 1996, when a Senate* above).

Meanwhile, Ecobank donated . . . : Annual report of the Foundation for Florida's Future, 1996; Denver Stutler, "Ecobank: Conservation Is Good Business," *Outside the Lines,* Foundation for Florida's Future, March 6, 1996, 9–14. Foundation records do not specify exact amounts, but it was listed as giving more than $5,000.

In an effort to create . . . : Clerk of the House Lobbyist Directory, 1996; interviews with Fred McCormack and Vicki Tschinkel.

One block of credits sold . . . : Data courtesy of Florida State University law professor J. B. Ruhl, who assembled it from permit files. Ruhl mapped the data; we measured the distance from the project to the bank border.

Then there's the Little Pine . . . : Interviews with Raymond Pavelka, Ron Silver, and James Boyd; Corps permit no. SAJ-1994-00037; James Boyd and Lisa Wainger, "Measuring Ecosystem Service Benefits: The Use of Landscape Analysis to Evaluate Environmental Trades and Compensation," Resources for the Future Discussion Paper 02-63, April 2003, http://www.rff.org/documents/RFF-DP-02-63.pdf.

On December 30, 1996, Ecobank . . . : Corps permit no. SAJ-1995-06135.

About 15 minutes outside . . . : Interview with Tom Odom and tour of Lake Louisa, September 2006; Corps permit no.SAJ-1995-02208; interviews with Alan Fickett, Dennis Benbow, and Todd Gipe.

In the decade after . . . : Permit files for most mitigation banks include a credit ledger showing who purchased how many credits.

Corps regulations say . . . : Corps of Engineers, "Federal Guidance for the Establishment, Use and Operation of Mitigation Banks," November 28, 1995, http://www.nww.usace.army.mil/html/offices/op/rf/Mitigation_Banks/Mitigation_Banking_Guidance.pdf.

The nonpartisan Environmental . . . : The Environmental Law Institute report is *Banks and Fees: The Status of Off-Site Wetland Mitigation in the United States*; interview with Jessica Wilkinson. ELI also set up a searchable database of mitigation banking permits at http://www2.eli.org/wmb/search.htm.

Some banks constitute . . . : Florida Department of Environmental Protection permit no. 43029983; interview with Don Ross.

EarthBalance vice president . . . : DeFoor took us on a tour of EarthBalance's Myakka River Mitigation Bank—a more traditional restoration project—and promptly got his ATV stuck in the mud. One question we asked him during that tour was what his job was, since the company is based near Sarasota and he lives outside Tallahassee. His response: "I'm not sure most days what I do for a living." His boss, Don Ross, told us: "I would say his job is marketing. He is identified with the good side of the environmental community as opposed to environmental consultants. We're trying to build a firm that's about serving the public interest. Allison is able to steer a lot of people to us and keep an eye on what's going on as far as environmental policy."

Peace River is one of 10 . . . : The rest are Lake Louisa-Green Swamp Mitigation Bank, East Central Florida Wetland Mitigation Bank, Colbert-Cameron Mitigation Bank, Lake Monroe Mitigation Bank, Barberville Wetland Mitigation Bank, Reedy Creek Mitigation Bank, Sundew Mitigation Bank, TM-Econ Mitigation Bank, and Farmton Mitigation Bank. Interview with Stuart Bradow.

McCarthy and Fickett's second bank . . . : East Central Florida Wetland Mitigation Bank permitting files.

The closest they ever came . . . : Transcript of Dec. 16, 1997, meeting of the Florida Cabinet, http://www.myflorida.com/myflorida/cabinet/agenda97/1216/trans1216.html; Ecobank bankruptcy files; interviews with Alan Fickett, Howard Seitz, Seminole County Commissioner Randy Morris, and Dennis Benbow.

One such "elephant" . . . : Interviews with Randy Morris and William Colbert; minutes from Orlando-Sanford Airport Authority meeting, June 2, 1998.

"He had a natural aversion . . . ": Testimony of Jim Stelling in *James H. Stelling and Randall C. Morris v. Ecosystems Land Mitigation Bank Corporation*, Orange County Circuit Court, case no. CI-99-9039.

McCarthy and Fickett hired . . . : Interview with Randy Morris; documents and testimony in *Stelling and Morris v. Ecobank*; application of Kenneth Wright for the state Environmental Regulation Commission.

We wanted to hear from Wright . . . : We tried for six weeks in late 2006 to get Wright to comment, but he did not respond. Then, in the summer of 2007, Governor Charlie Crist appointed Wright to the Florida Fish and Wildlife Conservation Commission. When we called about that, he finally spoke to us, admitting he should have responded earlier and at last offering his version of what happened with Ecobank. Interview with Howard Seitz.

The check to Ecobank was . . . : A copy of the check and Stelling's testimony are part of the record in *Stelling and Morris v. Ecobank* (see chapter 16 note, *"He had a natural aversion,"* above); interview with Randy Morris.

Ecobank's one big success . . . : Interview with George Howard.

Because mitigation banks . . . : Bank permits say the land must be preserved "in perpetuity." Most people would take that to mean forever, but in Florida it means "until someone needs it." Dennis Benbow spent more than $6 million to launch the Wekiva River Mitigation Bank, but as he was trying to get his federal permit in 2006, he learned that the state wanted to route a four-lane expressway through his bank, which could cost him as much as a third of his expected credits—enough to doom the bank. Another Central Florida bank, the Reedy Creek Mitigation Bank, lies in the path of a road a developer needs for a subdivision. As Steve Brooker told the *Orlando Sentinel* regarding that road, "Perpetuity now has a date."

Still, it wasn't enough . . . : Interview with Howard Seitz; Seitz' testimony in Ecobank bankruptcy case, confirmed by Ecobank's credit ledgers in permitting files.

Though Ecobank's Chapter 11 . . . : Corps permit no. SAJ-2000-04530; interviews with Ron Silver and Ernest Hale.

For 34 years, the site . . . : Interviews with William Casey, Beverly Birkett, Ron Silver, and Clark Hull; tour of the Tampa Bay Mitigation Bank site, Sept. 29, 2006; Southwest Florida Water Management District Environmental Resource permit no. 43020546; Corps permit no. SAJ-1998-00796.

Even when the state and Corps . . . : Interviews with Howard Seitz, D. Miller McCarthy, Alan Fickett, Denver Stutler, and Sheri Lewin.

Congress has spent more . . . : The Intermodal Surface Transportation Efficiency Act of 1991 allowed the use of federal highway money to set up banks. A transportation bill in 1998 and a defense bill in 2003 steered more money and pushed more federal projects toward mitigation banks. Stetson University law professor Royal Gardner, in a recent article regarding the U.S. Supreme Court's decision in *Rapanos v. United States*, argues that these repeated endorsements of mitigation banking show that the court missed the boat with its ruling: "Congress was aware of how the agencies were interpreting the geographic scope of the Clean Water Act. Instead of reining in or reversing the agencies, Congress enacted laws directed at how wetland impacts should be mitigated, thereby implicitly accepting the agencies' interpretations." For more, see "Rapanos and Wetland Mitigation Banking," http://it.vermontlaw.edu/VJEL/Rapanos/8-Gardner.pdf.

The bankers say their biggest . . . : Interview with George Howard; HR 1588, National Defense Authorization Act for Fiscal Year 2004, Section 2694b(1); no byline, "Measure would set standards for wetlands 'banks,'" *Raleigh News & Observer*, June 8, 1996; Representative Jones press release, "House Passes Jones Provision For Wetlands Protection That Has Been Ten Years In The Making," Nov. 7, 2003, http://jones.house.gov/release.cfm?id=124.

The proposed regulations drew . . . : On March 31, 2008, the Corps and EPA unveiled the new regulations, with the EPA's Benjamin Grumbles trumpeting them as the most important development in wetland protection since the first announcement about no net loss. As expected, the new rules give preference to mitigation banks above all other methods of making up for wetland loss and include a "recognition that upland areas may provide important ecological functions within a mitigation bank, and compensatory mitigation credit can be provided by those functions."

The first such research . . . : J. J. Mack and M. Micacchion, "An Ecological Assessment of Ohio Mitigation Banks: Vegetation, Amphibians, Hydrology, Soils," Ohio EPA Technical Report, WET/2006-1, Ohio Environmental Protection Agency, Division of Surface Water, Wetland Ecology Group, Columbus, Ohio, 2006, viii, 22, http://www.epa.state.oh.us/dsw/wetlands/Bank_Report_Ohio_Final.pdf; interview with George Platt.

Chapter 17. Toward a More Honest System

In May 2007, Florida . . . : Patrick O'Driscoll, "A drought for the ages," *USA Today*, June 7, 2007.vv

And that's when the Corps . . . : Interview with David Hobbie. Although the Corps sent a letter in May saying the permit would be approved, the permit was not issued until October when a court challenge to the state permit ended.

Two weeks later, the Corps . . . : Public notice on Permit Application SAJ-2006-6656-IP-MD, June 4, 2007, for Babcock Property Holdings LLC. The project purpose says it will be "a self-sustainable, environmentally conscious, mixed-use community" of 20,000 homes, six million square feet of commercial development, roads, sewers, schools, a hospital, fire and police stations, golf courses, and an FGCU re-search facility.

The blame for the broken promise . . . : Interview with Estus Whitfield.

In 2006, Congress budgeted . . . : Corps Civil Works Regulatory Budget for 2007 (figures for previous year), http://www.gpoaccess.gov/usbudget/fy07/pdf/budget/corps.pdf; 2006 Jacksonville budget from public information office.

"Until the Corps takes . . . " : Government Accountability Office report GAO-05-898, 27.

Institute a pay-as-you-go . . . : This is hardly a new idea—it was included among the recommendations of the 1988 final report of the National Wetlands Policy Forum.

Save the priority areas . . . : OPPAGA, "Policy Review: Cumulative Impact Consideration in Environmental Resource Permitting," report no. 01-40, September 2001, http://www.oppaga.state.fl.us/reports/pdf/0140rpt.pdf; Century Commission for a Sustainable Florida, *First Annual Report to the Governor and Legislature*, Jan. 16, 2007, 45, https://www.commentmgr.com/projects/1148/docs/First%20Annual%20 Report%20-%20Version-9%201-31-07.pdf; interviews with Tom Pelham and Steve Seibert.

Where there is no consequence . . . : Interview with Roy "Robin" Lewis.

Some of the most stringent . . . : In mid-2007, a pro-development majority on the Hillsborough County Commission voted 4 to 3 to eliminate the wetlands protection division. The four, led by pro-wrestler-turned-politician Brian Blair (formerly of the duo the Killer Bees), said they were simply cutting the budget. A public outcry forced them to reinstate the wetlands division, but with watered-down regulations.

Selected Bibliography

Adler, Robert W., Diane M. Cameron, and Jessica C. Landman. *The Clean Water Act 20 Years Later*. Washington, D.C.: Island Press, 1993.

Allen, Frederick Lewis. *Only Yesterday: An Informal History of the 1920s*. New York: Harper & Brothers, 1931.

Allen, Leslie, Beryl Kuder, and Sarah L. Oakes. *Promised Lands*. Vol. 2, *Subdivisions in Florida's Wetlands*. New York: INFORM, 1977.

Andreen, William L. "The Evolution of Water Pollution Control in the United States—State, Local, and Federal Efforts, 1789–1972: Part II." *Stanford Environmental Law Journal* 22 (2003): 215–94.

Antonini, Gustavo A., David A. Fann, and Paul Roat. *Placida Harbor to Marco Island*. Vol. 2 of *A Historical Geography of Southwest Florida Waterways*. FLSGP-M-02-003. Gainesville: Florida Sea Grant, 2003.

Bingham, Gail, Edwin H. Clark II, L. V. Haygood, and Michele Leslie, eds. *Issues in Wetlands Protection: Background Papers Prepared for the National Wetlands Policy Forum*. Washington, D.C.: The Conservation Foundation, 1990.

Blake, Nelson Manfred. *Land into Water, Water into Land*. Gainesville: University Presses of Florida, 1980.

Blumm, Michael C. "The End of Environmental Law? Libertarian the Federal Circuit." *Environmental Law* 25 (Winter Property, Natural Law and the Just Compensation Clause in 1995):171–98.

Blumm, Michael C., and D. Bernard Zaleha. "Federal Wetlands Protection Under the Clean Water Act: Regulatory Ambivalence, Intergovernmental Tension and a Call for Reform." *University of Colorado Law Review* 60 (1989): 695–772.

Brickey, Kathleen. "Wetlands Reform and the Criminal Enforcement Record: A Cautionary Tale." *Washington University Law Quarterly* 76 (1998): 71–84.

Buker, George. *Environment—The Third E: A History of the Jacksonville District U. S. Army Corps of Engineers 1975–1998*. Jacksonville: U. S. Army Corps of Engineers, 1998.

Clark, John. *The Sanibel Report: Formulation of a Comprehensive Plan Based on Natural Systems*. Washington, D.C.: The The Conservation Foundation, 1976. Online version published by Sanibel-Captiva The Conservation Foundation by permission of

World Wildlife Fund, http://www.worldpolicy.org/projects/globalrights/environ-ment/report/index.html.

Cocke, Karl, et al., compilers. *Department of the Army Historical Summary: Fiscal Year 1981*. Washington, D.C.: U.S. Army, Center of Military History, 1988.

———., et al., compilers. *Department of the Army Historical Summary: Fiscal Year 1982*. Washington, D.C.: U.S. Army, Center of Military History, 1988.

Committee on Characterization of Wetlands. *Wetlands: Characteristics and Boundar-ies*. Washington, D.C.: National Academies Press, 1995.

Committee on Mitigating Wetland Losses. *Compensating for Wetland Losses Under the Clean Water Act*. Washington, D.C.: National Academy Press, 2001.

Comprehensive Everglades Restoration Plan. U.S. Army Corps of Engineers, Jackson-ville District, and South Florida Water Management District. April 1999.

Connolly, Kim Diana, Stephen M. Johnson, and Douglas R. Williams, eds. *Wetlands Law and Policy: Understanding Section 404*. Chicago: American Bar Association, 2005.

Cowdrey, Albert E. "Pioneering Environmental Law: The Army Corps of Engineers and the Refuse Act." *Pacific Historical Review* 44 (1975): 331–49.

Crewz, David W. "Wetlands Mitigation Evaluations for Manatee/Sarasota Counties: Final Report to ManaSota-88." Sarasota, Fla., 1992.

Crouse, Timothy. *The Boys on the Bus*. New York: Ballantine, 1973.

Dahl, Thomas E. *Florida's Wetlands: An Update on Status and Trends 1985 to 1996*. Washington, D.C.: U.S. Department of the Interior, Fish and Wildlife Service, 2005.

———. *Status and Trends of Wetlands in the Coterminous United States 1986 to 1997*. Washington, D.C.: U.S. Department of the Interior, U.S. Fish and Wildlife Service, 2000.

———. *Status and Trends of Wetlands in the Coterminous United States 1998 to 2004*. Washington, D.C.: U.S. Department of the Interior, U.S. Fish and Wildlife Service, 2005.

———. *Wetlands Losses in the United States 1780s to 1980s*. Washington, D.C.: U.S. De-partment of the Interior, Fish and Wildlife Service, 1990.

Davis, Jack E., and Raymond Arsenault, eds. *Paradise Lost?: The Environmental History of Florida*. Gainesville: University Press of Florida, 2005.

Derr, Mark. *Some Kind of Paradise: A Chronicle of Man and the Land in Florida*. Gaines-ville: University Press of Florida, 1998.

Douglas, Marjory Stoneman, with John Rothchild. *Voice of the River*. Sarasota: Pine-apple Press, 1987.

Environmental Defense Collection. Attachments to the deposition of Bernard N. Goode ((*Deltona v. Hoffmann*, docket no. 76-473-CIV-JT), Environmental Defense Collection, Ms. Collection 232, Record Group 2, Subgroup 5: Legal Papers, Series 1: Litigation Files M–O (Marco Island), Box 11, Frank Melville Jr. Memorial Library, Stony Brook University.

Environmental Law Institute. *Banks and Fees: The Status of Off- Site Wetland Mitigation in the United States*. Washington, D.C.: ELI, 2002.

Erwin, Kevin. "An Evaluation of Wetland Mitigation in the South Florida Water Management District, Volume 1." Contract #C89-0082-A1. South Florida Water Management District, West Palm Beach, 1991.

Finnell, Gilbert L., Jr. "The Federal Regulatory Role in Coastal Land Management." *American Bar Foundation Research Journal* 3, no. 2 (Spring 1978): 169–288.

Fjellman, Stephen M. *Vinyl Leaves: Walt Disney World and America*. Boulder, Colo.: Westview Press, 1992.

Foglesong, Richard E. *Married to the Mouse: Walt Disney World and Orlando*. New Haven, Conn.: Yale University Press, 2001.

Fried, Charles. *Order and Law: Arguing the Reagan Revolution—A First-Hand Account*. New York: Simon & Schuster, 1981.

Glendenning, Travis Reid. "Presidential Campaigns and Environmental Policy." Master's thesis, Miami University, Oxford, Ohio, 2006.

Goode, Bernard N. Depostion of Bernard N. Goode (*Deltona v. Hoffmann*, docket no. 76-473-CIV-JT). Environmental Defense Collection, Ms. Collection 232; Record Group 2, Subgroup 5, Series 1—Litigation Files M–O (Marco Island), Box 11. Frank Melville Jr. Memorial Library, Stony Brook University.

Grathwol, Robert P., and Donita M. Moorhus. *Building for Peace: U.S. Army Engineers in Europe, 1945-1991*. U.S. Army Center for Military History, CMH Pub 45-1-1. Washington, D.C.: Government Printing Office, 2005.

Griffith, Leon Odell. *Ed Ball: Confusion to the Enemy*. Tampa: Trend House, 1974.

Gross, Liz. "Why Not the Best? How Science Failed the Florida Panther." *PLoS Biology* 3, no. 9 (August 23, 2005): e333.

Grunwald, Michael. *The Swamp: The Everglades, Florida and the Politics of Paradise*. New York: Simon & Schuster, 2006.

Harper, Harvey H., and David M. Baker. *Evaluation of Current Stormwater Design Criteria within the State of Florida*. Final Report, prepared for the Florida Department of Environmental Protection, FDEP Contract No. SO108. Orlando: Environmental Research & Design, Inc., June 2007.

Hedeman Jr., William N. "The Evolution of Federal Legislation to Protect the Nation's Wetlands." In *Guide to Environmental Law in Washington, D.C.*, edited by Charles Openchowski. Washington, D.C.: Environmental Law Institute, 1990.

Heuvelmans, Martin. *The River Killers*. Harrisburg, Pa.: Stackpole Books, 1974.

Jamieson, Kathleen Hall. *Packaging the Presidency: A History and Criticism of Presidential Campaigning*. New York: Oxford University Press, 1996.

Johnson, Haynes. *Sleepwalking Through History: America in the Reagan Years*. New York: W. W. Norton, 1991.

Kendall, Douglas T., and Charles P. Lord. "The Takings Project: A Critical Analysis and Assessment of the Progress So Far." *Boston College Environmental Affairs Law Review* 25 (Spring 1998): 509–87.

Kindiger, Jack. "Lake Belt Study Area: High-Resolution Seismic Reflection Survey, Miami-Dade County Florida." U.S. Geological Survey, OFR-02-325.

Kozinski, Hon. Alex. "Honoring the Court's Past." "Proceedings of the 15th Judicial Conference Celebrating the 20th Anniversary of the United States Court of Federal Claims," special issue, *George Washington Law Review* 71, nos. 4/5 (September/October 2003): 529–36.

Kusler, Jon. "Views on Scientific Issues Relating to the Restoration and Creation of Wetlands." In *Issues in Wetlands Protection: Background Papers Prepared for the National Wetlands Policy Forum*, edited by G. Bingham, E. H. Clark II, L. V. Haygood, and M. Leslie. Washington, D.C.: The Conservation Foundation, 1990.

Larson, Ron. *Swamp Song: A Natural History of Florida's Swamps*. Gainesville: University Press of Florida, 1995.

Marth, Del, and Martha J. Marth. *Florida Almanac 1998–1999*. Gretna, La.: Pelican Publishing, 1998.

Means, D. Bruce, Ellie Whitney, and Anne Rudloe. *Priceless Florida: Natural Ecosystems and Native Species*. Sarasota: Pineapple Press, 2004.

Miami-Dade County Lake Belt Plan Implementation Committee. *Phase II Plan*.

Mighetto, Lisa, and Wesley J. Ebel. *Saving the Salmon: A History of the U.S. Army Corps of Engineers Efforts to Protect Anadramous Fish on the Columbia and Snake Rivers*. Report to the U.S. Army Corps of Engineers, North Pacific Division. Seattle: Historical Research Associates, 1994.

Milazzo, Paul Charles. *Unlikely Environmentalists: Congress and Clean Water, 1945–1972*. Lawrence: University Press of Kansas, 2006.

Minkin, Paul, and Ruth Ladd. "Success of Corps-Required Wetland Mitigation in New England." U.S. Army Corps of Engineers, New England District, April 3, 2003.

Mormino, Gary. *Land of Sunshine, State of Dreams: A Social History of Modern Florida*. Gainesville: University Press of Florida, 2005.

Moser, Don. "Mangrove Island Is Reprieved by Army Engineers." *Smithsonian*. January, 1977.

Myers, Ronald L., and John J. Ewel, eds. *Ecosystems of Florida*. Orlando: University of Central Florida Press; 1990.

National Wetlands Policy Forum. *Protecting America's Wetlands: An Action Agenda—The Final Report of the National Wetlands Policy Forum*. Washington, D.C.: The Conservation Foundation, 1988.

Nolan, David. *Fifty Feet in Paradise: The Booming of Florida*. San Diego: Harcourt Brace Jovanovich, 1984.

Plager, S. Jay. "Takings Law and Appellate Decision Making." *Environmental Law* 25 (Winter 1995): 161–70.

Proby, Kathryn Hall. *Audubon in Florida*. Coral Gables: University of Miami Press, 1974.

Redmond, Ann. 1992. "How Successful is Mitigation?" *National Wetlands Newsletter* 14, no. 1 (February 1992): 5–6.

———. "Report on the Effectiveness of Permitted Mitigation." Florida Department of Environmental Regulation, Tallahassee, Fla., 1991.

Renken, R. A., K. J. Cunningham, M. R. Zygnerski, M. A. Wacker, A. M. Shapiro, R. W. Harvey, D. W. Metge, C. L. Osborn, and J. N. Ryan, "Assessing the Vulnerability of a Municipal Well Field to Contamination in a Karst Aquifer." *Environmental and Engineering Geoscience* 11, no. 4 (November 2005): 319–31.

Reuss, Martin. "Interview with William R. Gianelli." In *Water Resources—People and Issues: An Interview with William R. Gianelli.* U.S Army Corps of Engineers. EP 870-1-24, 1985.

———. *Shaping Environmental Awareness: The United States Army Corps of Engineers Environmental Advisory Board, 1970–1980.* Environmental History Series, EP-870-1-10. Historical Division, Office of the Chief of Engineers, U.S. Army Corps of Engineers, 1983.

Roberts, Diane. *Dream State: Eight Generations of Swamp Lawyers, Conquistadors, Confederate Daughters, Banana Republicans and Other Florida Wildlife.* New York: Free Press, 2004.

Rothchild, John. *Up for Grabs: A Trip Through Time and Space in the Sunshine State.* New York: Viking, 1985.

Schneider, Keith. "Guess What! Fake Wetlands Don't Work." *Great Lakes Bulletin* 14 (Summer 2001): 20–21.

Shaw, Samuel P., and C. Gordon Fredine. *Wetlands of the United States: Their Extent and Their Value to Waterfowl and Other Wildlife.* Washington, D.C.: U.S. Department of the Interior, 1956.

Stine, Jeffrey K. "Oral History Interview with Bernard N. Goode." July 26, 1983. Unpublished manuscript in the possession of Col. Don Wisdom.

———. "Regulating Wetlands in the 1970s: U.S. Army Corps of Engineers and the Environmental Organizations." *Journal of Forest History* 27 (April 1983): 60–75.

Stowe, Harriet Beecher. *Palmetto Leaves.* Boston: James R. Osgood & Co., 1873.

Strand, Margaret. *The Wetlands Deskbook.* 2nd ed. Washington, D.C.: Environmental Law Institute, 1997.

Train, Russell E. *Politics, Pollution, and Pandas: An Environmental Memoir.* Washington, D.C.:Island Press, 2003.

Vileisis, Ann. *Discovering the Unknown Landscape: A History of America's Wetlands.* Washington, D.C.: Island Press, 1997.

Wright, Tiffany, Jennifer Tomlinson, Tom Schueler, Karen Cappiella, Anne Kitchell, and Dave Hirschman. *Direct and Indirect Impacts of Urbanization on Wetland Quality.* Washington, D.C.: U.S. Environmental Protection Agency, Office of Wetlands, Oceans, and Watersheds, 2006.

Ziewitz, Kathryn, and June Wiaz. *Green Empire: The St. Joe Company and the Remaking of Florida's Panhandle.* Gainesville: University Press of Florida, 2004.

Selected Sources on Remote Sensing

Congalton, Russell G. "A Comparison of Sampling Schemes Used in Generating Error Matrices for Assessing the Accuracy of Maps Generated from Remotely Sensed Data." *Photogrammetric Engineering and Remote Sensing* 54, no. 5 (May 1988): 593–600.

Cox, James, Randy Kautz, Maureen MacLaughlin, and Terry Gilbert. *Closing the Gaps in Florida's Wildlife Habitat Conservation System*. Project Report 020. Tallahassee, Fla.: Office of Environmental Services, Florida Game and Fresh Water Fish Commission, 1994.

Houhoulis, Paula F., and William K. Michener. "Detecting Wetland Change: A Rule-Based Approach Using NWI and SPOT-XS Data." *Photogrammetric Engineering and Remote Sensing* 66, no. 2 (February 2000): 205–11.

Jensen, John R. *Remote Sensing of the Environment: An Earth Resource Perspective*. Upper Saddle River, N.J.: Prentice Hall, 2000.

———. *Introductory Digital Image Processing: A Remote Sensing Perspective*. 3rd ed. Upper Saddle River, N.J.: Pearson Prentice Hall, 2004.

Jensen, John R., Michael E. Hodgson, Eric Christensen, Halkard E. Mackey Jr., Larry Tinney, and Rebecca Sharitz. "Remote Sensing Inland Wetlands: A Multispectral Approach." *Photogrammetric Engineering and Remote Sensing* 51, no. 1 (January 1986): 87–100.

Levien, Lisa M., Chris S. Fischer, Peter D. Roffers, and Barbara Maurizi. "Statewide Change Detection Using Multitemporal Remote Sensing Data." Paper presented at the First International Conference on Geospatial Information in Agriculture and Forestry, Lake Buena Vista, Florida, June 1–3, 1998.

Lunetta, Ross S., and Mary E. Balogh. "Application of Multi-Temporal Landsat 5 TM Imagery for Wetland Identification." *Photogrammetric Engineering and Remote Sensing* 65, no. 11 (November 1999): 1303–310.

Mather, Paul M. *Computer Processing of Remotely-Sensed Images: An Introduction*. San Francisco, Calif.: John Wiley and Sons, 2003.

Ozesmi, Stacy L., and Marvin E. Bauer. "Satellite Remote Sensing of Wetlands." *Wetlands Ecology and Management* 10, no. 5 (October 2002): 381–402.

Pearlstine, L. G., S. E. Smith, L. A. Brandt, C. R. Allen, W. M. Kitchens, and J. Stenberg.

"Assessing State-Wide Biodiversity in the Florida Gap Analysis Project." *Journal of Environmental Management* 66, no. 2 (2002): 127–44.

Reese, Heather M., Thomas M. Lillesand, David E. Nagel, Jana S. Stewart, Robert A. Goldman, Tom E. Simmons, Jonathan W. Chipman, and Paul A. Tessar. "Statewide Land Cover Derived from Multiseasonal Landsat TM Data: A Retrospective of the WISCLAND Project." *Remote Sensing of the Environment* 82 (2002): 224–37.

Treitz, Paul, and John Rogan. "Remote Sensing for Mapping and Monitoring Land-Cover and Land-Use Change: An Introduction." *Progress in Planning* 61 (2004): 269–79.

University of Alberta Biological Sciences Department. Geographic Information Systems Web site. "Error Matrix for Map Comparison or Accuracy Assessment." June 28, 2004. http:// www.biology.ualberta.ca/facilities/gis/uploads/instructions/AVErrorMatrix.pdf.

Vogelmann, J. E., T. L. Sohl, P. V. Campbell, and D. M. Shaw. "Regional Land Cover Characterization Using Landsat Thematic Mapper Data and Ancillary Data Sources." *Environmental Monitoring and Assessment* 51 (1998): 415–28.

Index

Adams, James, 114, 147–48, 171–72

Adams, John, 44, 58, 114–15

Air Force, 44, 46, 172

Allen, Frederick Lewis, 12

Alverson, Melvin, 188–89

Anderson, Vic, 45, 60, 66–69, 71, 107, 112, 114–15, 121, 133, 137, 302, 305–7, 313–14, 316, 325–26

Army Corps of Engineers, 13, 19, 30–32, 34–35, 39, 53, 62, 64, 67, 285–86, 296, 299, 305–6, 330–32, 339–40, 342–43

Askew, Reubin, 38–41, 50–51, 55, 57, 130, 301

Associated Press, 83, 297–98, 308, 310–11, 320, 330

Association of Florida Community Developers, 207, 213

Association of State Wetland Managers, 119

Audubon Society, 51–53, 57, 78, 90, 176, 207, 215

Bacchus, Sydney, 124–26, 315

Baker, Edward, 147

Baker, Howard, 25, 29, 43

Baker, John D., 147

Backer, Rick, 281

Ball, Ed, 219–21, 328–29, 341, 348

Barberville Wetland Mitigation Bank, 335

Barron, Bob, 66, 103, 116, 137, 159, 246–47, 307, 313, 316, 330

Beever, Jim, 245, 332

Benbow, Dennis, 254, 258, 263, 272, 334–36

Bersok, Connie, 248, 333

Beter, Dale, 68

Billings, Leon, 26, 35–36, 298–300

Biological opinions, 186, 188, 194, 203, 324

Blackner, Lesley, 73, 140, 189, 234–35, 307, 316, 324, 330–31

Blanton, Donna, 81

Boler, Bruce, 63–64, 179–81, 206, 243–47, 305, 322–23, 332

Boyd, Allen, 223, 328

Brooker, Steve, 74, 120–21, 133, 137, 199–202, 276, 307, 314, 316, 326, 336

Browder, Joe, 15–16, 296

Browner, Carol, 97, 166–67, 178, 321

Bush, George H. W., 2, 90, 93–97, 166–67, 175, 255, 285

Bush, George W., 99, 212

Bush, Jeb, 69, 211–13, 223, 265, 272

Callaway, Howard, 38, 55

Carpenter, Robert, 71, 73, 75–76, 136, 182, 198, 201, 213–14, 235, 238, 306–7, 316, 326, 330

Casey, William, 232, 270–71, 336

Castille, Colleen, 214

Charles Green Rodes, 10–11, 57, 70, 72, 81, 98, 103, 116–18, 120, 128–29, 131–32, 134, 203, 232, 267, 336–37

Clean Water Act, 1, 6, 25, 29, 30, 35, 43, 70, 130, 147, 151, 153, 155, 159, 299, 301–2, 339–40

Clean Water Network, 109, 111, 226

Clinton, Bill, 97–99, 178, 311, 322

Colbert, Stephen, 3

Colbert, William, 264, 335

Colbert-Cameron Wetland Mitigation Bank, 264

Collins, LeRoy, 13

Conservancy of Southwest Florida, 246, 332

Conservation easements, 132–33, 254, 270

Conservation Foundation, 91, 93, 204, 339, 342

Cornerstone Group, 197–98

Corrigan, Timothy, 227

Courtelis, Alec, 198
Crenshaw, Ander, 212–13
Crewz, David, 85–86, 309, 340
Crist, Charlie, 215, 281
CSR Rinker, 142, 156, 165
Curran, Danny, 59, 305

Da Capo, 263, 266, 268–69, 272
Dahl, Thomas, 3
Dalrymple, George, 144, 317
Daltry, Wayne, 242
Davies, Steve, 3, 293–94
Davis, Gary, 246
Davis, Michael, 98–99, 109, 313
Dawson, Robert, 43–44, 203–4, 302, 326
Dean, Henry, 251, 263
Deason, Jonathan, 204–5
Deltona Corp., 49–53, 55, 57, 76, 100, 151, 303, 318, 340–41
Dingell, John, 26–27, 37, 298–99
Disney, Walt, 12, 84–85, 220–21
Dryden, Kim, 203–4
Dukakis, Michael, 91, 94–95, 309–10
DuPont, Alfred, 220–21, 329
Dwyer, Rob, 117

East Central Florida Mitigation Bank, 262, 267–69, 271–72, 335
Ecobank, 255–59, 262–69, 271–72, 334–36
Ecotour Lodge, 75
Eells, Barbara, 224, 329
Eller, Andy, 183–87, 194, 196–97, 204–6, 323–27
Environmental Protection Agency, 24, 27, 35–42, 63–64, 91–92, 95–97, 158–59, 165–68, 171–78, 180–83, 244, 246, 273–75, 310–12, 321–23, 331–32
Erwin, Kevin, 88, 114, 249, 309, 314
Evans, Mark, 72–73, 214
Everglades, 10, 14–15, 26, 31–32, 61, 79, 97, 106, 120–21, 141, 143, 145, 165–67, 192–93, 276, 348–49
Everglades National Park, 14, 16, 75, 99, 142–43, 146, 158, 160, 174

Federal Emergency Management Agency, 189–90, 281, 283, 312, 324
Federal Water Pollution Control Act, 18

Feeney, Tom, 200–202, 326, 328
Fickett, Alan, 251–52, 256–58, 263–66, 269, 272, 335–36
Fisher, Carl, 10
Florida Atlantic University, 71
Florida Chamber of Commerce, 140, 164
Florida Department of Environmental Protection, 84, 104, 118, 132, 157, 208–9, 211–12, 214, 218, 241, 246–47, 285, 328, 332–33, 335, 341
Florida Department of Environmental Regulation, 85, 87–88, 118, 166–67, 309, 342
Florida Department of Transportation, 116–18, 120–21, 123, 128–30, 134, 138–39, 164, 228, 258, 263, 272, 314, 316
Florida Fish and Wildlife Conservation Commission, 280, 286, 296, 336
Florida Game and Fresh Water Fish Commission, 345
Florida Gulf Coast University, 187, 191, 193–94, 219, 243, 325
Florida Home Builders Association, 78, 207, 209
Florida International University, 169
Florida legislature, 9, 12, 145, 156, 168, 191, 201, 210, 248, 277, 317, 321, 324
Florida Mitigation Bank, 254, 334
Florida panther, 174, 182–83, 186–88, 192, 194, 203–7, 277, 280, 324–26, 341
Florida Rock, 146–59, 162, 164, 175, 197, 277, 318–20
Florida State University, 334
Florida Supreme Court, 21, 150, 297
Florida Wetlandsbank, 253–54, 256, 274
Florida Wildlife Federation, 57, 70, 191, 306, 323
Foundation for Florida's Future, 256
Fredine, C. Gordon, 9
Freedom of Information Act (FOIA), 103, 285, 312–13, 317, 325, 330
Fried, Charles, 148–49, 318, 341
Frye, William, 19

Gallihugh, Jeanette, 184–85
Garbe, Udo, 200–201, 326
Gianelli, William R., 42–44, 302, 343
Giattina, Jim, 181, 323
Gilmore, Dan, 207, 213, 215
Gipe, Todd, 258

Gluckman, David, 38–39, 80–81, 84, 301, 308–9

Goode, Bernard N., 50, 52–55, 303–4, 340–41, 343

Goss, Porter, 92, 197, 204–6, 325

Graham, Bob, 39, 146, 150, 195–97, 203–5, 226, 255, 276, 318, 325

Gribble, William, 37, 40, 54–56, 76, 84, 301, 304

Griffin, Ben Hill, III, 191–94

Grubbs, John, 73

Hale, Ernest, 270, 336

Hall, John, 59, 60, 62–68, 75–77, 107, 131–32, 138, 156–57, 179, 185, 192–93, 235–37, 275–76, 305–8, 313, 316, 323–25

Hankinson, John Henry, 178–80, 243, 322

Hanmer, Rebecca, 172–73, 321–22

Harling, Hugh, 201–2

Harper, Harvey, 244–46

Harrison, William, 223

Harvey, Richard, 167

Hastings, Alcee, 197–98, 326

Hauck, Ann, 64, 305, 323

Henderson Act, 84–85, 88, 196, 309

Henderson, Warren, 78–79, 81–83, 309

Herrin, Barbara, 233–34, 331

Heuvelmans, Martin, 34, 300, 341

Hobbie, David, 275–76

Hodges, Don, 217, 219, 328

Hoeveler, William, 159–64, 277, 319–20

Hoffman, Al, 210, 327

Holland, Spessard, 168–69

Holland, W. Langston, 27–28, 36–38, 168, 298–99, 301

Hooker's Prairie, 66, 114–15

Howard, George, 268–69, 273, 336–37

Hughes, Vance, 27–29, 36, 38–39, 299, 300

Hummer, Chuck, 31, 33

Hydrogeomorphic Method (HGM), 136–37, 316

IMC Agrico, 115–16

Interama, 168–70, 321

Johns River Water Management District, 106, 178, 234, 243, 249–51, 258, 280, 331, 333

Johnson, Haynes, 178, 180–81, 301–2, 316, 322–23

Jorling, Tom, 21, 26, 35, 297–300

Keep Florida Rockin, 164, 320

Kimley-Horn, 124, 233–35

Kozinski, Alex, 149–54, 318, 342

Krentzman, Ben, 22, 28, 37–39, 299, 300

Lake Belt, 142–47, 153, 155–56, 161–62, 164–65, 191, 197, 208, 278, 317, 319

Lake, Bill, 34, 300

Lake Louisa, 258–59, 262–63, 268–69, 271–73, 335

Landsat, 105, 286

Lee Ranch, 262–63

Legere, Richard, 230

Letellier, Carroll, 54–55, 58

Levin, Allen, 108–12, 313

Lewis, Roy, 121–23, 315

Little Pine Island Mitigation Bank, 257

Mack, Connie, 193–94, 203–6, 325, 337

Mackle, Frank, 50, 55, 57, 303–4

Mackle, Frank, Jr., 46, 48, 51, 57, 130, 304

Mackle brothers, 46–51, 53–57, 207, 303–4

Maehr, Dave, 186–87, 204–5

Mangrum, Norm, 102

Marco Island, 46–55, 57–60, 65–66, 68, 130, 184–85, 192, 207, 209, 214, 228, 243, 303–5, 339–41

Marshall, Art, 16

Marshall, Howard, 170–73

Matthews, Frank, 207–10, 213–14, 228, 243

McCarthy, D. Miller, 251–53, 256–58, 262–66, 268–69, 272, 334–36

McCormack, Fred, 79, 80, 308–9, 334

Meadow Pointe, 201–2, 264

Middlebrooks, Donald, 70, 277

Miller, Mike, 202

Mills, Jon, 79–81, 83–84, 146, 221, 301, 308–9

Mitigation: creating wetlands for mitigation, 85–88, 108–20, 123–27; early efforts at mitigating wetland losses, 84, 114, 118–19; enhancement as mitigation, 136, 138–39, 278; required by Henderson Act, 84–85; preservation as mitigation, 128–35, 138–39, 260, 278; warnings by scientists about problems, 85–89, 119, 274. *See also* No net loss policy

Mitigation banks, 252–60, 262–63, 267–74, 334–37

Moore, Sue, 117

Morris, Randy, 264–68, 299, 335–36

Morse, Chandler, 4

Munisport, 170–73, 321–22

Muskie, Edmund, 24–25, 29, 35–36, 167, 298, 300

Naples Reserve, 183–85, 196, 323

Narkiewicz, Joseph, 327

National Association of Home Builders, 4, 155

National Association of Realtors, 155

National Defense Authorization Act, 273

National Marine Fisheries Service, 41

National Mitigation Banking Association, 272

National Park Service, 64, 145–46, 180, 317

National Wetlands Inventory, 3, 101–3, 105, 280,
    286, 288, 312

National Wetlands Policy Forum, 93, 96, 119, 310,
    338–39, 342

National Wildlife Federation, 2

Natural Resources Defense Council, 38, 40, 51, 55,
    159, 226, 300–301, 306, 316, 330

Nelson, Bill, 205–7, 215–16, 223, 327

New Jersey, 92–94, 310

No net loss policy: adopted by George H. W.
    Bush, 94–96; agreement by EPA and Corps of
    Engineers, 96, 130; Bush Administration fail-
    ure to go beyond no net loss, 97; corps officials
    unable to say whether it's working, 100, 122–
    23, 131, 136–38; dealing with the policy's failure,
    276–78; embraced by George W. Bush, 99–100;
    embraced by Bill Clinton, 97–99; GAO reports
    on flaws, 122–23, 136, 270, 276–77; claims goal
    had been achieved, 1–3; National Research
    Council report, 100, 113, 122, 277; New Jersey
    model, 92–93; recommended by National
    Wetlands Policy Forum, 93; wetlands lost in
    Florida, 106–7, 199, 234, 262, 271; why it should
    be abandoned, 277–78

Nicewonder, J. D., 181–82, 206, 327

Nicklaus, Jack, 175–76

Nixon, Richard, 16, 23, 25, 35

Norton, Gale, 1–3, 100, 113, 293–94, 341

Nowicki, Mike, 75, 131–32

Old Cutler Bay, 176, 182, 184

OPPAGA (Office of Program Policy Analysis and
    Government Accountability), 248–50, 281,
    333, 338

Overflowed Lands Act, 9, 10, 30

Palenchar, John, 121

Palmer, Jimmy, 180, 182, 206, 323

Parker, Blake, 101–2

Parker, Michael, 157

Pavelka, Raymond, 257–58, 334

Payne, Lyal "Clif," 110, 112, 138, 313

Peace River, 115, 117, 260, 335

Peace River Mitigation Bank, 260

Peck Sink, 229–32, 330

Pennsuco, 147, 322

Plager, Sheldon Jay, 154–55

Planas, Raul, 176–77

Platt, George, 253–54, 256, 274, 334, 337

Portofino, 108–10, 112, 138

Property rights, 30, 40, 54, 57, 79, 81, 149–50, 152,
    175, 281, 283, 301, 319

Rametta, Dan, 128, 134–35, 139–40, 316

Range, Jim, 28–30, 42

Ray, Jerry, 225–27, 329–30

Reagan, Ronald, 41–42, 90, 149, 152, 173, 302

Redmond, Ann, 84–89, 167, 249, 309, 342

Reed, Nathaniel "Nat," 15–16, 34, 49, 70, 90–91,
    300

Reedy Creek Mitigation Bank, 335–36

Reese, Tom, 85–86, 288–89, 309, 323, 325, 346

Refuse Act, 19, 20, 30, 39, 340

Reilly, William K., 92–97, 168, 175–77, 310–11,
    321–22

Rice, Terry, 32–33, 61–63, 73, 120, 122, 156, 192–94,
    243, 300, 305, 307, 314–15, 325

Ridge Road, 134–35, 139–40, 195

Rist, Karsten, 176–77

Rivers and Harbors Act, 19, 26, 35–36, 148

Robinson, Aubrey, 24, 39

Rodes, Charles Green, 11

Ross, Don, 260

Royal Gardner, 67

Rummell, Peter, 221–24, 228, 328–30

Russell, David, 20, 22–23, 50, 297, 345

Sanibel, 91–92, 204, 326

Schnepel, Charles "Chuck," 69, 74, 199, 307, 311,
    313, 326

Scripps Research Institute, 69, 70, 277, 306

Seitz, Howard, 263–64, 266, 269, 272, 335–36

Seney, Jennifer, 5

Serenova, 130, 134–35, 208

Shaw, Samuel, 9

Sierra Club, 15, 24, 70, 78–79, 90, 140, 159, 214, 226, 240, 249, 306, 316–17, 319–20, 330, 333

Silver, Ron, 257–58, 269–71, 334, 336

Sinkholes, 217, 219, 221, 223, 225, 227, 229–33, 235, 328

Slack, Jay, 185, 187, 196, 205, 323, 326

Smathers, George, 46, 168

Smith, Kenneth, 184, 323

Smith, Loren, 149, 152

South Florida Water Management District, 59, 88, 205, 210, 242, 246–48, 275, 326, 332–33, 340–41

Southwest Florida Regional Planning Council, 242, 245, 305

Southwest Florida Water Management District, 118, 126, 130, 134, 139, 230, 240, 242, 271, 315, 330, 332, 336

Souza, Paul, 188, 324

Speth, Gus, 300–301

Sports Afield, 90–91, 95, 310

St. Joe (town), 219

St. Joe Company, 71, 213, 217–19, 222, 307, 329, 343

St. Johns River, 19, 61, 63, 72, 222, 236, 238, 243, 250, 262, 296, 331

Status and Trends of Wetlands, 293–94, 312, 340

Stelling, Jim, 264–68, 336

Strand, Margaret, 67–68

Strock, Carl, 76, 195, 215

Studt, John, 189, 317, 324

Stutler, Denver, Jr., 116, 255–57, 272

Suncoast Parkway, 128–32, 134, 140, 195, 234

Sundew Mitigation Bank, 270, 335

Supreme Court, 19, 23, 57, 148, 150, 153–54, 157, 230, 298, 304

Sweeden's Swamp, 91

Tabb, Robert, III, 21, 23, 26, 28, 56–57, 194, 297, 318

Tampa Bay Mitigation Bank, 87, 270–71

Task Force on Regulatory Relief, 42

Train, Russell, 37

Tripp, Jim, 80, 308

Tschinkel, Victoria, 80, 257

Uniform Mitigation Assessment Method (UMAM), 136, 138

University of Central Florida, 199, 201, 244, 251

URS Greiner Woodward, 129

Varn, Jake, 230, 232

Wal-Mart, 123–27, 232–35, 280, 282, 315, 331

Washington, George, 6, 7, 31, 220

WCI, 213–14

Wellborn, Tom, 181

Wetlands Rapid Assessment Protocol (WRAP), 136

Wetlands types, 287, 289

Whitfield, Estus, 276

Wilkinson, Jessica, 260, 273–74, 335

Williams, 200, 210–15, 228, 298, 322, 327

Williams, Trudi, 210–15, 228

Williams, Warren, 200, 326

Winchester, Pam, 232–35, 331

Wisdom, Donald, 48–49, 51–58, 68, 73, 192, 303–6, 343

Wood storks, 158, 162–63, 165, 183

Woodley, John Paul, 212, 312

Wray, Robert, 27–28, 39, 299

Wright, Ken, 202, 264–68, 295, 336, 343

Wrublik, John, 188, 324

Young, Don, 98–99

Young, Linda, 109, 111, 226, 228, 313, 330

Yulee, David Levy, 9

Zabel, Alfred, 20, 23, 26, 28, 50, 56–57, 150, 297, 318

Journalists Craig Pittman and Matthew Waite are reporters for the *St. Petersburg Times*. Their stories on Florida's wetlands won the top award for investigative reporting in 2006 and 2007 from the Society of Environmental Journalists, as well as the Waldo Proffitt Award for Excellence in Environmental Journalism in Florida.

The Florida History and Culture Series

Edited by Raymond Arsenault and Gary R. Mormino

Al Burt's Florida: Snowbirds, Sand Castles, and Self-Rising Crackers, by Al Burt (1997)

Black Miami in the Twentieth Century, by Marvin Dunn (1997)

Gladesmen: Gator Hunters, Moonshiners, and Skiffers, by Glen Simmons and Laura Ogden (1998)

"Come to My Sunland": Letters of Julia Daniels Moseley from the Florida Frontier, 1882–1886, by Julia Winifred Moseley and Betty Powers Crislip (1998)

The Enduring Seminoles: From Alligator Wrestling to Ecotourism, by Patsy West (1998), first paperback edition, 2008

Government in the Sunshine State: Florida Since Statehood, by David R. Colburn and Lance deHaven-Smith (1999)

The Everglades: An Environmental History, by David McCally (1999), first paperback edition, 2001

Beechers, Stowes, and Yankee Strangers: The Transformation of Florida, by John T. Foster Jr. and Sarah Whitmer Foster (1999)

The Tropic of Cracker, by Al Burt (1999)

Balancing Evils Judiciously: The Proslavery Writings of Zephaniah Kingsley, edited and annotated by Daniel W. Stowell (1999)

Hitler's Soldiers in the Sunshine State: German POWs in Florida, by Robert D. Billinger Jr. (2000)

Cassadaga: The South's Oldest Spiritualist Community, edited by John J. Guthrie, Phillip Charles Lucas, and Gary Monroe (2000)

Claude Pepper and Ed Ball: Politics, Purpose, and Power, by Tracy E. Danese (2000)

Pensacola during the Civil War: A Thorn in the Side of the Confederacy, by George F. Pearce (2000)

Castles in the Sand: The Life and Times of Carl Graham Fisher, by Mark S. Foster (2000)

Miami, U.S.A., by Helen Muir (2000)

Politics and Growth in Twentieth-Century Tampa, by Robert Kerstein (2001)

The Invisible Empire: The Ku Klux Klan in Florida, by Michael Newton (2001)

The Wide Brim: Early Poems and Ponderings of Marjory Stoneman Douglas, edited by Jack E. Davis (2002)

The Architecture of Leisure: The Florida Resort Hotels of Henry Flagler and Henry Plant, by Susan R. Braden (2002)

Florida's Space Coast: The Impact of NASA on the Sunshine State, by William Barnaby Faherty, S.J. (2002)

In the Eye of Hurricane Andrew, by Eugene F. Provenzo Jr. and Asterie Baker Provenzo (2002)

Florida's Farmworkers in the Twenty-first Century, text by Nano Riley and photographs by Davida Johns (2003)

Making Waves: Female Activists in Twentieth-Century Florida, edited by Jack E. Davis and Kari Frederickson (2003)

Orange Journalism: Voices from Florida Newspapers, by Julian M. Pleasants (2003)

The Stranahans of Ft. Lauderdale: A Pioneer Family of New River, by Harry A. Kersey Jr. (2003)

Death in the Everglades: The Murder of Guy Bradley, America's First Martyr to Environmentalism, by Stuart B. McIver (2003)

Jacksonville: The Consolidation Story, from Civil Rights to the Jaguars, by James B. Crooks (2004)

The Seminole Wars: The Nation's Longest Indian Conflict, by John and Mary Lou Missall (2004)

The Mosquito Wars: A History of Mosquito Control in Florida, by Gordon Patterson (2004)

Seasons of Real Florida, by Jeff Klinkenberg (2004)

Land of Sunshine, State of Dreams: A Social History of Modern Florida, by Gary Mormino (2005)

Paradise Lost? The Environmental History of Florida, edited by Jack E. Davis and Raymond Arsenault (2005), first paperback edition, 2005

Frolicking Bears, Wet Vultures, and Other Oddities: A New York City Journalist in Nineteenth-Century Florida, edited by Jerald T. Milanich (2005)

Waters Less Traveled: Exploring Florida's Big Bend Coast, by Doug Alderson (2005)

Saving South Beach, by M. Barron Stofik (2005)

Losing It All to Sprawl: How Progress Ate My Cracker Landscape, by Bill Belleville (2006)

Voices of the Apalachicola, compiled and edited by Faith Eidse (2006), first paperback edition, 2007

Floridian of His Century: The Courage of Governor LeRoy Collins, by Martin A. Dyckman (2006)

America's Fortress: A History of Fort Jefferson, Dry Tortugas, Florida, by Thomas Reid (2006)

Weeki Wachee, City of Mermaids: A History of One of Florida's Oldest Roadside Attractions, by Lu Vickers and Sara Dionne (2007)

City of Intrigue, Nest of Revolution: A Documentary History of Key West in the Nineteenth Century, by Consuelo E. Stebbins (2007)

The New Deal in South Florida: Design, Policy, and Community Building, 1933–1940, edited by John A. Stuart and John F. Stack Jr. (2008)

Pilgrim in the Land of Alligators: More Stories about Real Florida, by Jeff Klinkenberg (2008)

A Most Disorderly Court: Scandal and Reform in the Florida Judiciary, by Martin A. Dyckman (2008)

A Journey into Florida Railroad History, by Gregg M. Turner (2008)

Sandspurs: Notes from a Coastal Columnist, by Mark Lane (2008)

Paving Paradise: Florida's Vanishing Wetlands and the Failure of No Net Loss, by Craig Pittman and Matthew Waite (2009)

Embry-Riddle at War: Aviation Training During World War II, by Stephen G. Craft (2009)

The Columbia Restaurant: Celebrating a Century of History, Culture, and Cuisine, by Andrew T. Huse, with recipes and memories from Richard Gonzmart and the Columbia restaurant family (2009)

Ditch of Dreams: The Cross Florida Barge Canal and the Struggle for Florida's Future, by Steven Noll and David Tegeder (2009)